RADIO STATION OPERATIONS

Management and Employee Perspectives

From the **Wadsworth Series in Mass Communication**

General

The New Communications, 2nd, by Frederick Williams
Media/Impact: An Introduction to Mass Media by Shirley Biagi
Media/Reader by Shirley Biagi
Mediamerica: Form, Content, and Consequence of Mass Communication, 4th, by Edward Jay Whetmore
The Interplay of Influence: Mass Media & Their Publics in News, Advertising, Politics, 2nd, by Kathleen Hall Jamieson and Karlyn Kohrs Campbell
Technology and Communication Behavior by Frederick Williams
Media Writing: News for the Mass Media, 2nd, by Doug Newsom and James A. Wollert
Mastering the Message: Media Writing with Substance and Style by Lauren Kessler and Duncan McDonald
Uncovering the News: A Journalist's Search for Information by Lauren Kessler and Duncan McDonald
When Words Collide: A Journalist's Guide to Grammar and Style, 2nd, by Lauren Kessler and Duncan McDonald
Interviews That Work: A Practical Guide for Journalists by Shirley Biagi
Mass Media Research: An Introduction, 2nd, by Roger D. Wimmer and Joseph R. Dominick
Communication Research: Strategies and Sources by Rebecca B. Rubin, Alan M. Rubin, and Linda J. Piele
Creative Strategy in Advertising, 3rd, by A. Jerome Jewler
Fundamentals of Advertising Research, 3rd, by Alan Fletcher and Thomas A. Bowers

Broadcast/Cable/Film

Stay Tuned: A Concise History of American Broadcasting by Christopher H. Sterling and John M. Kittross
World Broadcasting Systems: A Comparative Analysis by Sydney W. Head
Broadcast/Cable Programming: Strategies and Practices, 3rd, by Susan Tyler Eastman, Sydney W. Head, and Lewis Klein
Radio Station Operations: Management and Employee Perspectives by Lewis B. O'Donnell, Carl Hausman, and Philip Benoit
Broadcast and Cable Selling by Charles Warner
Advertising in the Broadcast and Cable Media, 2nd, by Elizabeth J. Heighton and Don R. Cunningham
Copywriting for the Electronic Media: A Practical Guide by Milan D. Meeske and R. C. Norris
Writing for Television and Radio, 4th, by Robert L. Hilliard
Writing the Screenplay: TV and Film by Alan A. Armer
Newswriting for the Electronic Media: Principles, Examples, Applications by Daniel E. Garvey and William L. Rivers
Newstalk II: State-of-the-Art Conversations with Today's Broadcast Journalists by Shirley Biagi
Communicating Effectively on Television by Evan Blythin and Larry A. Samovar
Announcing: Broadcast Communicating Today by Lewis B. O'Donnell, Carl Hausman and Philip Benoit
Modern Radio Production by Lewis B. O'Donnell, Philip Benoit, and Carl Hausman
Audio in Media, 2nd, by Stanley R. Alten
Television Production Handbook, 4th, by Herbert Zettl
Directing Television and Film by Alan A. Armer
Sight-Sound-Motion: Applied Media Aesthetics by Herbert Zettl
Electronic Cinematography: Achieving Photographic Control over the Video Image by Harry Mathias and Richard Patterson
Immediate Seating: A Look at Movie Audiences by Bruce Austin

RADIO STATION
OPERATIONS

Management and Employee Perspectives

Lewis B. O'Donnell *State University of New York at Oswego*

Carl Hausman *Free-Lance Writer and Producer*

Philip Benoit *Dickinson College*

Wadsworth Publishing Company   Belmont, California
A Division of Wadsworth, Inc.

Senior Editor: Rebecca Hayden
Editorial Assistant: Melissa Harris
Production Editor: Jane Townsend
Interior Design: Andrew H. Ogus
Print Buyer: Barbara Britton
Photo Research: Stuart Kenter
Cover Design: Stuart Paterson/Image House
Cover photograph: © Ray Pfortner/Peter Arnold, Inc.
Photographs by Philip Benoit unless otherwise credited.

Printed in the United States of America   49
1 2 3 4 5 6 7 8 9 10—93 92 91 90 89

Library of Congress Cataloging-in-Publication Data

O'Donnell, Lewis B.
   Radio station operations: management and employee perspectives /
Lewis B. O'Donnell, Carl Hausman, Philip Benoit.
      p.   c.m.
   Bibliography: p.
   Includes index.
   ISBN 0-534-09540-2
   1. Radio broadcasting—Management.   2. Radio stations—Management.
I. Hausman, Carl, 1953–   .   II. Benoit, Philip, 1944–
III. Title.
HE8696.036 1988   88-13962
384.54'53'068—dc19   CIP

PREFACE

Many readers of this book are probably under the impression that radio is a glamorous, exciting business. Those readers are, of course, right.

But modern radio is as complex as it is glamorous. Dealing with reams of research is hardly exciting, and tedium—as well as excitement—is a part of the business. In short, *radio is a business,* and that is the primary focus of *Radio Station Operations: Management and Employee Perspectives.* Chapter 1 outlines how this business evolved from an electronic novelty to a major enterprise. Chapter 2 shows how program elements such as music, personality, and news were developed and how they are used today.

Chapter 3 tackles the business of formats and programming, supplying detailed summaries of major formats, along with their advantages and disadvantages. Chapter 4 explores how people put the elements of radio into operation. The facilities of radio are often somewhat intimidating because of their apparent complexity, but Chapter 5 takes the mystery out of equipment and facilities by offering walk-throughs of several typical radio stations.

Production—the tool that creates a station's sound—is examined from a management perspective in Chapter 6. Market analysis and development, another critical aspect of modern radio management, is the subject of Chapter 7. Chapter 8 demystifies a subject of concern to every radio station manager or sales executive: ratings and audience analysis.

Sales is the subject of Chapter 9; the mechanics of sales and the techniques of persuading clients and closing deals are discussed. Chapter 10 focuses on the often-neglected subject of personnel management and ties modern management theory directly to radio station operations.

Chapter 11 fills what is a void in radio textbooks: It deals exclusively with finance, examining such subjects as budgeting, ownership structures, and cash flow. Finally, Chapter 12 takes a common-sense, management-oriented approach to the realities of regulation.

A word about the structure of this book: One of the difficulties related to us by many educators is that radio courses—whether they are titled *Management, Sales,* or *Operations*—deal with widely varying subject matter and have an equally wide-ranging student constituency. In light of this, we have written the book in such a way that most chapters can be assigned out of order or read and understood in isolation. Duplication of material, however, has been kept to a minimum. Terms introduced in previous chapters are usually redefined, but this is done as quickly and unobtrusively as possible. Histories that may have been addressed in previous chapters are slanted to specifically address the relevant concept in the current chapter, so that repetition is kept to a minimum. Chapter 1, for example, provides quite a thorough history of radio and will be helpful to students with little media background (business or management majors, perhaps). Readers who have studied radio history can simply scan the material and move on. If they move to Chapter 2, they will encounter a brief recap of the history of some program elements with certain *specifically relevant* background material added. In Chapter 3 the background is laid out with a fresh angle—the development of radio's modern format.

We hope that this book meets the needs of radio professionals, students, and faculty. If it does succeed, it is largely due to the efforts of those who offered their assistance throughout the entire process of conceiving and writing this work. We thank John Baxter, Southern Oregon State College; A. Vernon Lapps, Mansfield University; Hugh McCarney, Western Connecticut State University; Jay P. Pappas, Ashland College; and Frank E. Parcells, Eastern Illinois University.

CONTENTS

RADIO TODAY:

AN INTRODUCTION

Modern radio is fully a creature of its time. The ability of radio to tie into the life-styles of its listeners has been greatly developed since programmers first discovered the commercial value of the youth culture in the 1950s. Fragmentation of the audience has allowed radio programmers to hone in on relatively small segments of the population. The success of all news operations and black, Hispanic, and religious formats, for example, has demonstrated over and over the marketing potential that lies in catering to the interests and tastes of audience segments that constitute relatively small percentages of the overall population.

Radio's ability to read these interests and to program with such precision reflects the extensive knowledge that programmers have of their audiences. One effect of this increased sensitivity is the tendency to shift attention from one audience segment to another. A station that is struggling among several other stations in a large market to attract the interest of the twelve- to twenty-year-old age group, for instance, suddenly may decide to cater to an underserved audience segment whose tastes run more to country music.

The result of this kind of management decision is that the WXXX of today may have a completely different sound tomorrow. The era in which stations were known to listeners by the names and voices of its announcers has been supplanted by a volatility that makes it difficult for stations to build listener loyalty. A given station's format may change many times in a relatively short period of time. In short, it has become necessary for station management to monitor market conditions continuously. Programmers must know the tastes and interests of the audience segment served by their stations, and every element of the on-air product must be geared accordingly.

There is more competition to keep track of than there was even two decades ago. When AM radio dominated, as it did for years, the FM spectrum was of little concern to most commercially successful radio operations. Today, with its superior sound quality and commercial success, FM dominates. Increasingly, AM operations are struggling for survival, and that sector of radio is now searching desperately for technologic innovations such as AM stereo, which will help it compete more effectively with FM.

Many view the efforts of AM to compete as futile. These skeptics point to the fact that AM stereo reduces the station's coverage area and that the minimal improvement in sound quality is not worth such a sacrifice.

In programming as well, today's radio station is radically different from its predecessor of a few years ago. Whereas radio of the 1950s and 1960s was largely locally programmed, today the vast selection of syndicated music formats and other feature and information services makes it risky to compete without some professional guidance.

THE MODERN STATION AND THE MODERN MARKET

Modern radio has fully accepted the proposition that to succeed all the elements of the on-air product must contribute to the creation of a well-thought-out station sound. The sound of the station is carefully built to mesh with the life-styles of the audiences it seeks to serve. Easy Rock (EZ Rock), WARM 103, Hit Radio 100, "Where the hits just keep on comin'," Magic 99—all these promotional phrases uttered continuously are typical of today's station (see Chapter 3). All the elements of the on-air product are fine-tuned to produce the desired effect for the listener. The frequency with which music is played during a given hour is carefully thought through. The production elements contained in the commercials, the selection of news stories, the writing style and method of delivery in news (if indeed the station carries news at all), the style of the disc jockey, and the length of the disk jockey's patter between records are carefully orchestrated to support the "sound" of the station.

Many stations are automated to a greater or lesser degree. At present, there is a trend away from the nonpersonal sound of automated music that swept the industry during much of the 1970s. Personalities are back in vogue, and automated formats are sophisticated enough to provide the advantages of syndication while making the product personal. At the same time, there is an increase in the variety of program material available through syndication.

Because of the centralized availability of programming, the distinction between the sound of stations in a medium or small market and a large market is less obvious. In fact, stations that were once shoestring operations in small communities often have become major, market-ratings leaders simply because their signals can be received in a nearby large market. By programming a well-conceived format and creating a sound that is devoid of traits that once earmarked a station as a small-town operation, these stations can compete easily with larger competition when an audience niche is found and catered to.

This pronounced ability for stations to dramatically rise in popularity has changed ownership patterns in radio today. Group ownership has increased notably because astute investors realize that professional programming and marketing savvy can reap handsome returns on investment dollars. Selling prices of stations have soared in recent years, and the art of station buying and selling has become a whole segment of the industry in itself. Stations that would have gone begging on the auction block two decades ago are now selling for millions of dollars because perceptive management can turn losers into winners almost overnight.

SMALL, MEDIUM, AND LARGE MARKETS

A look at a modern large market today reveals a vastly changed set of circumstances from what one would have encountered in the 1960s. There may be as many as twenty or thirty stations, programming ten or fifteen different formats. Given the widespread audience preference for FM, top stations are likely FM operations, and some of these may be licensed to communities outside the geographic limits of the market as it has been traditionally configured. Look at the same market three months later and you might find that a station that hardly appeared in the ratings reports is now one of the top two or three, while the former number one station may be slipping quickly to the bottom.

Small- and medium-market operations, far from being the locally owned, small-budget operations they once were, may be owned by a group that also owns a dozen other stations. The record library of a small-market station may consist of a satellite dish that receives a service that runs the station's automation equipment, which feeds in local commercial messages produced by the station's sales manager at appropriate intervals.

News may emanate from another satellite service, supplemented by reports prepared by the single full-time newsman. Indeed, it would be difficult to tell that this is a station licensed to a community with a population of under 10,000. The facilities may be newly constructed, and equipment is likely to be state-of-the-art.

The configurations described above do not tell the whole story. There are still small-market operations providing service to small communities and orienting themselves very carefully toward servicing the community to which they are licensed. There are still prosperous AM operations in large markets, and many show no signs of impending misfortune. The point is that there is great volatility in today's radio. The flux of today's radio industry is the product of a sophisticated approach to a business that has the potential of reaping vast fortunes for those with the skill and knowledge to bring about success. At the same time, however, the stakes are such that failure can come suddenly and with little warning.

AM AND FM

As noted previously, there has been a dramatic reversal in the fortunes of AM versus FM operation. Listeners of the 1940s and 1950s barely knew that FM existed. Receiver manufacturers, facing higher manufacturing costs, were reluctant to move aggressively into set production. Moreover, the FM band was either programmed with classical offerings, which served a very small segment of the audience; with so-called dinner music (inoffensive instrumental music, usually heavily dominated by strings); as educational radio, later to develop into a highly professional service under the rubric of public radio; or as a way to transmit paid services (such as Muzak) as a multiplexed signal on the FM subcarrier (see Chapter 5).

When FM stereo was perfected, receiver manufacturers (who were discovering the nation's appetite for sound systems of high quality) gave impetus to the FM band by producing receivers of sufficient quality to maximize the superior quality of music on FM. Because FM was allocated a wider band of frequencies than was AM, it was possible for FM to transmit a greater portion of the dynamic range of music. That is, the difference between loud and soft could be more pronounced on FM than on AM. FM allowed listeners to hear more of the range of frequencies that comprised the original music source. The greater bandwidth of the FM channel (as explained in Chapter 5) also made it possible to transmit in stereophonic sound. With high-fidelity stereo-recordings now dominating the record industry, FM was poised to provide a greatly improved sound service on the air for listeners.

The result is that FM has achieved great popularity among the nation's radio listeners. Automobile manufacturers have made AM/FM radios readily available, and buyers have responded. Portable receivers added FM reception to the traditional AM offerings on such equipment. Recent miniaturization of electronic components has made high-quality sound available in units that can be stuffed into shirt pockets or hung from the waistband of jogging shorts.

The automation boom made it possible to run the FM operation with little extra staffing, and the format services provided programming designed to attract highly desirable audience segments. In short, FM's quality has become the overwhelming choice of those among today's radio listeners who are interested in music programming. Accordingly, FM's profits have soared.

AM did hang on for a while, but in the past five years many AM operations have foundered. Many modern listeners never investigate the AM band to sample its offerings. Although formats like all-news and nostalgia radio (music of the big band era) do not suffer greatly from the loss of quality imposed by AM's technical limitations, most music simply sounds better on FM.

In attempting to fight back, AM operators are looking for technical improvements that will allow for stereobroadcasting and better frequency response. These innovations are in the works, but meanwhile FM's fortunes continue to improve, while AM as a whole, languishes in hard times.

RADIO AS A BUSINESS

Radio's development as a commercial medium has meant that it always has been destined to operate as a business. When television threatened radio with extinction, there were many who mourned the impending loss of an important form of entertainment. But it was those whose livelihood depended upon radio's continued viability as a commercial medium who had the greatest stake in finding new directions for the medium.

Radio's rebirth brought changes in the economics of the industry, which initially saw less money flowing to stations from networks, and a growing localization of the profit sources that ran radio. To be profitable the station had to depend on resources available locally. The strong audience pull of network programming was gone. With that went the network compensation that once provided a considerable portion of the revenue that once bolstered the profits of many stations.

Radio's new structure meant that it was sink or swim at the station level. As it turned out, this mode of operation worked. Radio found its new role in catering to the musical tastes of its listeners, and there was no need for expensive mass-appeal programming. Music could be easily and successfully programmed at the local level. Local and national advertisers quickly saw the benefits of radio in reaching audiences in new ways. The business picture brightened considerably for stations that had been wallowing in premature predictions of doom just a few years before.

The economics of today's radio industry have changed again. In both programming and profitability, the center of activity has expanded beyond the scope of the local station. Syndicated programming suppliers, corporate ownership of stations, nationally produced programming supplied to stations with commercials intact, and ad hoc networks linked by satellites have contributed to a situation in which it is difficult to see the individual station as an independent operation.

At the station level, the business still operates essentially as it always has. Salespeople persuade clients who advertise products and services to purchase time on the station. The revenue thus produced is used to operate the station, that is, pay for music sources, news services, talent, clerical support, station promotion, and administrative support. What is left over after expenses are covered is profit. This basic formula for success remains unchanged. But an examination of modern station operations shows that the basic financial structures of the industry have changed considerably in recent years.

With radio stations changing hands with greater frequency than ever before, there is less of a tendency for the owners of a station to be in the business of operating a single station for the purpose of making a reasonable profit. More commonly in today's radio business, stations are owned by larger business entities such as a group of investors or a corporate headquarters with other holdings in communications or other businesses. These are owners who are looking at the operation in terms of return on investment.

Even when a station is purchased by an individual today, it is often viewed in terms of its ability to provide a good return on invested capital. For such owners, it is of great importance to improve the overall worth of a station in a fairly short period of time. Fewer people are looking at radio station ownership merely as a comfortable way to make a living, as a typical small-business owner might look at a shoe store or an appliance business in a small community.

This concern with improving the value of the property results in several important factors governing the operation of the enterprise. Profitability is very important but not the sole criterion for success. Profits can be postponed in order to build the potential for even greater profit. Given the size of many of the businesses that invest in radio properties today, it is possible for a particular radio station to withstand losses that would cripple a small entrepreneur.

A profitable station that ranks lower than it should in a given market is not necessarily an unattractive station to potential buyers. Such a station might be stable from the standpoint of producing a steady flow of income for its owners. However, large investors interested in rapid growth may find that there is more money to be made from the station if it operates at a loss for several years while it builds new studios, hires highly paid talent, or installs satellite-receiving equipment. Such changes, well-managed, can lead to success in building an attractive audience, which can greatly improve the ranking of the station in its market. The selling price a top-rated station can command will more than make up for short-term losses incurred by the added investment.

Besides changes in ownership structures, there have been changes in the costs involved in radio station operation. In the past there was relatively heavy investment in station facilities and equipment. Personnel costs also accounted for a large share of operating budgets. Of less impact in earlier times were the costs of music, which was often available free from record companies interested in airplay, and for promotion, which was largely limited to announcements aired on the station itself.

Today activity in all these areas has increased not only in dollar amounts required but also in terms of the proportions of operating budgets that are required to support them. Equipment costs, for instance, have grown as a percentage of operating expense. Several factors account for the increase. Competitive forces have made it necessary for many operations to upgrade substantially the quality of their sound reproduction. Moreover, the advent of compact discs and the impending debut of digital audio tape (DAT) have meant that stations have had to augment existing studio and production equipment to maintain the high-quality sound reproduction demanded by today's audiences.

As AM finds ways to compete more effectively with FM, there will be additional costs ahead for that segment of the industry. Physical facilities are being renovated and rebuilt by many stations because group ownership allows for capital outlays that can be absorbed more easily and written off corporate tax returns. Even in small markets, many stations are finding it expedient to abandon facilities that have been used effectively for years in favor of new sites that can be designed more precisely for the technical and business requirements necessary for successful operation.

In the programming area, satellite services have added considerably to costs. Music and other programming services no longer can be a minimal part of the budget. There is a considerable burden placed on technical budgets by the necessary earth-station equipment and automation equipment needed to integrate program services into program schedules.

Personnel costs have increased. Growing professionalism among those trained in the skills demanded by today's radio operations have driven labor costs higher. Small reductions in the on-air staff needed in some automated operations have been offset largely by an increased need for clerical support and for hiring the necessary personnel support for the increasingly complex technical aspects of station operations. In addition, many stations now require computer-operations people and technicians familiar with computer maintenance.

Benefits packages for employees have increased in recent years. Corporate ownership structures have brought attractive benefits packages to employees at stations in markets of all sizes. To compete successfully for personnel, even relatively small operations have had to improve their offerings in this area.

Costs of operating the business end of radio have increased as billing and bookkeeping operations have become more sophisticated. Beyond the personnel requirements of computerization, there is the cost of the equipment itself and the need for additional space to house the equipment.

Another major area that has imposed growing demands on station budgets is station promotion. To compete and grow in today's volatile radio market, stations must let people know that they are there, enticing listeners in ways that will lead them to sample the station's offerings and to keep them coming back for more. Advertising budgets at radio stations include funds for heavy television campaigns and newspaper, magazine, and billboard advertising. Printing costs of slick brochures and full-color packets designed to attract advertisers are becoming a routine expense for stations wishing to remain competitive.

Besides the categories above, there are expenses for consulting services purchased regularly by many stations, heat, light and electrical power, and plant maintenance, to name some. Of course, the bottom line is that all the expenses involved must ultimately produce a profit. In today's radio station, the sophistication of the business practices (and the complex financing resulting from new structures of ownership along with heavy competitive forces) make the operation far more complex than the small-business configuration that was typical of radio just a few years ago.

PUBLIC AND NONCOMMERCIAL RADIO

The noncommercial sector of radio today is a very exciting segment of the radio industry. The modern public broadcasting system (PBS) has advanced exponentially from the relatively unsophisticated service that characterized its operations in the 1960s.

Once known as educational radio, many of the system's early stations were licensed to colleges or municipalities. Some operated as little more than training facilities for broadcasting students. Program quality was, at best, uneven. Many stations were on the air for only part of the day. Little thought was given to the audience. This was the service that provided what was "good"—whether there were two or two million listeners mattered little.

Primarily, financing often was accomplished through allocations from the operating budget of the institution to which the station was licensed. There was some, but very little, network programming; even that was often of dubious quality. Broadcast schedules often comprised a hodgepodge of local music programming, instructional material available on tape (which was "bicycled" from station to station), and occasional public affairs offerings produced with varying quality by well-meaning community organizations.

Public radio has overcome those shaky beginnings to become a first-rate service that responds to the needs and interests of its audience while still providing an alternative service that is not available on commercial radio. Public radio produces programming of the highest quality, funded by a combination of quasi-governmental, listener, and foundation and corporation sources. Programs such as *All Things Considered,* the retired *A Prairie Home Companion, Morning Edition,* and many others have found substantial audiences.

Programming is structured to appeal to wide interests, and the level of listenership is an important criterion in determining whether a program remains on the air. Stations originate programming and supplement it with network offerings from National Public Radio based in Washington, D.C., and American Public Radio based in Minnesota. State-level programming services produce material for public stations in the state and often produce programs that are distributed nationally. From market to market, stations vary in levels of staffing and sophistication of operations in accordance with their budgets. Fund-raising still remains a vital source of financial support, and this results in some variations in quality. Equipment is sometimes not state-of-the-art, and inadequate staffing can contribute to less-than-ideal conditions. As a whole, however, increasing numbers of listeners seek out the noncommercial sector of radio as a high-quality alternative to the commercial realm.

Two factors can explain the unprecedented level of popularity enjoyed by public radio. First, the rise in the popularity of FM—the frequency spectrum assigned to the public sector since it's beginning—helped improve the likelihood that listeners would sample the offerings of the service. Second, public broadcasters have generally recognized the need to serve the audience with satisfactory production values and programming that attracts a following.

RATINGS AND RESEARCH

The fortunes of radio today revolve around the ability of station operators to know as much as possible about the audiences that exist. Armed with this knowledge, programmers have succeeded in developing formats that appeal to almost any musical taste or programming interest imaginable. The need for a station to know its audience doesn't stop when an audience niche is found and attracted to the station's programming. The audience must be continually monitored. How are listeners responding to the programming being offered? Is your station gaining or losing audience? Are you getting your full share of the audience? What can you tell your advertisers about the characteristics of your audience in relation to, for example, income levels and life-styles?

To meet these needs and to respond to the questions raised above, an industry has grown up. Audience research for radio, like television, is conducted by commercial organizations that specialize in gathering and reporting data on a regular basis for use by stations and advertisers. These firms survey each radio market in the country on a regular basis. The data are then sold to stations and other clients for their use.

Computer use has greatly expanded the ability of stations to manipulate data to demonstrate such things as the cost to an advertiser of reaching a certain number of people of a certain age group or of how many spot announcements it will take to reach a given number of separate individuals with an advertising message.

At one time it took hours, even days or weeks, of analysis to read the data to this fine a degree. It was primarily large-market stations, advertising agencies, and national sales representatives that ran such analyses. But today most stations, large and small, have microcomputers with easy-to-understand software that provides the ability to analyze audience data very quickly and easily (see Chapter 5). It is a very simple matter for a sales manager in even the smallest of markets to show the proprietor of a local shoe store exactly how station WXXX can help him reach the customers he is interested in.

Sophistication in audience analysis and measurement has been responsible to a great degree for the proliferation of formats and station sounds that characterizes modern radio. Because of rapid analysis of data and expert integration of qualitative information about audiences, it is possible to predict with considerable accuracy what kinds of programming will appeal to listening audiences. This knowledge combined with the use of heavy promotion to attract listeners has greatly developed radio as an efficient and effective advertising medium.

PART ONE

PROGRAMS

———————

———————

CHAPTER 1

———————

RADIO:

———————

BIRTH AND REBIRTH

———————

Radio has captured the imagination of the public since its earliest inception. The idea of invisible signals flashing through thin air to be heard by people sitting next to a small box in their homes seemed to radio's early listeners to be the stuff of science fiction. It had become possible, in a world in which geography could severely limit one's awareness of human events, for information to be passed through space, penetrating walls and other physical barriers to reach listeners far away from the source of the original sound.

In its earliest expression, radio offered to free us from the insulation imposed by such boundaries. Any form of human expression that could be conveyed through sound was now available to the most isolated farmhouse and the most sophisticated city dweller. All you needed was the box, and your home became a concert hall, a theater, a classroom. The romance of the idea is undeniable.

1.1

GENESIS OF THE BROADCAST ERA

Radio's magic did not spring full-blown into the American cultural mainstream. Like other major social phenomena, radio at its birth gave no indication of its future impact. It would shape society far beyond the wildest dreams of those who first discerned its technical feasibility. The story of radio's birth and development starts in the nineteenth century.

From Marconi to de Forest to Sarnoff

It was the theoretical physics of James Clerk-Maxwell in the late-nineteenth century that set the stage for the emergence of what was much later to become radio. Clerk-Maxwell's "A Treatise on Electricity and Magnetism" in 1873[1] postulated the existence of electromagnetic phenomena. Using mathematic formulas, Clerk-Maxwell determined that an invisible energy, which behaves like visible light, must exist. Several more years would pass, however, before an actual demonstration of this theory would occur.

Little more than a decade later German physicist Heinrich Hertz conducted a laboratory demonstration that confirmed Clerk-Maxwell's theory. Hertz's proof of the existence of such phenomena, however, provided no hint of the practical applications of this form of energy. In fact, it was widely believed that there was no practical use of these waves.

It was the dogged persistence of the young Guglielmo Marconi (Figure 1.1) that produced the first evidence that electromagnetic energy could be put to practical use as a means of transmitting information. As a teenager in Italy, Marconi spent long hours in his workshop experimenting with the hertzian waves that so fascinated him.

Other scientists also were experimenting with the waves. Ultimately, it was the young Marconi who first demonstrated that it was possible to manipulate these waves to send telegraphic messages. This was accomplished by using the Morse system of dots and dashes. The wave was generated and then interrupted in a pattern conforming to the coded message. It was the same on–off configuration of existing telegraphy. The difference, and hence the distinct advantage to Marconi's system, was that wires were not required.

Messages could be transmitted across expanses of water. Receivers no longer had

Figure 1.1

Guglielmo Marconi's experiments with electromagnetic energy led to the development of
radiotelegraphy and later radiotelephony. Here he is shown with David Sarnoff (left) of
RCA at RCA's transmitting center at Rocky Point, Long Island, New York, in 1933.
Courtesy of The National Broadcasting Company, Inc.

to be wired directly to the sender. The utility of telegraphy had been greatly enhanced.
What had been an interesting scientific observation had become a practical system of
communication. Wireless, as it came to be known, meant that ship-to-shore communication was now possible, a considerable advantage in an age of increasing inter-
oceanic travel and commerce.

When the Italian government expressed no interest in Marconi's discoveries his
British-born mother took Marconi to England. The British government was very interested in a technology that offered such a rapid communications system for its far-
flung empire.[2] Quickly, the practical success of Marconi's invention was translated into
commercial success. A company was formed, and Marconi became one of six directors
and a major stockholder. Patents were obtained, and financial success followed in due
course.

Following up on his success in England, Marconi brought his invention to the United States, where the United States Navy took a strong interest in it. Marconi formed an American company, and radiotelegraphy became an American commercial venture that would form the basis of an entire industry.

Meanwhile, wireless had begun to capture the imaginations of other inventors and experimenters. If hertzian waves could convey telegraphic messages, why not sound? The challenge was to discover how to manipulate radio waves in a way that would allow sound to travel through space the way it travels through wires.

An inventor named Reginald Fessenden argued that it was the use of an interrupted wave, which served well to convey telegraphic codes, that was hindering the development of sound transmission via electromagnetic waves. Fessenden teamed up at General Electric (GE) with F. W. Alexanderson. Together they developed an alternator that could transmit a continuous wave. They found that, by altering the characteristics of this wave, sound could indeed be transmitted through space. The signal could be detected in much the same way that telegraphic signals were, and the sound could then be reproduced and heard through the earphones connected to the receiver.

The alternator developed by Fessenden and Alexanderson was put into operation at Brant Rock, Massachusetts. From that location in 1906, Fessenden broadcast a Christmas Eve program. There was violin music played by Fessenden and a phonograph recording of Handel's "Largo." Fessenden also read a passage from the Bible. After wishing the audience a Merry Christmas, Fessenden said he would broadcast again on New Year's Eve. Shipboard wireless operators, who were listening for dots and dashes, were astounded to hear voices and music coming through their earphones.

In the early part of the century, numerous individuals were working on radio experiments. Prior to 1910, Thomas E. Clark in Detroit and Charles D. "Doc" Herrold in San Jose, California, were beginning to shape radio's future. Herrold, who opened a college of engineering, provided a weekly schedule of programs that attracted loyal followers. Herrold's operation ended with the onset of World War I, but after the war others took over. Today Herrold's small, low-powered station operates as KCBS, San Francisco.

Another experimenter, Lee de Forest (Figure 1.2), worked to improve transmission capabilities of this very promising technology. What was needed was a way to amplify broadcast signals. De Forest's invention of the audion tube (later called the vacuum tube) dramatically advanced radiotelephony, as it was becoming known.

Beyond de Forest's significant advances in radio technology, he was also providing early radio programming to a scattered group of experimenters and amateurs who were becoming devoted followers of this exciting new form of entertainment. What these early listeners heard was a collection of live musical performances, lectures, gramophone recordings, and reports of events. It was entertainment mostly because it was novel. To pick music from the air and hear it on a crude receiver was fascinating to

Figure 1.2

Lee de Forest's invention of the audion tube resulted in major advances
in radio transmission.
The Bettmann Archive, Inc.

those who lived in an era in which the primary source of musical entertainment in the
home had been limited to the sounds evoked from the piano in the parlor or from a few
wax cylinders played on a gramophone (Figure 1.3).

Despite the novelty of the experience, there was little in the way of radio programming that would suggest that there was commercial value to such entertainment.
Commercial applications were perceived to lie solely in the sale of transmitting and
receiving equipment to governments that needed to communicate for military or other
purposes. This was an area of enterprise that was being vigorously pursued by Marconi,
de Forest, and others. But there were some who perceived another role for radio, a role
that ultimately would make government applications seem relatively insignificant by
comparison.

A young man named David Sarnoff (see Figure 1.1), who had relayed telegraphed reports of the sinking of the Titanic to an anxious America (and who was to

Figure 1.3

Radio receivers once occupied a prominent place in the American home.
Courtesy of The National Broadcasting Company, Inc.

become one of the giants of the radio-broadcasting era), was one of the first to see the potential for radio transmission.

In 1915 Sarnoff was the first to identify the commercial prospects of what he called a "Radio Music Box."[3] His "plan of development" looked at the eventual prospect of making radio a household utility rather than the experimental toy of those who were becoming known as radio "amateurs."[4] Sarnoff's proposal was to bring to every home in America the offerings of the nation's centers of culture.

"The idea," he wrote to his superiors at American Marconi, "is to bring music into the house by wireless. . . ." He went on to describe the commercial potential of such a service. "The main revenue to be derived will be from the sale of the 'Radio Music Boxes' which if manufactured in lots of one hundred thousand or so could yield a handsome profit."[5]

Sarnoff's idea was to await further development of the radio-manufacturing industry before broadcasting became a thriving commercial operation. When Radio Corporation of America (RCA) came into being as a cooperative venture among several competing manufacturers, Sarnoff's idea was adopted and became the basis for a booming business in his "Radio Music Boxes." The stage was now completely set for broadcasting to become a major part of modern life.

The First Commercial Stations

During World War I, technology advanced rapidly. By the end of the war, technologic development had progressed greatly. The efforts of Lee de Forest to provide listeners with crude programming schedules were soon imitated by many other amateurs. Sending music and voice into the "ether" was a romantic and fascinating phenomenon. Many found an all-consuming hobby in hovering over simple crystal receiving sets to pluck signals from the air that could be heard dimly through the headphones, which were eagerly passed around from person to person so that all could listen.

Because the general public lacked the means to receive radio signals, there was little incentive for anyone to develop a regular program schedule. It was the usual chicken-and-egg problem. Without listeners there was little incentive to develop better service, but without better service there was little impetus for audience growth. The resolution of this situation began to take shape in Pittsburgh.

Pittsburgh was the home of Westinghouse, a firm that had carved out a strong role in communications and electric power. During World War I, Westinghouse prospered as it acquired numerous government contracts. But when the war ended, Westinghouse needed a way to compete effectively in a market now dominated by the conglomeration of RCA, and American Telegraph and Telephone (AT&T), which together controlled a lion's share of the patents needed for commercial success in the growing radio industry.

In 1920 Westinghouse engineer Frank Conrad, who had played a major role in wartime radio development, began a series of radiotelephone transmissions from a workshop in his garage. Like other amateurs around the country, he eventually began transmitting programs on a somewhat regular basis. He received mail from other amateurs, and his enterprise gradually grew more sophisticated. Phonograph records were supplied by a music store, and family members served as announcers.

Meanwhile, a Pittsburgh department store saw profit potential in these broadcasts. Conrad's programs could be used to promote sales of amateur wireless sets, which the store had on sale for $10.00. Soon a newspaper ad appeared in the *Pittsburgh Sun* (Figure 1.4) noting that Conrad's transmissions had been picked up at the wireless receiving station, which had been installed in Horne's department store, and that sets were on sale in the store.[6]

Westinghouse immediately recognized the implications of this. If the public could be assured of a continuing schedule of service, there could be "limitless opportunity" for the sale of receiving sets.[7] Westinghouse had been manufacturing receivers for several years, but there had been no thought of marketing them to the general public. However, here was an opportunity to bring to the everyday citizen what had been an avocation only for those with technical know-how. Accordingly, West-

Figure 1.4

An ad in the *Pittsburgh Sun* for Frank Conrad's early broadcasts.
Reproduced with permission of KDKA Radio, Pittsburgh, PA.

Air Concert
"Picked Up"
By Radio Here

Victrola music, played into the air over a wireless telephone, was "picked up" by listeners on the wireless receiving station which was recently installed here for patrons interested in wireless experiments. The concert was heard Thursday night about 10 o'clock, and continued 20 minutes. Two orchestra numbers, a soprano solo—which rang particularly high, and clear through the air—and a juvenile "talking piece" constituted the program.

The music was from a Victrola pulled up close to the transmitter of a wireless telephone in the home of Frank Conrad, Penn and Peebles avenues, Wilkinsburg. Mr. Conrad is a wireless enthusiast and "puts on" the wireless concerts periodically for the entertainment of the many people in this district who have wireless sets.

Amateur Wireless Sets, made by the maker of the Set which is in operation in our store, are on sale here $10.00 up.

inghouse moved quickly to build upon Conrad's amateur activities and established a broadcast service.

Westinghouse applied to the U.S. Department of Commerce for an operating frequency for a new transmitter. The station was assigned the call letters KDKA. KDKA's maiden broadcast was on November 2, 1920; it aired the presidential election results, in which Warren G. Harding defeated James M. Cox. Information was received by telephone at the transmitter site from **wire service** reports arriving at the *Pittsburgh Post*. Recorded music filled the intervals between election reports.

The audience was there, and the concept was born. Westinghouse could stimulate set sales by providing a service of regular broadcasts. Although some dispute KDKA's claim of being the first broadcast station, there is little doubt that it had developed a revolutionary concept. KDKA was now equipped to exploit fully the potential of this new medium.

The commercial relationship between a broadcast service and the sale of radio receivers had broken new ground in the field of communications. Recognizing that radio broadcasting could promote a commercial enterprise was something new. The commercial radio station had been born.

Soon listeners could receive a regular schedule of live music, lectures, and sporting events. The public's enthusiasm grew, and radio receivers were suddenly in great demand. They became widely available through stores or through the industry of amateurs who were increasingly asked to assemble sets for friends and neighbors.

Following up on KDKA's success, other commercial stations sprung up quickly in the early 1920s. The term *commercial stations,* however, meant only that they were licensed by the U.S. Department of Commerce. Advertising still played no role in radio. Westinghouse established an additional station in Newark, New Jersey, with the call letters WJZ. Programming was supplied by major entertainment figures from New York. Other stations popped up in New York, and more followed in other parts of the country. The instant popularity of these stations led to the rapid development of stations by department stores, newspapers, colleges and universities, and religious organizations.

The boom in radio broadcasting left little time to think about where all this progress might lead. The major benefits to these early broadcasters were goodwill and publicity for the sponsoring organization. Some educational institutions had vague notions of educational applications, but the real fascination was in the magic of the medium itself.

It was not until AT&T came up with a new concept in 1922 that the first inkling of radio's true potential began to emerge. The concept was radical: The telephone company would provide no programs, only facilities. Just as the telephone was provided to AT&T customers for their own uses, so would broadcast facilities be made available to paying customers for whatever they wished to put on the air. AT&T's profits would come from the charges made for this service. The concept was named **toll broadcasting,** and it originated in Manhattan from a station with the call letters WEAF.

AT&T soon discovered that the concept was incomplete. The problem was the same one faced by radio in general. If there was no programming, there was no audience. With AT&T's concept, programming was to be supplied by paying customers. But without an audience, who would be willing to pay for using the facilities? AT&T decided that they needed to supply a certain amount of programming to kick the system into action.

That evidently provided the necessary stimulus to attract toll users, for soon WEAF was thriving. WEAF's first income-producing message was hardly a demonstration of radio's power to sell products, but it signaled the beginning of radio's future as an effective advertising medium. That first commercial announcement was for an apartment building in New York City. It was what might be termed today a "soft sell" on the merits of the spacious living afforded by an apartment complex, in the Jackson Heights section of Queens.[8]

WEAF found that its concept of toll broadcasting was virtually an instant success. Toll broadcasts were reaching many customers for commercial clients, and business was improving dramatically. AT&T responded by building new studios and improving the technical quality of its transmissions. Inevitably, pressure was building for broader use of radio as an advertising medium.

The Rise of the Networks

The concept of hooking stations together for simultaneous broadcasting came about when AT&T's station in New York, WEAF, was persuaded to supply its programming to WMAF in South Dartmouth, Massachusetts.[9] The owner of WMAF paid a fee to WEAF for the programs that were unsponsored; the sponsored programs he received free.

There were obvious benefits for commercial sponsors if, rather than having their messages broadcast by a single station, there could be several stations broadcasting their messages at the same time. So AT&T seriously began to develop what was first known as **chain broadcasting,** which later became network broadcasting. AT&T's control of telephone lines gave it immediate dominance in this field.

The concept developed rapidly, and by 1924 it was possible to broadcast coast to coast simultaneously over a chain of twenty-six stations.[10] Other station owners came to recognize the advantages of chain operation, but AT&T's control of telephone lines effectively prevented substantial competition.[11] Moreover, other stations were still operating noncommercially.

The revenues brought in by toll-broadcasting operations were substantial. In 1925 AT&T profited $150,000 from its broadcasting operations.[12] In other ways, however, AT&T's broadcasting operations were proving costly to the company. Controversies regarding the company's restrictions on the use of telephone lines by other broadcasters were heating up. These and other disputes were bringing unfavorable publicity to the firm; as a government-regulated industry, this was of increasing concern to AT&T.

To resolve these disputes, AT&T decided to retire completely from the broadcasting field. A new company was formed with joint ownership among GE, RCA, and Westinghouse. The purpose of the new entity was to provide programming for a network of broadcasting stations. Regular programming service would be fed via telephone lines leased from AT&T. WEAF, purchased from AT&T, would serve as the origination point for programs that were distributed throughout the country. The new company, formed in 1926, was called the National Broadcasting Company (NBC).[13]

Radio's Coming of Age as an Advertising Medium

There was considerable resistance at first to the widespread use of radio as an advertising medium. Critics saw advertising as a compromise to radio's potential as a cultural force. Some proposed that legislation be passed prohibiting the use of radio for advertising messages. Many newspapers refused to carry announcements of sponsored programs, and many radio stations refused to sell airtime to advertisers.

One reason for this opposition was the aura of sophistication surrounding radio. The medium was seen as being somehow above the type of enterprise that would use this valuable cultural tool to sell products. Announcers wore tuxedos. Studios were plush and elaborately furnished to the extent that microphones were hidden in lampshades and large plants. This gave rise to the label often applied to this time in radio's history: the "potted-palm" era of broadcasting (Figure 1.5).

The fact that radio came directly and saliently into the home resulted in a reluctance on the part of program creators to risk anything that might offend. Even those who presented commercial messages through toll broadcasts were carefully monitored by radio executives to prevent unseemly excesses of a commercial nature. Was tooth brushing too personal a function to be discussed in messages promoting tooth-care products? Should one mention price?

This early reticence led to the creation of a fascinating tactic among early advertisers. To gain the advantages of frequent mention of the sponsor of a program without being accused of offensive excess, entertainers frequently were named after the sponsoring organization. Thus came into national prominence The Gold Dust Twins, Goldy and Dusty sponsored by Gold Dust laundry detergent, and the Clicquot Club Eskimos, named after a soft-drink manufacturer. There was also the singing duo Jones and Hare, who appeared on radio under several names. The Happiness Boys for Happiness Candy Stores, The Interwoven Pair for Interwoven Socks, and The Taystee Loafers for Taystee Bread were a few of their names.[14]

The power of the medium to reach potential customers, combined with the formation of NBC, meant that such subtlety would not last. Slowly, the commercial sales pitch became a common feature of radio, and through the remainder of the 1920s, direct-selling messages were confined largely to regular business hours. However, there was no doubt that commercialism was to become the basis of the broadcasting industry.

The formation of NBC made it possible for advertisers to reach vast audiences.

Figure 1.5

Radio studios of the 1920s and 1930s reflected the formality of the medium.
Courtesy of The National Broadcasting Company, Inc.

Because NBC had been formed from two competing broadcasting operations, it now owned two stations in New York and in several other locations. To deal with the problem of feeding the same program over two stations in the same city, NBC formed two networks. One was designated as the "Red Network" and the other as the "Blue Network." Program schedules of stations in cities all over the country thus consisted of heavy doses of network-supplied programming, and much of that programming was sponsored.

Stations carrying network programming were becoming more and more intrigued with the idea of commercial sponsorship. Many stations that had operated as publicity vehicles for newspapers, department stores, or other business ventures made the move into commercial sponsorship.

Following the stock market crash in 1929, many restrictions on how advertising could be conducted began to fall by the wayside. Competition for NBC's two networks, in the form of the struggling Columbia Broadcasting System (CBS), hastened the demise of restrictions on radio advertising.

Government restrictions on advertising threatened to become a reality shortly after the election of Franklin D. Roosevelt in 1932. A bill drafted by the Food and Drug Administration proposed to deal with misleading advertising messages. A successful fight by the advertising industry and the National Association of Broadcasters, however, had the result that advertising was exempt from the provisions of the act, which essentially called for better product labeling.

Sponsorship of entire programs was the norm in the early 1930s because the networks were beginning to play a major role in broadcasting. This eventually gave way to an increase in the number and frequency of what became known as spot announcements. By the late 1940s and into the early 1950s, network-sponsored programs were interspersed on local radio stations with locally sponsored programs and commercial announcements.

As advertising agencies became increasingly accustomed to funneling clients' advertising funds into radio, agencies began to assume a large role in the production of programs. Gradually, production of sponsored programs began to shift from being a network responsibility to being an agency responsibility. Radio departments were created at leading agencies, and agency personnel coordinated scripts, hired talent, and generally controlled all aspects of the programs. The networks, which received the revenue for the airtime, were quite willing to cooperate in this arrangement.

By the mid-1930s commercial radio was well-intact. Stations were selling time locally and carrying large blocks of network programming. Radio began to be perceived by newspapers as a strong threat to their continued prosperity as a major advertising medium. However, efforts to stop this success were futile despite feeble attempts by newspapers to fight back through tactics such as refusing to publish radio program schedules.

Radio had developed into a commercial giant. The rise of commercial networks and radio's steady development as a unique entertainment medium meant that prosperity lay in store for the medium as it entered radio's golden age.

1.2

THE GOLDEN AGE OF BROADCASTING

The creation of the major radio networks meant that for the first time in history the collective attention of vast numbers of people could be focused on the same event at the exact time that event was taking place. And, those people could participate without having to leave the comfort of their living rooms.

Initially, high-blown predictions were made about how radio would bring historical moments to those who would otherwise have gained only secondhand awareness of them long after the events had taken place. Cultural offerings from the world's leading artists could be imported to remote, isolated areas. People could be informed and culturally enriched without having to reside in the nation's population centers. These lofty purposes were incorporated into much early radio programming. But as the medium evolved and became a commercial voice for advertisers, it became evident that it was not to be the cultural elite of society who would be the sole arbiters of the types of programming.

Sponsors bought *people,* not programs. When Lucky Strike purchased sponsorship of the *Jack Benny Program,* it did so because of the large audience who tuned in week after week. As far as Lucky Strike was concerned, the program was merely the bait that attracted the attention of people who could systematically be exposed to messages regarding the attributes of Luckies. This was true from the earliest commercial entry into this exciting mass medium.

For a time it was fine to keep the programming fare at an elevated level. It was inevitable, however, that if radio was to gain the following and devotion of a broad audience to attract large amounts of advertising revenue, programmers would have to develop a sensitivity to popular tastes in entertainment. Eventually, radio would have to cater to those tastes.

Radio's Role as a Mass Entertainer

Along with the need for programmers to meet popular tastes, there was increasing realization that radio's appetite for program material was enormous. When one hour had been filled, there was yet another to be filled immediately. And, audiences always waited anxiously to devour more programs.

New forms of entertainment had to be created to meet the unique demands of this mass medium. There were models. Newspapers had discovered economies that kept a steady flow of material with which to fill their pages. Columnists could be found regularly in the same space. Comic strips provided readers with running stories that needed only small amounts of development from day to day, week to week, year to year. The motion picture industry had discovered the serial. Multipart adventures and dramas could be depended on to draw crowds into movie houses week after week to follow the adventures of Tarzan or Flash Gordon or to chronicle the *Perils of Pauline.* It was this kind of program form that radio needed to attract listeners and keep them loyal to a certain sponsor or to a spot on the dial.

With the involvement of ad agencies in programming came the development of the forms that would become uniquely radio's. Programs were developed in serial fashion, often bearing the imprimatur of the sponsor. For example, *Jack Armstrong, the all-American boy,* was sponsored by Wheaties, a cereal that could presumably help develop in young listeners the physical attributes that would enable them to perform the heroic feats documented in the series. *Sergeant Preston of the Yukon, The Shadow, The Green Hornet, Mr. Keene: Tracer of Lost Persons, Gangbusters,* and other radio series soon occupied a dominant place in American life.

The programs gave listeners a set of characters who were developed gradually over time. Story lines needed only to allow the characters situations and predicaments to negotiate. Dialogue and sound effects, unique and creative devices, were all that was necessary to relate vast amounts of information. The imaginations of the listeners completed the story. All that was needed to visualize even the most exotic landscapes and strange lands was a few words of description, a few sound effects, and the expressive interpretation of dialogue. If recapitulation of the plot was needed, an announcer provided a resonant recitation of the key elements of the story.

The variety format, which became a mainstay of radio programming, took its cue from vaudeville. Instead of the lighted stage in a darkened theater, there was the magic sound of laughter and good times emanating from some distant theater where a studio audience could see what the radio listener could only imagine. But it was the listener who often had the advantage. When Jack Benny tried to start his tempermental Maxwell automobile, the radio listener had a far more vivid picture of what was taking place than did the studio audience.

Situation comedy, musical variety, adventure, high drama, and game formats became staples of radio in its heyday during the 1930s and 1940s. Audiences became devoted fans of stars they had never seen. Social events were organized to make allowances for favorite radio programs. Some programs acquired large national followings. Numerous motion picture theaters, reacting to the competitive force of radio, would interrupt their feature films when *Amos 'N Andy* came on the air. To do otherwise would mean empty theaters on a certain evening of the week.

America was partaking of a cultural phenomenon that it had never had the opportunity to experience. Sponsors were reaping the benefits; sales of products advertised on radio soared. More Americans were smoking Lucky Strikes and using Rinso Blue. Ipana Toothpaste and Pepsi Cola swept their respective markets on the heels of constant exposure on radio.

Radio's Role as an Information Source

Along with the explosion of entertainment programs came a revolution in the way Americans learned about events. The first commercial broadcast in 1920 on KDKA was a report of election returns. Early programming was replete with news of events, including the voices of the newsmakers. However, the regular reporting of events as a newspaper might report them was a slower development.

Initially, many stations reported news only when obliged to fill programming time that unexpectedly became vacant because a performer failed to arrive at the studio at the designated time. At such times, it was not unusual for an announcer to read the local newspaper, simply to have something to broadcast until the next performer arrived.

It was not until World War II that radio became a regular source of "hard" news. But for all of radio's halting entry into the forms that ultimately would become a full-blown broadcast news service, news was very much a part of the emerging medium. This fact greatly alarmed the owners of newspapers: A public who could hear news read to them might not want to buy papers to read for themselves.

The reaction of the newspaper industry to this perceived threat was an attempt to influence news services to impose severe limitations on radio's use of wire service material. This was successful only for a short time. In 1935 the United Press syndicate broke ranks and began to serve radio stations as they had in the past. The other two, International News Service and Associated Press, soon followed suit. It eventually became evident that newspapers had little to fear and much to cheer, for news reported on radio stimulated interest in learning more about events by reading newspapers, which usually supplied more detail.

News Finds a Unique Voice

Radio's great contribution to news coverage was its ability to take the public instantaneously to the scene of a breaking news story. One of the most dramatic examples of the power of radio news coverage literally came home to radio listeners who had tuned in to hear a routine news report describing the docking of the dirigible Hindenburg as it arrived in Lakehurst, New Jersey, from Germany in 1933. The descriptions by the rattled announcer, as he witnessed burning passengers falling to the ground following the explosion and fire that occurred while he was on the air live, was preserved in recorded form. Even to modern listeners it is an example of the powerful drama that can characterize unfolding events, broadcast as they happen.

Those who presented news reports over the air came to have an increasingly larger role in the nation's life. It soon became evident that considerable influence could be exerted by those with access to the airwaves. This sometimes presented problems for those who operated broadcasting facilities. When H. V. Kaltenborne, who had a background as a newspaper editor, began to give "talks" on the air, those controlling radio had to face the problem of what constituted proper editorial criticism. Could government officials be targets for criticism? Kaltenborne weathered the controversies and went on to become well-known as the dean of radio news commentators. Commentary, which presented the news with interpretation and opinion, supplemented the objective reporting of events and became a mainstay of radio's news offerings.

Radio greatly depended on printed news sources to provide information. There was widespread use of wire service material and newspaper reports during the 1920s and 1930s. The implementation of news gathering capabilities awaited the advent of World War II. Meanwhile, news coverage was spotty and of widely varying quality. Even in the live reporting of news events, radio was slow to explore the full capabilities of the medium.

Radio's Coming of Age in the Murrow Era

When Edward R. Murrow began his famous broadcasts from London in the late 1930s, American radio had been broadcasting from Europe for almost a decade. By 1930 CBS, under the watchful eye of the young William Paley, had begun to be a competitive network force against NBC. CBS newsman Ceasar Searchinger pioneered the development of broadcasts from Europe, and it was his activity that led to the first opportunity for Americans to hear the voice of the British monarch. Later came the voice of George Bernard Shaw, who used the opportunity to make castigating remarks about the American social system.

As Europe became embroiled in Hitler's activities, Edward R. Murrow (Figure 1.6) and CBS made these distant events real for American listeners. The voices of the principal European leaders—Hitler, Mussolini, Chamberlain, and Churchill—were heard by Americans while they ate dinner or sat in their living rooms. Gradually, European events began to seem more like American events. The isolationism that had been the hallmark of American diplomacy since the end of World War I was dissolving before the increasing knowledge that the world was growing smaller. There was a growing sense that what affected Europe affected America.

When the German Blitzkrieg began in London, Murrow was there to describe the devastation of the nightly German bombing raids. He described the people of Lon-

Figure 1.6

Edward R. Murrow's broadcasts of the "Battle of Britain" depicted
the devastation of the London Blitzkrieg.
The Bettmann Archive, Inc.

don searching for household belongings amid the rubble and destruction of bombed-out dwellings. He conveyed to Americans sitting in the comfort and security of their homes the stark fear that accompanied the sound of air-raid sirens in the night. Radio listeners heard the sirens, the explosions, and the screaming while Murrow's rich, clipped, baritone voice described the scene in vivid but economical phrases. Murrow departed from the stilted style that characterized the carefully scripted reports of his predecessors. He was "talking" to the radio listener, and he was a captivating presence.

Gradually, Americans grew convinced that Hitler must be stopped. Europe had been at war for some time before significant public opinion arose in favor of United States involvement. The compromises of Munich had turned out to be a sham, and Hitler, unchecked, had pressed his plans to dominate Europe. War had broken out, and America was sitting on the sidelines. American public opinion, however, was being altered by the vivid news from Europe that came into their homes in such an immediate fashion. Thus, when Pearl Harbor was bombed and the Axis powers became the enemies of the United States, there was widespread American sympathy for the justice of the cause.

Throughout the war, radio reported the action from Europe and the Pacific. The names of Larry Lesueur, Charles Collingwood, and Eric-Sevareid became familiar to American radio listeners who looked to these correspondents to convey a sense of what it was like to witness, firsthand, momentous events. Radio reporters landed with allied troops on the beaches of Normandy on D-Day and followed the advancing armies through France to Berlin, where the end came in Europe. In the Pacific, island-hopping American troops were accompanied by radio reporters. Americans were kept in touch with everything from MacArthur's return to the Philippines to the dropping of atomic bombs on Hiroshima and Nagasaki to the ultimate signing of the Japanese surrender.

By the end of the war, radio journalists had become proficient at gathering and reporting news in a fashion that fully utilized radio's immediacy. The organizational structures that reported on world events had become well-oiled machines. Murrow's seasoned team of correspondents formed the nucleus of a news organization that would come to represent a major force for excellence in American journalism.

CBS became the model for other networks as they developed worldwide news organizations of their own. In the late 1940s and into the early 1950s, radio had reached its full potential as a news medium. This would carry over into television and form the basis for the network news operations of today.

Radio news was now a journalistic form unto itself. Its impact was vast, and the public would come to be increasingly influenced by its presence as a major force in everyday life. The American public could now participate in events as they were happening. People could experience momentous events with greater immediacy because they heard the *sounds* of news. No longer did distant events seem remote and unconnected to the daily lives of ordinary people. Radio supplied the presence that written reports could never convey. It had become very difficult for anyone to live quietly on an isolated farm in rural America and view world events as remote and unrelated to individual concerns.

Program Forms

While news was coming of age in radio, other program offerings were developing into forms of entertainment that were becoming as unique to the medium as radio news was in the journalistic realm. The era of the potted palm, which heavily depended on the willingness of performers to use material that was adapted from the concert hall or the

Figure 1.7

The predictability of Gracie Allen's responses to George Burns's straight lines eased
the problem of creating fresh material week after week.
Courtesy of The National Broadcasting Company, Inc.

theatrical stage, had given way to forms of entertainment that would keep the voracious medium satisfied with a steady diet of entertainment fare.

The series concept solved the problem of filling long hours, daily and weekly, with material that would attract audiences. Tired vaudeville formulas, which depended on fresh audiences for old material, had to be abandoned. In radio the audience wasn't changing. The same people returned week after week, so a constant supply of new material had to be created, used, and abandoned.

It was noted earlier that the amount of new creative material required could be reduced by setting up an ongoing story line and a set of characters whose major traits could be established and continued, episode after episode. A number of interesting devices actually made this work. In comedy, for example, dialogue could be written that played off of previously established character traits. Gracie Allen's (Figure 1.7) famed bubble-headedness was a given. Thus, when George Burns asked a straight question, the listening audience was already primed for the misinterpretation Gracie would apply to her response.

Jack Benny's propensity for penny-pinching provided a ready-made vehicle for very minimal use of dialogue. An example of this is the long silence that followed a

Benny situation in which a burglar made the famous demand, "Your money or your life." The silence in itself was hilarious to listeners, and the comedy was compounded by the line Benny eventually delivered following the long silence, "I'm thinking, I'm thinking."

Radio depended on such devices for survival. The process was refined to high-level efficiency. The most efficient example of this type of conservation of material was the soap opera. Whereas action/adventure series and situation comedy usually engaged in plot development that involved either resolution of a dilemma or movement of the action forward, the daytime serial focused on the lives and problems of fictitious individuals and how those characters and their situations were affected by other characters.

The announcer's opening lines of the long-running *Romance of Helen Trent* are illustrative of the simple premise behind this form. "The Romance of Helen Trent. The real-life drama of Helen Trent who, when life mocks her, breaks her hopes, dashes her against the rocks of despair, fights back bravely, successfully to prove what so many women long to prove in their own lives, that because a woman is thirty-five or more, romance in life need not be over. That romance can begin at thirty-five." *Our Gal Sunday* asked if a "girl from a small mining town in the west could find happiness as the wife of a wealthy and titled Englishman." *Just Plain Bill* was about just plain Bill. *Mary Noble, Backstage Wife* described the hardships and heartaches of being married to a famous actor.

Plot movement was agonizingly slow in soap opera, and yet there was no more loyal audience to be found in any medium. Characters received voluminous quantities of mail. Letters came from listeners suggesting ways to deal with the fictional situations posed in the dramas. And best of all for radio, this devotion was achieved with minimal strain on the creative reservoirs of writers and producers.

The listener loyalty engendered by network programs in the 1930s and 1940s made the networks a dominant force in the broadcasting industry. The role of individual stations in programming was continually shrinking during this period of time. Networks extracted contracts from affiliates, giving the network the right to take over the affiliate's airtime at the network's discretion. From the stations' standpoint, the advantages of network affiliation were an acceptable trade-off for the strictures imposed by affiliation contracts. High-quality popular programming was continually available, and stations received compensation for the use of their airwaves by sponsors who had bought time in network programs.

While there were still many stations that were not network affiliates, the industry as a whole was becoming strongly identified with network stars and programs. Large salaries were paid to top stars. Networks began to vie with one another for celebrities by staging talent raids on competing networks.

Radio became a glamorous and romantic institution in American society. Millions built their social lives around the network schedules. Variations on the series idea took the form of action series, western drama, situation comedy, comedy/variety, audience participation, panel shows, live dramatic presentation of stage classics adapted for radio, drama written especially for radio presented in repertory format with showcase formats in which a new play was produced each week, mystery programs, detective shows, and radio equivalents of the scary story and horror-film variety, the latter typified by the very popular *Lights Out*.

The enthusiasm with which Americans embraced these new programs and the vast popularity of radio can be explained in part because imagination allowed the listener to individualize and tailor the effect to experiences and emotions that spoke uniquely to the individual. The voice of a romantic lead left it to the listener to fill in the physical features that complemented the picture for him or her. The awkwardness of a comedian standing in his underwear before a studio audience was funnier because it could be imagined. Literalness could have lessened the impact considerably.

Programs and stars became part of daily life. Everyday conversations of Americans were becoming sprinkled liberally with expressions heard on radio. "Tain't funny McGee" from *Fibber McGee and Molly*, "Vas you dere Scharlie" from a character known as Baron Munchhausen, and Joe Penna's refrain "Wanna buy a duck?" were to that era what "Sorry about that Chief" became when Don Adams played Maxwell Smart on television decades later.

Radio, then, had become a mass medium. Those who created radio programs were shaping our national culture. New products found vast markets overnight. Presidents could address the entire nation at once. Leaders could exert profound influence on national and international affairs with a single utterance. No longer was it necessary to travel all over the country to reach the American people.

Entertainers became nationally known, literally overnight. Vaudeville, which had long served as a training ground for aspiring entertainers, would die out; it would become more difficult for struggling young performers to develop. You could no longer "bomb" in Sheboygan and come back on another night to "wow" them in Peoria. If you bombed in radio, you could be finished for good.

Yet, it was indeed a golden age for those who could make this medium work. There was a fortune to be made by opening a microphone key. Radio entertainers rose to superstardom. Life in show business became easier and more lucrative for more people. People got rich in radio.

But there was change in the wind as World War II ended and peacetime technology brought itself up to speed once again. Television, which had been demonstrated as early as the 1920s and which was a phenomenon of the 1936 World's Fair, was being perfected. In the mid-1940s, television was on the verge of becoming a reality for the American public. When the first television sets became available to consumers in 1946, few sensed the magnitude of change in store for radio.

Those who operated radio stations went into television, and as the 1950s were born, it was becoming clear that television was soon going to take the magic out of radio. America was caught up in the idea that progress meant vitality. Technology was making it possible to escape the drudgery attached to many of the chores of everyday life. Television was the icing on the cake.

Although many would argue later that radio entertained us more vividly because our imaginations created much of the effect, television lured us with its ability to provide entertainment minus the effort. Television was part of the good life that came with prosperity and technologic innovation.

Many in radio panicked as they witnessed the fascination with which the public greeted television. All the forms that worked so well for radio worked better for television. The diminished role of the imagination was to be overcome easily by the magic of watching pictures emanate from a box in the home.

The principle of programming economy that resulted in the series concept in radio programming was applied to television. Stars of radio became even bigger stars when they could be seen. Jack Benny and Fred Allen made the transition to television easily. Programs like *Our Miss Brooks* and *Boston Blackie* made the crossover. Comedian Milton Berle exploited the increased potential of television for effective slapstick comedy. Ernie Kovaks pushed television to its fullest. For example, he would often tie up expensive studio time for hours to produce sight gags that lasted only seconds on the air. As a result, the viewing audience was no less fascinated than Kovaks, and the new medium was the message for the public. But for many in radio, the message was doom.

Radio listenership was plummeting. The network shows that a few years before had attracted millions moved to television or were being discontinued because advertisers withdrew in the wake of low audience figures. A few programs hung on longer than most. The soap opera *Ma Perkins* carried a loyal following into the 1960s. *Don MacNiel's Breakfast Club,* a variety/talk show from Chicago, stayed on the air after other shows of its type were long gone.

But by and large, radio was on the ropes. The magic was gone. The public had turned to television, and there wasn't room for both as competing media of mass entertainment.

1.3

RADIO'S COMEBACK

As it turned out, radio was far from dead. Its salvation was to come from various factors that led to its modern vitality as a healthy medium serving millions.

Radio's Search for Identity

It was not immediately apparent, in the wake of the rise of television, how or if radio would pull out of its tailspin. The seeds of radio's recovery, however, were present in the programming of the 1940s and 1950s. Recorded music had long been a staple of radio. Martin Block popularized the form with his *Make Believe Ballroom* on WNEW in New York City. Block is credited widely with creating the concept of the disc jockey, and the long-standing American interest in popular music had been reflected in radio over many years. Recording artists had been featured on many of radio's most popular programs. Long-running forms like *Your Hit Parade* presaged a later development that would become known as the "Top-Forty" format.

The focus for many in radio was on *how* the medium could continue to attract enough listeners at one time to entice the interest of advertisers to keep the industry alive. To many it did not appear that the playing of recorded popular music was going to do it.

Once it became evident, however, that mass audiences need not be tuned to centrally produced programming for radio to be a success, the stage was set for radio's rebirth as a different kind of medium. This awareness came about gradually, but the seeds of the success were contained in the idea that music would form the basis of the new life that radio needed.

Finding the Formula

Martin Block's pioneering activity in the establishment of the record show needed the added force of a separate social phenomenon in order to cast the disc jockey into the role of radio's savior. As the rhythm-and-blues sound that grew out of country music took hold and began to displace the big band craze that dominated the 1930s and 1940s, radio took note.

Most of the recorded music that was being played in the early 1950s featured artists and music that had been spawned by the big band era. The records receiving airplay were standards performed by artists like Frank Sinatra, Tony Bennett, Peggy Lee, Patti Page, and others who appealed to the adult tastes of that period. Geographic variations produced strong pockets where country music, for example, was heard frequently, and many stations would play jazz during the late evening, piano music at dinnertime, or classical music on Sunday afternoons.

The modern concept of a music format was not yet fully formed. Music on radio was generally eclectic. Not too much thought went into what was played. Most often air personalities selected music on the basis of their own tastes or in response to feedback from listeners. The record show host of this era was the precursor of the full-blown disc jockey/personality who was soon to emerge as a major force in radio.

The announcer of the past era—who was often perceived as a disembodied voice, reciting information almost as a singer would voice a song—was being replaced by announcers whose primary function was to introduce the records being played. Announcements of title and artist were soon supplemented with the notation of the time and the temperature. Soon other information was included in the announcer's running commentary. Weather forecasts, baseball scores, and commercial spot announcements were read.

Announcers became adept at weaving all these elements into a unified presentation. Ad libs about the artists or the music became commonplace. Matters were no longer so formal between an announcer and the audience. This voice belonged to a person, who could be very interesting; a person of wit and knowledge, who could speak about many topics. The announcer could be viewed by the listener as a friend, a companion.

Thus did the modern disc jockey come into being. Personality became the name of the game. The music was important, of course, but equally important was cultivating listeners as loyal fans of the air personality. Styles evolved. The friendly and witty announcer who was knowledgeable about music and recording artists gave way to the wild personality who carried on between records with zany patter designed to augment the fun factor of radio. All this fed very easily into an emerging cultural phenomenon that was to sweep the nation and tie into the revolution in music known as Rock and Roll.

The New Youth Audience

As Rhythm and Blues evolved into Rock and Roll, the youth of the nation became enthralled with this new form of musical expression. The slightly rebellious nature of this music and the artists who performed it drew a fast following among the young and sparked the formation for the first time in our nation's history of a teenage culture.

The prosperity of the 1950s allowed teenagers more disposable income than ever before. They had grown up with mass communication and were receptive to focusing on phenomena that helped define their identity as a force to be reckoned with in society. Rock and Roll was the perfect expression of the culture that sought and quickly found such a salient identity.

The phenomenon of this distinct and definable cultural group, combined with the affluence of the 1950s, made teenagers attractive as consumers. They had money to spend, and their tastes could be easily assayed to determine what kinds of products they could be persuaded to purchase.

As the recordings of early Rock-and-Roll artists like Ferlin Husky, Carl Perkins, Bill Hayley and the Comets, and Elvis Presley began to sell in great numbers to teenagers, radio was responding. Now the disc jockeys were dealing with more than simple musical taste. There was a *life-style* to be tuned into. The hit parade format was used to program records and to chart the relative popularity of Rock-and-Roll artists.

The Top-Forty format swept the country in the mid-1950s. Local radio stations kept in touch with record stores in their markets and charted the hits. Publications of the music industry reported from week to week on national record sales. Program directors began to assemble playlists that would ensure that the proper amount of play was given to the hits.

Those who were tracking the market potential of the teenage culture found the new music formats to be the natural vehicle for touting wares to the youth of America. Products that appealed to the youth culture were the accoutrements of fun living. Soft-drink marketers, who had, not long before, discovered the effectiveness of tieing into the life-styles of audiences in the "Pepsi generation," found this new group of consumers equally responsive to its appeals to having fun. Grooming products, the quickly rising fast-food industry, and others were fueling the recovery of radio.

Radio's new voice had been found. Disc jockeys like Allen Freed, who developed the concept of "personality" as a central feature of Top-Forty radio, and Dick Clark (Figure 1.8) rode the teen/rock phenomenon to superstardom. The payola scandals, in which disc jockeys accepted money in exchange for pushing certain records on the air, revealed the level of economic impact involved.

Not all radio went to Rock and Roll. Some stations stayed with the adult audience. The companion phenomenon was not exclusive to teens: Adults had discovered radio's utility as a companion. In the car, at the beach, and in the back yard—where television could not reach or where full attention could not be given—radio could still entertain.

The Segmented Audience

The youth culture and Rock and Roll had demonstrated convincingly the ability of radio to live comfortably without the mass audience appeal that it had lost to television. Advertisers were able to see the efficiency of targeting the audiences they

Figure 1.8

Dick Clark's ability to tune into the youth culture has made him one of America's most
enduring broadcast personalities. He is pictured here on the set of *American Bandstand*
in 1956 at WFIL in Philadelphia.
Courtesy of Dick Clark Productions, Inc.

wished to reach and the effectiveness of gearing an advertising pitch directly to consumers who shared common traits that could be exploited.

This worked not only with teenagers, but also with other groups of consumers. Radio was discovering the means of attracting discrete segments of the audience by programming to the tastes of these various groups.

Market research firms and audience analysis techniques arose in the wake of radio's new found role. Researchers latched onto the concept of demographics, a term that came from the academic study of population. Groups of consumers could be characterized and located. Using data about such groups, those who sold products could improve the effectiveness with which products were developed and sold.

By tieing this concept to radio's efficiency in attracting listeners according to musical tastes, prosperity was in the wind for an industry that shortly before had been written off by many as being on the verge of extinction.

New Formats

Radio managers and programmers quickly became adept at programming to the musical tastes of the particular audience they wished to attract. No longer did radio stations offer a variety of musical genres to its audiences. The decision as to what type of music to air became a management decision rather than leaving it to the disc jockey. Soon a station could be identified by its **format,** a term that came to mean the type of music played on the station. A station was known as a Top-Forty station or Country-and-Western station. Those that stuck with the so-called standards were known as Middle-of-the-Road (**MOR**) stations.

Like all enterprises, some succeeded while others did not. The fortunes of any given station could rise and fall in relation to the competition's format changes or by carving out previously untapped audience segments and programming for that group.

As the methods of audience analysis improved and the methods for gathering and reporting data on levels of listenership became more and more sophisticated, finer and finer distinctions were made among audience segments. By the mid- to late-1960s, fine tuning programming to the musical tastes of increasingly narrower segments of the audience was possible. In major metropolitan areas, where perhaps four or five different formats had at one time dominated the market, there was now room for more stations to succeed. Several factors, which resulted in a proliferation of formats that fragmented audiences into more and more discrete bits, were at work.

Prior to the 1960s, the major action in radio's phenomenal growth had been in the **AM** sector. There were several reasons for this. To a considerable extent, **FM** licenses had been acquired by AM operators wishing to preempt the possibility of competition. A long stall, imposed by **FCC** inaction, in the authorization for FM and the ultimate assignment of the service to the high-frequency range of the frequency spectrum had deflated enthusiasm for the service considerably. Through the major part of the postwar development of radio, FM programming primarily consisted of what the AM side was programming or simply enough program material of some sort to keep the license active.

The audience for FM, in the years prior to 1965, was limited because the overwhelming majority of automobiles were equipped with AM-only receivers. FM was an expensive, undesirable option. Home receivers were of minimal quality as well. So FM, for all of its higher fidelity, languished in AM's shadow while the rest of the radio industry was finding its new niche in American life.

In the 1960s, however, great improvements were made in the quality of receivers. Many FM stations implemented stereo **multiplexing,** and several entrepreneurs developed automation systems to air program material without the need for full-time operators. FM's potential was evident. Better sound was possible, and listeners could now take full advantage of FM's capabilities.

Many firms that supplied music tapes to automated stations began to engage in audience research, which told them the ideal number of music cuts that should be played back to back and what sequence of cuts would best hold the attention of the desired audience segment. As a result of this growing knowledge of audience tastes in music, many firms began to produce music tapes that had been scientifically programmed for maximum impact.

Program suppliers became adept at using demographic data to determine the audience segment tastes and then designing finely tuned programming to attract that audience to the format. Format production companies began to produce music programming for all kinds of stations, not just for those that had automation equipment. Consulting services worked with stations across the country to help them define untapped audience segments that could lead to a dramatic turnaround for even the most unpromising of stations.

Today's radio is characterized by many formats. Fragmentation of markets is the rule. The science of determining audience tastes has led to systems of classification that go beyond simply fitting a particular piece of music into a category of musical taste that corresponds with a demographic group. It is equally important today to know how music should be arranged within a format and how it should be presented as an ingredient in an overall station sound.

1.4

SUMMARY

The evolution of radio from its earliest beginnings as an experimenter's toy to the sophisticated communications medium of today reflects the development of twentieth century America (see Figure 1.9). Radio was shaped by the strong commercial and regulatory forces that emerged during a period of extremely rapid growth and development in this country. While it is true that radio today reflects the society in which it developed, it is equally true that radio played a major role in forming some of the major characteristics of that society.

Figure 1.9

SIGNIFICANT EVENTS IN THE DEVELOPMENT OF RADIO

1873

James Clerk-Maxwell posits the existence of electromagnetic energy in "A Treatise on Electricity and Magnetism."

1888

Heinrich Hertz publishes "Electro-Magnetic Waves and Their Reflection" in which he reports laboratory proof of the existence of electromagnetic waves.

1896

Guglielmo Marconi applies for a British patent for his wireless apparatus.

1900–1904

Reginald Fessenden and Lee de Forest conduct experiments.

1906

Lee de Forest develops the audion tube.

1909

Charles D. "Doc" Herrold opens a college of engineering in San Jose and conducts radio experiments.

1910

The Wireless Ship Act requires ships to have wireless operators.

1912

The Radio Act empowers the Secretary of Commerce to issue radio licenses.

David Sarnoff relays wireless reports of the Titanic disaster to the American public.

1919

RCA formed.

1920

KDKA in Pittsburgh broadcasts election returns.

1922–1924

Radio conferences held in Washington, D.C.

1923

WEAF forms the first network interconnection.

1926

NBC formed by GE, Westinghouse, and RCA.

1927

NBC operates "red" and "blue" networks.

The Radio Act passed by Congress. The Federal Radio Commission formed.

1928

William Paley takes control of CBS.

1933

Franklin Delano Roosevelt broadcasts the first "Fireside Chat."

1934

The Communications Act enacted by Congress.

The Press Radio Bureau formed.

1940

Edward R. Murrow broadcasts from London Blitzkrieg.

1941–1945

Radio covers World War II.

1944

First disc jockey-style programming is heard.

1945

FCC moves FM to VHF portion of frequency spectrum.

1946

Television sets are first sold to the general public.

1949

Top-Forty radio debuts.

1952

FCC lifts freeze on television licenses.

1967

The Public Broadcasting Act allows public radio to apply for funds from the Corporation for Public Broadcasting.

NOTES

1. Sydney W. Head, *Broadcasting in America: A Survey of Electronic Media,* 5th ed. (Boston: Houghton Mifflin, 1987), 44.

2. For an interesting account of Marconi's activities, see Erik Barnouw, *A Tower in Babel: A History of Broadcasting in the United States to 1933* (New York: Oxford University Press, 1966), 9–18.

3. Gleason L. Archer, *History of Radio: to 1926* (New York: American Historical Society, 1938), 112–113.

4. For an excellent discussion of the role of amateurs in radio's development, see Barnouw, *A Tower in Babel,* 33–38.

5. Archer, *History of Radio,* 112.

6. Barnouw, *A Tower in Babel,* 68.

7. Barnouw, *A Tower in Babel,* 68.

8. Archer, *History of Radio,* 397–398.

9. Archer, *History of Radio,* 144.

10. Archer, *History of Radio,* 145.

11. Those that could compete were restricted to using poor-quality telegraph wires, which were rented from Western Union. See Head, *Broadcasting in America,* 47.

12. Barnouw, *A Tower in Babel,* 125.

13. Barnouw, *A Tower in Babel,* 181–185.

14. See Barnouw, *A Tower in Babel,* 158.

CHAPTER 2

PROGRAM

ELEMENTS

The operation of a modern radio station involves weaving a variety of program elements into a unified pattern. Many elements make up the warp and weave. To comprehend the process of creating a coherent format, the first step is to understand the individual pieces that make up the station's sound.

From a management perspective, it is important to develop a rounded and complete view of the elements in a radio station's program schedule. Much of the friction among management and individual departments stems from a reciprocal lack of knowledge of departments' duties and expectations. Much of the blame for that discord must be shouldered by management. Why? There is no good reason to assume that the news director has a working knowledge of station finances, but the manager *is* expected to have a working knowledge of news. In actuality, though, this is not always how things work. A manager who came up through the sales ranks and has no knowledge of or interest in news can alienate the news staff and run the risk of diminishing the entire station's efficiency and profits. Programming people, often deeply involved in music, similarly must expand their view when moving into operations and management. Technical people frequently take a narrow view of radio station operations; a similar case could be made against specialists in financial matters.

The point is not that specialists are incompetent or by nature incapable of managing because each radio station employee is, to some degree, a specialist. What is meant by this discussion is that a manager's perspective must be reasonably all-inclusive. Although unrealistic to expect a manager to be an expert in every area, the extent of the manager's knowledge should be sufficient to determine when operations are deficient, to be able to improve the operations of individual departments, and to better integrate the workings of those departments into the overall operating scheme.

Basically, this chapter discusses the three major specialties—music, radio personalities, and news—which are actual program elements, the over-the-air product of a radio station. Other off-air functions such as sales, technical and financial operations, and management are addressed in separate chapters.

2.1

MUSIC

Music programming has two distinct advantages for a radio station: It is evocative and economical. In addition to having a powerful social and personal impact, music is really the only programming element that allows most stations to thrive. Very few stations make profits with anything besides a music format. Those that do have successful nonmusic formats usually are located in very large markets where a small and discrete segment of the listening population can translate into significant numbers.

From the Wireless to the Music Box

The history of radio's development is well documented in Chapter 1. However, from the standpoint of music's role as a program element, a certain historical frame of reference deserves attention.

Radio and the music industry have had a strange relationship—sometimes adversative, sometimes cooperative. An extension of this is a certain amount of tension, past and present, between the producers of music and the radio industry. In fact, radio has not always been the "music box" it is today. In the earliest days of radio, there were serious doubts about the suitability of music as a program element. At that time, any sound material was fair game: poetry readings, lectures, or live music recitals. All were novelties to the few people who were able to receive the radio signals.[1]

Gradually, as more receivers became available to the general public, substantive program forms began to emerge. Concurrent with the development of radio, growth in the technology of recording music occurred. The resulting movement of music into radio unfolded along four lines.

NOVELTY ERA   Until 1930 gaining exposure for the new medium was desired, and music was one of the options explored. Emerging radio networks had their own orchestras, a tactic that would continue into the next era.

LIVE ERA   From 1930 until the years of World War II, no really good mechanism for storage of sound, except on disc, existed. Those discs, called **electronic transcriptions,** were not of particularly good quality. Many stations were concerned about quality and were reluctant to use transcriptions. As a result, there was much live dramatic programming, news programming, and variety shows.

TRANSITION ERA   From World War II to 1950, recording devices become more available and technologically advanced. As the impact of networks declined, local programming became more important. Music was a major part of local programming. Initially, there was much resistance to using recordings; some broadcasters actually considered the practice deceptive. At the same time, record companies feared that radio would wipe out demand for store-bought records.

MODERN ERA   From 1950 to the present, recorded music became standard practice and the foundation of the station format.

PROBLEMS IN THE LIVE AND TRANSITION ERAS   The economies of music usage brought about problems in the live and transition eras. Were composers and publishers of music entitled to royalties from broadcasters? An organization representing composers and publishers, **ASCAP** (American Society of Composers and Publishers), made a compelling case for royalty payments. In essence, ASCAP argued that use of music by radio was not an eleemosynary function: It was not a charitable use guaranteed as a public right. Broadcasters argued that they were popularizing music and therefore were under no obligation to pay royalties.[2]

Broadcasting lost that particular battle. Later, broadcasters formed their own competing licensing organization, **BMI** (Broadcast Music Incorporated), arguing that ASCAP had no real interest in licensing popular music. Another organization, **SESAC** (Society of European Stage Authors and Composers), originally licensed only in Europe but now licenses some music in the United States.

Radio and the Music Industry

Today, both ASCAP and BMI are viable forces in music, and radio and the music industry still live in a state that alternates between peaceful coexistence and successful symbiosis. Broadcasting has proven to be a boon for artists, widely increasing the public awareness of popular music. Record companies and composers also have close ties with broadcasting, based on licensing agreements and the selection of music for airplay. Each is discussed next.

ARTISTS Who creates the raw material of radio music programming? The performing artists of popular music are the most visible element of the music business. The artist's stake, however, is primarily in the recording industry itself and not directly concerned with radio. In other words, popular music superstars are directly involved with recording contracts and concert opportunities; the radio airplay of their work is a valuable plus but not an immediate result of their efforts.

Although this may seem to be a hair-splitting distinction, it is important to reiterate that recording artists are connected to the radio business only through their association with record companies.

RECORD COMPANIES These firms have had many cycles of profitability. The field was once dominated, virtually to the point of monopoly, by large companies such as Columbia and RCA Victor. As is frequently the case with large, highly profitable firms, they became complacent and did not react quickly to changing public tastes. A number of smaller firms started up in the 1950s and 1960s; some, such as Atlantic, are now large firms. Once established, the potential of the "small label" stayed, and on occasion a small record company discovers a new artist and makes the big time. At present, record companies form a $4-billion-a-year industry, larger, by many estimates, than television.

COMPOSERS Credit for composing a song today is quite different than in the era of Irving Berlin. One reason is that although a songwriter's name generally appears somewhere on the record label, he or she does not receive full credit for all creative work on the effort—as did happen with the famous "Irving Berlin tunes." Today, there are very few songs so strongly linked with the composer as songs were in the 1920s and 1930s. The *actual* creation of a song is a collaborative effort among technicians, artists, and writers.

This could seem like a trivial point until one considers the fact that creation of a song is highly dependent on the production process, to the point where it's difficult to define exactly who the "composer" is. Some media historians think that the trend of heavy in-studio production began with the Beatles and reached an apex with Fleetwood Mac's $1.3-million effort known as *Tusk*.[3]

Although this point does not directly affect radio programming, it is worthwhile to understand that the complexion of the music industry has changed in lockstep with the advance of technology.

LICENSING AGREEMENTS   ASCAP, BMI, and, to some extent, SESAC are an everyday fact of life for today's radio station manager. The licensing firms charge a fee to radio stations (and to other users of recorded and written music) and distribute the collected fees among member artists and composers. This is done by a sampling technique where radio stations, during a specified period of time, keep notes of all music that has had airplay. The samples are collected and correlated, and weighted estimates are used to pay royalties.

SELECTING MUSIC FOR AIRPLAY   How does music bridge the gap from record company release to hit single? In a way, it is a chicken-and-egg evolutionary dilemma: Some stations make their decisions of which records to play based on record shop sales of a song, but there is no question that airplay increases record sales and in some cases creates a hit.

This question took on some sinister ramifications in the 1950s when it was revealed (although reveal might be a strong word because the situation was almost common knowledge) that some disc jockeys were receiving money and other inducements to give airplay to certain records. To this day, radio stations at all levels are highly sensitive to any sort of arrangement that could be construed as **payola,** and there are stringent FCC rules against such a practice.

In the modern radio station, music typically is selected by a music director or program director, who evaluates the music itself and its suitability for the particular station. This evaluation process is important to radio stations and is discussed fully later in this chapter.

Music, Life-style, and Demographics

It is practically impossible to underestimate the impact music has on Americans and American society in general. Music is a huge business and a highly personal form of entertainment. Music has a strong impact both from its immediate effect and its recall effect. It is no accident that "oldies" stations have many loyal fans because the music reinforces memories of a particular period in one's life. Everyone is familiar with the phenomenon of hearing a particular piece of music and instantly recalling a specific past situation associated with that melody.

The evocative power of music is vitally important to the business of radio broadcasting because radio's particular power is used to isolate and, in effect, sell an audience. The audience, of course, is packaged for consumption and "sold" to advertisers. This basic concept, however, was not always a universal given. In fact, the unique packaging power of radio was not fully realized until the emergence of youth-culture stars like Elvis Presley. In essence, the fans of these singers were riding the waves of a small-scale cultural rebellion, and the music became the standard that they bore. The music was a unifying factor.

Advertisers initially doubted the longevity of the new popular music and were skeptical of the youth culture as a purchasing entity. They soon found, however, a tremendous, undiscovered profit potential. Bolstered by the fact that people in general and young people in particular had more disposable income than ever before, advertisers began vigorously pursuing the youth market.

The story does not end with the youth movement. Music is an evocative tool for reaching many groups. Nostalgia, such as a feeling for big band music, is an effective mechanism for reaching a precisely defined audience. Easy-listening, country, classical, and religious music have similarly devoted and identifiable fans. Appealing to such discrete audience segments is what programming is all about, and the particulars of this effort are evaluated in Chapter 3. Now, it is sufficient to understand that modern radio utilizes music as a vehicle to reach a particular **demographic.** Strictly defined, a demographic is a statistical representation of an audience; in radio, the word is frequently used to indicate a discrete audience segment with unified emotional, life-style, and economic characteristics.

Life-style in particular has a linkage to music. Music reflects life-style and to some extent creates it. (Note how devotees of certain music adopt the dress, vocabulary, and sometimes the political beliefs of the artists.) Music has become a vicarious means of expression: Devotees say what they want to say indirectly by aligning with artists who make statements with which the fans identify.

Therefore, a broadcaster seeking to package a demographic segment reflecting a certain life-style must carefully select music that is reflective of the relevant characteristics. In simpler words, the programmer tries to identify music that the station's target audience will like.

How a Programmer Evaluates Music

"Playing what the audience likes" is nowhere near as simple as the concept might appear. Many factors must be weighed, including suitability of the music for airplay in general and for the format in particular and, finally the key factor, artistic acceptability.

AIRPLAY SUITABILITY   Some music borders on being unsuitable for airplay anywhere, at any time, usually because of sexually or drug-oriented lyrics. Obscenity is difficult to define, but in 1988 the pendulum was swinging perceptibly toward conservatism and tighter regulation relating to song lyrics and obscenity in general. For example, after many years of a virtual hands-off policy, the government recently imposed harsh restrictions on a station in Santa Barbara, California, claiming the lyrics of a particular song ("Making Bacon" by the Pork Dukes, if you must know) were unsuitable for airplay.[4]

FORMAT SUITABILITY   If, indeed, the piece is suitable for airing in general, the evaluator (usually the program director or music director) next judges if it is suitable for use within the format. To some extent, this is a subjective decision, especially when the piece of music does not clearly fall into a particular category. As noted in Chapter 3, those listeners who are loyal to a particular music style are sometimes quite vehement in protecting the purity of their music. A "crossover" country single (crossing into the realm of popular music) played on a so-called pure-country station could certainly alienate a substantial portion of the listenership.

Evaluating format suitability is based perforce, on broad musical knowledge and general programming experience. The call on a particular piece of music is not always easy, even for the most experienced radio experts. Although it takes minimum expertise to determine that Barry Manilow does not belong on a hard-rock station, other situations are not so clear-cut. Did "Don't It Make My Brown Eyes Blue" belong on a country station? Although it is ostensibly a country song, many program directors wondered, when the title was first released, whether it was a blues piece. Kenny Rogers created some confusion among the country programmers when he moved into some areas of social comment and popular mainstream music.

ARTISTIC ACCEPTABILITY   A cut perfectly suited to the format may not please audiences if it is poor music or if it lacks the nebulous magnetism of a potential hit. In

Figure 2.1

Billboard's use of a "bullet" indicates a record is likely to become a hit.
Reproduced with permission of Billboard Publications.

FOR WEEK ENDING JANUARY 30, 1988

Billboard® HOT 100® SINGLES™

Compiled from a national sample of retail store
and one-stop sales reports and radio playlists.

THIS WEEK	LAST WEEK	2 WKS AGO	WKS. ON CHART	TITLE / PRODUCER (SONGWRITER)	ARTIST / LABEL & NUMBER/DISTRIBUTING LABEL
				★ ★ NO. 1 ★ ★	
1	2	4	15	NEED YOU TONIGHT 1 week at No. One C.THOMAS (A.FARRISS, M.HUTCHENCE)	◆ INXS ATLANTIC 7-89188
2	3	5	10	COULD'VE BEEN G.E.TOBIN (L.BLAISCH)	TIFFANY MCA 53231
3	5	6	12	HAZY SHADE OF WINTER BANGLES,B.DRESCHER,D.WHITE (P.SIMON)	◆ BANGLES DEF JAM 38-07630/COLUMBIA
4	1	3	11	THE WAY YOU MAKE ME FEEL Q.JONES (M.JACKSON)	◆ MICHAEL JACKSON EPIC 34-07645/E.P.A.
5	8	11	10	SEASONS CHANGE L.A.MARTINEE (L.A.MARTINEE)	◆ EXPOSE ARISTA 1-9640
6	10	15	12	I WANT TO BE YOUR MAN R.TROUTMAN (L.TROUTMAN)	◆ ROGER REPRISE 7-28229
7	4	1	15	GOT MY MIND SET ON YOU J.LYNNE,G.HARRISON (R.CLARK)	◆ GEORGE HARRISON DARK HORSE 7-28178/WARNER BROS.
8	11	17	13	HUNGRY EYES (FROM "DIRTY DANCING") E.CARMEN (F.PREVITE, J.DENICOLA)	◆ ERIC CARMEN RCA 5315
9	6	7	13	CANDLE IN THE WIND G.DUDGEON (E.JOHN, B.TAUPIN)	◆ ELTON JOHN MCA 53196
10	7	8	17	TELL IT TO MY HEART R.WAKE (S.SWIRSKY, E.GOLD)	◆ TAYLOR DAYNE ARISTA 1-9612
11	13	16	12	I COULD NEVER TAKE THE PLACE OF YOUR MAN PRINCE (PRINCE)	◆ PRINCE PAISLEY PARK 7-28288/WARNER BROS.
12	18	24	8	WHAT HAVE I DONE TO DESERVE THIS? ◆ PET SHOP BOYS & DUSTY SPRINGFIELD S.HAGUE (TENNANT, LOWE, WILLIS)	EMI-MANHATTAN 50107
13	17	22	9	SAY YOU WILL M.JONES,F.FILIPETTI (M.JONES, L.GRAMM)	◆ FOREIGNER ATLANTIC 7-89169
14	15	21	9	TUNNEL OF LOVE B.SPRINGSTEEN,J.LANDAU,C.PLOTKIN (B.SPRINGSTEEN)	◆ BRUCE SPRINGSTEEN COLUMBIA 38-07663
15	21	25	12	DON'T SHED A TEAR C.NEIL (E.SCHWARTZ, R.FRIEDMAN)	◆ PAUL CARRACK CHRYSALIS 43164
16	14	18	16	CRAZY D.LORD (A.QUNTA, I.DAVIES, R.KRETSCHMER)	◆ ICEHOUSE CHRYSALIS 43156
17	20	23	13	I LIVE FOR YOUR LOVE D.LAMBERT (RESWICK, WERFEL, RICH)	◆ NATALIE COLE EMI-MANHATTAN 50094
18	23	29	10	EVERYWHERE L.BUCKINGHAM,R.DASHUT (C.MCVIE)	FLEETWOOD MAC WARNER BROS. 7-28143
19	12	14	13	THERE'S THE GIRL R.NEVISON (H.KNIGHT, N.WILSON)	◆ HEART CAPITOL 44089
20	9	2	14	SO EMOTIONAL N.M.WALDEN (B.STEINBERG, KELLY)	◆ WHITNEY HOUSTON ARISTA 1-9642
				★ ★ ★ Power Pick/Sales ★ ★ ★	
21	31	39	7	SHE'S LIKE THE WIND ◆ PATRICK SWAYZE (FEATURING WENDY FRASER) M.LLOYD (P.SWAYZE, S.WIDELITZ)	RCA 5363
22	26	30	14	POP GOES THE WORLD Z.HELD,MEN WITHOUT HATS (MEN WITHOUT HATS)	◆ MEN WITHOUT HATS MERCURY 888 859-7/POLYGRAM
23	25	27	13	HONESTLY S.GALFAS,M.SWEET,R.SWEET,O.FOX (M.SWEET)	◆ STRYPER ENIGMA 75009
				★ ★ ★ Power Pick/Airplay ★ ★ ★	
24	34	41	7	NEVER GONNA GIVE YOU UP STOCK,AITKEN,WATERMAN (STOCK, AITKEN, WATERMAN)	◆ RICK ASTLEY RCA 5347
25	30	37	10	PUMP UP THE VOLUME M.YOUNG (S.YOUNG, M.YOUNG)	◆ M/A/R/R/S 4TH & B'WAY 7452
26	27	32	11	PUSH IT H.LUV BUG (H.AZOR)	◆ SALT-N-PEPA NEXT PLATEAU 315
27	32	36	11	CAN'T STAY AWAY FROM YOU ◆ GLORIA ESTEFAN & MIAMI SOUND MACHINE EMILIO AND THE JERKS (G.M.ESTEFAN)	EPIC 34-07641/E.P.A.
28	16	9	15	FAITH G.MICHAEL (G.MICHAEL)	◆ GEORGE MICHAEL COLUMBIA 38-07623
29	35	38	11	I FOUND SOMEONE M.BOLTON (M.BOLTON, M.MANGOLD)	◆ CHER GEFFEN 7-28191
30	37	49	3	FATHER FIGURE G.MICHAEL (G.MICHAEL)	◆ GEORGE MICHAEL COLUMBIA 38-07682
31	19	10	15	IS THIS LOVE M.STONE,K.OLSEN (COVERDALE, SYKES)	◆ WHITESNAKE GEFFEN 7-28233
32	24	13	18	SHAKE YOUR LOVE F.ZARR (D.GIBSON)	◆ DEBBIE GIBSON ATLANTIC 7-89187
33	40	54	3	I GET WEAK R.NOWELS (D.WARREN)	◆ BELINDA CARLISLE MCA 53242
34	22	12	15	CHERRY BOMB ◆ JOHN COUGAR MELLENCAMP J.MELLENCAMP,D.GEHMAN (J.MELLENCAMP)	MERCURY 888 934-7/POLYGRAM
35	39	46	7	853-5937 E.THORNGREN,G.TILBROOK (C.DIFFORD, G.TILBROOK)	◆ SQUEEZE A&M 2994
36	42	45	10	BECAUSE OF YOU R.CLIVELLES,LITTLE LOU VEGA (D.COLE)	THE COVER GIRLS FEVER 1914/SUTRA
37	45	56	3	JUST LIKE PARADISE D.L.ROTH (D.L.ROTH, B.TUGGLE)	◆ DAVID LEE ROTH WARNER BROS. 7-28119
38	28	19	19	CATCH ME (I'M FALLING) (FROM THE FILM "HIDING OUT") K.WILLIAMS,JR.,K.SHORE (J.STARLING, W.COOLER)	◆ PRETTY POISON VIRGIN 7-99416
39	52	65	4	LOVE OVERBOARD R.CALLOWAY,V.CALLOWAY (R.CALLOWAY)	◆ GLADYS KNIGHT & THE PIPS MCA 53210
40	53	—	2	ENDLESS SUMMER NIGHTS H.GATICA (R.MARX)	◆ RICHARD MARX EMI-MANHATTAN 50113

◯ Products with the greatest airplay and sales gains this week. ◆ Videoclip availability. • Recording Industry Assn. Of America (RIAA) certification for sales of 1 million units. ▲ RIAA certification for sales of 2 million units.

deciding whether to program a cut and how often to program it, radio executives heavily rely on the bandwagon effect—the popularity of the song on "the charts."

Familiar sources include *Billboard, Cashbox, R&R, Gavin Report,* record store sales figures, and in-house research and listener surveys. *Billboard* is noted for its use of a "bullet" to designate a rising hit (Figure 2.1).

How a Station Stores Music and Assigns Airplay

Records arriving at the station typically are subjected to the tests described above, and then the songs that pass inspection are placed into rotation and/or categorized in the station's music library. Methods of categorization differ, but most libraries separate singles and albums into vocals and instrumentals; often the vocals are segregated in terms of male and female artists. Tempo considerations are used often in categorization: Up-tempo records may be filed in a different section from down-tempo records, or the tempo designation may simply be marked on the jacket. In stations where airplay and the library are eclectic, filing categorizations may include headings for jazz, classical, and so forth.

In many stations, the incoming music judged most suitable for production use (that is, background for commercials) is categorized separately. Also, some libraries have special sections for long and short cuts.

Often, music is dubbed on a cartridge, an endless-loop tape holder that can be inserted into a playback machine and started. Cartridge use has become so popular that in many stations an air personality may go through a day without ever handling a disc. **Compact discs** may change that situation. The new optically scanned discs produce a clean digitized sound and are finding their way into more station control rooms.

But for most stations, banks of cartridges are still the rule. Probably the most popular way of organizing cartridges is to color code them according to their musical style or popularity. For example, a piece of music rising in the charts is coded with a blue label and placed in the rack of "breaking" tunes. The entire song rotation follows a color-coded schedule, with a blue "breaker" scheduled to play after the top-ten hit that follows the news at the top of the hour. When the cut begins to lose popularity, it is reassigned—possibly to the yellow "fading" category—and its numbers of airplays are reduced. Perhaps someday the cut will return with a gold label—an "oldie."

Computers have made the task of assigning airplay more manageable. A programmer enters descriptions of the desired frequency of airplay and rotation among the dayparts, and the computer introduces the record into the playlist and prints out the list. Several firms supply hardware and software to accomplish this. Computer-aided programming has become so commonplace that even small stations are joining in the trend. Some stations, in fact, have a terminal right in the control room.

2.2

THE ON-AIR PERSONALITY

An interesting way to view the announcer's role in radio is to consider the uniqueness of the presentation. What we take for granted today was not always the case: Radio announcers in the early years were literally announcers. They "announced" events to an audience. The audience did not participate in the event, acting more like spectators. So in that connection, the radio voice was similar to the public-address voice that announced the players at a football game or cast changes in a stage play. Personality was not associated with the announcing voice.

With the emergence of the youth culture and the life-style factors of popular music, the entire perspective changed. The audience and the announcer *experienced the music at the same time,* and the announcer was less an announcer than a *companion.* Scrutiny of today's radio dial shows that the only real announcing that is practiced is done as a joke or is simply a reflection of no talent.

Today's on-air personalities are communicators. They must perform, entertain, and persuade—sometimes all within a few seconds. Communicators must reinforce the station's mission: reaching a target audience, affirming the station's hold on that audience, and, in effect, maintaining the overall sound of the station.

From a management standpoint, understanding talent and the requirements of effective on-air communication is very important. Simply stated, managers must understand the requirements of the job for which they will hire people. Not many managers come from the ranks of talent (although most program directors do), so the chance exists that a manager could have poor comprehension of the air personality's job, problems, and needs.

The Portable Companion

When radio changed from a mass-entertainment mode to a music-and-information mode, the way the audience interacted with radio changed dramatically. No longer was it necessary to commit a block of time to get the full impact of the scheduled program, as you would have to do with a soap opera or situation comedy. Rather, the audience could tune in and interact with the program and the program host for a short period of time. The essential result is that radio has become a presence that is not totally involving but provides instant and easy companionship for someone at the beach, in a car, or jogging.

This means that a heavy responsibility is placed on announcers. They must be companions—friends to listeners who are probably doing other things and who periodically tune in and out. Announcers are facilitators, people who accomplish an easy flow and exchange of information. In effect, announcers are the hosts and facilitators of a series of three-and-one-half-minute programs.

The Broadcast Communicator

The role of companion and facilitator demands that the presence of the radio personality be one of natural ease and comfort to the listener. Many managers describe the ideal announcer as sounding like an intelligent next-door neighbor or an engaging party guest. In any event, the formality and stylized delivery of the old-style announcer and the artificial intonations and expression that were the hallmarks of that style run contrary to the modern requirements of comfortable companionship.

A station manager obviously needs an announcer (the word is still a standard industry description of the position, so it is retained in our discussion) who is a communicator foremost. Exactly how does a manager evaluate a staff member or potential staff member in terms of that staffer's ability as a broadcast communicator? There are no inviolable rules, but some basic requirements are widely accepted:

1. *A clear speaking voice free of defects.* Although the job of a broadcast communicator is no longer limited to male baritones, a clear and pleasant voice is still essential.

2. *Normal delivery free of affectation.* The voice must not detract from the message. Artificiality and sing-song "announcer voices" are especially troublesome in this area.

3. *The ability to communicate one to one.* This is probably the key element in evaluating the broadcast communicator. The old-style announcer addressed the audience as a collection of people, a group presumably gathered for a common purpose. Today, as one major-market program director noted, ninety-nine

percent of all radio listening involves one person listening. Speaking "to all of the folks out there in radio land" is old-fashioned and ineffective.

The sum of these attributes is what allows an announcer to channel energy and talents into the goal of achieving a coherent station sound.

On-Air Personalities and the Station Sound Mix

In today's supersegmented and highly competitive market, the announcer is a key player in the drive to reach the *right* listener. The station "package" is an entire system of marketing a sound to that listener. It is not possible to isolate one element of the total recipe and identify it as the key ingredient. A format is more than music: It could include such facets as the amount of time between cuts, the style of the news announcer, the pace of the staff announcer, and the electronic processing of the signal. All aspects work in synergy.

An announcer may have a perfectly good technique but his or her work simply does not blend in with the other elements in a format. Management must be acutely aware of whether the announcer is able to effect that blend. There is no formula, but observation shows that different formats have specific requirements for an announcer's skills. Remember, too, that personality skills do not always translate intact from market to market: What is right for a Midwestern market may be totally wrong for California. The manager's task, then, involves evaluating how an announcer functions within a particular format and a particular market.

Although many success factors relating to the announcer and the format are purely dependent on chance and circumstances, some general characteristics have emerged for the different types of formats. (These categories are only a brief discussion of certain formats and how they specifically relate to the air staff. For an in-depth examination of formats, see pages 67–77.)

ADULT CONTEMPORARY FORMAT Adult contemporary music—a mix of light rock, former hits, and easy listening—requires an on-air personality to include a strong measure of one-to-one personalized communication skills. Companionship is strongly stressed by managers searching for top adult contemporary talent. These formats typically require a highly organized person who can handle a great deal of information exchange and who project adult intelligence. Young-sounding announcers with frenetic disc jockey deliveries need not apply.

HIT RADIO FORMAT   Hit radio music's format leans on frequent repetition of popular records for a young audience; emphasis is on energy and enthusiasm. The announcer must be able to relate to and communicate with a young audience; in this format, "young" can mean ages twelve or thirteen. This is not an easy task, and one of the essential requirements is that the announcer maintains interest in the music and in the life-style of that age group. On a more mechanical level, running this type of operation requires especially efficient command of the control panel and control room equipment in small and medium markets where the announcer may run the console.

COUNTRY FORMAT   Country music often has the same requirements for an announcer as does adult contemporary music. The announcer with an extremely "countrified" presentation is becoming a rarity, especially as country music moves into more urbanized markets. When the station's country format is specific and geared toward a particular strain of country music, the announcer must be expert in and have an appreciation of the music.

EASY-LISTENING FORMAT   Easy-listening music ranges from sanitized "elevator music" to some of the softer current hits. In most cases, an announcer needs a mature and reasonably "mellow" voice. A recent development in the easy-listening field is the expectation for an announcer to project a "chummy" personality. A manager of an easy-listening station knows that hiring accurate and polished announcers is essential. Hesitations and small errors that go almost unnoticed in a fast-moving format stand out in an easy-listening presentation.

ALBUM-ORIENTED ROCK FORMAT   Album-oriented rock format usually consists of long cuts and heavily relies on the intimate conversational style of the announcer. Managers of album-oriented rock stations demand that their announcers have full knowledge of the music and the life-styles it reflects.

TALK RADIO FORMAT   Talk radio recently has become as popular as it had been during any time in radio's history. It is a very demanding format for announcers (or, perhaps more appropriate, "hosts" or "personalities"). Managers must insist that announcers in this format be knowledgeable of current events and have the ability to engage in true one-to-one conversation.

SPECIALTY MUSIC FORMATS   Specialty music formats require broad knowledge on the part of the announcer and, consequently, on the part of the manager. For instance, classical music cannot be presented by an announcer who lacks knowledge of the music but has a facility for foreign pronunciation. This appears obvious; however, the number of announcers who feel they can bluff their way through classical music or any other specialty presentation makes the statement worth considering.

Effective On-Air Communication

Besides the specialized requirements mentioned above, a radio executive evaluates the quality of the announcing staff according to various criteria, including literacy, energy, consistency, dependability, adaptability, and conscientiousness. Management is also responsible for the training and professional growth of the announcing staff.

LITERACY   A knowledge of the language and a reasonable general education are essential for almost anyone doing on-air work. Mispronunciations and grammatical gaffes alienate even an unsophisticated audience. Increasingly, modern music formats require that the announcers discuss current events as well as back-announce records. Although such events may be less than earthshaking—last night's television schedule, perhaps—it is important that announcers display an overall awareness of the world around them. It is increasingly common for program directors to assign topics of conversations for certain shifts.

ENERGY   Effective staff announcers project an energetic demeanor while on the air; this is a universally accepted principle of broadcast communication. A person who displays a lackadaisical attitude is not likely to be a very interesting person off the air and certainly will be a disaster on the air. The medium itself is an enervating carrier, somehow "robbing" much of the energy of the performer. As a result, performers usually recognize the need for pumping up their energy supply, infusing an amount of energy far beyond what occurs in normal conversation. Radio managers generally recognize the importance of energy; during the hiring process they look for announcers who display energy both on the air and during a job interview.

CONSISTENCY AND DEPENDABILITY   The job of a radio announcer involves seemingly endless repetition. Although individual actions are repeated many, many times, there is almost no room for error. Air personalities who demonstrate occasional flashes of brilliance are typically less useful than announcers who do a less-than-sparkling but *consistent* job. This issue is a major one for managers because there are many announcers who suffer from frequent bad days or spells of inattentiveness, and such problems often are dumped squarely in the lap of management.

The essential point is that the average radio listener stays tuned to a station for only a short period of time. Hence, the person who stays tuned long enough to catch the occasional flash of brilliance is not characteristic of the audience as a whole. This is why inconsistency can do much damage and why long-term consistency is strongly rewarded.

Although not strictly a principle of effective on-air communication, dependability is a major concern. There are few other professions that require such rigorous standards of attendance, punctuality, and efficiency. Candidly, these characteristics are not always found in typical on-air personalities. Creative people frequently are free-spirited and sometimes unpredictable. Again viewing the situation from a management point of view, lambent wits who show up late for their air shift probably will be of less value to the station than their less-talented counterparts who manage to start the transmitter on time.

ADAPTABILITY   The wide variety of tasks that air personalities are called on to perform mandates an individual with an ability to quickly adapt to changing situations, especially unexpected situations. Radio staff announcing calls for men and women who are independent thinkers. They cannot wait for a supervisor to tell them what to do in every situation. In the event of a local or national emergency, the Sunday night, part-time fill-in announcer suddenly may become responsible for passing along critical information. In a less severe scenario, an announcer may be called on to quickly produce a commercial, to ad-lib when a piece of equipment fails, or even to fix a piece of equipment.

CONSCIENTIOUSNESS   Attention to detail is the name of the game in radio. Logs *must* be filled out correctly. Commercials *must* be played on schedule. Time commitments *must* be met, and every minute *must* be used to maximum efficiency. Although the timing involved in engineering an air shift becomes virtually a sixth sense, that skill always grows from meticulous planning.

When evaluating a current announcer or an applicant for an announcing position, it is imperative that the manager be able to judge in some fashion the announcer's attentiveness to detail. Sloppy work or falsification can be a serious problem. Meter readings—technical logs of transmitter parameters—must not be fudged.

TRAINING AND PROFESSIONAL GROWTH   The above examples show that a manager has a great deal of criteria on which to evaluate air talent and hire applicants. A manager also is expected to provide for the training and professional growth of announcers, regardless of whether the manager has had any experience on air. Although such evaluation and guidance are often done through an intermediary—that is, the program director—it is still the manager's ultimate responsibility.

A manager can directly or indirectly provide for training and professional growth of the announcing staff through a number of strategies, including the following:

1.   *Regularly scheduled evaluations.* Often this is done by the program director. Critique of tapes is a worthwhile endeavor not only for correcting mistakes but also for sharing ideas for new creative approaches.

2. *Clear guidelines.* Here is how one consultant, in a confidential report, summed up the plight of a talented announcer who was undersupported by management: "The announcer on the afternoon shift is very funny and creative, but he's handcuffed by the manager. What's happened is that the station manager has received some angry calls from one woman prominent in the community. . . . She complains when she hears anything she thinks is off-color and she thinks just about everything is off-color. Now, the manager reacts to the announcer's material only when he gets complaints. He doesn't make any objective recommendation or evaluation one way or the other. So the announcer is in the dark about what he can or cannot say. On Thursday, maybe, everything's okay, probably because the woman isn't listening. But on Friday, the material that was all right on Thursday is practically obscene. The manager is letting one member of the audience program the show, and the manager doesn't give any clear guidance to the announcer."

Such a situation is, unfortunately, not atypical. It is very important for managers to state guidelines up front. This causes much less trepidation than random objections. The manager also must stick to professional standards of objectivity and not bow to isolated complaints.

3. *Opportunities for flexible growth.* Usually, the wise manager allows or encourages a news announcer to try sports play by play or the Sunday disc jockey to do commercial production. Veterans of on-air work are virtually unanimous in their observations that their first type of on-air job was not always the one for which they were best suited. And even if they stuck with their original ambition, explorations into other areas were of long-term benefit.

Managers can benefit from a flexible approach because the news reporter just might turn out to be a superb play-by-play sports announcer. If not, little is lost. (Such flexibility is appropriate to small and medium markets; large markets have too many restrictions for much job flexibility.)

2.3

NEWS

Radio news often is not a large money-maker for a station. Radio newscasts simply do not attract the type of major advertiser investment as do television newscasts, primarily because they do not offer television's huge audience numbers. Also, there is less general awareness of the radio news medium among prospective buyers. Advertisers often are anxious to place their product on the local television newscast; they are often less inclined to seek out radio news. Advertisers may not be aware of the existence of radio news on some of the stations to which they (the local advertisers) don't listen.

Radio news is the most expensive programming element in terms of the relative investment of personnel hours and equipment versus the income returned to the station. As a result, some stations choose to air very little or no news at all. When news is a part of the programming effort, conflict between radio managers and news executives frequently occurs.

Both sides in the never-ending tug-of-war have valid points of view. Management believes that news operations often appear wasteful, highly overstaffed, and unsettlingly independent. Newspeople frequently regard management (the "suits") as insensitive bottom-liners who forsake the public good for a profit. There is some truth in both arguments, and the situation is not always adversative; however, a great deal of misconception flourishes in both camps.

Knowledge can help bridge the gap. A manager must have an understanding of news—the more intimate the understanding, the better. It is unrealistic for management to assume that newspeople can, or should, know the overall operational and financial picture of the station. It *is* realistic for newspeople to expect good management by an executive with an appreciation for quality journalism and an understanding of its mechanism.

What follows is an overview of the news operation. It is not a short course in journalism but a descriptive summary of what an informed nonjournalist should know about the workings of a radio newsroom.

Instant Information

Radio is the most flexible and adaptable of all news media. When a news story suddenly develops, radio offers the most immediate coverage. There are many reasons, but the most obvious is the physical delivery system of radio and its relative lack of complexity. Radio does not have to be printed, nor does it need a camera crew. A radio story can be phoned in, complete with taped interviews gathered at the scene. New hand-held, portable transmission units specially designed for radio newspeople are powerful and allow for on-the-scene coverage as quickly as a reporter can reach the event and think of something to say.

Radio news has a competitive advantage over newspaper and television in that it can be quickly assembled and edited, often by one person. A radio newsroom (Figure 2.2) is equipped with devices for recording off the phone and usually is equipped to record the signal of the station's remote news transmission devices. In addition, there are frequently incoming network lines from which audio emanating from national net-

Figure 2.2

A well-equipped radio newsroom.

works can be received. These feeds used to come exclusively from telephone lines from the network source. Today, most network transmissions come from satellites rather than "land lines."

Breaking news, the journalist's term for a story happening right now, can be put on the air virtually as fast as the story can be typed; in some cases, the newscaster will ad-lib from notes. Such a situation is a sharp contrast to television, where a staff of specialized personnel must team up to edit and assemble a newscast.

Another advantage in radio journalism is the flexibility of the medium in general. Looser program schedules and far greater ease of rearranging program elements allow for easy insertion of news bulletins and other information such as special traffic reports, weather information, cancellation of events, and even lost dogs. The news staff—like all people who provide the material for radio—can take justifiable pride in the fact that they provide information and companionship to an appreciative public.

Radio News Gathering, Writing, and Delivery

Techniques vary from station to station, as does the individual news department's staffing and function. But in many cases, the type of organization and presentation of news is the same. Let's follow the progression of events that leads to a newscast in a typical radio station.

Although most of WXXX's listeners think of the midday news as a program that airs at lunchtime, some of the newspeople who put the newscast together are actually wrapping up their working day at 12 Noon. Two staffers in the five-person news department arrived for work at 5 AM. After infusions of black coffee, they assembled the first newscast of the day, the 6 AM report. The newscast was assembled from various sources:

— Calls made to local police and fire agencies.

— Items rewritten from the local newspaper. (Although standard practice, rewriting often is frowned on and is sometimes a source of conflict between newspapers and local radio stations. Simply rewriting from the paper can be hazardous because newspapers can be wrong; when a radio reporter copies wrong news, the radio station is wrong, too. To make matters worse, the source of the wrong information is painfully apparent.

    Newspapers may very much resent wholesale appropriation of their news items, for obvious reasons. Of course, once a radio reporter follows up on a story found in the newspaper—verifying the information and adding to it—it is perfectly legitimate to run the story.)

— Material filed by other news staffers during the previous night. This can include a report on a city council meeting or on-the-scene coverage of a fire. The fire story will be followed up, and the on-the-scene tape will be used as long as reasonable (until it begins to seem badly dated).

— Wire service material. **Wire services** cover, write, and feed news to local stations that contract for the service. Two major wire services are United Press International (UPI) and Associated Press (AP). Most wire services also provide regional news during the "state split," when circuits of the wire service are turned over to regional bureaus and state and regional news is fed.

    Use of wire service material varies greatly. Some stations locally produce and read *only* local news and hardly use the wire service except for state and regionally oriented material. Conversely, some stations drastically overuse the wire service and engage in a "rip-and-read" operation where virtually no news-gathering is done except for ripping the copy off the teletype.

    Incidentally, *wire service* and *teletype* are vestigial terms from an era that only recently passed. Most services now transmit by satellite rather than wire, and the teletype has been largely replaced by the computer printer. An aerial dish located at or near the station picks up the feed from an orbiting satellite, and the feed is printed out on a high-speed printer.

— Other sources for stories include items from the futures file, a collection of items about events that will be taking place shortly. An example is a story to be announced later today about the appointment of a new city planner. Other stories are taken from press releases. Or, a short interview segment is recorded over the phone from a college's public relations news service.

The noon newscast includes some of the items used during the morning newscasts at 6, 7, 8, 9, 10, and 11. Most material is rewritten to give it a fresh *angle*, a fundamental concept in radio news. A new slant, or angle, to the story keeps listeners from getting the impression that all the station's newscasts are rehashes of the same old news.[5]

Sometimes, a great deal of news is held over and rewritten, but today is a busy day and many new stories have broken. The news director, who arrived at 9 AM and who will work until 6 PM, made several assignments for street reporters to cover in person:

—— A neighborhood demonstration against a planned trash plant.

—— A press conference about the selection of the new city planner.

—— The grand jury handing up indictments in a local corruption case.

—— A feature story on dieting for the summer. The story includes an interview with a nutritionist from a local college.

What happens with the material? Street reporters might phone the information back to the station and could elect to send the audio of their interviews, known as **sound bites,** over phone lines for editing and quick use at the station. In most of the stories covered this morning, the reporters did both. Short reports were filed from the scene of the demonstration for the 10 and 11 o'clock news reports. The 10 AM demonstration story was more or less a prewrite, because the demonstration was just getting under way. The 11 AM story was filed by the reporter, his voice alone, and concluded with the tag line, ". . . This is Marty Leroux reporting for WXXX News." This format—giving a report and signing off with the reporter's name—is known as a **voicer.**

The press conference concerning the city planner was a relatively routine affair. The reporter made a quick visit, recorded a short statement, and fed the statement itself back to the station over the phone (using a special clip to connect the recorder's output to the phone handset). Next, the reporter fed a story ad-libbed from her notes, with a lead-in to the tape-recorded interview segment and a closing remark to follow the statement. The editing was done back at the station, and the story incorporated the tape.

[reporter's voice:] . . . as expected, Myron Stein was appointed city planner. Also as expected, he immediately promised to end the city's building moratorium.

[Stein's voice:] I'll do everything in my power to get this moratorium repealed. The net effect of the moratorium was to encourage poor use of the land. We only allowed building of single-family houses, and that's the worst type of housing from a planning standpoint.

[reporter's voice again] Stein faces some stiff opposition from the city council, and right now it's anyone's guess as to whether he'll be more effective in ending the moratorium than was his predecessor. This is Lois Larsen reporting from City Hall.

In radio terminology, the taped interview segment of Mr. Stein is known as an **actuality.** Actuality is basically synonymous with sound bite, although sound bite is often used to refer to recorded sound effects, such as fire engine sirens and interview segments. When combined with Ms. Larsen's voicer, the report is known as a **voice actuality.**

Some other stories were written in the newsroom in preparation for the noon newscast. Reports of a traffic accident were written from information gathered over the phone during an interview with a police officer. The Associated Press wire service carried a story about declines in the nationwide, average SAT scores, and a WXXX news reporter called an area college for a local angle.

The noon newscast is ten minutes long. Despite the fact that it is a relatively short period of time, many person-hours of preparation are involved. Over twenty stories will be read. Some are only a few sentences in length, lasting fifteen or twenty seconds. The longer stories, such as the voice actualities, will run close to a minute; that minute might reflect about three hours' work.

The news director anchors the noon report. He is responsible for choosing the order of the stories, which is not a small task because broadcast news structure imposes a disproportionate importance on the lead stories. Which will be today's lead? After some debate, the news director chooses to lead with the demonstration story. Here, the judgment is not based solely on journalistic considerations. He likes the story because it contains interesting and evocative sound bites and poses some degree of human drama.

Two minutes before the start of the noon newscast, however, the situation changes entirely. A reporter assigned to cover the grand jury calls in with the news that a major city official has been indicted. The story was expected for the afternoon because indictments usually do not get handed up until after lunch, but no one anticipated the indictment of an important city official. The reporter now has about ninety seconds to prepare an ad-lib; because her story will be leading the newscast, it *must* go live. The demonstration story will follow next. The diet story is preempted because there is no time left in the lineup.

Partly because of the news director's experience in handling fast-changing news-

Figure 2.3

The inverse pyramid.

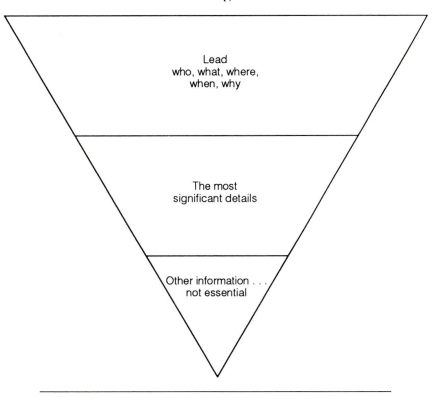

casts, the program goes smoothly and proceeds with a snappy flow of information. Much of the reason for the lively pace is the writing style of the stories. The news director is able to time himself and edit the copy as he reads; knowing the story is going to run long, the news director omits the last few sentences of several stories. This, by the way, is not an accidental accomplishment. The stories are written "from the top down" and meant to be cut from the bottom. In journalistic terminology, this is known as the inverse pyramid style (Figure 2.3).

The lead contains the most significant information; it might say "A fire of un-known origin swept the Atlas Tire Warehouse at 51 Chandler Street today, destroying the building but causing no injuries." The story then would continue with the most significant secondary details, such as the estimated damage, description of the fire, numbers of firefighters called in, and how long it took to put out the fire. In the structure of a radio news story, here is where an actuality from the fire chief might be inserted.

This story then would conclude with less immediate details such as information on the number of people left jobless by the fire, speculation from investigators on the possible cause, and information on plans to rebuild.

Radio stories are written for the ear and not the eye. The sentences are short in time and actual length, usually well under twenty to twenty-five words, and much less complex in structure than newspaper stories. Newspaper leads, for example, sometimes compress the who, what, where, when, and why into a one paragraph-long lead sentence. Such a strategy would be inappropriate for radio because the listener cannot take in so much information in one bite and cannot refer to a sentence that was not completely understood. Also, broadcast news is more conversational than print stories. One other major difference is **attribution**—the statement of where the information came from—is generally placed at the beginning of the sentence in broadcast news. In other words, a broadcast reporter would write "Fire officials said there were no injuries in this morning's fire," rather than "There were no injuries in this morning's fire, fire officials said." Attribution is placed at the beginning because it is a more conversational method, hence better suited for broadcast. When attribution leads the information, it can most easily be remembered by the listener.

As seen from the material presented, news is a complex operation that requires a tremendous amount of effort. Ten minutes of news represents much more of an investment of time and money than does playing three records. A thirty-second actuality can require sitting through an hour-long press conference and the hour spent driving the round-trip from the radio station to the event.[6]

News and the Station Sound Mix

One way to make the most of the news effort is to shape that news in such a way that it reinforces the message of the station, contributing to the overall sound and format. Album-oriented rock stations, for example, often present news very informally, and much of that news is oriented toward the slant of the audience. In fact, such a station might very well subscribe to a specialized news service that provides material oriented toward this audience.

Fast-moving music formats inevitably are tied to fast-moving news deliveries. The deliveries of news announcers in easy-listening stations, on the other hand, typically would be more slowly paced, and the voices themselves would reflect a more mature quality. The relationship between news and programming would at this extreme seem obvious; it is immediately apparent that listeners of an easy-listening station would be jarred by a "newsflash" type of delivery.

Reinforcing the sound of the station goes beyond copying the mechanics of delivery. Of more importance is the overall integration of the news effort into the station's *image*. Is this the station that "cares about you"? If so, one way to demonstrate that concern is with a high quotient of news and information, perhaps with consumer affairs and self-help features added for good measure. Does the station cater to the well-to-do businessperson? If that's the case, the news must include a generous helping of financial reports and stock quotations.

How Managers and Programmers View News

Besides the points of friction explored in this chapter and elsewhere in the book (such as conflict over news involving sponsors and the news department's high-level autonomy), some other issues frequently cloud relations between management and news and sometimes between programming and news.

A final idea to consider is that in some cases a news story endangers the financial structure of the station by exposing it to libel charges. This is not common, but it does happen. Unfortunately, our system of jurisprudence allows even an absurdly hollow nuisance suit to entail debilitating legal fees.

Managers need good advice on libel, much more than can be presented in the pages of a textbook. Incomplete or dated advice on libel can be worse than none at all. Libel laws change; more to the point, interpretations change. In a legal system based largely on the concept of precedent, the ebb and flow of current legal philosophy plays a profound but difficult-to-understand role.

Libel can be defined broadly as the act of issuing or publishing a statement that damages a person's reputation, defaming his or her character, or exposing that person to ridicule. (Libel differs from slander in that libel refers to a published statement; in broadcasting, a statement is deemed to be "published" when it is put over the air.) There are three well-known defenses against libel: truth, privilege, and fair comment. However, these categories are not easy to define (were they clear-cut, there would be a noteworthy reduction of legal cases). The seemingly obvious concept of truth, for example, can be quite difficult to evaluate. The idea of **truth** entails proof, and as any reporter knows, there are many gradations of proof. Calling a contractor corrupt, for example, means that the alleged corruption must be documented. But how much documentation is enough? Where are the lines drawn? Can this alleged corruption be proved in court? These are questions best discussed with competent counsel and experienced news executives.

Fair comment is not easily defined, either. Fair comment's basic tenet is that public figures expose themselves to a certain amount of criticism, and we recognize that in a free society much of that criticism may be harsh and less than completely accurate. But who, exactly, is a public figure? Many court cases, including the landmark case *New York Times vs. Sullivan,* have sought to clarify that issue. *New York Times vs. Sullivan* essentially held that even false statements made against public figures were not actionable as long as those statements were not made with reckless disregard for the truth. Since that decision, other cases have broadened the rights of the press and minimized those of public figures, although the pendulum has vacillated on occasion.

Privilege is another defense against libel. Essentially, there are certain "privileged" statements not actionable under any circumstances such as a fair and accurate reporting of a court proceeding and remarks made by legislators from the floor of a legislative chamber. The principle of the law is to encourage full and robust debate.

Do not be left with the impression that all radio station managers and news departments live in a state of barely contained hostility; many radio stations regard their news departments as the highest-quality component of the organization. News *is* expensive, and the interests of journalists and salespeople inevitably will come into conflict. However, a proper appreciation of the critical role of radio journalism and support for the news department's goals will serve the interests of the radio station *and* its listening public.

EXERCISES

1. Inventory the music in your personal record and tape collection. In a brief paper, about two pages, tell why you like this type of music. Are your tastes in music exactly the same as others of your age and financial and social status? Or, are those tastes similar but not identical? Explain why your music appeals to you. Be specific. Evaluate how the music reflects your personal experiences and life-style.

2. Evaluate a local air personality (your instructor may assign a personality, or the choice may be left to you). Your task is to write a brief evaluation of this announcer as if you were considering hiring this person. Write a two- or three-page memo to the station owner explaining your recommendations. Evaluate the following points:

a. The announcer's ability as a one-to-one communicator.
b. How well the announcer reinforces the format of the station. For the purposes of this exercise, assume that your station's format is similar.
c. What sort of constituencies does this announcer appeal to? Be specific: ages, life-styles, occupations. Back up your judgment with examples taken from your monitoring of the station.
d. What would you recommend to improve the announcer's abilities?

3. Do the same assignment but evaluate a local newscaster. Incorporate these points:
a. The newcaster's credibility. Does the newscaster appear to understand the news?
b. The newscaster's ability as a writer. Assume that the newscaster wrote all the copy that was read.
c. The newscaster's skill in structuring the newscast. Were stories in the proper order of importance? Was the proper amount of time allocated in relation to the relative importance of each story?
d. How good is the newscaster's interpretation? Were moods and phrasings appropriate?

NOTES

1. An eloquent example of the obscure role of the early medium is the following: Television pioneer Fred Friendly, speaking in Boston, recently recalled his first experience with radio. "My father brought home the first set on the block. I asked him what it was for, and he said, 'So we can listen to Pittsburgh.' So I asked him, 'Why do we want to listen to Pittsburgh?'"

2. For a lively discussion of the licensing struggle, see Erik Barnouw, A Tower in Babel: A History of Broadcasting in the United States to 1933 (New York: Oxford University Press, 1966), 119–120.

3. For a discussion of the trend of in-studio composition, see Edward Jay Whetmore, The Magic Medium: An Introduction to Radio in America (Belmont, CA: Wadsworth, 1981), 79–84.

4. One aspect of the new rigor in regulation of obscenity is that the government is now explicitly stating what is and is not, in its view, suitable. An argument against obscenity rulings has been that the government has never specified

exactly what is obscene. All that is changing, as the article "FCC Launches Attack on Indecency" in *Broadcasting* (20 April 1987): 35 points out. For the first time, *Broadcasting* listed "the words you can't say" over the air.

5. For a clear summary of newswriting principles, see Ted White, Adrian J. Meppen, and Steve Young, *Broadcast News Writing, Reporting, and Production* (New York: Macmillan, 1984), 55–75; see pp. 90–101 for examples of leads that provide new slants on dating stories.

6. A parenthetical but relevant discussion concerns the debate over gathering of actuality and the expense of the effort. Some radio station news departments have a policy against gathering actuality over the phone and always send reporters in person to conduct interviews. In some stations the quality of that day's news effort is judged, in part, by the amount of actuality gathered.

   The conventional wisdom of gathering actuality has held that hearing the voices of newsmakers brings the news to life and makes it more informative and immediate. A recent study, however, showed that a group of college students who listened to a three-and-one-half minute simulated newscast that had no actualities "scored significantly higher on a multiple choice test of recall and rated the newscast more interesting" than did students who listened to a newscast that had actualities. See K. Time Wolfemeyer, and Lori L. McFadden, "Effects of Actualities in Radio Newscasts," *Journal of Broadcasting and Electronic Media* 29, no. 2 (Spring 1985): 189–193.

CHAPTER 3

FORMATS AND

PROGRAMMING

Radio formats began after World War II. Radio was the mass medium—an unchallenged giant in popular entertainment. Lurking in the background was an upstart technology known as television. But television was viewed as a novelty, an interesting way to combine radio with pictures. Its commercial possibilities were doubted.

This chapter examines how formats originally came into being, how formats helped radio achieve a new-found commercial success, and how formats are implemented today. Before beginning the examination, a definition of terms is in order. Formatting and programming often are used synonomously and interchangeably to mean arranging the program elements from hour to hour and within the hour. There is no classical definition. In popular usage, the term **formatting** pertains to the entire overall strategy of the station, whereas **programming** refers to the placement of elements within the broadcast day. This is, admittedly, a general definition, but it does seem to reflect the typical usage of terms that have no exact denotation.

3.1

EVOLUTION OF THE MODERN FORMAT

Radio had reached its peak of popularity because of its ability to capture the imagination and serve as the center of family entertainment, especially in the pre–World War II era and the spartan war years. A listener in 1938 would approach the radio in an entirely different way than would a listener today because the overall appeal and strategy of the medium *was* different. Long-form entertainment such as the half-hour comedy show was the norm, and the family would gather around the radio for an evening of programs that would also include variety, music (often live broadcasts of popular orchestras), and adventure.

The format was geared entirely to mass appeal, much the way television is today. Networks dominated the broadcast schedules, providing a consistent source of quality mass-appeal, national-interest entertainment, which could not be duplicated at the local level. News programming gained in importance during the war, and radio had developed a deserved reputation for magically transporting the listener to the scene of breaking news.

The point is that radio programmers presented the big stars to the mass audience and, in effect, waited for the audience to come to them. Advertisers were attracted by the presence of this mass audience and often became identified closely with the entertainment presented during the shows they sponsored. The serial form, for example, was dominated by soap companies and hence developed the name "soap opera."

Death of the Old Formats and Birth of the New

In the late 1940s through the mid-1950s change was, literally, in the air. Television evolved into a medium that inherently had the advantage when it came to mass entertainment. Aside from television's riveting novelty effect, technology and modern consumer production were making the home television much more affordable. With postwar prosperity taking hold, consumers had built up an enormous backlog of savings and consumer demand and were ready to purchase some luxuries. Advertising of the era vaunted the benefits of vacuum cleaners and juice squeezers. The woman with the old-fashioned carpet sweeper was portrayed as the victim of the worst kind of drudgery, whereas the modern housewife was freed from such indignity by the all-electric everything.

These factors—easing of the hardship of the war years and the capturing of imagination via technology—made it clear that nothing could catch the tidal wave of mass entertainment more effectively than television.

Format and Programming Developments

Early television broadcasts were constructed by programmers who brought their expertise from radio. As a result, early television tended to be radio with pictures. Arthur Godfrey went so far as to don headsets for his television show (which was simulcast on radio). Walter Winchell didn't see the necessity of removing his hat when appearing on camera. However, as more radio series began the crossover to television, the possibilities of producing truly captivating and visually oriented television became more apparent, and that is exactly what happened.

But what of radio? Radio was faced with the prospect of competing for a mass audience against a mass-appeal medium. The novelty of television increasingly fascinated the audience, even though many felt (and still feel) that radio was greatly superior to television in its ability to create an image in the theater of the mind.

Television required less effort because so much less imagination was involved: The images were explicit, and there were fewer details for the mind to fill in. The visual component was mesmerizing and could absorb more easily the attention of the audience. As television sets found a place in more homes, the set became part of the social structure. Proud owners of a new set would invite guests over for an evening of television, in much the same way as VCR (videocassette recorder) get-togethers became popular in the mid-1980s.

Radio, meanwhile, was going belly-up in a hurry. Advertisers were deserting the floundering medium in droves. To make matters worse, many radio executives were completely resistant to change, holding a death grip on those old, long-form programs.

It became apparent that something must be done, and radio's dilemma ignited the wildfire of the disc jockey era. The genesis of the disc jockey phenomenon predates the dominance of television and it is traced by many to a program called the *Make Believe Ballroom.* This originally was a live band show, or *supposed* to be a live band show on the night that the band didn't show up. Recordings were substituted.[1] The success of this type of inexpensive and practical format extended into the hit-parade program structure, where top musical numbers were played in order of popularity.

This structure produced what came to be known as the Top-Forty format and appeared to be a viable solution to the problems facing radio. The Top-Forty format soon emerged at various outlets throughout the country. It was not a sudden and stunning invention, in the sense that it was completely new and totally unheard of, but the idea of a "jockey riding the controls" and "spinning discs" did enjoy a bit of novelty and a surprising spurt of popularity. Talented entertainers were attracted to the concept, and soon-to-be network television stars such as Dave Garroway were pioneers in the disc jockey format.

Top-Forty would, of course, evolve. In the 1960s, for example, programming pioneer Bill Drake nipped and tucked the existing Top-Forty into a smooth, flowing, and some would say "robotic" presentation. Most Top-Forty outlets would follow Drake's lead, and his firm—Drake–Chenault Enterprises—would eventually become one of the most successful providers of formats and programming.

Social Significance of the New Formats

Fanning the flames of the disc jockey phenomenon was the fact that the popular music of the 1950s was undergoing a transition from the big band era to Rock and Roll. The youth culture became a social force to be reckoned with; young people were buying recordings like never before. Fans diligently followed the careers of rising young artists. The Rock-and-Roll station assumed a more personal relevance to the listener. The disc jockey's presentation of music combined with friendly chatter *was* the event, a common experience shared among listeners.

Equally intriguing was how advertisers viewed this phenomenon. It was possible, by exploiting this strange new music, to isolate young listeners, the young market of rabid devotees of the Top-Forty stations across the country. Advertisers found that there was indeed a market among young people for certain types of products, and they clamored for airtime.

Meanwhile, disaffected holdouts from the big band era also became targets of the advertiser. Many stations clung to music of the big band era, and the musical standards attracted an adult audience searching for the so-called **middle-of-the-road (MOR)** sound. They, too, had discrete buying habits and proved a valuable audience to "sell" to an advertiser.

Mass-entertainment radio still existed, but the trend was inevitable: The medium was evolving, and executives in charge of programming increasingly recognized that it would be necessary to pursue a *particular* and not a *mass* audience.

Another principle of the new science of programming became clear. Advertising agencies and the emerging radio programmers found that selected audiences could be reached during specific portions of a station's broadcast day. In other words, the audience available in the morning, both in the house and in the automobile, was very much different in composition than at midday. Thus, the advertiser looking to sell some laundry detergent began to appreciate the fact that he could exploit the midday **daypart,** that portion of the broadcast day that ostensibly would reach a preponderance of homemakers, a segment of the audience much more predisposed to buy laundry soap.

Radio people, sensing a renaissance of medium, quickly seized the opportunity offered by this kind of advertiser interest. Therefore, programming that was increasingly efficient at attracting and identifying specific audience segments, audiences with demonstrably skewed constituencies within dayparts, was developed. Some would say that programming became, at this point, "scientific."

The age of radio as mass medium faded. Mass-market radio, which had fallen ill in the early 1950s, was figuratively declared dead in 1960 when the last radio daytime serial went off the air. Spelling the end of long-form entertainment as it existed then, the cancellation ended the era when station owners would try to attract advertisers to a general and broad audience. Rather, time sales were based on delivery of an audience tailored to the needs of the specific advertiser and the advertiser's specific marketing strategy.

Evolution of the Art of Programming

Radio station managers who, at one time, might have left the choice of programming pretty much in the hands of the air personality began to realize the economic hazards involved in that strategy. In the 1950s the hazards of payola—record companies paying disc jockeys to air certain cuts—also played a major role in bringing programming authority to the management level. Procedures were eventually refined, and playlists were handed to disc jockeys by the **program director,** a programming executive. The position of program director effectively removed much of the threat of payola because accountability for playlists was more visible and centralized.

Besides the factors cited above, the construction of the playlist was based on the idea of *keeping* an audience tuned in. Research in tune-out factors began to play an increasing role, and programming moved in the direction of using surveys of record store sales for more sophisticated soundings of what listeners liked and what they didn't like. The essential question was, Do our listeners tune out when they hear a particular kind of record, or during a newscast? How do we compensate?

In the case of news, the answer often was to place the news at times where listener tune out, if any, would not be as damaging. In other words, it would not be detected as readily by the methodologies of ratings services. Ratings are taken in terms of quarter hours, so the goal is to keep the listener on board into the next quarter hour.

Programmers, at all costs, avoid elements that might spur tune-out at quarter after the hour, at the half hour, or at quarter to the hour. Chapter 8 has a detailed explanation. To keep listeners' attention, so the theory went, a programmer could compensate for the dulling effects of the news by coming out of the newscast with a strong, upbeat vocal.

What emerged was the development of a station sound, a way in which the production and air personalities were oriented toward developing an overall trademark identity. A station with a strong, *cohesive, and recognizable* sound could be picked out readily from among the competition. No longer was the station's sound and format simply the kind of music played; it was strongly geared to what was between the cuts. The air personalities, the commercials, and the news had to reflect and reinforce the overall station sound. This trend was manifested by major stations that even went so far as to hire air personalities who sounded surprisingly alike. WHAM in Rochester, New York, for example, was a clear-channel station noted in the 1960s for its totally cohesive MOR sound. The sound was refined to the point where listeners would know that they were listening to WHAM the instant they tuned in, regardless of what was being aired at the time. Some technical devices also were used to create that recognizable sound, such as the addition of echo on WABC, New York, during the 1960s and early 1970s.

What is the modern incarnation of these developments in radio? First is the paramount supremacy of the format. Although the word *format* can technically be taken to mean simply the way in which something is structured, the modern interpretation of the word format has taken several meanings.

—— *Music genre:* Today, the genre is far more specific than a simple categorization of Top-Forty or MOR. Those people engaged in format development recognize many variations of the Top-Forty structure and have split it into supersegmented categories with formats designed to appeal to the devotees of particular kinds of music—hard-edged rock, softer popular tunes, and so forth.

—— *The sound of the station:* What types of program elements does the station use to establish a distinct identity from among the competing stations? Often this category of format definition entails the use of certain jingle packages, the style of announcing, and the style and sound of commercials. Many stations, for instance, do not accept prerecorded commercials that do not reinforce their station sound. Advertising agencies are well-aware of this, and many will supply commercials in various styles such as country or hit-radio. The content is the same, but the style and packaging is different.

—— *Program element timing:* Closely related to the sound of the station is how rapidly program elements are presented and how long those elements typically are. For instance, a Top-Forty station typically uses very short news summaries, if news is used at all. Top-Forty is a very fast-moving format; therefore, long news reports would, in theory, detract from the format's effectiveness. The pace of program elements is frequently a matter of standard operating procedure, and often the program director gives specific instructions about the "tightness" of the desired on-air mix.

The programmer refining musical genre and the sound of the station draws on a variety of sources at many levels of sophistication. The small local station may simply develop an overall guideline of the music style to be played. The major-market station may use audience research undertaken by the station's in-house research department and develop detailed playlists. In any case, the program elements coalesce into an overall program strategy, one of the major radio formats.

3.2

MAJOR FORMATS

Many major *categories* of formats have emerged in radio broadcasting. Many subcategories are within these broad catchalls. One person's adult contemporary, for example, often sounds like harsh rock music to another listener. In other words, a comparison could be made among adult contemporary stations that shows some of these stations include "harder" rock more than other stations. Another listener might favor an adult contemporary format that leans more toward easy-listening. Country music might heavily rely on crossover hits at one station, but another country music station may reject crossovers in favor of "pure country."

Of primary importance, recall that formats and programming carry far beyond the simple selection of a category of music. As examined in this and following sections, formats involve the capture of a specific audience and methods for producing good ratings numbers.

Before discussing the broad categories of formats, it is worthwhile to point out that the modern concept of formatting and programming has come to mean, in the eyes of some, a tool for a quick fix. Formats have, in fact, revolutionized the radio industry. The development of narrowcasting (broadcasting to a narrowly defined audience) and commercially packaged formats (provided by syndicators) has meant that even the sleepiest operation can, given the right combination of events, zoom to a profitable place in the market—*if* the station is found and identified by a specific audience.

First, let's take a broad look at these formats. Again, a reminder: These categories are not definitive in their scope, nor are they meant to be. Each heading will give a brief summary of the format, its ranking in terms of *how many individual stations in the United States use the particular format*,[2] a summary of the format's strengths and weaknesses from the standpoint of the programmer, and a brief analysis of current trends within the particular format category. Remember, the numeric rankings reflect only the number of stations using the format at the particular time the tally was made. They are used here simply as an arbitrary way to order the list.

Country Format

RANK: 1

SUMMARY   At one time country was fairly well-defined. The artists typically had a Grand Old Opry style, and the country sound was clearly distinct from popular music. It was often characterized by steel guitars, a twanging sound to the instrumentals, and whining vocals.

Radio stations typically presented the music in a rural context, relating the music to country life. This tradition has been modified as country has become much more popular and adapted by stations in many locations, including highly urban markets.

Country music has splintered significantly among several forms, and country artists popular in one specific country genre might not be heard at all on a station preferring a different country-programming strategy. Some stations, for example, favor country that has a distinctly rock flavor, while others opt for music with a stronger country twang.

ADVANTAGES   Country music has a broad appeal to wide age groups. The audience is increasingly upscale. There is strong advertiser identification with certain products (pickup trucks, for example), and country is typically a solid performer in the market, although not usually the ratings leader. The pickup-truck example is not meant to stereotype the country listener. It is one product that meshes well with the audience, but country listeners do come from a broad range of backgrounds and buy a wide range of products.

DISADVANTAGES   Advertisers sometimes believe that country is exclusively a blue-collar commodity and not an ideal vehicle for many products. The audience for a country station is usually characterized by strong likes and dislikes, making programming a difficult task. Although a programmer may be able to generate strong appeal to an individual segment, an error in programming (such as crossover artist on a vehemently "pure-country" station) might just as efficiently drive listeners away.

CURRENT TRENDS   There is a movement toward a so-called pure sound among certain stations, and a strong fussiness about the use of music by crossover artists exists. The gravitation to specific formats is stressing an identifiable strain of country music, and new formats might lean to such strains as country oldies.

Adult Contemporary Format

RANK: 2

SUMMARY   Adult contemporary (AC) covers a broad range of musical styles, sometimes favoring a good share of oldies, sometimes based in more contemporary rock. It is highly adaptable to molding around strong air personalities. AC is mostly designed to reach relatively young adults and is generally quite distinct in its rejection of hard rock. Often, AC is heavily geared toward information exchange and places great emphasis on weather, news, and traffic. There is typically some use of music sweeps: going through two or more cuts and back-announcing them at the conclusion of the set.

ADVANTAGES   AC has a direct appeal to primary and powerful buying groups, groups with major purchasing power. There is less of a tune-out factor in AC than in many other formats. The broad range of the public who listens to this format typically tolerates a variety of styles. AC is not as prone to the quick-changing vagaries of public taste as are stations catering to highly homogenized musical likes and dislikes. AC is frequently a leader in the ratings and lends itself well to effective promotion. It is also a good format for exploiting the talents of a highly skilled air personality.

DISADVANTAGES   The competition is very tight, and the situation is aggravated by the fact that other formats may overlap into the AC station's audience appeal. The station playing the easier styles of Top-Forty, for example, can erode an AC station's audience. AC is often highly dependent on personalities, making it somewhat risky from the station programmer's point of view; in general, it is not an easy format to program. Top air personalities in this format can be expensive. There is a great deal of music available, and deciding what to play and why to play it is often a formidable task. The recent trend of AC stations to splinter into subformats makes it difficult for a programmer to isolate a profitable niche. It is common to find AC stations at the top and the bottom of the ratings charts in a particular market.

CURRENT TRENDS   There is a continuing movement toward fragmentation of the AC format, an attempt to more narrowly define target audiences. Many stations are programming more oldies in AC. AC stations sometimes lean toward the older, age thirty-five and up audience. There is a perceptible move toward heavy marketing efforts to display the individual characteristics of stations and distinguish them from the competition. This competition is increasingly heavy as more stations seek particularly desirable demographics. A case in point is the current popularity of the light contemporary version of AC, which is strongly geared toward familiar pop artists and aimed at the older segment of the AC audience, particularly females.

Middle-of-the-Road/Nostalgia Format

RANK: 3

SUMMARY   Middle-of-the-road (MOR)/nostalgia is a very broad category. Not all MOR is nostalgia, and not all nostalgia is MOR; however, there is enough overlap so that programmers today tend to view this as a distinct category. Because of the difficulty in obtaining nostalgia music, station executives often go out of house to obtain a syndicated format. Al Hamm Productions is one of the firms most noted for catering to this need. The MOR/nostalgia format has heavy dependence on big bands and the pop standards of the 1940s and 1950s. Most of these formats also include a generous helping of fairly recent music that fits within the general sound of the station. There is typically heavy use of ballads. Music generally takes the forefront; personality often is not emphasized to any great extent.

ADVANTAGES   This format is a good tool for capturing a segment of the radio audience who views itself as disfranchised from current radio offerings. Some of the audience characteristics are easily identifiable and therefore have appeal to certain categories of advertisers. The discovery by marketers that people over age forty-five retain considerable buying power has spurred the development of such formats. With the aging of the population in general, MOR/nostalgia appears more attractive to advertisers. Another major advantage is that listeners have a strong loyalty to this format. Some format syndicators, for example, publish newsletters and encourage member stations to sponsor events for audience members. Although this is certainly not the format for a market-ratings leader, it has been proven that in large-enough markets MOR/nostalgia can capture a significant and profitable share of the audience.

DISADVANTAGES   Advertisers sometimes feel that an aging audience is not as affluent and therefore less likely to spend money. Although some segments of the typical MOR/nostalgia audience (ages thirty-four to forty-nine) are traditional money-makers, many listeners are older. The total numbers are limited, and the overall audience of people who remember the standards of the 1940s has no alternative but to eventually shrink in numbers. A minor disadvantage is the difficulty of finding announcing personnel who are familiar with the music. However, there are some very well-done satellite feeds available if this type of format cannot be done by the station itself.

CURRENT TRENDS   Some younger people are gravitating to the format. There is also an increasing amount of attention paid by advertisers to the use of format blocks, almost a return to long-form programming, within MOR/nostalgia stations. Special programs, often running a half-hour to an hour, seem to be gaining in appeal, especially when they use long-established MOR/nostalgia personalities as hosts.

Top-Forty/Contemporary Hit Radio Format

RANK: 4

SUMMARY   Top-Forty/contemporary hit radio (CHR) is a format designed to appeal to younger listeners, ranging from ages twelve to forty-nine years with the prime target being eighteen to thirty-four years old. Younger listeners, ages twelve to eighteen, are also an important component of the demographic because they control a rapidly increasing amount of disposable income. The Top-Forty/CHR approach is characterized by narrow, rigidly constructed playlists and a rapid, highly blended sound. Top-Forty/CHR is typically a heavily produced sound, moving at a swift and energetic pace. There are many contests and promotions and a strong bias against inserting any unproven music, which could be a tune-out factor. Young audiences are notorious for their lack of loyalty.

ADVANTAGES   This format is considered by many programmers and advertisers to be the fundamental format of radio. The music and research involving the music is easily available; the rankings are listed in any issue of *Billboard* or *Cashbox*. Music programming itself is generally simpler than in other formats. The selection is limited, and programmers do not have to choose from a universe of music. They can concentrate on working with a small playlist and fine-tuning it.

DISADVANTAGES   There is an extreme amount of competition that has been aggravated by the growing number of Top-Forty CHR stations on the FM band. As mentioned, there is a serious lack of loyalty among listeners. Current programming strategists are adamant in their contention that listeners to Top-Forty/CHR are loyal to the *music* but not the station or the personalities. The possibility of tune-out, then, is an ever-present threat. Although determining what music to play is relatively simple, the highly competitive nature of this format can entail the need for sophisticated research into how often and when to play certain cuts. There is a certain lack of advertiser appeal attached to this format because the audience is not sufficiently upscale.

CURRENT TRENDS   The number of stations using this format rises and falls and has recently dipped, although this does not mean that the format as a whole is declining because many Top-Forty/CHR stations are powerhouse operations. Increasingly, station owners worry about oversaturation and competition from AC. KKHR-FM in Los Angeles was one of several major stations to revert to soft rock because of that market's oversaturation with Top-Forty/CHR and encroachment by the more contemporary strains of AC. There is a strong trend in urban markets of adding music oriented to blacks to current Top-Forty/CHR formats, and the increased availability of such music is fortifying this trend.

Religious Format

RANK: 5

SUMMARY   Stations adhering to religious music formats are strongly based in the AM spectrum because increasingly profitable music formats are shifting to FM. Many stations have had a long-standing trend of airing religious programming at some point of the broadcast day or week, but the 1970s showed a strong growth in the trend of station ownership by organizations specializing in religious programming. This format was also spurred by the increasing availability of gospel music, although many religious stations air country or even soft rock as part of their overall programming effort. There has been a recent growth in the marketability of music known as Christian contemporary, personified by artists such as Amy Grant.

ADVANTAGES   Most religious stations are nonprofit organizations, but some are commercial and frequently produce a reasonable return to their sponsoring organizations. In many cases, revenue is raised through over-the-air pleas for money. Audiences for this type of station are among the most loyal.

DISADVANTAGES   Commercial religious stations are not traditional profitmakers, and the format certainly is not a good alternative for all markets.

CURRENT TRENDS   Group ownership is increasing, as is the availability of program material. Often, stations are tied into a network arrangement.

Easy-Listening Format

RANK: 6

SUMMARY   Programmers who construct an easy-listening format have moved away—and make a conscious effort to stay away—from the concept of "elevator music," or "beautiful music." In fact, the term *beautiful music*, popular in station slogans a few years ago, now virtually is banished from the the broadcaster's vocabulary. Apparently, "beautiful music" is perceived as "background music," and the advertising contained therein is not really listened to. In easy listening there is heavy dependence on instrumental music with lush string arrangements and orchestrations of popular music. Although many stations use syndicated material and automation, observers note a movement away from anything that smacks of a "canned" format. The live host is frequently expected to introduce some mild elements of personality into the presentation.

ADVANTAGES   This format appeals to the most affluent of all audience segments. Although the listeners may be older than those of other formats, the higher-income segments have an affinity for this type of music. Easy listening has relatively low staffing requirements because the less important parts of the broadcast day can be automated. Such formats generally lend themselves well to automation, appearing more natural and graceful than other formats might. An additional advantage to the programmer and station manager is the underrealized fact that advertisers themselves often like and listen to this kind of music, a great plus when a station's salespeople call on potential advertisers.

DISADVANTAGES   Here again, as is the case with country music, the programmer must walk a tightrope between the strong likes and dislikes of the audience. At one end of the spectrum, the elevator music fan might object to even the most unobtrusive vocal, finding it distracting. On the other end of the spectrum is the listener who is presumably younger and likes music a bit more up-to-date. From a purely mechanical perspective, the station programmer who wants to use easy listening must have an FM station: The lower-quality AM signal does not adequately reproduce the nuances of orchestral music. To a certain extent, the programmer also must be concerned more with the competency of on-air talent and operators than in some other formats. Young, untrained, and inexperienced voices are highly intrusive in an easy-listening format. Mistakes in operations are not well tolerated by listeners or advertisers. A fair amount of audience research is essential to fine-tune this format to appeal to a traditionally fussy audience.

CURRENT TRENDS   One recent trend has been experimentation with so-called New Age music, instrumental music with jazz roots, which some programmers refer to as "yuppie Muzak." Stations in such cities as Santa Cruz, California, and Washington, D.C. have implemented New Age formats.

News/Talk Format

RANK: 7

SUMMARY   The news/talk format evolved from the concept of an all-news format—a format prohibitively expensive in all but the largest markets. News requires enormous resources; one minute's worth of news can involve one hour of a newsperson's time to gather, write, and produce. The talk aspect—live in-studio interviews and/or call-in opinions from listeners—melds well with news and enables a programmer to maintain the verbal thrust of the programming but decrease expenses. The format is clear to a listener: Talk and exchange of information are what is aired. Personalities of hosts are a strong factor in attracting and keeping audiences; their views of the world are a major element in how the listeners view the station.

Another factor in the development of the news/talk format was the perplexing questions of what to do with stations in the AM band as FM showed increasing dominance in music programming. In most cases, the news is featured in the drive-time hours, with talk relegated to the less profitable dayparts, although there are exceptions.

There are other related format options available to the programmer of an AM station; sports broadcasts are among these options. Small-market AMs can compete quite well against FMs when broadcasting high school, college, and professional sports. Other services, such as network-fed talk shows with national toll-free numbers, contribute to the options available to programmers. The total picture relates to the emerging small-market format, which can involve many of the elements discussed above and cross over into several music categories. Highly local and community-oriented programming might, some feel, be the ultimate salvation of AM.

ADVANTAGES   The station programmer who opts for a news/talk format can generally create an immediately distinguishable format, a different product from other offerings in the market. The way ratings are taken often is to the advantage of the news/talk station; it is possible to develop a high cume (see Chapter 8) by counting listeners who tune in occasionally for headlines but actually do not listen to the station for an extended period.

DISADVANTAGES   There is a high expense for the news component and high start-up and technical costs. The programmer is highly dependent on good-quality air

Figure 3.1

WCAU–AM in Philadelphia has used top-quality air personalities to succeed with a talk/ news format.

people. An argument could be made that disc jockeys are relatively interchangeable, but the same could not be said for talk-show hosts. No less a luminary than Larry King has noted that there is a shortage of good hosts for talk radio. "To do a good job, you need good interviewing skills," King says, "which few hosts possess. They just talk to a guest for two minutes and then throw the show open to callers. It becomes pandemonium."[3]

Very few would disagree that talk hosts have an exceedingly difficult job. News/ talk formats frequently fail in part due to the lack of top-class talent. Where the format is durable, such as the long-standing tradition of WCAU in Philadelphia (Figure 3.1), it is because on-air talents are highly professional and well-paid.

CURRENT TRENDS   Abusive talk-show hosts are back in style, apparently. Following in the legacy of such 1960s television standards as Joe Pyne, the aggressive talk-show host is today pulling in ratings by stimulating argument.[4] Some view this as a natural outgrowth of healthy controversy. Other observers liken it to the appeal of slowing down to take a close look at an auto wreck.

Other important trends unrelated to the abusive-host syndrome include a generalized growth of the talk medium. *Westwood One's Talknet* programs, information-oriented, call-in shows that focus on such topics as finances and love lives, are carried across the nation.

Album-Oriented Rock Format

RANK: 8

SUMMARY   Album-oriented rock (AOR) originally was known as free-form or progressive rock, an eclectic mix of music that was a reaction against the rigid playlists of Top-Forty. Longer cuts of rock were used, often including blues, some jazz-style music, and folk. AOR has traditionally been characterized by the laid-back style of the announcer and is almost always an FM phenomenon. AOR is intensely geared to the attitudes and mores of the listeners. Music sweeps (several cuts played without interruption) play a major role in this type of format.

ADVANTAGES   To an advertiser, and therefore to station management, the advantage of AOR is a highly distinguishable and almost always well-researched audience. The audience strongly identifies with the life-style portrayed by the station, a factor appealing to advertisers who want to reach the adherents of this life-style. There is a good measure of listener loyalty, observable from, among other indicators, the number of bumper stickers on the autos of listeners who like to proclaim themselves fans of this music.

DISADVANTAGES   The music appeal is often very narrow. In fact, certain types of music will offend certain members of the audience. Because programmers must go to great lengths to please this audience, research is paramount. The advertisers, in general, view the AOR audience as less affluent. The numbers of stations programming AOR are increasing, meaning cutthroat competition for what is intrinsically a relatively small audience. One major objection to AOR is the advertiser perception—based on typical trends reflected in rating figures—that this format does an inadequate job of reaching females. Also, there is an increasing syphoning of the typical AOR audience by Top-Forty/CHR and AC.

CURRENT TRENDS   An increase is noted in the use of oldies, usually called "classic rock" in AOR parlance. Classic rock is aimed at attracting ages twenty-five and older and is considered more attractive to advertisers.[5] Jazz-style music is making a strong comeback and is often programmed in blocks. An increasing awareness of the so-called purity of the music and a splintering of audience fragments among the various styles of AOR, such as those mentioned above, are observed.

Specialty Format

Each specialty format is a format within its own right; they are placed together here for easier consideration. There are many specialized formats, and extended discussion of each would be ponderous.

In larger markets, it is frequently feasible for one station to wrest a small but monetarily significant segment of the audience by means of a specialty format. For example, all news (as distinguished from news/talk) can survive well in a large market. The successes of WCBS, New York, and WEEI, Boston—to name only two all news stations, illustrate the viability of this format in urban areas. Oldies are also becoming a format in themselves, with about 500 stations in the United States formatting oldies full-time.[6] Black, urban contemporary, jazz, classical, and other specialty formats are aimed at seizing a particular part of the audience. In some cases, these formats can command premium commercial prices because they are capturing a particularly affluent segment of the market. Classical music stations, for example, often claim high profits for paltry numbers because of the affluence of their listeners. Ethnic programs can often convert a small number of extremely loyal listeners into high profits. In smaller markets, it is often usual for the Polish polka program to be one of the best time-per-dollar segments in the station's schedule. Ethnic programming is also strong in major urban markets.

The disadvantages of specialty formats are obvious. In a business dominated by numbers, numbers are hard to come by with such finely targeted formats. However, elements of the specialty programs are appearing with greater regularity within other formats such as urban contemporary finding its way into the Top-Forty.

3.3

DESIGNING FORMATS

Determining the format for a particular station is the first step, obviously predating the design of the particular program strategy with which it is implemented. Some factors that relate specifically to the selection of a format are discussed in the chapters on measuring market potential (Chapter 7) and audience research (Chapter 8).

Other considerations are purely circumstantial. Is the station AM or FM? An AM station is not the best choice for easy listening or AOR, although it has been done; FM's high fidelity might be considered to be wasted with a news/talk operation, although there are examples of that programming on FM. Operating limitations play a part, too. A station without presunrise authorization (meaning it cannot go on the air before local sunrise) would be hard-pressed to make a go of an all-news operation because the listeners expect news early in the morning.

Budget, of course, is another consideration. A well-financed station can always out-promote a less-endowed rival, a situation especially relevant to the competing AC stations; AC stations typically rely on heavy promotion.

Clearly, the *primary* consideration is the competition within the market. Is there an obvious gap in the formats currently offered? Is the gap exploitable by an innovative programmer? How well is the competition doing with the formats currently in operation? Can shock value—a weird and outrageous format—demand attention, figuratively grabbing listeners by the lapels?[7]

For those involved in programming or planning to be involved in programming, the factor that cannot be overstressed is the need to learn all about the marketplace and the potential of the format before making a change. Experience has shown that frequent format changes are expensive and risky. In realistic terms, a station that drastically changes the format must begin recruiting listeners from scratch, although a station needing a format change is obviously not doing well to begin with. A station going from easy listening to Top-Forty/CHR (portrayed in surprisingly realistic terms in the engaging television series *WKRP in Cincinnati*) will initially lose almost *all* its listeners.

Such decisions are made with the input and guidance from research tools and marketing judgments (discussed in other sections of this book). Often, these decisions are beyond the realm of the duties of the person usually thought of as the programmer, and sometimes are beyond the purview of the station manager. The role of the programmer, which is addressed in the remainder of this chapter, is often fulfilled in the actual design and implementation of the format chosen.

Designing format entails determining the basic arrangement of the program elements within the **sound hour** (the pattern of elements such as music, jingles, and news, within each hour) and the program clock along with development of the playlists. Playlists range from very rigid, computer printouts of what will play at any given second to more loosely constructed guidelines for on-air talent.

The Program Clock and Sound Hour

Program clocks have been designed in endless configurations, and there probably are as many of them as there are successful radio stations. A **program clock** (Figure 3.2) is a basic visual representation of where the music, commercials, and news fit within a sound hour. The music mix is highlighted on a program clock. Often, a pie slice of the clockface instructs the operator to play an up-tempo vocal at a particular point in the hour. In many cases, songs keyed to the clock are color-coded. A rack of blue-coded cartridges, for example, would correspond to the blue-colored pie slice on the clock.

In some stations, the songs are coded and indicated in the clock by various names, such as power rotation, oldies, or bulleted new cut. The operator frequently has the latitude to choose any cut in the particular category, an especially useful option when juggling time schedules.[8]

Remember that a program clock can exist without a diagrammed clock adorning the studio wall. In many formats, the rotation is indicated by other means but the effect is the same. One popular syndicated format, for instance, has song cuts arranged in order on a long reel-to-reel tape. The cuts are played in order until the tape finishes, and then another tape is used. Additional music is on cartridge, and the operators are provided with specific instructions on when to play cartridge and when to play tape. The ultimate goal is to provide a mix of music that produces variety, avoids duplication, and avoids a jarring, abrupt change from one style of music to another. Such a format can be automated easily in whole or in part.

The overall tendency in construction of what programmers like to call the sound hour might involve guidelines in clock, automated, prerecorded, or informally noted form; in any event, the overall goal is the same. A program in any configuration achieves consistency throughout the broadcast day. This is important in order to achieve a recognizable sound and to put listeners into a comfortable listening mode: After a while, they know to expect music after a jingle and are gratified by the consistency.

Top-Forty formats usually are characterized by more rigid adherence to programming formulas. AC stations also often have intricate program arrangements. A typical sound hour in an AC station might, for example, start with a short news segment and station identification, followed by a lively vocal to give the audience a boost back into the programming, followed by an oldie, followed by two commercials. After the commercial, the operator would be instructed to play a bulleted (rising) hit, followed by a lighter vocal. The next slot is reserved for weather, another commercial, and a station promo. Up next is a "B-list" song, meaning one that's fading from the charts, followed by a top-ten hit. The reasoning for the order of elements in any format partially relates to consistency from hour to hour and partly because it is believed that certain types of

Figure 3.2a

Program clocks can be structured in a traditional clock configuration (left) or as a chart
to be filled in by air personalities. The chart arrangement is used by WNNK–FM in
Harrisburg, PA.
Chart reproduced with persmission of WNNK–FM, Harrisburg, PA.

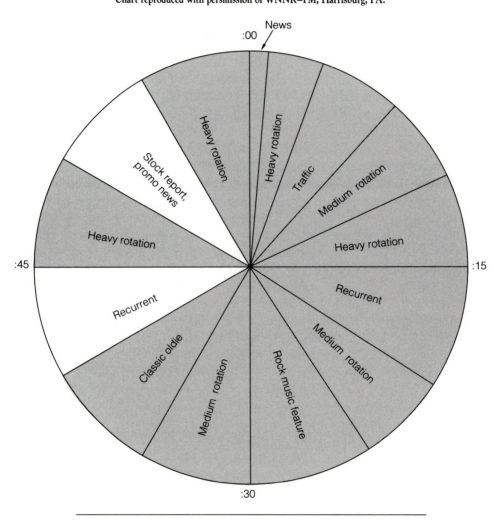

Figure 3.2b

```
                                         FOR: AFTERNOON DRIVE w/NEWS HOURS
                                             (MONDAY THRU FRIDAY)
                                              3PM - 6PM ONLY!!
     CLOCK - "C"....w/NEWS
     -----------------------------------    -----------------------------------
     DATE:_____ HOUR:_____       DATE:_____ HOUR:_____
     -----------------------------------    -----------------------------------

     (NEWS)

     C OR A_____  _____

     E_____       _____

     A_____       _____


     HIP- E_____  _____

     B_____       _____

     C_____       _____


     A_____       _____

     HIP- E_____  _____

     D_____       _____


     B_____       _____

     (WHAT YOU NEED
      TILL TIME UP TO_____  _____
      NEWS)

     NOTES:
```

program elements work best at certain times. The lively vocal, for instance, is believed to break the perceived listener boredom that has developed by the end of the newscast.

As another example, consider a program clock for an MOR format. Typically, the song rotation guards against abrupt changes in song style or leaps across decades (as related to the era of the song). One popular MOR/nostalgia syndicated format almost always begins a set of song with a standard from the 1940s and moves forward to modern versions of MOR music cut in the 1980s. After each stop set (a group of commercials), the sequence starts over again.

Other program elements must be in harmony with the overall thrust of any program-rotation scheme. Announcers, for example, frequently are given precise instructions on what to say and how to say it—often having their remarks written out for them on index cards. To cite another case, a confidential memo from one program syndicator explicitly instructs announcers *never* to use the word nostalgia, *never* to remark about the age of the music (and remind the listeners of their age), and *never* to swerve from the scheduling scheme. Such situations, of course, depend on the contractual agreement between the station and the syndicator.

To the listener, the mechanics are generally not obvious. To the air person, the mechanics of the format often seem hopelessly cumbersome and limiting. Most operators, however, would admit to the necessity of such format restrictions and operating procedures.

Playlists

The printed representation of these format mechanics is the playlist. A **playlist** is the music available within the chosen format, arranged in the order of play. Frequency—the number of times a cut is repeated—is also factored into the list. Depending on the format and the programmer, extensive research might be undertaken to determine how much of what plays and how often. In the highly competitive Top-Forty format, programmers consult industry publications, most notably *Billboard* and *R&R,* to determine the relative popularity of hit records and consult local record store surveys. Telephone-request lines typically are monitored, and surveys are made among listeners. The names of such listeners are often culled from the ranks of contest winners, callers, and writers to the station. Music research done at the station can involve playing a music sample over the phone and gauging the listener's reaction.

Increasingly, playlists are maintained on a computer.

Do these scientifically designed formats work? The question is open to some debate because it is very difficult to prove conclusively that the reputedly scientific mix is the main ingredient in a station's success. Many radio people feel that there is some validity to the argument that experienced air personalities could program their shifts just as effectively. The current state of radio, however, is such that all announcers are not experienced professionals with an in-depth knowledge of the music that they play. Nor are they always sensitive to market forces. In light of this, a certain amount of scientifically scheduled programming *is* essential for the station attempting to capture a segment of the market.

3.4
IMPLEMENTATION OF A FORMAT

The most obvious way to implement a newly designed format is to post the clock, playlist, or both and make the records available to announcers. In actuality, this scenario is not as simple as it might seem.

In-House Programming

Putting the music on the air can involve a large staff to select the music, catalog it, arrange it, and, in many cases, rerecord it on cartridge. Putting the music into the program schedule is a highly time-consuming affair. Designing the playlist in-house can easily occupy a full-time staffer and an assistant. The task can be aided greatly by use of a computer, but the fact that each hour must be programmed differently complicates the job enormously.

As one example, note how the programmer's lot is complicated by the changing audience composition during the night. Early evening is often considered to be the domain of teenagers, whereas late night can be, at a particular station, assumed to be populated by audience members who cannot sleep. But programming in the middle of the night, say 2 AM to 4 AM, reaches a new class of listeners: the night workers. After that, programs must appeal to the very early risers. (This is overgeneralized but is useful as an example of segmentation within an audience, and of how programmers try and reach listeners with a certain demographic profile.)

In summary, programming is not a simple nor an obvious task. That much may be readily apparent, but what is not always immediately visible is the enormous amount of time, effort, and money that must be invested to implement a format successfully. That is one of the primary reasons why consultants and **syndications** have enjoyed a measure of success in recent years.

Consultants and Syndications

With the splintering of audiences and the fragmenting of the formats designed to reach those audiences, there has been a simultaneous growth in the business of advisors on programming—advisors who offer services ranging from general guidance to a completely prepackaged format. This growth industry was pioneered by such figures as Jim Drake of Drake–Chenault Enterprises; syndicated services such as Drake–Chenault's prospered by providing a complete range of programmed elements that were aimed at capturing a particular audience segment.

Consultants look very carefully at the client's station and make a marketing analysis that helps determine the type of format to be implemented. The process then involves providing the service on an ongoing basis and fine-tuning it over time. Consultants observe station operations in a very objective manner because they are not a part of the operation and have no personal stake in their recommendations, except for the success of those recommendations.

A consultant—sometimes known as a "format doctor"—may provide no program material but simply act as an evaluator of a station's talent and format and sometimes of the technical signal clarity and strength.

Station management receives a comprehensive report making recommendations on personnel and/or programming changes; fees typically amount to several hundred dollars a day for the consultant's time. Critics of consultants often indicate that it does not take high-powered evaluative skills to determine the relative abilities of air talent. However, even the harshest critics of consultants agree that a consultant is usually better-equipped to evaluate and sometimes undertake research than is the program director at the local level.

Today, there is a wide range of services available to any station executive, from both the advice-giving consultant and the program-providing consultant. In terms of programming, some syndicator/consultants specialize in very narrow formats; others offer a variety of formats that can be tailored for different stations. At the time of this writing, for example, about thirty-five specialized networks exist, up from only fifteen six years previous.

An outgrowth of the format-marketing industry has been the recent capability to directly feed service via network connections rather than providing the stations with tapes. The newest aspect in this area has been the use of satellite feeds. Satellites in geostationary orbit (orbiting the equator in exact synchronization with earth, thus maintaining a constant relative position) "beam down" programming to any station with a relatively inexpensive receiving dish. Satellite Music Network, a highly successful example of this type of operation, provides seven formats to hundreds of affiliates. Stations pay a fee for the programs and split the advertising revenue under a prearranged agreement. This has been a boon to many ailing stations, especially small stations with personnel and money problems. One particular advantage of satellite (versus land-line) transmission is the growing fidelity of signal transmission. Executives of Satellite Music Network, for example, claim that their new satellite transmission system provides "compact disc quality audio."[9]

Of course, a disadvantage of any type of syndicated service is that it displaces personnel. If local stations lean extensively toward prepackaged programming, there are fewer announcing jobs. Aside from the direct impact on announcers, there is a secondary effect in that the "farm system" for beginning announcers would be disrupted.

Transtar Radio Networks typically look for stations in somewhat larger markets than those served by Satellite Music Network. Transtar currently offers a choice of three formats. Other examples of syndicated services:

—— Bonneville Broadcasting System offers an easy-listening taped format. Currently, this format is used at more than 150 stations, more than half of which are in the top 100 markets in the nation.

—— All Star Radio offers drop-in comedy packages. About 200 stations subscribe.

—— Creative Radio Networks offer such long-form programs as the Elvis Hour, the Rock Files (history of rock), and country music programs, which include interviews with the artists.

In summary, the art and science of programming is a tough and booming business. It is, above all, a precise business. In today's highly competitive world of radio broadcasting, it is incumbent on the programmer to know the audience as well as the music.

An important final point to consider is the crowding of the marketplace. Stations in the United States number over 10,000, up about 1000 stations from ten years ago. As a result, competition is keen. With the need to narrowly target a specific audience, the role of the modern programmer appears to be firmly established.

EXERCISES

1. Look up the radio stations serving your hometown, or other locality with
    which you are very familiar, in the *Broadcasting/Cablecasting Yearbook.* This
    publication, available in most larger libraries, contains listings of broadcast and
    cable outlets by city.

    First, write a brief summary of your best ideas of why the stations that serve
    your hometown are segmented into the formats listed in the yearbook. For
    example, what would explain the presence of two classical music stations? Per-
    haps your city has a strong tradition of catering to the arts and a broad follow-
    ing for symphonic music. Three AOR stations? Does the preponderance of
    colleges in your town have anything to do with it? Do major ethnic groups play
    a role in the types of formats available to listeners?

    Second, compare your locality to two cities or towns of similar size. If in
    doubt, use the *Standard Rate and Data Service* or similar reference works that
    list cities and populations. Is the distribution of formats roughly the same? Is it
    exactly the same? If not, why? Is the city of 30,000 in which you live domi-
    nated by larger radio stations from outside the area, leading to an apparent
    shortage of stations in your city, in contrast to the city of 30,000 located in an
    isolated area of the Midwest that has several more stations?

2. Design a hypothetical sound hour for a radio station. Use music with which
    you are familiar, be it rock or classical. Program the news, commercials, music
    (identify the specific selection and try to estimate times for the cuts) entirely
    at your discretion.

    The important point is not so much *what* you choose but *why* you choose it.
    Explain your format selection and justify each program element. Why do you
    think these elements would appeal to listeners, and why do you place them in
    that particular order? What kind of listeners are you appealing to? Use your
    imagination and sound reasoning.

3. Monitor two stations in your market and take notes of each station's sound
    hour. Keep track of every program element and record its starting and stopping
    time. Be sure you monitor the stations during the same time of day; in other
    words, if you listen to Station A at from 8 AM to 9 AM Monday, monitor Sta-
    tion B from 8 AM to 9 AM next Monday or on another weekday.

    Compare the two stations. Are the formats different? Is there a distinct simi-
    larity in the type of music played at fifteen minutes after the hour? How do you
    contrast the air personalities and their approach? What about the overall sound
    of the station? Write a four- or five-page paper contrasting the approaches.

NOTES

1. A very readable history of the evolution of the disc jockey format can be found in Christopher H. Sterling, and John M. Kittross, *Stay Tuned: A Concise History of American Broadcasting* (Belmont, CA: Wadsworth, 1978).

2. "Format Tally," *Broadcasting* (28 July 1986): 60. These rankings change from year to year, but ranking in terms of numbers of stations using various formats at the time of this writing shows some interesting distributions.

3. Larry King quoted in "Radio Talk Shows, Where America Speaks Up," *U.S. News and World Report* (16 January 1984): 55.

4. "Audiences Love to Hate Them," *Time* (9 July 1984): 80–81.

5. "Oldies on Rise in Album-Rock Radio," *New York Times* (18 June 1985): C26.

6. *Los Angeles Times News Service,* story distributed 4 November 1986.

7. "Radio's Wacky Road to Profit," *Newsweek* (25 March 1985): 70, 71.

8. For an extended examination of programming strategies, see Susan Tyler Eastman, et al., *Broadcast/Cable Programming,* 3d ed. (Belmont, CA: Wadsworth, 1989) passim; and Edd Routt, et al., *The Radio Format Conundrum* (New York: Hastings House, 1978) passim. Routt's book, although dated, provides an excellent insight into the overall strategy of radio programming.

9. "Satellite News Network Moves to Westar V Satellite," *The Pulse of Broadcasting* (8 September 1986): 4.

PART TWO

OPERATIONS

CHAPTER 4

DEPARTMENTAL RESPONSIBILITIES

AND ORGANIZATION

Personnel in a typical radio station have widely diverse backgrounds and skills. One of the peculiarities of the business is that employees with little in common must work closely for a mutual goal. Engineering specialists, for example, are typically highly trained in technical operations and maintenance; besides the jobs for which they were trained, they must work closely with on-air personnel—people who often fail to appreciate the technical complexities of the station's equipment. Salespeople typically have backgrounds 180 degrees removed from news staffers, yet they must work toward the same overall objective. Financial people must interact with creative staff, and, of course, the viewpoints of those groups can be strikingly different.

This chapter provides an overview of the people who work in radio and, more importantly, shows how they interact in typical operations. It is more important to have a general understanding of the people and jobs involved in the radio business than it is to memorize detailed configurations of the radio hierarchy.

A secondary point: It is useful to view the departments and people of a radio station as an *organization* in the literal sense of the word—that is, a living organism, an interactive entity. In that regard, this chapter focuses on interrelations of station staff.

4.1

RADIO STATION STAFF

The following categories of station personnel are the most immediate representation of job function. Almost all radio stations, regardless of size or format, have job duties aligned within

— *Management and administrative:* These personnel are concerned with the actual work flow within the station. Employees in this category see to it that what must get accomplished actually gets accomplished, whether that entails meeting profit goals, sending out invoices, issuing paychecks, assuring that correspondence from management reaches staff members, meeting FCC requirements, composing logs, or hiring and firing personnel. Members of this department include the general manager and the general administrative staff such as personnel, traffic (discussed shortly), and payroll staff.

— *Technical:* People in this category are concerned with the operation and repair of the station equipment. Under the direction of the chief engineer, technical staffers assure that what goes out over the air is of the proper technical quality level. Sometimes, this involves electronically tailoring the sound of the station.

— *Programming:* These employees are charged with the important task of putting together coherent and correct combinations of program elements. People in this category include the announcers, the production staffers, the program director (also a management function), music librarian, and, under most categorizations, news reporters.

— *Sales:* The members of this department actually produce station revenue. In effect, they rely on the programming department to provide the bait for gathering a significant audience. That audience is what the sales department "sells" to advertisers. The structure and size of a sales department varies from market to market.

Within the categories above, there are many discrete job descriptions, to be explained in detail in a following section. Be aware at this point that the *functions* of the staff are virtually identical regardless of market size. What will differ among markets is the number and amount of responsibilities assigned to a particular person or position and the specificity of the job. In small-market radio stations, for example, research might be handled by program directors. Because program directors' time is limited and because of many other duties, the research component might involve only a couple of hours (if that) a week making calls to the local record stores, scanning *Billboard,* and reviewing what material is available from the local ratings report, if there is indeed a local report in the market.

In a large market, a station heavily involved in research might employ one or more persons whose jobs revolve entirely around research. Before examining some other radio jobs in detail, we'll take a brief look at how those duties differ among various-size markets.

Large Markets

The key personnel difference between a large and a small market is that key areas of responsibility in large markets are assigned to specific positions. Sales managers in a small market may be responsible for making calls, billing orders, and other duties. In a large market, sales managers would exclusively be managers, coordinating the overall sales effort with several submanagers who report to them. In general terms then, large-market employees are highly specialized and perform a limited range of duties. A possible organizational chart (there is no "typical" arrangement) is pictured in Figure 4.1.

Medium Markets

There is likely to be a significant conglomeration of responsibilities in most positions. The chief engineer in a medium-market station, for instance, might be the only engineer on staff (and perhaps only a part-time consultant). In a large market, the chief

106

Figure 4.1

A typical large-market radio operation.

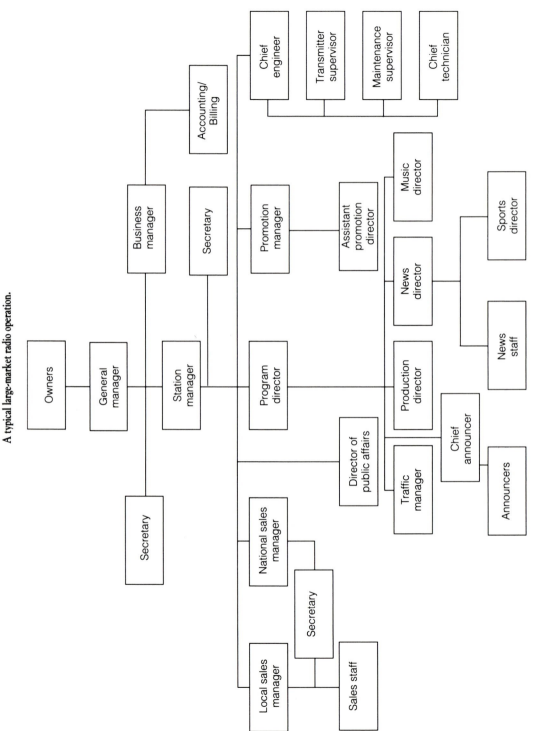

107

Figure 4.2

An organizational chart for a medium-market radio station.

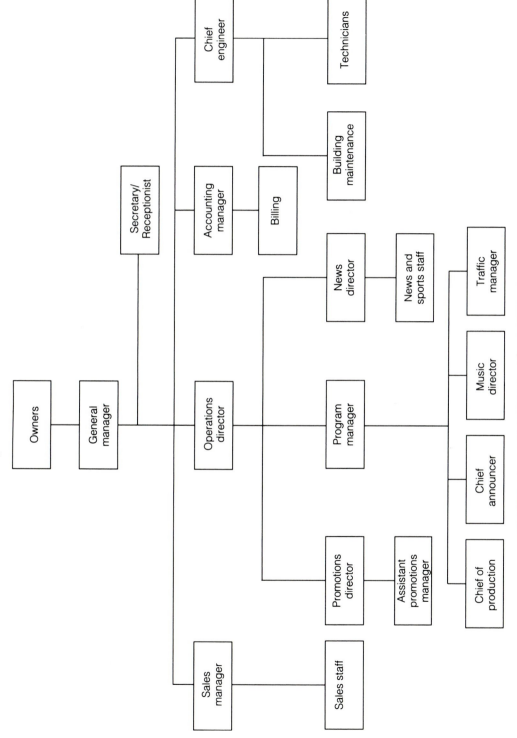

Figure 4.3

A typical organizational chart for a small-market radio station.

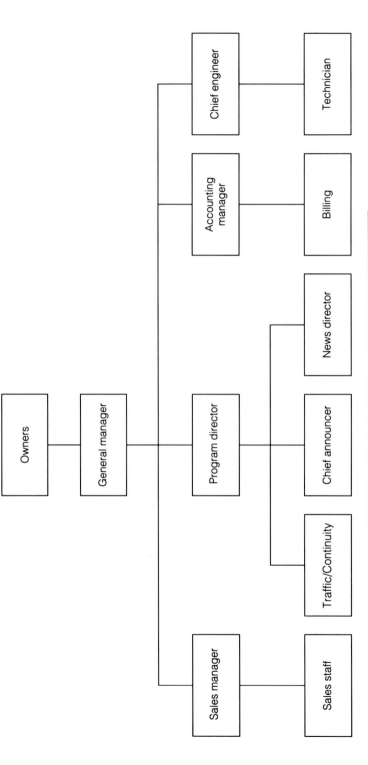

will supervise a staff of engineers—some of whom are assigned highly specific tasks such as working with the transmitter or repairing control room equipment.

News departments are smaller in a medium market than in a large market, although many medium markets support reasonably sized news departments. To have seven or eight reporters on staff in a high-quality medium-market operation is not unusual. A medium-market organizational chart is shown in Figure 4.2.

Small Markets

Usually, any given position has many responsibilities. General managers in small-market stations perform a much different job than their counterparts in a major metropolitan area. Small-market managers may be actively involved in sales, programming, and even engineering. An engineer, if there is one on staff, might pull an airshift. Versatility is the key in small-market operations. An organizational chart for this market is shown in Figure 4.3.

4.2
DUTIES OF KEY PERSONNEL

The descriptions above were nonspecific for a reason: It is essential to understand first that departments in small, medium, and large markets have the same overall functions. In general, things work the same way at almost any radio station. It is only the specific duties and the groupings of duties that vary.

Now, let us examine the specific functions of key personnel with the goal of understanding their typical areas of responsibility, their usual professional backgrounds, and their interactions with the rest of the station staff.

Managers

Radio managers are most often referred to as general managers (GMs). In large markets, GMs may be vice presidents of the parent corporation. In smaller markets, GMs also may be owners. Managers' primary mission in commercial radio is maintenance of profit. Many other duties are involved in management, but the profit statement is the yardstick by which commercial radio success is measured. In most cases, GMs are first and foremost chief fiscal officers. Even in nonprofit organizations, GMs are in charge of finances, including those raised through fund-raising. In large markets, many of these functions are delegated to business managers.

Managers' responsibilities extend to personnel management; oversight of legal matters, labor relations, sales supervision, and facility management; and final responsibility for programming. There is a community relations component to the position. Managers are the final arbiter of disputes and disagreements and, in general, set station policy.

BACKGROUND AND QUALIFICATIONS GMs usually have come up through the ranks of sales departments and may or may not have had experience in other aspects of the radio business. Sometimes GMs in medium and small markets rise through the ranks of programming or, more infrequently, through news. Most often GMs are college graduates and may have an advanced business degree. In larger markets and in chain ownership situations, GMs may be financial specialists with no broadcast background.

INTERACTION WITH THE OVERALL ORGANIZATION Because managers are in charge of the organization *in toto,* they interact with almost all aspects of it. Conversely, each employee knows and to some extent deals with the GM. This has the practical effect of making GMs the highly visible villain in many operations. Managers must enforce budgetary restrictions and are saddled often with the reputation of being a "bottom liner." The actions GMs must take at times can appear ruthless and, in fact, may be ruthless. It is a difficult position to have to say no and to enforce regulations, but that is simply the nature of the job.

Program Directors

Program directors (PDs) are some of the most visible and most important members of the management team in almost any radio station. The responsibilities in this area have grown considerably over the past two decades. In simpler times, implementing a format was a relatively clear-cut matter. Little choice was involved because there were only a few basic formats, and those extant formats were mix-and-match affairs. But today's programming department is by necessity a complex and protean operation. Heading this department requires knowledge of music and popular culture and the ability to interpret research data.

PDs have overall charge of the format construction. This job extends to select-ing music (which sometimes is done through subordinates, music directors), maintain-ing the music collection (again, a task frequently delegated), producing commercials (via production directors), and scheduling music for airplay.

In almost all organizations, PDs are in direct charge of the announcing staff. PDs typically take an active role in hands-on supervision. In larger markets, PDs can have overall responsibility for hiring, firing, and critiquing announcers. In medium and small markets, PDs often are working announcers or chief announcers, but might have their duties extended only to the scheduling of announcer airshifts. Many organization hierarchies place PDs in charge of news and public affairs, but this is not always the case.

A final and important element of PDs' job is monitoring. It is PDs who keep an ear tuned to the sound of the station and evaluate how that sound makes the station competitive in the market.

BACKGROUND AND QUALIFICATIONS   By and large, PDs have come up through the announcing ranks. In small and medium markets, PDs are often the most experi-enced announcers (as one small-market PD suggested, the only announcer who is not a teenager). In larger markets, there is a trend for PDs to be research-oriented execu-tives; in this case, they may not have on-air backgrounds. Educational backgrounds vary widely, although increasingly college educations are becoming the norm for PDs. Many PDs went through college media or broadcasting sequences.

INTERACTION WITH THE OVERALL ORGANIZATION   PDs are more removed from many aspects of station operations than are general managers, but PDs come into frequent contact with members of the engineering staff and news department. In some cases, PDs have jurisdiction over these departments. PDs' tie-in with the sales depart-ment revolve around the suitability of on-air products for the consuming public (the audience) and, by extension, the purchasers of advertising (merchants and agencies). Special events are frequently coordinated through PDs and the sales department. There often may be promotion directors who report to PDs.

The PD spot is a very visible and often lucrative one. However, the PD position may or may not be on the ladder to the GM's job. PDs do operate with reasonable amounts of autonomy and reward, so they may in fact not desire promotion into gen-eral management. The strong orientation of PDs toward the programming function may account for the typically lateral mobility of PDs, who move from station to station with great regularity. PDs' upward mobility often comes from moving to jobs in larger markets rather than advancing to general management.

In broad terms, PDs do not have quite as onerous a job as GMs. Although some hiring and firing and other personnel matters may come under the PDs' jurisdictions, their jobs are primarily the frontline work of radio—forming the on-air product. Because PDs are generally younger than GMs and have more similar professional backgrounds to the people they supervise, PDs are often viewed by the staff as being more approachable.

Operations Directors

Some stations have an employee known as an **operations director** (OD), or operations manager. Typically, ODs handle nonprogramming functions, although it is clear that many stations that employ an executive with the title of operations manager delegate program-related duties to that person. In fact, sometimes PDs are replaced by individuals who have more duties and responsibilities. Operations managers are occasionally administrative lieutenants to general managers; in some stations, the position is known as assistant general manager. Some organizations place operations managers above PDs. In others, the terms *operations director* and *program director* seem to be synonymous in practice.

In certain situations, managers functioning directly below GMs are called *station managers* and may have similar duties to operations managers.

BACKGROUND AND QUALIFICATIONS The operations director may, depending on the particular station, be an executive charged primarily with financial and personnel duties; in such a case he or she will generally have a background similar to that of the station manager. In many stations, though, the operations director has come up through the on-air ranks. See the section "Program Directors" for relevant background and qualifications.

INTERACTION WITH THE OVERALL ORGANIZATION Because the position combines varying elements of GM and PM functions, the interaction with staff and individual qualifications will reflect those of either or both positions.

Sales Managers

Executives in charge of sales work very closely with GMs to ensure that adequate revenues are produced. In the context of station operations, sales managers are key employees and often experience intense pressure to produce.

In most stations, sales managers are directly responsible for the entire gamut of airtime sales. This includes monitoring all levels of sales—local, national, and retail—and assigning responsibilities among the sales staff. One of the more burdensome parts of the job is development of sales quotas and projections. There are many factors affecting the success of the sales effort, many of which are difficult to foresee, but sales managers who fail to meet sales quotas are little comforted by the fact that the situation is unpredictable. Major job functions of sales managers are assignments of accounts to salespeople. This can sometimes involve taking an account from an unproductive salesperson and reassigning it. Other typical duties include developing rate structures for advertising and developing sales materials such as brochures. In many cases, sales managers supervise all promotional activities.

Perhaps the most overarching role of sales managers is in training and motivation of salespeople. This function extends to all levels of sales department supervision and includes such duties as role-playing sessions and formal training in sales techniques.

Although the jobs of sales managers are demanding, there are also the opportunities to earn very high monetary rewards.

BACKGROUND AND QUALIFICATIONS   Sales managers universally have worked their way up through the ranks of sales. There is no college program that prepares students for immediate entry as a sales manager. Promotion to sales management is usually based on past performance as a salesperson. Many broadcast salespeople have worked in other areas of sales before coming to broadcasting; some worked as announcers before moving into sales.

INTERACTION WITH THE OVERALL ORGANIZATION   Sales managers interact most closely and frequently with sales staff and GMs. The jobs of GMs and sales managers are strongly intertwined.

Sales managers have little direct interaction with many other departments, and those interactions are often of a negative, adversarial nature. When sales managers interact with news, for example, it is often to express displeasure at the news department's handling of the latest story that involved a sponsor. Sales managers and sales staff, in general, do interact with announcers on a regular basis, often working with announcers during the production of a commercial. Production directors also work closely with sales staff.

Salespeople are among the most personally visible of station employees (that is, seen in person by members of the community). They deal with a wide variety of people; in small and medium markets, those people are often community leaders. When community members visit the station, it is often in conjunction with a sales-related function.

Chief Engineers

The most pressing function of chief engineers is to keep the station on the air. In that connection, maintenance of equipment is a very heavy responsibility. It is also necessary for chief engineers to ensure that the on-air signal conforms to technical FCC requirements.

In larger operations, chief engineers supervise a staff of technical people. Some members of the staff may be devoted exclusively to studio maintenance; others may specialize in transmitter operations. Chief engineers become involved in planning when stations upgrade facilities or equipment. Purchases are a major duty of chiefs. (Incidentally, the position is usually called chief engineer even in small markets where the chief is the one and only engineer.)

Many stations, even medium-market stations, do not have staff engineers but retain "consultants" who do the required checks and undertake emergency maintenance on a retainer or per-call basis.

BACKGROUND AND QUALIFICATIONS   Chief engineers typically hold an FCC general-class license, which up until a few years ago was known as a first-class broadcast license. Many engineers are self-taught, although that is less common today than in past years. Hands-on experience is the most pressing requirement for engineers, and the levels of formal education vary. Some engineers have two-year technical degrees, others may have bachelor degrees, whereas some may have no formal training whatsoever. There are no formal educational requirements to pass FCC tests.

Chief engineers are almost always more experienced than those they supervise. Engineering is an experience-intensive job, and work background seems to count more than specialized training.

In major markets, equipment operations are added to the duties of engineering departments, although this is not done by chiefs. Certain large markets require that engineers operate control room equipment during an airshift (that is, put records on the turntable and open the microphone switches, for example). Computer knowledge is becoming much more important to chiefs because engineering staffs are often called upon to operate computer hardware for automation and other functions.

Rules for FCC certification of engineers have been loosened considerably in recent years. Today, there is a general industry trend toward a system of industry self-certification. The Society of Broadcast Engineers (7002 Graham Rd., Suite 118, Indianapolis, IN 46220) offers certification upon successful completion of a written test. The SBE's test is regarded by many managers as superior to past and present FCC tests; managers feel it more accurately measures the qualifications needed for broadcast engineering and is less reflective of the test taker's ability to memorize details and "psych out" the test.

Recently the responsibilities of chief engineers in the area of signal quality have risen sharply. This is especially true for AM stations, many of which are literally fighting for survival. FM dominates listening habits in very large part simply because of the better quality of its signal. A recent survey, for example, showed that 65 percent of the public surveyed would listen to FM instead of AM even if the two broadcast identical programming.[1]

This means, essentially, that a better signal can translate to better ratings. Engineers now spend an increasing amount of time and energy trying to make that signal stronger and clearer. The ultimate goal of the growing field of AM-technical improvement is viewed by many as a stereo signal that sounds as technically "lively" as FM. While the difficulties involved—and there are many—are being sorted out, improvement of existing signal quality and strength is an important job.[2] Chiefs' roles in this task can range from maximizing the signal strength of the transmitter and antenna array to electronic manipulation of the signal by filters and processors.

INTERACTION WITH THE OVERALL ORGANIZATION   Engineers and engineering management interact often with programming, but that interaction is often contentious because it frequently involves engineers fixing something the programming staff has broken. Top management places a heavy responsibility on engineering, and station managers are frequently in contact with engineers about technical standards and equipment purchases. Buying equipment is a very time-consuming and difficult task, requiring much reading and research.

It is important for radio managers to realize that engineer staff members, by and large, come from a very different background than do programming staff or salespeople. Frequently, engineers hold a much different outlook on life in general. This can sometimes result in the engineering staff feeling alienated from other station employees.

Traffic Managers

Traffic managers and traffic departments work at the "nerve center" of station operations. The job of traffic is not well understood by the general public and even, to an extent, by other radio station staffers. Traffic is primarily responsible for preparing station logs; within this context, the major duty is scheduling commercials. Commercial scheduling, a highly complex matter, has many factors to take into account. Client separation, for instance, is paramount: Commercials for similar products or services, such as car dealerships, cannot be run close to each other and certainly *never* back to back. Traffic managers also are charged with the responsibility of assuring that commercials receive an adequate rotation through various dayparts. Traffic must sometimes make quick adjustments in scheduling to make good on a missed commercial or, as happens when airplane disasters make the news, to take airline commercials off the air for a specified period and reschedule them later.

Traffic managers or managers' designees are also responsible for routing of copy (written scripts) and tapes. It is critical to ensure that commercial copy and prerecorded spots reach the control room on time for scheduled airplay.

An overall duty of the traffic department is to supervise order processing (orders for commercials to be scheduled) from the sales department and to ensure that those orders get logged. In this regard, traffic is pretty much what the name implies: The traffic department monitors the flow of information between and among departments, particularly management, production, and sales. In some cases, the sales department has a separate traffic department.

BACKGROUND AND QUALIFICATIONS   Traffic managers often rise through the clerical ranks. A college education is not a requirement in most cases. Frequently, traffic is a stepping stone to other areas of station operations. A newly emerging qualification for traffic managers is computer literacy. Almost all large stations and most medium markets have computers involved, to some degree, in scheduling. (For details, consult Chapter 5.) These computers use special software designed specifically for radio scheduling. This software accomplishes such tasks as ensuring separation of spots and scheduling workable rotations. Using these computer programs requires some skill on the part of the operator.

INTERACTION WITH THE OVERALL ORGANIZATION   Traffic managers' most direct and ongoing interactions are with the sales department—processing orders and scheduling commercials. Traffic interacts with programming to a slightly lesser degree and interacts with news infrequently.

There are various positions at which traffic managers are located within the radio station hierarchy. Traffic might report directly to the general manager, the sales manager, or to the program director, and in some cases to both the general manager and the sales manager.

News Directors

In a large market, news directors are executives in charge of journalistic matters as well as a good deal of budgetary and personnel duties. Large-market news directors supervise specialized employees such as sports directors or traffic reporters.

In small markets, news directors might supervise only part-timers or actually may be the only news person on staff. But regardless of market size, news directors' primary responsibility is story assignment (unless it is a one-person department, in which case the news director more or less fulfills the assignment). Story assignment is a much more difficult task than might be assumed. News directors or subordinate assistants must correlate appointments, staff availability, travel times (factoring in traffic congestion), and lunch breaks.

BACKGROUND AND QUALIFICATIONS News directors and news reporters are usually college-educated. College degrees are required for many news jobs, including entry-level positions. However, the fact that applicants have degrees doesn't automatically qualify them for any news position. Possession of a journalism degree rarely, if ever, allows entry into radio news at a supervisory level.

News is highly experience-intensive. Surveys have shown that when faced with the choice of hiring news people with extensive education or extensive experience, experience usually wins. This, incidentally, is also the case with most other positions in radio.

A final qualification—and one that is virtually impossible to overstate—is *the ability to write well*. Many newcomers to the field are under the misconception that broadcast news is read but not written. The majority of time and effort expended in the news operation is in interviewing, note taking, and writing. An additional requirement is that the news person must write for the ear, not the eye.

INTERACTION WITH THE OVERALL ORGANIZATION The news business is referred to as a profession, in general because it is regarded by the public as having an elevated status. In terms of relations with other members of the radio station organization, news is often regarded with some envy and resentment for two reasons. First, news operations use a disproportionate share of the budget in relation to revenue returned to the station. Second, news people are often by nature very serious people; although they may be pleasant and sociable away from the job, they are bound by certain inflexible codes of conduct on the job. Often, this leads to some misunderstanding on the part of other employees, who may regard news staffers as stiff-necked and unfriendly.

In many ways, news people are more aggressive than many other employees; they are also more questioning of authority and skeptical in general. From a management perspective, personnel matters involving the news department are sometimes nettlesome. Managers in overall charge of all station operations must realize that news people are, in effect, trained to question authority and often expect a large degree of autonomy in the operation of their department. Conflict between news directors and general managers is sometimes bitter and probably inevitable. Issues pertaining to news coverage involving sponsors is generally at the heart of the conflict.

Other Directorial Positions

The categories described are not all-inclusive nor do they represent the sum total of all management and employment functions. There are, in large markets, many other management-related positions. A production manager in a large market may have a staff of several producers and technicians. In a small market, however, the production manager may run a one-person shop or may work in a combined position; the program director, for example, may assume the production director's duties. Small stations often have no formal production manager position. Instead, those duties are shared among the PD and on-air personnel.

Duty sharing is common in almost all levels of radio, and it is important to remember that job descriptions are not always inflexible. Jobs grow to suit the people who assume them just as people grow into jobs.

4.3

DAY-TO-DAY OPERATIONS OF TYPICAL RADIO STATIONS

The meshing of the components of a radio operation is something that requires an active effort. Experience and observation show that this simply doesn't happen by chance. Indeed, the entire purpose of having a management structure is to ensure that the various parts of the station work together smoothly.

The Realities of Radio

A newcomer to radio is often surprised and sometimes dismayed by the amount of work involved in radio. Although radio appears glamorous to the observer—and, no doubt, there is a certain amount of glamour involved—the majority of the work is simply *hard work*. Radio management in particular can be a trying and tedious task. Some examples are discussed next.

UNION NEGOTIATIONS   Negotiations pertaining to unionizing a shop are sometimes bitter affairs. In-place union regulations and traditions can thrust a barrier between management and employees. Keeping track of rules, regulations, and procedures relating to unions is almost a job in itself.

PROFESSIONAL RELATIONS   Radio managers belonging to national associations sometimes become heavily involved in lobbying or other professional organizational practices such as committee work within broadcasters' organizations. Although not necessarily a difficult or unpleasant task, attending national conferences and meetings can be time consuming.

TECHNICAL REGULATIONS   Such functions can be a can of wriggling, multiheaded worms for the radio manager. Compliance with technical rules and standards is an ever-present task and requires careful coordination with the engineering department.

COMMUNITY INTERACTION   A radio manager must often deal with members of the community and not always on an entirely friendly level. The job of fielding complaints often falls to the GM.

SUPPLIER RELATIONS   This includes the interaction with program suppliers and consultants. Such interaction typically involves negotiation, analysis, and research.

Management and Interaction of Staff

Operation of a radio station cannot be a one-person job. A manager cannot dictate each individual aspect of operations nor follow up to ensure that each task is done competently and completely. One person cannot substitute for a chain of command.

WORK FLOW   That chain of command is inextricably linked to a web of connections in which tasks are shared, policies communicated, and creative contributions made. From a management view, the flow of decision making and job performance should not be a strictly downward process.

Many observers of management techniques feel that vertical lines of implementation result in many good ideas being lost.[3] This means that military-type chains of command do not work well in a facility peopled by exceptional employees, many of whom are highly creative. It seems clear that this situation—the relative excellence of radio personnel in general—is brought about in large part because of the tremendous competition for radio jobs. It is rare, even in fairly small markets, to find an excessive level of incompetence or a significant lack of motivation. In short, an evaluation of management within the framework of departmental responsibilities and organization shows that delegation of authority and responsiveness to employee ideas and suggestions is an essential tool for a radio manager.

Competition for Available Funds and Resources

The very qualities that make many radio station staffers creative and highly motivated are the same factors that often make them the bearers of strong personalities. Often they are extremely vigorous in pursuit of their goals and their department's goals. Just as it is necessary for a manager to deal effectively with the advantages of a motivated and creative staff, it is also essential to deal with the related negative consequences. There is always tough competition for limited resources. In any market, there is an intrinsic limit on available funds and on the upward ceiling for career advancement of staffers. Some limits on flexibility and autonomy of various departments are also imperative.

Balancing the situation—dealing with the pluses and minuses of a radio station staff—is really the crux of effective management. The material presented in this chapter is obviously only a starting point. Of further interest are Chapter 5, which examines facility management; Chapter 9, which deals with sales and sales management; Chapter 10, which focuses on personnel matters; Chapter 11, which deals with the techniques of allocating limited financial resources; and Chapter 12, which examines regulation and control from a management perspective.

EXERCISES

1. Assume that you are the manager of a new facility slated to go on the air in several months. You must hire a staff. One of the questions asked of you by the station owner is, "Should the news director report to the program director or to the general manager?" What are your thoughts? Write a one- or two-page defense of your position.

2. Write a help-wanted advertisement (as you would expect it to appear in *Broadcasting* magazine) for a program director for your new station. The ad should be a maximum of 100 words. Invent whatever particulars you desire but be sure to

address the specific qualifications you would seek in a program director, the goals for that position, and what you would expect the new program director to accomplish.

3. You are the general manager of a medium-market station and must resolve a dispute between the sales manager and news director. There is a large rodeo coming to town in two weeks, an event that typically generates several thousand dollars of advertising revenue. Local animal-protection agencies have been demonstrating against the rodeo, and the news director is running a series citing what he says are documented cases of injury and death to animals in this rodeo. The marketing director for the rodeo is threatening to pull advertising if the remaining four parts of the five-part news series are aired.

    The sales manager contends that the reports are sensationalized, and she further charges that the news director is motivated by personal advancement—in other words, looking for good audition tape material.

    Do you tell the news director to discontinue the series? Do you ask him to modify it? Would you ask to listen to the pieces? If so, do you feel qualified to make a journalistic judgment? Answer these questions in a three- or four-page paper or discuss in class how you would handle the situation. Be specific.

NOTES

1. "The AM Stations Go for a Facelift, *The New York Times*, 8 March 1987, 19.

2. For a comprehensive summary of materials available in the complex field of AM-technical improvement, consult AM Improvement Subcommittee of the Engineering Advisory Committee, AM *Technical Improvement Bibliography* (Washington, D.C.: National Association of Broadcasters, 1985).

3. For a discussion of policy implementation see Ward L. Quaal, and James A. Brown, *Broadcast Management: Radio and Television* (New York: Hastings House, 1976), 50. The policy implementation discussion is still valuable, although much of the book is dated. For extensive discussion of general management, consult Barry Sherman, *Telecommunications Management* (New York: McGraw-Hill, 1987).

CHAPTER 5

TECHNOLOGY, TRANSMISSION,

AND FACILITIES

The physical aspects of radio broadcasting are basic to the industry. An understanding of how transmission takes place and the limitations imposed by physical principles is an essential element of effective and efficient radio management. Without an appreciation for the rationale of regulation and a basic familiarity with the technologies that maximize the quality of the station's sound, even the most creative programmers and the most productive salespeople can fail to fully use the substantial potential of this fascinating medium.

In its earliest form, radio broadcasting was a scientific and technical phenomenon that gave no hint of the kind of entertainment, information, and profit-making venture it would eventually become. When Heinrich Hertz first demonstrated the existence of electromagnetic waves in 1873, he wanted to describe what was to that point theoretical. Guglielmo Marconi in the 1890s found that these waves could be useful for conveying telegraph messages without the need of wires.

In 1906 Lee de Forest's development of the audion tube made made it possible to control and shape radio energy. At about this same time, Reginald Fessenden contributed to the improvement of radio reception with his development of the heterodyne circuit. These advances created the conditions necessary for the emergence of modern radio broadcasting.[1]

Modern radio operations, though far more sophisticated than anything dreamed of by the earliest experimenters, still depends on the same basic physical principles to supply programs for its audiences.

5.1

BASIC TECHNOLOGY

Radio's value as a communication system depends on the hardware that performs the complex series of operations necessary to get a signal from a broadcast studio to a radio listener. To understand radio completely, it is necessary to understand the functions performed by that hardware. It is not necessary for everyone in radio to be intimately familiar with the procedures used to repair a transmitter or to align the heads on a tape machine. But it is helpful (indeed, some would say, necessary) for those who work in radio to be familiar with the basic principles of broadcast transmission.

Fundamentals and Regulations of Radio Transmission

Radio transmission is a way of sending messages using radio wave propagation. The basic task is to convert sound information into electrical form so that it can be transmitted using electromagnetic energy. The term ascribed to the process of changing sound into a form in which it may be transmitted is **transduction.**

Transduction involves two basic steps. First, the sound is converted (encoded), in this case, into an electrical pattern. Second, the electrical signal travels through a channel that allows the encoded sound to get from the point of transmission to the point of reception.

Figure 5.1

A microphone element moving through a magnetic field.

Diaphragm   Magnet

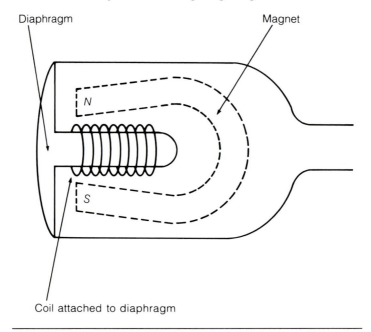

Coil attached to diaphragm

It is the task of studio equipment such as microphones, turntables, and tape players to transform sound from the physical vibration of molecules into a form that can be transmitted. The element of a microphone, for example, moves in response to vibrations of air produced by sound energy. The movement of the microphone (mic) element through a magnetic field produces an electrical pattern that corresponds to the original sound wave (Figure 5.1).

The electricity pattern produced by the microphone corresponds to the pattern of the original sound. In the form of electricity, a signal is conducted along a cable to a broadcast transmitter. There it is transduced again into a pattern of electromagnetic energy. These radio waves are produced by rapidly alternating electrical current generated by the transmitter. The encoded sound wave travels into the atmosphere, where it then can be detected by radio receivers.

The same process takes place when the stylus of a turntable senses the patterns of a record groove and translates that physical vibration into an electrical signal. Even the most modern equipment such as a compact disc (CD) player is no more than a sophisticated method of detecting and transducing what started out as sound.

Figure 5.2

This chart represents the portion of the electronic spectrum that includes frequencies used for broadcast transmission (EHF = extremely high frequency; SHF = super high frequency; UHF = ultra high frequency; VHF = very high frequency; HF = high frequency; MF = medium frequency; LF = low frequency; MHz = megahertz; kHz = kilohertz).

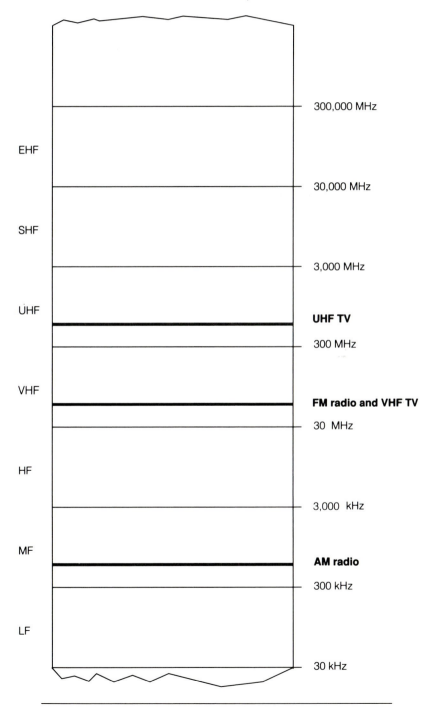

A channel in radio transmission is the group of radio frequencies used to transmit the encoded sound. The carrier is the group of frequencies assigned to the station for use in transmitting its signal.

ELECTROMAGNETIC ENERGY   A basic understanding of electromagnetic energy is necessary for an understanding of how transmitters encode what was originally sound.

Electromagnetic waves can be represented on a chart depicting them in relation to other forms of electromagnetic phenomena, which include visible light, infrared radiation, and X rays (Figure 5.2). Similar to visible light, radio waves travel through space at the constant speed of 186,000 miles per second, or 300 million meters per second.

Radio waves, like other forms of electromagnetic energy, can be characterized graphically as variations on either side of a zero point. The number of times the wave varies from zero to a certain height above and below the zero line back again to zero in a given amount of time is designated as its **frequency** (Figure 5.3). One such oscillation either side of the zero point is a single cycle. In point of fact, radio waves oscillate many times in the space of a single second. Radio waves also have **amplitude,** represented in Figure 5.3 as the distance from the peak of the wave to the zero point. Amplitude describes the intensity of a given wave. Alterations in the amplitude and the frequency of a wave can be controlled. The ability to control the variations in amplitude and frequency makes possible the transmission of sound information produced in the broadcast studio.

Figure 5.3

A single cycle.

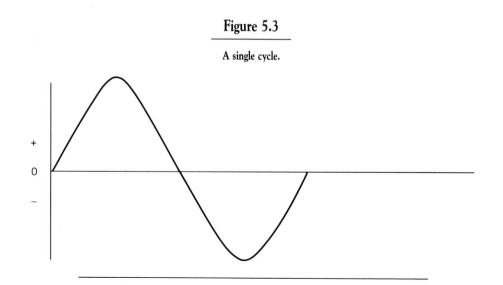

MODULATION   In order for a broadcast station to use its carrier for transmission, it alters the pattern of the carrier in a way that replicates the pattern of the original sound information. When this happens the carrier is said to be modulated.

The two systems of **modulation** used in radio broadcasting make use of amplitude and frequency to encode and transmit sound information. Amplitude modulation varies the amplitude of the carrier while the frequency remains constant. Frequency modulation occurs when the frequency is changed to encode the sound information while amplitude remains constant.

AM BROADCASTING   Because AM broadcasting uses variations in the strength (amplitude) of the signal to encode information, it is susceptible to static interference. Atmospheric static interacts with the amplitude of the modulated wave, producing audible noise in AM receivers.

The portion of the frequency spectrum allocated to AM broadcasting runs from 535 to 1605 kilohertz (Figure 5.4). This is divided into 107 different channels, each of which is 10 kilohertz wide. The width of a channel determines how much information can be transmitted. We can use the human voice to illustrate how this concept affects radio broadcasting. Different voices singing the same musical note, for example, have the same fundamental frequency. But there are variations in timbre and color of the voice, which make one voice different in quality from another. These characteristic qualities are produced by multiples of the frequency and are known as overtones, or harmonics.

In order for radio listeners to differentiate among sounds of various quality, more than a single frequency must be transmitted. A group of radio frequencies, then, is necessary if radio is to reproduce sound in close approximation of its original character. The 10 kilohertz width of AM broadcast channels has been set by government regulation to provide enough channel capacity to ensure adequate sound quality, or fidelity. The restriction of AM radio to 10 kilohertz limits the range of sound frequencies that can be reproduced, giving it less than full-range frequencies for ideal fidelity.

Ideally, all broadcasters would have available to them channels sufficiently wide to provide the greatest fidelity possible for transmission of encoded-sound information. In practice, however, there are only a certain number of frequencies available for use by commercial broadcasters. In response the federal government has developed regulations restricting the use of the spectrum by individual broadcasters. The guiding philosophy of the restrictions imposed by the government is to allow a maximum number of stations to operate with minimum interference.

AM broadcasting in the United States has been assigned to the medium frequency band (MF) of the radio spectrum. The term *medium band* distinguishes this segment of the frequency spectrum from those designated as extremely high frequen-

Figure 5.4

The AM broadcasting band consists of the frequencies 535 to 1605 kilohertz.
(NOTE: There are some regional variations of the listings.)
FCC documents 47 CFR 73.25; 73.26; 73.27.

Class I Operating Frequencies

640	720	820	890	1120
650	750	830	1020	1160
660	760	840	1030	1180
670	770	870	1040	1200
700	780	880	1100	1210

Class II Operating Frequencies *

670	780	1020	1120
720	880	1030	1180
770	890	1100	1210

Class III Operating Frequencies

550	620	960	1280	1360	1440
560	630	970	1290	1370	1460
570	790	980	1300	1380	1470
580	910	1150	1310	1390	1480
590	920	1250	1320	1410	1590
600	930	1260	1330	1420	1600
610	950	1270	1350	1430	

Class IV Operating Frequencies

1230	1340	1450
1240	1400	1490

* In special circumstances these stations can operate on the remaining frequencies used by Class I stations.

cies (EHF), ultra high frequencies (UHF), and very high frequencies (VHF) or those that are lower, such as low frequencies (LF) and very low frequencies (VLF). Besides AM and FM broadcasting, various other radio services use portions of the frequency spectrum. Amateur radio transmission, citizens' band, marine radio, and emergency channels are some of the additional services competing for use of radio frequencies.

The physical characteristics peculiar to the medium band of radio frequencies

Figure 5.5

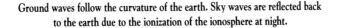

Ground waves follow the curvature of the earth. Sky waves are reflected back
to the earth due to the ionization of the ionosphere at night.

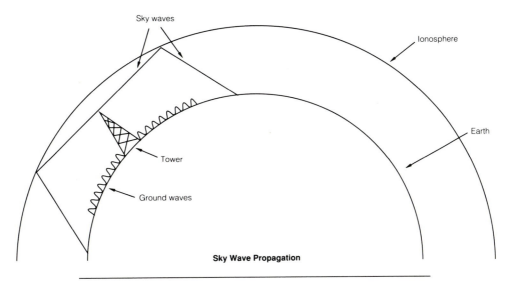

cause them to travel through space, or propogate, in two ways—through ground waves and sky waves. **Ground waves** follow the curvature of the earth and travel anywhere up to seventy-five miles from the transmitter (Figure 5.5). Because a broadcast signal radiates in all directions, signals travel up as well as out. Normally those traveling up continue out into space. But because electrical properties of the ionosphere change at night, some of these signals are reflected back to earth after sundown. These reflected waves are known as **sky waves** (Figure 5.5). Often a pattern develops in which sky waves "bounce" back and forth between the ground and the ionosphere in a way that causes the signal to "skip" over great distances, hitting the earth at several points many miles apart. Sky waves give some AM (medium wave) stations the ability to be received over a large geographic area at night.

As radio broadcasting was developing, the FCC gave certain stations the right to use unusually high power to make use of ground waves and sky waves. This broadened the coverage pattern of the few operating stations so that radio signals could be received in sparsely populated sections of the country that had no local radio stations. This was part of a plan to ensure that everyone had some broadcast service.

These stations, which were given the role of providing this expanded service, were protected from interference from other stations operating on the same frequencies. As more radio stations came into being, areas that once had no local broadcast service began to support profitable radio operations. Because of the protection afforded these clear-channel operators, however, many smaller stations have been restricted to daytime operation or to very low power or both.

In order to make sense of the various types of restrictions placed upon radio stations in the United States, the FCC uses a system of station classification. Each AM station in the country is assigned to a particular level of service that corresponds to its frequency assignment, the power limitations under which it operates, and any restrictions on hours of operation.

AM STATION CLASSIFICATION   AM stations are assigned by regulation to one of four categories of classification. Class I stations operate with the highest authorized power. Class IV stations are low-powered stations. Because they serve small areas, there are many stations in this class. Class II stations operate at slightly more power than Class III stations, but both are designated as regional in their service areas.

The FCC also classifies AM channels. Three general categories of AM channels are designated: clear, regional, and local. Clear channels are afforded protection from interference by other stations operating on the same frequency. This is done by severely restricting power and by placing limitations on nighttime operations of other stations assigned to the same frequency. Stations operating on clear channels are either Class I or Class II stations.

The FCC's system of station classification is grounded in some very thorny realities. The restrictions and limitations imposed by this system work in favor of some broadcasters (those operating on clear channels, for example) and against others (stations restricted to low power and daytime-only operation). The issues that arise in connection with this system transcend national borders. A recent agreement reached by the United States with the Mexican government illustrates how the physical behavior of radio waves makes it necessary for governments to take the lead in sorting out the issues that emerge from the attempts to deal fairly with many competing interests.

On August 28, 1986, the United States and Mexico signed a pact that allows extended operation by both United States and Mexican commercial AM radio stations.[2] About 2000 daytime stations benefit. Under terms of the agreement, stations can extend their broadcasting hours, subject to individual restrictions. Previously, stations were restricted under blanket regulations pertaining to all classes of radio stations. However, it was apparent that on a case-by-case basis, increases in operating hours and sometimes operating power could be accommodated if those increases were kept within strict technical standards.

The practical effect is that these stations can now use a limited amount of power at night. That power, however, can provide significant coverage. Some 2000 AM

United States daytime stations, previously ordered to cease operations daily at 6 PM, can now broadcast up to two hours past sunset. Of those 2000 stations, 220 of them can operate as full-time stations with power of up to 300 watts. Those stations are on the channels allocated to Mexican clear-channel stations. Mexican stations on United States clear channels can now operate full-time. Relaxation of the previously stringent clear-channel rules reflects the realization that previously heavily restricted stations on these channels can operate without significant interference to their international neighbors if strict guidelines are followed.

Such international pacts are common in the Western Hemisphere. The United States concluded a similar agreement with Canada in 1984. A plan negotiated between the United States and the Bahamas provided for operation of a Bahamian clear channel. Agreements have been reached with other Caribbean nations, although frequent skirmishes are fought with Cuba.

Motivation for such a pact is obvious. Extended operations both for United States and Mexican stations mean greater income. More time is available, hence more time for scheduling commercials. To the already fragile world of AM broadcasting (AM listening is at an all-time low),[3] having to cease operations in the midst of an afternoon drive time can be crippling.

This agreement not only affects border stations but also extends to stations like WPAL in Charleston, South Carolina, and WNAK in Naticoke, Pennsylvania. Such stations cite the increased availability for commercial airtime and increased opportunities for public service.

OTHER RESTRICTIONS ON AM BROADCASTING   As noted previously, the 10-kilohertz band width of AM stations reduces the fidelity and the dynamic range of the sound that is transmitted. While this allows for greater flexibility by far than telephone, it restricts AM radio from producing sound above frequencies of 5000 cycles per second. The result is a loss of overtones that provide richness and warmth, which give fullness to sound. Another disadvantage to restricted channel capacity is the reduction in dynamic range or the difference in volume from soft to loud sound.

The radio industry has been working to establish new standards that would result in better sound reproduction for AM. Several initiatives to improve AM sound have recently been pursued vigorously by the radio industry.

AM STEREO   For several years the radio industry has pushed to bring about a system of AM stereo broadcasting. Although authorization for AM stereo has been in existence for several years, the FCC never adopted specific standards that designate a particular type of system to be universally implemented throughout the industry.

As a result, there are two major systems now competing for dominance. They

for FM stations. In fact, for many years SCA services were the only revenue producers for many FM operators. The FCC treats SCA services as secondary to the broadcast service, but it has special regulations for SCA services. These regulations state that it is the licensee's responsibility to exercise control over material broadcast as subsidiary services and give the licensee the right to reject material it deems as inappropriate or undesirable (47 CFR 73.295).

To the average listener, however, the most obvious advantage of multiplexing is that it makes possible stereophonic broadcasting. In FM stereo, the right and left channels are transmitted on separate subcarriers. Stereo receivers detect both signals and reproduce right and left channels through twin speakers. The monaural signal, or the combined right and left signals, leaves the transmitter as a single signal, which is detected by monaural receivers.

Unlike AM broadcasting, FM transmission varies the frequency of the signal and keeps the amplitude constant (Figure 5.7). Because static interference interacts with variations in amplitude of radio signals, FM is free of interference.

One of FM's disadvantages is that American FM occupies the VHF band of the frequency spectrum. Because of their shorter wave length, VHF signals attentuate, or lose power, rapidly. This means that FM signals in the United States are easily interfered with by terrain features and they propagate best in a line-of-sight pattern (Figure 5.8). The direct-wave propagation pattern and the sensitivity of these frequencies to attenuation means that the reach of FM signals depends on the height of the antenna and the power of the transmitter.

The FCC classifies FM stations, as it does AM stations, to prevent interference with one another. FM coverage patterns are much easier to control than AM signals. There is no sky-wave problem with FM, so nighttime restrictions are unnecessary. The signal travels no farther than the horizon; thus, FM stations are classified according to power and antenna height.

Despite the advantages that FM gains from its superior bandwidth, there are disadvantages posed by propagation characteristics. Less power is needed by AM operators to serve the station's coverage area, and sky waves give some AM stations a substantial and marketable nighttime listenership, which is unavailable to FM operators. These disadvantages, however, have not prevented FM from developing into the dominant American radio service in the minds of today's radio audiences. This is a dominance, however, that was not achieved without a struggle.

FM OVERTAKES AM   The early years of FM broadcasting were lean despite its superior technical quality. One factor was that television had captured the public's imagination and FM just didn't compare as an overall entertainment medium. Another factor was that most of the radio-listening public had only AM receivers. Not until the late 1960s did automobiles come factory-equipped with optional AM/FM re-

Figure 5.7

Amplitude modulation (AM) varies the amplitude while the frequency remains constant. Frequency modulation (FM) varies the frequency in relation to the pattern of the original sound information.

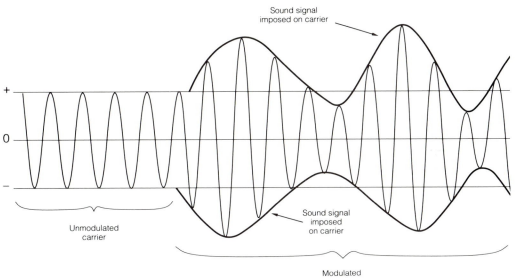

Sound signal imposed on carrier

Sound signal imposed on carrier

Unmodulated carrier

Modulated carrier

Amplitude Modulation

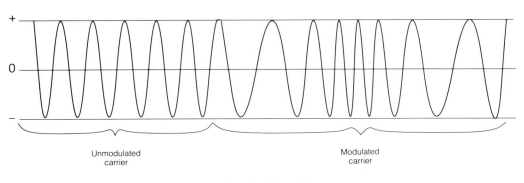

Unmodulated carrier

Modulated carrier

Frequency Modulation

Figure 5.8

FM signals travel no farther than the horizon.

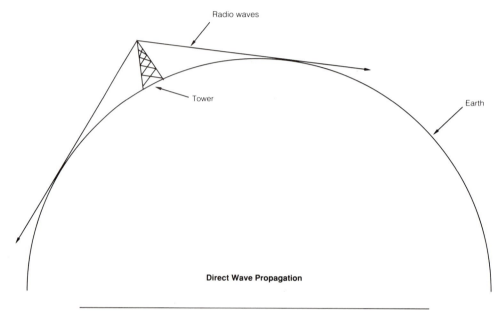

Direct Wave Propagation

ceivers. And, the FM receivers that existed in the earliest years of its development were not designed to take maximum advantage of the greater fidelity of FM.

In the area of programming too, FM lagged behind its potential. Much early FM programming was an exact duplication of AM service. This practice, **simulcasting,** reflected the desire of broadcasters to protect their more profitable AM operations from competition. It also allowed operators to keep their licenses active without incurring the expense of a separate program schedule.

Perhaps the mechanism that unleashed FM potential was the development of automation. Automation had a major impact because it gave programmers new ways to fill broadcast schedules. Music formats were developed to take advantage of this new technology, and the availability of program material increased dramatically. FM was the logical outlet for this increase in program product.

About this time (the early 1960s), the FCC enacted regulations limiting the extent to which FM operators were permitted to simulcast. Partly in response to this situation, various firms began to produce programming specifically for use in automated stations.

FM operators began to use this new programming in their automated operations. As listeners began to sample these new FM offerings, they found that they were attracted by FM's superior sound quality and that music was presented with fewer interruptions. When commercials became more numerous in FM, automation systems made it easy to cluster them, keeping a feeling of relatively long periods of uninterrupted musical segments. Formats such as Album-Oriented Rock were developed and were virtually exclusive to FM, and audiences became accustomed to tuning in to FM stations.

Meanwhile, FM receivers were improved as was broadcast technology in general. By the 1980s FM had overtaken AM broadcasting as the most listened-to form in radio broadcasting. Today, FM licenses that went begging in the 1950s are changing hands at enormous prices and are reaping high profits for what once were regarded as second-string operations.[8]

The on-going efforts of electronics manufacturers to achieve ever-improved sound reproduction has resulted in a public demand for high-level sound quality in radio. The development of digital sound, through CDs and soon **digital audio tape (DAT),** has captured the attention of the American public. Broadcasters are keeping abreast of developments in sound reproduction and rapidly are integrating the latest innovations into their operations.

Basic Equipment

There is wide variation in the sophistication of the equipment used by broadcasters today. In any large market, you will find everything from modest facilities with ancient equipment to the most elaborate physical plants with state-of-the-art equipment. Essential to the discussion of broadcast equipment is an understanding of which basic types of equipment perform which functions in a radio broadcast operation. All studio equipment in a radio station is designed to allow sound to be transmitted. Chapter 6 deals fully with the use of broadcasting equipment in station production. This chapter deals with equipment in relation to how particular types of equipment relate to other aspects of a station's facilities and examines the overall role of various items of equipment with regard to their general applications in station production.

CONSOLES   The function of the console is to mix together and route the output of other pieces of studio equipment. For example, the console allows production people and on-air staff to combine the music from a tape cartridge machine with the voice pickup of a microphone. The signals that come into the console from many sources are fed out as a single signal. The signal is fed to a transmitter or to a tape machine.

Radio stations commonly have several consoles, some units more sophisticated than others. Some production tasks (for example, news production) can be accomplished with relatively simple consoles. At the other end of the scale are large, multi-track consoles used for sophisticated recording projects.

In production situations, the console functions as the nerve center. The various sound elements that combine to create the effect that makes a commercial work or a station promotion effective are controlled and mixed at the console. Experienced production people have learned how to "play" the console in a way that makes the production process far more than a simple mechanical operation.

MICROPHONES   Microphones act as **transducers** to pick up physical sound vibrations and convert them to electrical energy that can be fed to a transmitter, a recording device, or loudspeaker system. Several methods are used to transduce sound with microphones, but the basic result is that an electrical pattern is produced when sound is detected by the element of the mic (see Figure 5.1).

Microphones have differing designs and operating characteristics, and there is a great deal of difference among mics as to which type is most effective for a given task. Variations in frequency response, pickup patterns, and operating characteristics make it possible to be very selective in the use of mics for production purposes. A good knowledge of the individual characteristics of microphones can make an important difference in production and on-air sound quality. In attempting to produce a desired effect, choice of mic is a vital component in achieving desired results. Proper mic selection is an important but often neglected skill among radio professionals.

TAPE RECORDING AND PLAYBACK EQUIPMENT   Tape-recording and playback equipment are essential to radio operations. Taping makes it possible to store sound elements so that they can be integrated into the programming at the appropriate time. Tape and tape-recording hardware have changed significantly over the years, but the basic process remains the same.

In principle, the process of tape recording is similar to the operation of a microphone. That is, it acts as a transducer. When tape recording, the sound is picked-up by the microphone or other source and is converted to an electrical pattern, as in live broadcasting. In tape recording, however, the electrical information is transduced into an arrangement of metallic particles on a strip of acetate, or Mylar. When the tape is played back, the electrical pattern is reproduced and fed to the transmitter, speaker, or both.

Tape-recording and playback equipment commonly found in broadcast operations are cassette machines, cartridge units, and reel-to-reel tape decks. All these modes use the basic principles of recording and playback. They differ in the size of the tape, in the mechanical operation of the equipment, and in fidelity. The job that must be done dictates the choice of which option will best serve the purpose.

Recently, **cassettes** have become a more commonly used format in broadcast

Figure 5.9

Radio news reporters have come to rely heavily on portable cassette recorders for news-gathering activities.

operations. Improvements in the fidelity and the quality of hardware have made this format a staple of news-gathering operations and music reproduction at many stations (Figure 5.9).

Cartridge units use a tape format consisting of a continuous loop of tape fed past the heads of the cartridge (cart) machine. Cart machines were once used almost exclusively for short announcements such as commercials and public service announcements. Today, they are commonly used in place of discs for recorded-music playback. In fact, cartridge tapes form the basis of many automated operations in which all program material is stored on cart and integrated automatically into the program schedule at the appropriate time. In production, carts are used both as a convenient middle step in assembling small bits of recorded information for integration into the production and as the format in which the produced material is delivered to the studio for airplay.

Reel-to-reel tape decks play a decreasing role in day-to-day radio station operations. Other formats have supplanted it as the standard for on-air operations, but there is still a large role for this format in production situations requiring precision editing. A major advantage of the reel-to-reel format is the relative ease of cutting and **splicing** in the editing process (Figure 5.10).

Figure 5.10

Reel-to-reel tape recorders are still widely used in modern radio stations.

TURNTABLES AND CD PLAYERS   Until recently, music was stored on either tape or, more commonly, vinyl discs. The term *disc jockey* originated because the traditional activity of the announcer was to introduce and play records. Playing discs is by no means a thing of the past, but as noted, many stations are storing music on carts, which make it easier to handle on-air situations. Most recently, many stations are playing all the CD–recorded music that they can get.

Broadcast **turntables** differ from those used in most home stereo sets. Radio stations select turntables with heavy-duty playing capability and reliable performance. Modern broadcast turntables are easily started and come up to speed quickly. A typical on-air studio is equipped with two or three turntables, allowing one to be in use while another is cued and ready to go.

Compact disc players differ from other types of sound storage systems in that sound is encoded in digital form. This form samples the original sound source and creates a pattern of responses that encode the sound. Most listeners consider digital recordings to be superior in sound quality to analog recordings.

An added plus of CD players is that they use a laser beam for pickup of the recorded sound. Because nothing physically touches the disc, scratches are not heard. There is no wear on the disc itself, and the noise that is produced when a stylus glides over the grooves of a vinyl disc is not heard on CD players. CD players resist skipping caused by imperfections in discs and are less sensitive to jarring.

Broadcasters have encountered some difficulties with CDs. When CDs first came into broadcast use, the problems were related to cueing selections for airing. In response, manufacturers quickly developed equipment with the capacity to rapidly search for desired selections and to cue them properly for airplay. Present CD units are considerably easier to use than are the turntables of the past.

Much production work is still done using standard turntables. Music used in production is commonly on disc as are the leading sound-effects recordings. In sound effect use, disc far surpasses tape because of the difficulty of locating short audiocuts on tape. On disc, cuts that last only a few seconds can be spotted visually.

OTHER DEVELOPMENTS   Manufacturers of audio equipment have recently developed digital cassette equipment, which does for tape recording and playback what CDs have done for disc reproduction.

Analog systems for music recording and playback soon may be replaced altogether. These developments go hand in hand with other recent technical innovations that have improved drastically the quality of broadcast sound.

OFFICE EQUIPMENT   Beyond the equipment that it takes to get sound on the air, equipment is needed to run the business operations of the station, including standard office equipment and hardware to perform the functions common to any business operation. There are some areas, however, that require specialized forms of equipment because of the unique requirements of the broadcasting industry.

5.2
STUDIO, OFFICE, AND TRANSMITTER FACILITIES

The physical plant from which a radio station operates is a major element of the station's success or lack of it. Inadequate facilities, which do not allow adequate space for important functions to be performed, can reduce quality of the station sound and hamper the productivity of the staff.

Tours of Various Facilities

Tours of radio station facilities (Figure 5.11) show that good planning for the physical layout and construction of stations contributes significantly to the potential for smooth, efficient operations. In planning facilities for radio operations, managers must work closely with all station personnel. Good facilities planning can result in conditions that allow staff to concentrate entirely on the responsibilities of the job without having to deal with inadequate surroundings.

Comparison Among Small, Medium, and Large Markets

Whether a station is located in a large, medium, or small market, efficient design of facilities is important. Relatively modest facilities working on a small budget can still make the best use of available space to enhance working conditions and ensure productivity.

In very small markets, space sometimes can be at a premium. There are still some stations where production is done after sign-off, when the on-air studio becomes a production studio. Such stations often have a single station secretary who handles traffic and billing from a desk near the entrance, where one of the additional secretarial chores is to greet visitors. Salespeople at such facilities often work out of a briefcase and share office space with the station manager. One station of modest size even uses a corner of the general manager's office for a news announcer's booth.

Such stations are often very profitable for the owners, and salespeople are well compensated. If the space is used efficiently and if equipment is maintained, there is often no discernible disadvantage to such modest accommodations.

Stations in medium markets usually have more studio space and more spacious facilities. But often such stations operate from facilities originally intended for other purposes. Many old hotels still house radio stations that have been located there since they first went on the air many years ago. Conversion of such space is often less than ideal. At the medium-market level, there is often sufficient revenue produced that new construction can take place to upgrade inadequate facilities; often stations at this level are fairly elaborately equipped.

The large-market level has the most elaborately designed operations. At this level, stations are often large revenue producers. Moreover, the owners of these profitable operations are very often large corporate entities with substantial resources for building state-of-the-art facilities.

At any market level, however, wide variations in station design are found. Every major market has its share of struggling stations operating in far less lavish surroundings than many stations in smaller markets. The major considerations in facility design remain the same, however, for all market sizes.

CONSTRUCTION CONSIDERATIONS   Besides taking care to purchase and install equipment with a sensitivity to the special requirements of radio broadcasting, there are construction considerations in radio facilities that can make or break the effective operation of a station.

LOCATION   A station that is located adjacent to a heavily traveled interstate highway or a railroad switching yard is going to encounter noise and electromagnetic-interference problems that may make it impossible to operate without elaborate and expensive soundproofing. Therefore, when selecting a construction site, careful consideration should be given to the special requirements of a broadcast facility.

Try to isolate the facility from environmental features that cause noise vibration. Buffers of trees or terrain features between the studio building and major highways, for instance, reduce the noise hazard considerably. Noise from factories and low-flying aircraft can also present problems that might not be noticed when first looking at a site.

Figure 5.11

Radio facilities.

WHEN-AM and WRRB-FM in Syracuse, New York, are housed in a brick one-story building. The AM transmitter and towers are located adjacent to the main building. The FM transmission facilities are in a remote location. The satellite dish provides a network news feed. There is ample parking for employees and visitors.

The reception area is located just inside the main entrance to the building but outside the main portion of the station's studios and offices. It is well-lighted and gives a good presentation of the station to visitors.
Photo by Wade B. Lamb.

The general manager's office is a well-appointed business office.

Accounting adjoins the general manager's office. Accounting operations
are completely computerized.

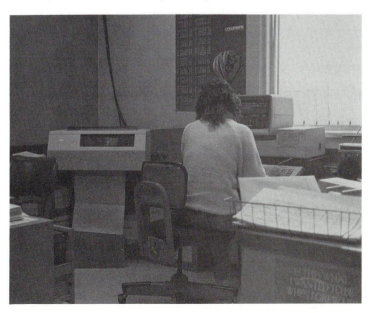

The sales office provides a cubicle arrangement for each salesperson. The sales department is located at the end of the wing containing the general manager's office, the accounting area, and the administrative offices.
Photo by Wade B. Lamb.

Air personality Jay Flannery in the programming office. Production work is coordinated from this office and assigned to individual announcers.

The FM air studio is located next to the program office. It has a view to the outside.

The AM air studio looks through the hallway to the open door of the program office. The announcer works "combo" (runs his own console). The console can be operated standing up or from a high stool.
Photo by Wade B. Lamb.

The production studio has a double window, which looks into an adjoining studio.
Soundproofing material lines the walls. The large studio is equipped with mic hook-ups
for voice recording, but it can be used for private meetings
when the sliding soundproofed panel is closed.

The newsroom is provided with its own production equipment.
Photo by Wade B. Lamb.

The news announcer's booth is equipped with its own cart machines to allow the news announcer to control the integration of "sound bites" while on the air. The window looks into the AM air studio.

A lounge facility located in the studio wing provides a convenient place for station employees to meet, relax—and even work.
Photo by Wade B. Lamb.

HEATING AND AIR CONDITIONING   Other than plumbing, heating and air conditioning comprise the major ongoing service influencing the quality of life in all parts of the station.

In approaching the problem of heating and air-conditioning equipment, broadcasters must deal with the fact that studio equipment produces heat in excess of what might exist in a typical office setting. This can be an advantage in the winter, as illustrated by one radio station in Ashland, Ohio, that uses heat from the operation of the transmitter to help heat the station. But this also means that more cooling is necessary in the summer. More importantly, it means that centralized control of these functions does not work well. Separate thermostats and separate air-circulating systems help solve this problem.

A separate studio system also allows this system to be custom-designed to reduce the noise from air-circulation equipment. One way to do this is to increase the volume of circulated air without increasing the flow rate.

SOUND ISOLATION INSIDE THE BUILDING   The desirability of having separate air-conditioning and heating systems for studios has been noted. It is equally important to provide sound isolation for other aspects of studio operations.

In the best-constructed studio facilities, there is complete separation of the studio from the rest of the building. To achieve this, studios are often constructed on springs and surrounded by materials that protect against vibration and sound transference. This can also be accomplished by providing for air space between double-wall construction. Some studios have rubber cushions installed between walls; another option is double-wall, staggered-stud construction (Figure 5.12). Acoustically laminated glass is available where glass is needed to see between studios and control areas.

WIRING SPACES   Because of the number of wires and cables necessary to get programming on the air, many studios have space under the floors to run cable. Raised floors or computer floors make it possible to run cable where it won't be in the way of other operations. At the same time, easy access to the cable areas allows for easier maintenance.

FLOOR PLANS   The use of space in a radio station requires careful consideration of the operations that must take place. In an all-news operation, there is no need to have a music library near the on-air studio. However, the news machines and production studios should be as close as possible. Both on-air and production studios often are located in the center of a building, where outside noise is less of a factor.

Sales offices are often located near entrances so that clients don't have to be directed through endless corridors. Engineering and technical support facilities are usu-

Figure 5.12

Staggered-stud construction.

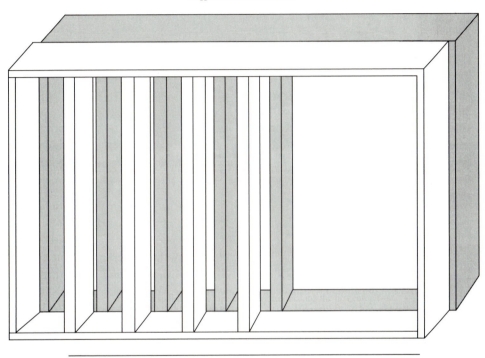

ally near studios. Production studios are best located near on-air studios and control rooms.

NEWS DEPARTMENT CONSTRUCTION CONSIDERATIONS   Location of the newswire facilities is now less of a noise consideration than it was a few years ago. Modern, quiet operating newsprinters have replaced early chugging, clunking machines, which had to be carefully isolated from studios and office space. Newsprinters in stations of ten to twenty years ago often were installed in boxes lined with soundproofing materials. They were opened only to clear copy.

One station that operated from an old bank building installed the wire service machinery within the thick reinforced walls of what was formerly the bank's main vault.

Modern machinery needn't be that isolated. But there are police and fire monitors, phones ringing, and the other noisy activities that accompany the operation of an active newsroom. Some consideration should be given to a newsroom location somewhat isolated from other operations that would suffer from disruption. News production facilities are best located in the same general location of the newsroom; in small stations, news production can be done effectively in a general production studio.

COMPUTER FACILITIES   Computers are becoming essential to the efficient operation of radio stations of any size. Whether a station is using microcomputers (personal computers) or more elaborate systems, consideration must be given to the physical accommodation of the equipment.

Stations that heavily depend on computers often have central processing hardware that requires an entire room for housing. Personal computer users need to think about office configurations that will best make computer workstations accessible and free of interference from other activities. Noise and heat control can also be considerations.

OFFICE CONSTRUCTION   The bread and butter of any station operation is the bookkeeping, billing, and traffic functions, which are normally performed using space and facilities similar to standard office environments. Office facilities needn't take up very much space. At some small stations, the clerical work of getting out bills, typing the program log, handling correspondence, and answering the telephone is handled by one station secretary. Larger stations have a clerical department with several office employees supervised by an office manager.

The equipment that supports the business functions of a radio station includes standard office machines such as typewriters or more modern word-processing equipment. Most stations soon will be equipped with some degree of computer capability if they don't have it already. Computer equipment may consist of one or two microcomputers, or there may a central mainframe with terminals providing access from various office stations and equipment that links office operations to on-air operations and satellite feeds. Later in this chapter, computers are discussed in relation to the central role they can play in station operations.

In designing office space, the comfort of the people who must work there all day is paramount. Well-lighted, well-ventilated areas are essential. There should be adequate room for the work to be performed comfortably without having employees tripping over one another. The station reception area may not be the place to locate the business office.

A reception area of some kind for receiving guests is a very important part of the operation. This space must be congenial, with space for guests to sit while waiting for the person they are visiting. A receptionist who performs routine clerical duties may be seated in this area to make guests feel welcome.

Figure 5.13

The engineering facility for WRVO FM in Oswego, NY.

A limited number of key station personnel may require private offices. The general manager, the station manager, and the sales manager are positions most often assigned private offices. The news director may be assigned a desk in the news room; program managers are often located in or near the music library. On-air personalities usually have a central gathering place where they can relax when not on the air.

TRANSMITTER FACILITIES Transmitter facilities often are not located in the same building or even at the same site as the studios. Remote transmitter locations are usually in a small building located next to the tower. They are equipped with very little in the way of furnishings, though there may well be technical work areas used for equipment repair and maintenance.

ENGINEERING AND TECHNICAL FACILITIES With the exception of very small stations, there is always an area set aside to house the equipment and tools necessary for equipment repair and maintenance (Figure 5.13). This facility also may be the location of the equipment used to route the signals produced in the studios. This equipment feeds on-air material to the transmitter correctly and routes the output of produc-

Figure 5.14

A patch bay functions like a switchboard to route audio signals.

tion facilities to where it is needed. It is common, however, to locate such equipment in or near the on-air studio. **Patching** equipment (Figure 5.14), which functions much like a telephone switchboard to reroute signals from a particular source to various pieces of equipment, sound-processing equipment, and signal-processing equipment may also be located in the engineering area.

ANTENNAS   Antennas are the radiating elements that allow the signal to travel from the transmitter to receivers. In AM radio the tower serves as the radiating mechanism. In AM operations more than a single antenna often is needed to direct the signal in a way that creates the proper-shaped pattern, known as the signal contour. Radiations from one tower are cancelled out by the signal from other towers when they are in phase with one another, thus directionalizing the signal. AM towers improve the quality of their authorized signal by installing radiating elements, which are buried in the ground around the tower.

FM antennas are smaller because of the much smaller wavelength of FM signals. The actual antennas for an FM operation are mounted high on the tower so that the necessary height is achieved to enable the signal to reach the authorized coverage area (Figure 5.15).

Figure 5.15

On the right is a typical AM broadcast antenna. On the left is an FM antenna. Note the short radiating elements (see insert) on the FM tower.

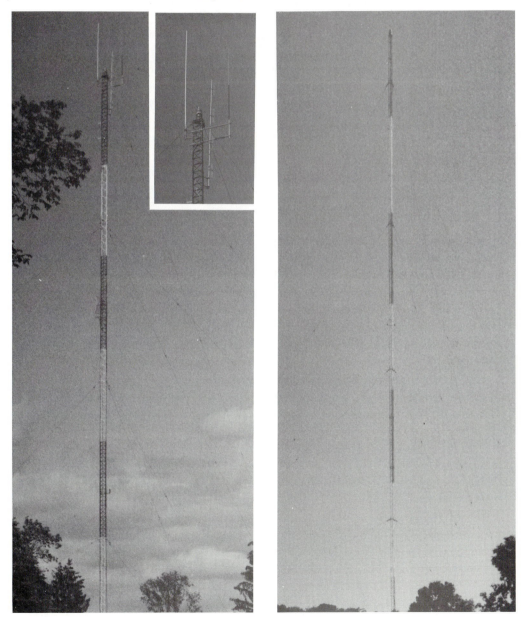

Some Well-Designed Stations

The secret of creating an effective design for a radio facility is to arrange space in such a way that the station functions in a well-integrated fashion. Such stations reflect thoughtful placement and use of equipment, adequate space for work to be carried out, and elimination of anything that results in the discomfort of employees. As one might expect, stations in larger markets have the resources to build and equip facilities more elaborately than smaller market stations, which often must make the best of modest budgets. Nevertheless, even small-market stations can make very effective use of available resources.

With the assistance of *Broadcast Management/Engineering* magazine,[9] several radio stations that have been particularly successful in designing facilities that demonstrate sound principles of operations-oriented facility design are presented. The descriptions that follow point out some of the most interesting features of these stations.

KVOO-AM, TULSA, OKLAHOMA   KVOO, an AM operation located in the fifty-sixth-ranked market in the United States, moved into new studio facilities in November, 1985. This particular facility is very interesting because it is located adjacent to a six-lane expressway with a railroad running down the middle.

The designers of this station considered the room within a room style of studio construction to deal with the noise problems but opted not to go this route. Instead, the station decided to use screening of studios from the outside walls as a major defense against noise and made heavy use of soundproofing materials to isolate sound-sensitive areas (Figure 5.16).

Four-inch block walls were used to construct the main walls of the studios. Two panels of five-eighths-inch gypsum board form the interior walls; they are separated from the block wall by a three-fourths-inch dead space. Specially designed carpeting lines the studio walls to reduce reverberation.

Offices are arranged around the outside walls to provide additional insulation of noise-sensitive areas. The station has three production studios equipped with consoles, turntables, reel-to-reel tape machines, cartridge record and playback units, and cassette machines.

All studios are wired to the engineering area and any of them can be used as the on-air studio. The studio that normally functions as the on-air studio includes equipment such as console, turntables, cart machines, and speakers. Storage racks for tape cartridges are mounted on the wall. Music is played on the air by remote control of a cartridge unit located in the office of the air staff. The music library is near the production areas and doubles as an office for the production director.

Transmitter facilities are located separately from studios (like most larger market operations), and the station plans to rebuild those facilities soon.

Figure 5.16

Floor plan for KVOO-AM, Tulsa, OK.
Reproduced with permission of BM/E.

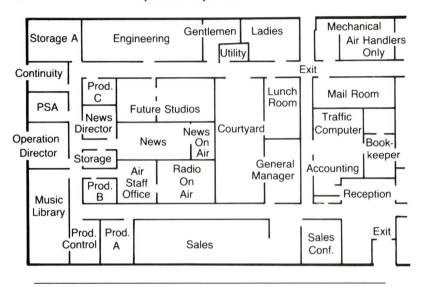

KLKK-AM, WILLITS, CALIFORNIA   KLKK is located in a small market in Northern California. It operates on 5400 watts daytime and 2700 watts at night. A relatively new station (it went on the air in 1985), KLKK had the opportunity to build all new facilities from the ground up (Figure 5.17).

To achieve sound isolation, double-wall, staggered-stud construction was used. Over one inch of sheetrock is on each side of the double wall. Double windows provide visibility between studios. Carpeting on the walls provides sound deadening and attractive decor.

This station is equipped with used, reconditioned studio and on-air equipment. There is also a mobile studio, which consists of a small building that can be transported in the back of a pickup truck and assembled at the site of live remote broadcasts.

KLKK's transmitter facility houses a Harris SX-5A transmitter. Audioprocessing equipment enables the station to maintain a consistent sound. An equalized telephone line provides a studio/transmitter link, and an automatic switcher kicks in the auxiliary transmitter if the main one should fail. A three-tower antenna array creates the assymetrical coverage patterns required by the station's license.

This station was constructed on a low budget, but its owner maintains that it

Figure 5.17

Floor plan KLKK-AM, Willits, CA.
Reproduced with permission of BM/E.

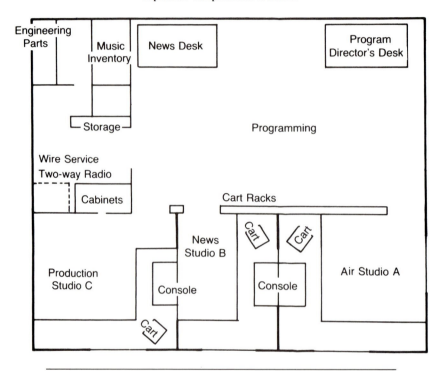

operates comparably with larger facilities costing ten to twenty times more to build. He credits this to simplicity in design and construction.

WLVE-FM, MIAMI, FLORIDA   Located in the eleventh-ranking metropolitan area in the United States, WLVE-FM built new studios designed to combine efficient operation with modern interior design (Figure 5.18). Some thirty-five different colors of paint are used, and all furnishings and carpeting are coordinated with the color scheme.

Four studios are built with a "dead" studio, which is linked to all of them. The dead studio is used for interviews and as a multitrack studio. The studio complex and the engineering area have computer flooring (raised flooring) to provide routing for wires and cables. Two- and three-wall construction provide sound isolation; studio windows have at least two layers of one-half-inch glass, and most have an additional three-fourths-inch layer of glass.

Figure 5.18

Floor plan for WLVE-FM, Miami, FL.
Reproduced with permission of BM/E.

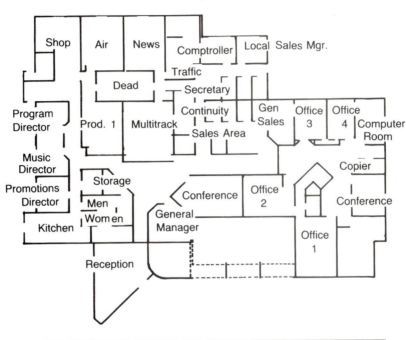

The studio complex is served by a separate air-conditioning system, which uses a low-velocity/high-volume flow of air to keep blower noise at a minimum. Each studio has separate air-conditioning circuits with ground returns. A generator provides power to the studios in the event of a power failure.

On-air music is supplied primarily by CDs, and a CD player is used that allows for manual cueing and presetting of the console faders.

The on-air studio is elaborately equipped. Besides a state-of-the-art console, there are six cart machines, three CD players, two top of the line reel-to-reel machines, two standard turntables, a cassette deck, three condenser mics, amplifiers, processors, a computer terminal, and three announce positions.

There is a studio, which is used as a production facility and as a back-up for the on-air studio, that is identical to the on-air studio. A news studio is equipped for stereo production and contains a console, condenser mics, turntables, cassette decks, CD players, reel-to-reel machines, speakers, and amplifiers.

In the rear of the news studio is a news-gathering area equipped with a satellite earth station, television monitor, and police scanner.

A fully equipped multitrack production studio is used primarily by outside clients, but it is also used for complex, on-air production projects. Along with the standard taping equipment, this studio has a music synthesizer and a drum synthesizer.

A microwave link sends the air signal to the transmitter site in digital form, and it is backed-up by a radio link.

SUMMARY   These three outstanding facilities are excellent examples of stations in small, medium, and large markets that operate from carefully planned facilities. There are, of course, many stations that must make do with less than ideal facilities. The task, however, is the same for all radio operators. That is, make efficient use of the available space. The primary considerations remain the same for those modifying existing spaces as for those with the luxury of building from the ground up.

Studios must be constructed to meet on-air and production needs of the station, and they must be protected from extraneous noise. Ease of operation is the key factor to consider in layout of equipment. Support of the on-air product is paramount, of course, but it is also extremely important to provide for effective operation of the support services that exist to support the on-air product. And, of course, the business operations must work effectively if the whole venture is to produce a profit.

5.3

AUTOMATION AND DATA PROCESSING

Automation in radio station operations developed because FM licenses, which were acquired by broadcasters as protection against the possibility of competition, might be worth something if a cheap source of programming were available. The earliest radio station automation equipment was designed to let a station program long hours of music while significantly reducing the station's need for personnel.

The first generation of automation equipment was designed to operate like a jukebox that played record after record and allowed spaces for the insertion of commercials, announcements, and promos. In fact, the earliest automation equipment was made from two Seeberg Jukeboxes hooked to an Ampex 350 tape recorder.[10] Commercials and spot announcements were recorded on reel-to-reel tape and when a sensor passed over the playback heads, the jukeboxes played records.

Early Automation

The technology described above was the brainchild of Paul Schafer, who is credited with being the father of radio station automation. Schafer's first system was developed in the 1950s, before the introduction of the first cart machine.[11] Other systems quickly came into existence from a variety of manufacturers. Later systems made major use of tape cartridge machinery and developed what became known as the workhorse of automation systems, a cartridge **carousel.**

Carousels solved the major problem faced by early automation equipment, which was how to get the spots integrated into the music. Music had become easily programmed by simply arranging it on large reels of tapes that played on cue from the control system. With the introduction of carousels, carts could be rotated into position easily and played in response to the preset command stored in the control system.

As automation came into heavy use from the mid-1960s to the mid-1970s, larger, more complex units that were designed to automate more and more operations and to improve the integration of program elements evolved. FM operations were becoming enormously popular with listeners, and the successful stations were those playing more music and less talk. Personality radio as typified by the fast patter of a glib disc jockey was disappearing in favor of wall-to-wall produced sound.

In today's automated station, operations are different from the automated station of the 1970s. Today, often an automation system that costs about $5000 performs as well or better than systems that sold for $80,000 in the 1970s. The key, of course, is the advent of microcomputers.

Computer-Aided Programming, Billing, and Communications

Automated program functions that were once controlled by bulky, complex switching mechanisms now can be coordinated by a personal computer. **Software** provides the flexibility to control hundreds of events with the capability to easily make last minute changes in events scheduling. A system developed by IGM, one of the leading automation manufacturers, called the EC (Economical Controller) system runs on any IBM–compatible microcomputer.

Using this system, an operator on duty sits before a computer monitor that displays the last event played, the event on the air, and the next several events programmed. The operator checks to ensure that cartridge tapes are in their proper positions and loads and unloads carts into the carousels. The on-air program is controlled by the automation program.

Figure 5.19

Touchstone 2000 in use at WEEI-AM, Boston. The top photo shows the air personality
using the screen to put a commercial on the air. The bottom photo is close-up of the
screen of the microcomputer used to prepare the broadcast schedule.

COMPUTERIZED ON-AIR OPERATION One station has taken computer-controlled programming beyond simply automating the control of a predetermined schedule of events. WEEI-AM in Boston, which programs an all-news format, uses a touch-screen system to allow the on-air announcer to control the airing of events.[12]

The central element of the WEEI system is a touch-sensitive computer monitor that displays the program elements available to be aired. When the on-air announcer touches the place on the screen where it lists a commercial, for example, a signal is sent to a cartridge machine, and the commercial is aired (Figure 5.19).

Known as the Touchstone 2000 series, the system is the product of Media Touch located in Salem, New Hampshire. An IBM computer runs the system at WEEI. The computer stores the program log and displays it on the touch screen while another IBM computer automatically logs all events as they are placed on the air. Another monitor in the on-air studio provides copy for live announcements, which the announcer reads from the screen.

The system at WEEI gives the announcer complete control over the air product.[13] Unlike the traditional **combo** operation, the on-air announcer doesn't need to cue and manipulate tapes and carts. Formerly, all-news operations had to employ a technician to play commercials and announcements. With the microphone open much of the time in the on-air studio, it was very difficult to manipulate program materials. With this technology, the operation can be combo-operated easily.

The program **log** is produced by the station's traffic department and downloaded onto the computer file where it is stored until it appears element by element on the touch screen. Each morning the billing department is provided with a printout of the previous day's log, which gives the starting and ending time of each element that went on the air.

In essence, what computers have done for radio stations is to remove the gap separating live from automated operations. By allowing the program events to be prepared in advance and stored in a computer program, the station can opt to have it placed on the air either by a preprogrammed set of instructions or by an air-personality operating the system from a studio.

TOTAL STATION AUTOMATION Today's computer technology is creating a revolution in broadcast operations that promises to free radio from many inconvenient and inefficient structures. Modern radio stations are rapidly becoming computerized and automated in every aspect of their operations. The result is a vast improvement in sound quality and a streamlining of office functions.[14]

In the programming area, the large quantity of program materials available to stations via satellite has spurred the development of sophisticated automation systems that can interface with satellite-delivered programming. These sophisticated systems use microcomputer hardware in conjunction with software packages designed to control station programming in response to predetermined schedules.

In stations where music programming is received by satellite, the software senses cue tones fed with the program material. When the satellite signal is received at the station, the cue tone is separated from the program signal and fed to satellite-interface equipment. The cue tones activate the local program elements that are integrated into the satellite-fed programming in accordance with instructions programmed by the computer.

In operations that use their own program material or taped syndicated material, microcomputers and software packages can be used to greatly streamline operations. These packages provide advantages that formerly could only be performed by using cumbersome systems of relays or mechanical switching devices. These modern systems require less hardware, provide greater flexibility, and are easier to operate than earlier automation systems.

In both satellite-fed systems and in-house operated systems, manufacturers are responding to the desire of stations to localize the sound of programming. Satellite networks have developed services that feature station promos fed to affiliates through the network and local weather forecasts by program hosts.

In stations where major portions of the broadcast schedule originate in-house, there is a trend toward a type of automation referred to as "live assist." In these systems, computer software is geared to controlling studio operations that formerly were performed by on-air personalities, such as cuing records and loading cart machines. Computer-driven systems now make it possible for these tasks to be done with the touch of a button or, as in the case of WEEI, by touching a part of the computer monitor screen.

There are several configurations of automation equipment that automatically create the program log that tells the air personality when program elements are scheduled; the equipment also generates a record of what was broadcast. These systems can be accessed by traffic managers who can schedule commercials as sales orders are received. The system automatically schedules the commercial in accordance with instructions to prevent scheduling it near times when competing products are scheduled. For example, the computer may be programmed not to schedule two competing airline commercials within fifteen minutes of each other. The traffic person no longer has to physically examine the log to guarantee this kind of protection.

Discrepancy reports are prepared to show any commercials or other program elements that were scheduled but not aired so that the accounting department can make the necessary billing adjustments. The report also notes the reason for the discrepancy. If a piece of equipment fails, engineering is notified so that repairs can be made.

WHGH-AM in Boston uses an IBM system with Columbine software to coordinate its sales functions and billing procedures with on-air scheduling. The system generates the program log and keeps track of commercial availabilities so that salespeople can identify instantly what time periods are available for commercials.

National sales representatives in major marketing centers can access the station's computer to find spot availabilities. Local salespeople completing a sale for a schedule of spots can enter the order immediately and let the client know when those spots will air.

Once a spot has been scheduled, aired, and properly logged by the computer, a bill is computer-generated for the client. Revenue reports can be run to determine progress toward meeting monthly, quarterly, or yearly sales quotas. Sales managers can get sales figures for individual people and compare current figures with past performance.

There are also computer programs that allow salespeople to use ratings and audience data for use in selling. Comparisons can be made among stations in the market and with other advertising media such as newspapers and television.

In essence, the entire station can be automated using computers. It is possible for group-owned stations to link all their operations using dedicated telephone lines. This technology lets us envision a time when the standard on-air studio might consist of little more than an announce booth with a computer screen. All equipment and source material can be located in other parts of the station or in another city. Production will still be important, and the traditional functions of recording and playback of music and other sound elements will still be required. However, the on-air manipulation of program elements, which can be very distracting for on-air talent, may soon be a thing of the past. There can also be a great reduction in the tedious paperwork involved in maintaining the business operations of stations. Office personnel will still be required, but increased computerization of business functions will allow for much greater efficiency and productivity.

The integration of program operations with sales and accounting functions can provide more productive salespeople and happier clients. The streamlining of studio operations can greatly enhance the "live" sound of automation systems whether they are satellite-driven or programmed in-house. For stations with live studio presentation, on-air personalities now can be freed from many of the tasks that tend to distract them from their on-air presentations. Another advantage of simplified on-air functioning is a reduction in the number of mistakes made by operators. The net effect should be an improved overall sound.

The economics of computerization are a primary factor in making decisions on the extent to which a station should automate. To completely automate a station can be an extremely expensive operation, but many automation configurations allow the process to proceed on a phased-in basis so that the costs can be amortized over time. Most installations, however, pay for themselves within two or three years.

It is important to remember that computers at this level of sophistication require facilities and personnel to support them. Computer technicians with troubleshooting capabilities must be on hand, and clerical and sales personnel must be capable of operating computer systems. Facilities must be adapted or constructed to accommodate the necessary wiring and the housing of processing equipment.

EXERCISES

1. Assume that you are the owner of a medium-market AM radio station. The station is new and hasn't yet gone on the air. You have been given the necessary budget to construct studio and transmitter facilities from the ground up. Do the following:

    a. Describe how you will program the station. Do not explain why you have chosen this particular programming plan; just list and describe all sources of programming material that you will be using. The importance of determining the source of program material at the outset is that there will be important decisions to be made on factors such as storage of music and facilities for computer operation and satellite equipment, depending on the sources you select. The usefulness of your facilities and equipment planning will depend on how well you have thought through your programming needs.

    b. Describe the major pieces of equipment that you will need to run the station and describe the facilities that you need to run the operation. Justify your facilities and equipment needs in relation to the specific functions that they will perform in the station operation. For example, if you plan to automate your operation, describe the equipment that you will need to support the program service you will offer. (NOTE: An all-news operation requires different facilities and equipment than does a station programming a satellite-delivered rock format. Do not overlook the office and business aspects of the operation.)

    c. Draw a floor plan showing the layout of the office and studio facilities that you will need to run an efficient operation. Show the location of all studio, engineering, program support, and business functions of the station.

2. For the station types listed below give the advantages and disadvantages for operation of each station as an AM facility and an FM facility. Consider only the physical and technical aspects of each form of transmission, but relate your technical analysis to what you know about the market considerations of radio.

    a. A country music station
    b. An all-news station
    c. A talk station
    d. A nostalgia or music-of-your-life format station
    e. An adult contemporary station
    f. A classical music station
    g. A rock music station

NOTES

1. A concise review of the history of radio's early development can be found in
    Sydney W. Head and Christopher H. Sterling, *Broadcasting in America: A Sur-
    vey of Electronic Media,* 5th ed. (Boston: Houghton Mifflin, 1987), 39–102.
    For a more comprehensive historical review see Erik Barnouw, *A Tower in Babel:
    A History of Broadcasting in the United States to 1933* (New York: Oxford Uni-
    versity Press, 1966).

2. "More Stations, More Power, More Hours," *RadioActive* (November 1986):
    18–19.

3. *Channels, The Business of Communication, Fifth Annual Issue* (1987).

4. "NAB Hosts Upbeat Radio Show," *Broadcast Management/Engineering*
    (November 1986): 67.

5. Ibid.

6. Ibid.

7. Head and Sterling, *Broadcasting in America,* 77–78.

8. *Broadcasting* regularly lists recent station sales in its "Changing Hands" section.

9. Stations listed were among those featured in "The Best Station and Facility
    Design," *Broadcast Management/Engineering* (December 1986): 27–57.

10. James C. Woodworth, "Reminiscing About Automation," *Radio World* (15
    February 1987): 23.

11. Woodworth, *Radio World:* 23.

12. Larry S. Vidoli, "WEEI Enters Touchscreen Age," *Radio World,* (15 February
    1987): 27.

13. Interview with John Rodman, WEEI-AM (23 February 1987).

14. Much of the material for the discussion of station automation is drawn from
    Jerry Whitaker, "Program Automation for Radio," *Broadcast Engineering* (April
    1985): 38–48.

CHAPTER 6

PRODUCTION

In the most basic terms, **production** means use of studio equipment to combine sounds into a finished product. The physical act of production involves recording with microphones, use of tape-recording and playback equipment, routing and mixing of signals through a broadcast console, and the actual cutting and splicing of audio tape.

But the real thrust of production transcends physical actions. Production in modern radio involves creating a special and evocative sound—a finished product that communicates a feeling and a message, creates an effect, and reinforces the sound of the station.

This chapter explores the basics of production primarily from the standpoint of what a manager must know. Production techniques are extensive and varied and cannot be capsulized in one chapter.[1]

6.1

FUNDAMENTALS OF PRODUCTION

Chapter 5 introduced the primary pieces of equipment used in production. Here, we expand on the use of equipment in production, building sequentially on the material presented earlier.

Console

Newcomers to production are often intimidated by the **console.** Indeed, it is a formidable piece of machinery (Figure 6.1). Its banks of switches and dials seem to defy comprehension at first glance, but it is a simple piece of gear. Unfortunately, the seeming complexity of the console prevents many people not directly involved in on-air work from understanding its use. There is a simple method of learning console operations that involves understanding the concepts of routing, mixing, and amplification; keying; and delegation.

ROUTING   The **routing** function uses the knobs and switches to take the output of a source—such as a microphone—and to send that signal to the transmitter or to a tape recorder. In the most basic terms, a microphone in a control room does not send a signal anywhere until the routing mechanism, the console, sends the signal to its final destination. In effect, the switch on the console turns the microphone on and off. A device called a **potentiometer** (or pot in radio's verbal shorthand) adjusts the volume of a signal. A pot is a variable resistor, much like the familiar rheostat—the wall-mounted knob that controls the brightness of household-lighting fixtures. In a typical console the pot is governed by an on–off switch. In other words, a switch turns the signal on or off, whereas the connected pot governs the loudness level.

MIXING   The **mixing** function is a direct extension of the routing function because the console is capable of routing *more than one signal* to the tape recorder or transmitter: The operator can mix voice and music from separate inputs through the console. The console channels them into one source, and the operator adjusts the proper volume of each source. For example, the signal from the microphone being used by an announcer might be routed into pot 1, and the signal from the turntable

Figure 6.1

The mixing console is the nerve center of radio. It can be intimidating at first glance.
Courtesy of Harris Corporation, Quincy, IL.

might be governed by pot 2 (Figure 6.2). Turning on both pots results in a mix, and the relative levels would be controlled by the levels of the pots.

AMPLIFICATION   **Amplification** is primarily a technical function that is not of direct concern to the producer. **Audio** signals—electrical signals carrying sound information—are weak when they leave a microphone, turntable, or other source. The amplification function of the console boosts the signals to usable levels. Note that by extension the amplification principle also enables the producer to increase or decrease the relative level of sound sources.

KEYING AND DELEGATION   **Keying** is the second concept. The on–off switch is more properly called a key, and it does more than turn on the pot. The key is located directly above the pot and is usually a three-position switch (Figure 6.3). "Off" is in the middle. Throwing the switch to the right puts whatever source is governed by the pot into the **program channel.** Throwing the key to the left puts whatever sound source is governed by the pot into the **audition channel.** Audition is an off-air channel used for private listening or, sometimes, off-air production. There is one other channel: the **cue channel.** When the pot is turned all the way counterclockwise, it can be clicked into the "cue" position, and the output is heard through a small speaker located in the board. Cue, as you might guess, is for "cueing" up a sound source—that is, finding the beginning of the sound signal on a tape or record and putting the tape or record in position to start correctly when the signal is needed on air.

Figure 6.2

The signals of a microphone and a turntable can be routed and mixed by manipulation of the pots.

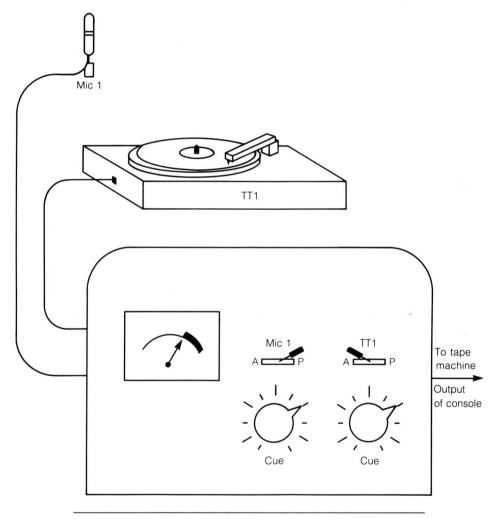

Figure 6.3

The key is located above the pots. The key on the left is in the program position. The key on the right is in the off position. Audition is to the left of center on both keys.

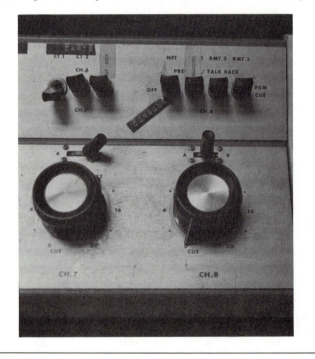

Delegation is the final concept. Delegation allows a few knobs on the console to control the sound output of many pieces of equipment. For example, one pot might control either tape recorder 1 or cartridge machine 2. The switch above the key—the delegation switch—would be labeled TAPE 1 to the left and CART 2 to the right. Infrequently used sources might be bunched four to a pot if the console is configured to allow this. Infrequently used sources include the over-the-air telephone line and the network newsline. (In the on-air control room, the network news incoming line might be used only once an hour for three minutes during the network newscast.)

In summary, delegation allows the producer to choose which piece of equipment is controlled by the pot. Keying allows the source to be turned on and off and into program and audition channels. Both the delegation and the key switches feed the signal through the pot, which is used to control the volume of the source.

USING THE CONSOLE   Any console can be deciphered using these principles. Although console designs differ, the basic functions are the same. Does a console use vertical slide faders instead of pots? Don't let the difference throw you; if you use the principles above and think through the operation, you can learn to run the board. Are there push buttons instead of keys? Again, remember the basic principles, and the board will not be a mystery.

It may seem that a disproportionate amount of explanation is being presented relative to console operations, but "consolephobia" is the primary stumbling block for most people learning production operations. Once the console function is understood, however, the rest of production comes logically and easily. With this in mind, a brief and practical illustration of how a producer might use a hypothetical console for production of a simple commercial is presented. The commercial involves three elements:

—   A script (copy) that the announcer reads over the microphone

—   A sound effect of a winter snowstorm taken from a sound-effects record, a standard long-playing (LP) disc

—   Tropical-type music taken from a standard LP

The commercial is for a travel agency. It opens with five seconds of the winter snowstorm sound effect, some announcer copy sympathizing with the listener about the terrible weather, and then the background music fades in under the announcer's copy, which is about the travel agency's Tahiti vacations.

Three basic console-operation sequences accomplish this task:

1.   The pot governing the turntable is keyed to program, and the delegation switch is set to TT1 (turntable 1). The pot itself is set to a volume level deemed appropriate by the producer, who listened to the cut and predetermined a volume level before starting the commercial production.

When enough of the sound effect is heard ("established," in radio terminology), the producer gradually lowers the volume level on the pot and begins to fade out the sound effect.

2.   Next is "opening up" the mic, meaning keying the mic pot to program and selecting the appropriate delegation. It is worthwhile to note that not all pots are delegated on a typical board. Frequently used pots, such as the one governing the announcer's mic, may not have any other sources wired into it.

3.   The final step involves starting the turntable, which can be done when the microphone is open because broadcast turntables are specially designed to start

quietly. The producer uses the pot marked TT2 to govern the loudness level of the tropical music cut, which is mixed underneath the announcer's voice. When the message is complete, the producer brings the music up full for a second by increasing the volume on TT2 and then fades the music down and out.

Most operations are really no more complicated than this. They may involve more sound sources, but the principles remain the same. You can figure out any board by careful examination of the labels and some experimentation.

Tape-Recording and Playback Units

Recording and playback units are mechanisms for storage of an audio signal. The audio signal is transduced—changed in form—to a magnetic impulse; that impulse is fed into one of the heads on a tape recorder. A head is a magnetic conductor that forces the audio impulse to bridge a small gap; when the signal bridges the gap, it imposes a pattern on the audio tape. Most tape machines have an erase, record, and playback head.

How can a pattern be imposed on a tape? The tape is made of a Mylar, or acetate base, that is coated with iron oxide (which is rust). The iron oxide particles are forced into a pattern as the audiotape is moved across the magnetic field and the particles are microscopically realigned.

In radio production there are two basic forms of tape machines: reel-to-reel and cartridge. Reel-to-reel units range from simple devices, which record only one or two channels, to highly complex sound studio–type machines, which can record four, eight, sixteen, twenty-six, or thirty-two channels. Why would one want to record so many channels?

Most applications of such multiple-track recording involve the mixing of music. Individual singers and instruments in a combo are recorded individually so that their respective levels can be remixed and adjusted until the proper balance is achieved. In addition, sophisticated multitrack (Figure 6.4) machines have various technical devices for shaping sound.

Some production work in the modern radio studio is done on multitrack equipment. Although the function of a multitrack console is somewhat different from that of the standard broadcast console discussed earlier, the fundamental operating principles are roughly the same.

Cartridge machines, which were introduced in Chapter 5, have many applications in the production process. Examples are the following: First, the cart machine

Figure 6.4

A multitrack mixing console.

allows the producer to instantly start a recorded segment. Second, using a cart machine for short program segments eliminates the need to thread up and cue reel-to-reel tape or cue a disc on a turntable.

Microphones and Sound

A microphone transduces the physical motional energy of a sound wave into an audio signal, usually by means of a diaphragm within the mic. Essentially, the soundwave— vibration of molecules in air or other medium—causes the diaphragm to vibrate in sympathy with the sound wave. This is the same physical principle that allows the diaphragm of skin at the end of the ear canal to perceive sound.

Microphones are classified typically into three types—moving coil, ribbon, and condenser—that reflect the instruments' internal workings. Microphones are classified by pickup patterns—omnidirectional, bidirectional, and cardioid—that relate to the directions from which the mic "hears" sound. Finally, all mics are described in terms of their frequency response. All characteristics are discussed next.

MOVING COIL MICROPHONE   The diaphragm in a **moving coil microphone** is attached to a conducting coil, and the vibration moves the coil through a magnetic field. As a result, an electrical signal is generated, and this signal carries the audio imprint of the sound. Moving coil mics are rugged and dependable.

RIBBON MICROPHONE   A **ribbon microphone** produces a signal via a thin foil element mounted between two poles of a magnet. Vibrations move the foil ribbon, and the ribbon produces an electrical signal as it vibrates between the magnetic poles. Ribbon mics are usually delicate but they produce a sound that producers regard as warm and rich. Many announcers feel that ribbon mics accentuate their voice quality.

CONDENSER MICROPHONE   *Condenser* is an antiquated term for *capacitor,* an electrical element that stores an electrical charge. Vibration of the diaphragm causes a change in capacitance, which is translated into an electrical signal. A **condenser microphone** typically provides very high-reproduction quality but is expensive and somewhat delicate.

OMNIDIRECTIONAL PICKUP PATTERN   As you might deduce from the prefix, a mic with an **omnidirectional pickup pattern** picks up sound equally well from all directions. There is, however, a slight loss at the rear because the physical mass of the mic blocks some of the sound signal. Figure 6.5 shows an omnidirectional pickup pattern. The concentric rings indicate sound level in decibels. A decibel is a relative measure of volume, the derivation of which is quite complicated. But the basic concept of a pickup pattern, also known as a polar pattern, relates simply to the fact that as the pattern dips toward the center of the circle, the sensitivity declines by the indicated number of decibels.

BIDIRECTIONAL PICKUP PATTERN   A mic with a **bidirectional pickup pattern** accepts sound from the front and the rear but not the sides, as shown in Figure 6.6. Ribbon mics have a bidirectional pattern unless some special acoustic manipulation is built into the mic's workings (which is quite common).

CARDIOID PICKUP PATTERN   Cardioid means heart-shaped, a rough approximation of the pattern shown in Figure 6.7. Visualize the pattern in three dimensions—remember, *all* the patterns are three-dimensional—by imagining the mic as the stem of a huge apple. The **cardioid pickup pattern** is directional and thus cancels

Figure 6.5

An omnidirectional pickup pattern.

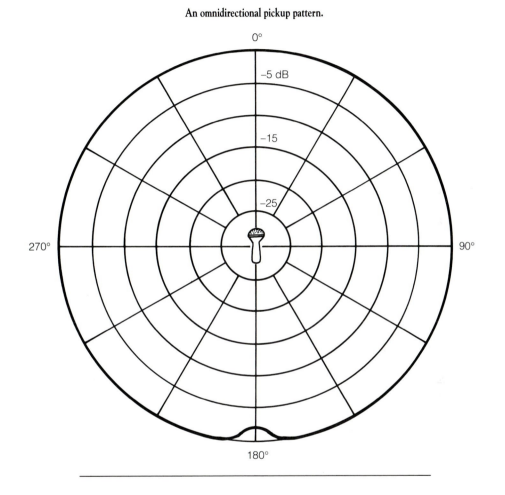

out noise from the rear, making such a mic useful for combo operations, in which a disc jockey operates the equipment.

FREQUENCY RESPONSE   Some mics reproduce a wider range of sound than do others. In general, the wider the range of pitches reproduced by the mic, the better the sound quality. Certain mics boost various frequencies and minimize others. Although this is a *very* complex area, it is worth noting that cardioid mics tend to boost bass

Figure 6.6

A bidirectional pickup pattern.

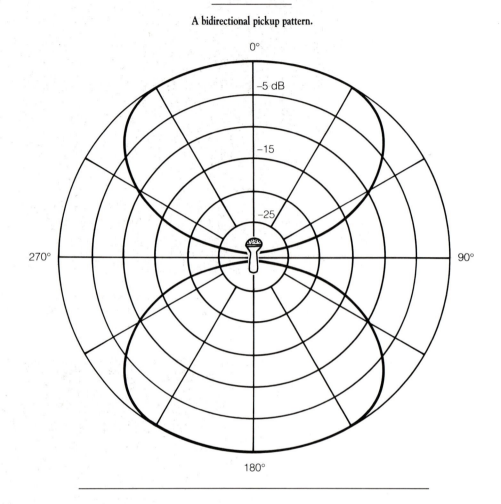

frequencies when the sound source moves closer to the mic. Known as the proximity effect, this bass-boosting function makes cardioids popular with announcers who desire a deeper sound.

Some popular mics used in modern radio are illustrated in Figure 6.8, along with brief descriptions relating to their type, pickup pattern, and other factors.

Figure 6.7

A cardioid pickup pattern.

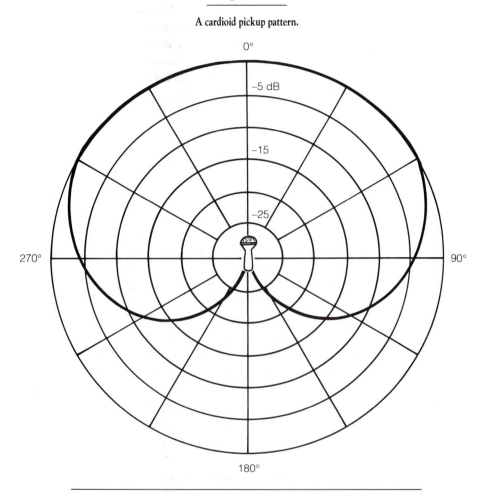

Splicing and Dubbing

Two final factors relating directly to the production function are splicing and dubbing.
Splicing is the act in which audio tape is physically cut and taped back together again.
Splicing is most commonly used when a producer wants to eliminate a certain segment
of the tape or wants to rearrange the order of elements on a tape. Splicing is also done
when a tape accidentally breaks.

Figure 6.8

Microphones used in modern radio.

Microphone	Pattern	Description
Neumann U-47	Condenser	Cardioid pickup pattern; excellent voice mic; flat response; warm sound; blast filter; bass roll-off 
Sony C-37P	Condenser	Omnidirectional/cardioid; four adjustments for bass roll-off; good for voice pick-up and musical instruments 
Sennheiser 416 (middle), with 417 and 418	Condenser	Supercardioid; usually boom mounted; flat response; eliminates unwanted ambient sound; excellent for remotes, where directionality is desired 
Electro-Voice RE-30, RE-34	Condenser	RE-30 is omnidirectional, RE-34 is cardioid; power supplied by 9-volt battery or phantom power supply; feeds line-level or mic-level signal; graphite in handle improves comfort in cold conditions
Electro-Voice RE-18	Moving coil	Supercardioid; excellent shock protection makes this a good choice for hand-held use; blast filter; bass boost with close use

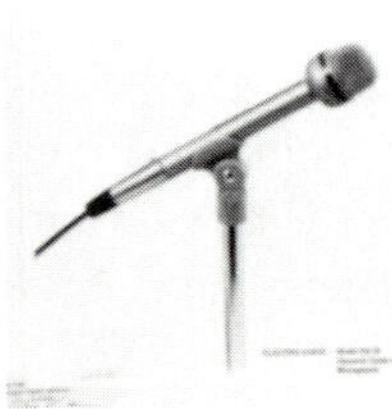

© Gotham Audio Corp.

© Sony Corp. of Am.

© Sennheiser Electronic Corp.

© Electro-Voice, Inc.

© Electro-Voice, Inc.

Microphone	Pattern	Description	
Electro-Voice RE-50	Moving coil	Omnidirectional; similar to popular 635A; shock resistant; excellent all-purpose mic; internal wind screen; blast filter; rugged	© Electro-Voice, Inc.
Shure SM-58	Moving coil	Cardioid; good studio mic; rugged; pop filter	© Shure Brothers, Inc.
Shure 300	Ribbon	Bidirectional; warm sound; pop prone; very good voice mic	© Shure Brothers, Inc.
Shure SM 33	Ribbon	Cardioid; mellow sound, bass enhanced with proximity; excellent voice mic; favorite of many announcers	© Shure Brothers, Inc.
RCA 77DX	Ribbon	Omni-, bi-, or unidirectional (switch selector); classic mic of radio's golden age; switchable bass response; delicate; very fine mic for voice and many musical instruments	

A splice is made by locating the spot at which the first edit point passes over the play head, marking that spot, spooling off the unwanted portion of tape, and then finding and marking the second edit point—the part that you want to rejoin to the first edit point. An illustration and brief explanation are shown in Figure 6.9.

Dubbing refers to transferring sound from source to source electronically—for example, copying it from a tape onto a cart. Dubbing from tape to cart is a common production practice, which is why tape and cart functions were reviewed earlier in this chapter. As an example, a producer who has constructed a news introduction on reel-to-reel tape certainly would elect to dub it onto cart to avoid the complications of finding and threading the tape reel every time the news is about to be aired.

Dubbing can be used to electronically remove an unwanted section from a tape, rather than cutting and splicing the tape. First, dub the good first section of the tape to tape B, stop tape B, and fast-forward the original tape past the unwanted section. Next, start the original and start recording on tape B, and the electronic edit is completed.

Figure 6.9

a. The tape is positioned in the channel of an editing block with the edit point (previously marked in grease pencil) over the groove.

b. The tape is cut at the mark with a single-edged razor blade.

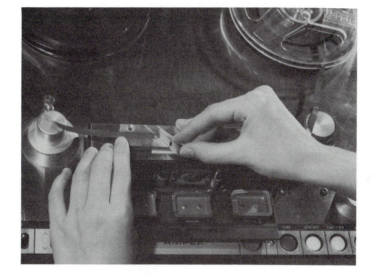

c. Tape is spilled off the tape machine after making the first cut.
The second edit point is found.

(*continued*)

d. After the second cut is made, the two ends are butted together in the channel of the editing block and joined with editing tape.

e. The spliced tape is removed from the channel and the edit is checked.

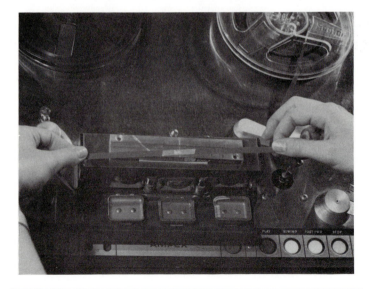

Production Skills

Production is a technical and artistic endeavor, and creativity is at a premium among production directors in modern radio. But how does production affect a manager's job? Knowledge of the following factors is important:

—— *Station equipment.* Radio managers, operations directors, and/or program directors frequently are responsible for equipping various departments; this requires some knowledge of the hardware. For example, a manager of an FM AOR station probably would elect to use a control room mic that is highly sensitive and provides that intimate presence that characterizes AOR. (Consult Figure 6.8 and you will see that a Neumann U-47 would be a good choice.)

Perhaps mics are being ordered for the news department; a manager must know enough about mic characteristics *and* the characteristic duties of the news department to conclude that an Electro-Voice RE-50 is a wise choice.

—— *Programming logistics.* Managers must know the logistics of programming. Assigning a production task to an announcer or production manager entails a knowledge of how long that task will take. Also, someone making an assignment must be able to judge the quality of the finished product in relation to the task assigned and the available equipment.

—— *Commercial production.* In a related note, managers must have a thorough understanding of commercial production. Commercials are the economic backbone of the station; the manager must understand not only how commercials are constructed but also how they persuade to achieve an effect. Factors relating to the communication of ideas through production techniques are the subject of the remainder of this chapter.

—— *Financial considerations.* Perhaps the most salient point relates to budgetary matters. As one radio station owner puts it: "Every engineer or production person I've ever known wants the absolute latest, most expensive item on the market. It's the manager's job to understand what will do the *job,* not what will make these people happy. The bottom line is still the name of the success game."

6.2
CREATING PROGRAM ELEMENTS

All elements in a produced radio program, such as commercials, are used to support the theme, to act in concert with other production elements to get a message across to the listener. In the most general terms, the goal of production is to communicate a message. The individual techniques of production are used within this framework to achieve an effect.

Communicating a Message: Techniques of Copywriting

Consider the case of a shoe store. Is the goal of an effective radio commercial to communicate the message that the shoe store has many different kinds of shoes at various prices? Think carefully, because this type of question commonly arises and sometimes separates the true producer from the knob-twisting mechanic. The answer typically affects the success of the station's economic growth in general.

The answer? Of course not. Any shoe store has a lot of shoes, some cheap and some expensive. There are, however, many merchants who believe that an effective commercial involves reciting every brand of shoe and price that can be crammed into sixty seconds of copy. More dismaying, some managers and producers feel the same way.

Experienced **copywriters,** people who produce the written scripts for radio, know that effective advertising involves much more than a simple declaration of what's for sale and how much it costs. The typical cram-and-jam shoe store commercial could be vastly improved by a number of approaches such as the following:

—— A commercial with bouncy vibrant music, extolling the listener to "swing into spring" with the new line of Acme shoes. Such commercials typically are effective because they create a connection in the mind of the listener between the end of winter and a new spring wardrobe. After all, what motivates *you* to shop for spring clothes? Is it always pure necessity?

—— A commercial aimed at mothers and fathers with a "back-to-school" nostalgic motif. Here is how one advertising copywriter used that approach:

Remember the excitement of going back to school when you were a kid? There was the slight sadness that summer was over, but there also was the sense of anticipation . . . new beginnings and a feeling of good times ahead for the new school year.

Along with that sense of excitement came the time when you went shopping for new clothes. They always had a special kind of "new" smell to them. And when you smell it today, you probably think of going back to school.

Best of all, though, was getting new shoes. Your old reliables had just about made it through the past year. And now it was time to get those brand new ones that would get you off to a good start.

Well, _____ Shoes, at _____ etc.

Note how each paragraph tugged at an emotion, how it communicated an idea. Such is the basis of advertising. Let us be realistic: To a great extent, shoes are shoes, toothpaste is toothpaste, and cars are cars. An advertiser must sell other factors than simply the pure physical features of price and construction. Perhaps the commercial "sells" an atmosphere of prestige or reinforces our desire to go along with the crowd.

Effective copywriting incorporates the atmosphere; in advertising parlance, it "sells the sizzle and not the steak." To produce an effective piece of copy, remember these elements:

1.   Write for the ear, not the eye. Long sentences, convoluted grammar, and phrases such as "the latter option" (a radio listener cannot go back and refer to the former and the latter) have no place in radio copy. Write in short, conversational sentences. Write the way you speak.

2.   Write in such a way that the announcer is able to read your copy gracefully. In basic technical terms, this means to write in all capital letters for easy viewing; in a more artistic vein, it means that you must impart a proper rhythm to the words. Watch, in particular, your use of commas and dashes.

3.   Think *radio:* Make your commercial an effective play in the theater of the mind. Use sound effects when appropriate. Sound effects are usually indicated in copy by the abbreviation SFX; for example, (SFX: cherry dropped in to giant pile of whipped cream). However, use sound effects only when there is a purpose. Never use them as a reflex or simply because they are available.

A sound effect is particularly useful when it serves to compress time. For instance, a two-second sound effect of a howling blizzard makes the point much quicker than does a half page of copy describing the miserable weather. (Details on sound effects and other related production techniques are presented later in the chapter under "How Production Elements Are Used to Achieve an Effect.")

scenes you feel are appropriate. (Use Figure 6.10 as a model.) If production equipment is available, produce the spot.

2. Cast celebrities as radio talent for the following commercials. For each spot, choose a celebrity and then write a paragraph on the reasons for your choice.
    a. Spokesperson for a decaffeinated coffee. (HINT: If you choose a reassuring and fatherly figure such as Robert Young—still famous in reruns as Marcus Welby, M.D.—you probably would have a great deal of company in the advertising world. Why do you suppose advertising executives did choose Young?)
    b. Spokesperson for a line of affordable yet stylish clothes. You decide if they are men's or women's clothes. Find a spokesperson who reflects common sense and value.
    c. A tough-minded woman who tells listeners it's all right to take cold medicine whenever they need it. The theory is that many women "tough out" colds because they feel it's wasteful to spend money on remedies for symptoms. Find a convincing person to counter that idea.
    d. Spokesperson for a line of very expensive ice cream. He or she must express the idea that quality is worth paying for.
    e. Spokesperson pitching a magazine subscription for a highbrow periodical that analyzes current events. The goal is to convince *average* people that they should take a stronger interest in world affairs and become expert through this magazine.

3. If a portable tape recorder and microphone are available, make a collection of at least five different sound colorations. Read fifteen seconds of copy (the choice of copy is unimportant) in various locations, seeking to get as wide a divergence as possible. For starters, you might try recording in a locker room, then in an open field.

   During a class discussion, compare and contrast the sound colorations. Also, try to imagine situations in which the particular coloration would be useful. (Actually, the most enjoyable part of this exercise is playing the recordings to the class and having classmates attempt to guess where the recordings were made.)

NOTES

1. For detailed information, see Lewis O'Donnell, Philip Benoit, and Carl Hausman, *Modern Radio Production* (Belmont, CA: Wadsworth, 1986); and Stanley Alten, *Audio in Media,* 2d ed. (Belmont, CA: Wadsworth, 1986).

Modern Radio Production specifically addresses techniques used in radio; *Audio in Media* presents a wider array of applications for audio equipment and goes into greater technical depth.

(A note on the sequence of this chapter: If you are reading selected chapters of this book and did not read Chapter 5, it would be helpful to read Sections 5.1 and 5.2 at this time. This chapter is structured to stand alone, but reading Sections 5.1 and 5.2 will provide greater depth of understanding.)

2. Earl R. Hitchinson, Jr. (ed.), *Writing for Mass Communication* (New York: Longman, 1986), 396. This citation is within a chapter written by Robert L. Bishop, a section that provides a good summary of the thrust of advertising copy.

3. Alec Nisbett, *The Technique of the Sound Studio*, 4th ed., (New York: Focal/ Hastings House, 1979), 271.

4. Several years ago, the conventional wisdom held that humor was not a good advertising tool, but the phenomenal success of humorous radio commercials by such creative teams as Dick and Bert and Bob and Ray seemed to have disproved that theory. Today, the consensus seems to be that humorous commercials can do just as well as serious commercials, tending to invoke a good level of attention and a moderate level of recall, a finding supported by Calvin P. Duncan, and James E. Nelson, "Effects of Humor in a Radio Advertising Experiment," *Journal of Advertising* 14, no. 2 (1985): 33–40, 64.

5. Many similar recommendations can be found in Michael C. Keith, *Production in Format Radio Handbook* (Lanham, MD: University Press of America, 1984). This book analyzes ten of the most widely employed formats from a production perspective.

CHAPTER 7

MARKET ANALYSIS

AND DEVELOPMENT

Radio stations simply cannot and do not exist in a vacuum. They draw their lifeblood from the market in which they operate. What are the characteristics of a radio market? How does money flow from advertisers in a market? How can a station estimate and expand its base of listeners and its income base within a market?

Those types of questions can only be addressed by a manager who is very well-versed in the population and economic characteristics of the community. Only such knowledge can enable a station to thrive within its market base and expand that base.

This chapter does not focus on measurement of the audience as such; the process of counting and determining constituencies of the audience is discussed in the Chapter 8. Here, we examine ways in which audiences and advertisers relate with the various media competing for attention and advertising. We also deal with the intramarket impact of competing advertising media.

The market—the overall universe from which a medium draws its income—is not entirely a fixed entity. Within limits, it can be broadened, honed, and tailored to fit specific goals. Not only can the radio station sales executive *find* customers but also can *create* customers by making a segment of the community more aware of radio and of one station in particular. Such an effort can be targeted at potential advertising customers or potential listeners. Either way, it constitutes development of a market through promotion, a topic addressed later in this chapter.

7.1

ASSESSING AUDIENCE POTENTIAL

Audience potential is measured many ways. Basic tools in this analysis are general-population data, available through numerous government and community sources and private reports. Most of the material that deals with advertising and advertising research is tied into audience measurement, addressed fully in Chapter 8. Assessing the *potential*, as opposed to measuring current listenership, is a far less precise endeavor than the polling of audiences and the manipulation of sales figures. Many experienced sales and management executives often say they rely on a "seat-of-the-pants" feel for the market.

What those executives actually do is probably more "scientific" than they might at first believe. They keep an ear tuned to sources of information about the market, mentally filing their conversations with bankers and businesspeople. They are sensitive to any conditions that will affect the population base, such as a new industry moving into the region. Is there general economic development in the area? What about changes in the age of the population? These are the types of questions answered formally or informally by an executive's research.

Availability of Potential Listeners

Understanding the market is therefore more than a matter of figures. In terms of pure numbers of available listeners, for instance, the actual computation is simple. Census data—available from the local library, local government offices, or U.S. Representatives' local headquarters—show how many pairs of ears are within the station's signal range. Raw numbers, however, are of little intrinsic value without additional information to change the figures from *quantitative* to *qualitative* data.

An alert radio manager might change purely quantitative data into qualitative data by asking the following questions:

1. *What is the relative age of listeners?* Most radio advertisers would assert that the best possible audience is an audience with a high percentage of members in the desirable demographic range of ages eighteen to thirty-four. Some standardized thinking has held that older audiences are poor buying audiences, but that perception is changing. A seat-of-the-pants indication of this fact is the increase in all forms of advertising aimed toward older consumers; in general, it is safe to assume that major advertisers would not be placing such ads if they (the advertisers) did not perceive an audience. On a more scientific level, examination of any relevant body of sociologic data leaves no doubt as to the emerging "gray market" and its buying power. However, there is no denying that a healthy eighteen- to thirty-four-year-old demographic is an attraction to both the radio station seeking listeners and the advertiser "buying an audience" from the station. Relative age is one of the factors, but certainly not the only factor, in producing "quality numbers" for an advertiser. Other questions, such as the ones that follow, must also be posed.

2. *What is the relative affluence of the listeners?* Starting points in this determination include information on distribution of white collar versus blue collar, the number of families with two incomes, the quality of industry that supplies payroll dollars (note the difference between a high-tech firm employing many engineers and a service-based industry such as a hotel or fast-food chain paying many employees close to minimum wage). Looking beyond the numbers, a savvy radio executive can examine spending patterns, shopping habits, and banking habits. Local financial institutions can provide a wealth of information in this area.

Why bother assessing the relative affluence? For one thing, understanding the situation allows the station to intelligently adapt its promotions, sales, and marketing plans. A depressed market does not necessarily preclude the success of a radio station. Low-income listeners still buy groceries. It is certainly difficult to convince national buyers to purchase time in depressed markets, but not always. The argument posed by one sales manager for a station in a relatively poor area is that "everybody wears shoes." Even the poorest market must support some commerce.

3. *What are the characteristic life-style habits of the audience?* Is there a heavy empha-
    sis on outdoor activity? What other leisure activities are popular? From a more
    directly marketable perspective, do a great many people drive to work un-
    usually early in the morning? Although this may seem obvious, more than one
    station has been guilty of not precisely defining the local drive time. In some
    markets, such as one with a giant industrial plant where the first shift starts at
    6 AM, the drive time can actually begin at 4:30 in the morning.
        Other sleeping profits can be realized by an examination of life-style.
    One highly successful medium-market station in central New York, for ex-
    ample, was able to turn the traditionally lackluster hours of 4 to 6 AM into a
    profitable period by doing what no one else in the market did: appealing to a
    very large rural community encircling the city. One facet of this plan, which
    certainly could not have escaped the attention of station personnel, was the
    growing trend of area dairy farms to become modern, automated, and quite
    large. What a natural audience to "sell" to producers of fertilizers, feeds, and
    heavy equipment!

These examples and hundreds of similar cases point to the extremely important
precept that in today's supersegmented radio audience it is not always so important to
deliver a particularly large or affluent audience as it is to deliver a *well-defined* audience. A salesperson who can make a convincing case to potential buyers (local, regional, or national) that his or her station reaches a disproportionate number of rural
males can make a superbly persuasive presentation to the advertising manager pushing
a line of pickup trucks. Sales managers often point out that when examining audience
type and rating numbers, it is important to ask, "Is it more important to count the
people you reach or reach the people who count?"

Distribution of Potential Listeners

The term *distribution,* for the purposes of this discussion, does not apply to the geographic distribution of listeners but to their pattern of media use. Intrinsically linked
to the distribution factor is the problem of translating those potential listeners into
advertising dollars. Remember, we're discussing methods of assessing *potential, underde-
veloped* audiences and advertisers. Again, ratings are used to measure current audiences.
    In determining potential listenership and to some extent the potential number
of advertising dollars (specifically addressed in the following section), radio executives
typically take a number of factors into account.

RADIO VERSUS OTHER MEDIA   Can listeners be wooed from other media? Most research shows the patterns of media use across different media are firmly established. It is a difficult chore to attempt to swing a certain number of people from one medium to another or to take away a certain period of time spent on one medium activity and swing it to a different medium. Although immediate effects are difficult or impossible to bring about or measure, an overview of media-use patterns among consumers (listeners, viewers, readers, and so on) shows that newspaper circulations have been relatively stagnant in recent years, particularly among younger age groups. Some researchers theorize that there is less opportunity in active life-styles for newspaper reading. Regardless of the cause, it is interesting to observe that people are spending ever-increasing amounts of time commuting in cars today. The modern life-style would seem, then, to be a plus for radio.

Although statistical interpretation is quite variable in terms of the average hours of media use, most reliable figures show a rising amount of radio listenership. Some estimates place the amount of time an average American listens to radio at three-and-one-half hours a day.[1] This is a seemingly astoundingly high figure until you calculate all the radios in your house and cars and add up the time you spend listening to the clock radio in the morning, the car radio during the ride to work or school, the portable radio at the beach, the easy-listening music in the office or in elevators, and so forth.

In terms of the distribution of potential listeners in any market, it is important for a manager to realize that the majority of people everywhere in the nation are reached by radio in one way or another. Some estimates put the number of people who listen to radio at some point each day at 80.7 percent of the population of Americans age twelve and over. Over a weekly basis, the figure rises to 95 percent.[2] In this respect radio outpolls all other media including television.

Note too that in terms of time spent with the various media, radio leads in several demographic categories including those with $30,000+ annual incomes, college graduates, and women who work full time outside of the home.[3]

THE DISTRIBUTION OF POTENTIAL LISTENERS OVER DAYPARTS   Daypart assessment is another consideration in sizing up the market. (The specifics and mechanics of daypart segmentation were covered in Chapter 3.) From the standpoint of assessing audience potential, it is worth noting that a station has the opportunity to position itself using *daypart strategy*, meaning that a station can take advantage of a daypart distribution among listeners in the local market. In many major urban areas, for example, there is a sizable number of listeners during the overnight period, a daypart virtually ignored by programmers until recently. An insightful radio station manager takes such distributional patterns into account when assessing audience potential. If there is a constituency not being serviced, the analyst can recruit a profitable audience and deliver it to an advertiser. (Remember the example of the medium-market station appealing to farmers in the outlying areas of the region.)

THE DISTRIBUTION OF POTENTIAL LISTENERS BY FORMAT Radio stations live and die by the selection of programming, and such selection is, or should be, a result of careful evaluation of audience potential. In rural areas, for example, a considerably larger *percentage* of the audience would probably listen to country music than would an audience in an urban area.

But who, exactly, is out there? How much money do they have to spend? Can they be "packaged" and sold to an advertiser? Are there local advertisers who *want* this type of audience delivered? These are the kinds of questions that can be answered only after examining the market and matching market potential with particular formats.

Such strategy boils down to finding a niche and filling it. That strategy seems obvious, but it most certainly is not a cut-and-dried task—a task usually accomplished by finding an unfilled need in the market and filling that need. It has been the experience of many involved in radio that the assessment of potential is a delicate matter requiring considerable judgment and intimate knowledge of the community and raw data. Country music stations have done quite well in highly urbanized markets, to the surprise of many so-called experts.

DISTRIBUTION BY PSYCHOGRAPHIC CATEGORIES **Psychographics** are often referred to as representations of life-style and mental outlook. Psychographics relate to demographics in that psychographics use demographics (statistical representations of a population) to illustrate life-style factors. In some cases, psychographic categories have been colorfully designated as "minks and station wagons" or "shotguns and pickups."

On a deeper level, psychographics are tools to evaluate attitudes, mental processes, and the patterns of emotional likes and dislikes that motivate a consumer. The psychographic profile of likely buyers certainly would have played a role in the well-known television commercial for Volvos, where, in not-so-subtle terms, it was implied that Volvo owners are just plain smarter than people who drive other types of cars. It is not too difficult to see psychographic research behind recent commercials for pickup trucks that feature a rugged young man defying authority, musing on how he refuses to wear a tie.

Application of this type of information to a radio station is difficult at the smaller levels of the business. Major markets typically have in-house research departments that can use and interpret psychographic data; independent consultants also provide such services. Advertising trade literature, to an extent, deals with psychographics. Recognize, though, that psychographic analysis of a local market can certainly be made through approximations based on experience and judgment.

7.2

ASSESSING ADVERTISING PROFIT POTENTIAL

Up to this point, we primarily have been evaluating audience potential. A discussion of potential advertisers to buy that audience logically builds on the same foundation.

The first factor in a general assessment of the current state of advertising is to look at the overall picture. To begin with, why is advertising profit *potential* assessed in the first place? In some cases, an assessment may be undertaken in a situation where an ownership group or prospective station buyer is contemplating a move into the community. In such an instance, a full assessment of availability and distribution of advertiser dollars is crucial. Stations currently in operation must assess or reassess the situation from time to time. It is not uncommon for a smaller station to be limping along far below potential simply because no calculated effort was made to determine what kind of money was available for advertising and who had it to spend. The industry is rife with horror stories of situations where station managers and salespeople, for reasons unknown, virtually ignore the local retail market and focus on national sales. This certainly is not a reasonable method of operation unless there is a valid reason to believe that local retail business is not worth the effort (which may indeed be the case with very large, major market stations, but not always).

Sometimes categories of advertising revenue are underexploited. A frequently cited example of the problem is a sales operation that does not take advantage of cooperative-advertising money, an arrangement where a national manufacturer or distributor contributes to a local distributor's ad budget. This is a source of revenue that goes back into the advertiser's corporate till until a radio station makes an effort to obtain a share of it.

Availability of Advertiser Dollars

As is addressed more fully in appropriate sections of this book, there are a variety of channels of advertising revenue. They are summarized as follows:

—   *National.* National sales involve ads placed on behalf of products and services sold on a nationwide basis. The national advertiser secures spots on local stations through national sales representatives who typically do business in New York, Los Angeles, Chicago, or other major markets.

—— *Agency.* Ad agencies, which develop campaigns using all types of media, place ads on behalf of clients. While many of these agency buys may be on a national level, many are local and regional in scope.

—— *Local* (also known as retail). Local sales come from businesses located within the community, the confines of the coverage area. In a small market, the bulk of revenue comes from local sales. In medium and larger markets, local sales play a smaller role with the proportion of national and agency ads usually increasing in proportion with the market size.

Management in a given market must be fully aware of the potential of advertising dollars available from these categories and, perhaps more importantly, how the people who control these dollars distribute them.

Generally, retailers and other advertisers allocate dollars on the basis of sales revenues. Department stores, auto dealers, and furniture stores have industry guidelines that suggest a set percentage of revenues to be allotted to advertising. From this allocation, in-house ad managers or agency representatives decide how much goes to radio, how much goes to television, and how much to newspapers and other media. On a nationwide basis, radio gets about 7 percent of all advertising budgets; radio's share usually grows in smaller markets because television is less of a competitor.

Of a station's advertising revenue, 25 to 30 percent typically comes from national sources. (This can increase as the market size grows, but the total rarely tops 50 percent.) Most national ads are placed through national rep firms, some from ad agencies, and a small amount of advertising revenue is generated by compensation paid to affiliates from networks. It is important to note, however, that network revenue can carry a considerable price in support time and costs. Stations that insert local spots in network newscasts or choose not to run network news and play the network commercials that accompanied the newscast at another time (to fulfill contract obligations) must invest significant employee time in related traffic and production duties.

A manager looking for information on the amount of advertiser dollars available in the community can start with a publication called *Spot Radio Rates and Data,* a publication of the *Standard Rates and Data Service;* such a report lists household expenditures (Figure 7.1). *Standard Rates and Data Service* also publishes catalogs that are used to provide advertisers and agencies with information for planning and buying time and space on various media.

Another productive way to gather information on spot radio activity is the *Radio Expenditure Report, Inc. (RER),* a publication that reports on activities in more than 210 markets. (Figure 7.2). The results are projected to apply to all markets. *RER* undertakes individual market analyses on a contract basis.

There are many other sources of information available through libraries, such as

Figure 7.1

A sample page from *Standard Rates and Data Service* (SRDS).
Statistics published by Standard Rates and Data Service, Inc., *Spot Radio Rates and Data*, November 1987, as provided by National Decision Systems in Encinitas, CA.

PENNSYLVANIA — State, County, City, Metro Area Data

CITIES AND COUNTIES — This list shows counties in which cities are located. Cities are first, counties next.

Metro area / county designations:
Allentown—Lehigh · Altoona—Blair · Bethlehem—Northampton · Carlisle—Cumberland · Chester—Delaware · Erie—Erie · Harrisburg—Dauphin · Johnstown—Cambria · Lancaster—Lancaster · Lebanon—Lebanon · Philadelphia—Philadelphia · Pittsburgh—Allegheny · Reading—Berks · Scranton—Lackawanna · Sharon—Mercer · State College—Centre · Wilkes Barre—Luzerne · Williamsport—Lycoming · York—York

STATE / COUNTY—Map Loc. / City / Metropolitan Area	Population 4/1/87 (000)	Households 4/1/87 (000)	Gross HH Income 1986 ($000)	Per Household ($)	% Dist 0–14999	% Dist 15000–34999	% Dist 35000–49999	% Dist 50000+	Total HH Expend ($000)	Per Household ($)	Food ($000)	Drug ($000)	General Mdse ($000)	Apparel ($000)	Home Furn ($000)	Auto motive ($000)	Service Station ($000)	Passenger Cars 4/1/87 (000)	Black Pop 4/1/87 (000)	Spanish Pop 4/1/87 (000)
PENNSYLVANIA STATE TOTALS	11,891.5	4,439.31	131,741,839	29,676	31.2	38.1	16.1	14.6	68,538,079	15,439	14,823,695	2,311,244	9,895,678	3,273,698	3,547,399	11,638,017	6,057,782	6,415.22	1,020.2	154.38
ADAMS E-6	70.3	24.76	712,775	28,787	26.0	43.9	17.9	12.1	385,704	15,578	83,227	12,934	55,439	18,469	20,094	65,529	34,060	44.41	.7	.63
ALLEGHENY B-5	1,368.8	540.97	17,073,700	31,561	27.9	36.4	17.7	18.1	8,513,070	15,737	1,832,020	283,603	1,217,270	408,798	446,843	1,447,210	750,986	687.80	141.8	7.72
Pittsburgh	386.2	160.73	4,138,260	25,747	29.2	37.9	17.1	15.7	2,314,680	14,401	509,771	81,500	345,961	108,406	113,526	391,393	206,019	143.78	92.7	2.91
Pittsburgh Metro Area	2,120.6	821.44	24,570,900	29,912					12,738,300	15,507	2,751,760	428,314	1,834,920	609,222	661,545	2,163,610	1,125,360	1,114.56	162.7	10.89
Pittsburgh-Beaver Valley Consolidated Area	2,312.8	892.40	26,390,800	29,573	29.3	38.5	16.9	15.2	13,812,100	15,477	2,985,250	464,985	1,991,530	660,223	716,297	2,345,720	1,220,460	1,226.41	173.4	11.92
ARMSTRONG B-4	79.4	30.07	735,680	24,446	34.8	42.9	14.6	7.7	436,872	14,529	96,030	15,313	65,060	20,504	21,572	73,904	38,855	46.45	.7	.21
BEAVER A-5	192.2	70.96	1,819,890	25,647	30.6	45.0	15.2	9.1	1,073,800	15,132	233,470	36,672	156,612	51,001	54,752	182,114	95,100	111.57	10.7	1.03
Beaver County Metro Area	192.2	70.96	1,819,890	25,647	30.6	45.0	15.2	9.1	1,073,800	15,132	233,470	36,672	156,612	51,001	54,752	182,114	95,100	111.57	10.7	1.03
BEDFORD D-6	48.2	17.49	371,732	21,254	41.6	43.7	9.4	5.3	234,968	13,434	52,790	8,666	36,460	10,759	10,832	39,543	21,077	30.42	.1	.16
BERKS G-5	321.7	123.03	3,776,440	30,695	26.1	38.2	19.5	16.2	1,950,830	15,857	419,058	64,703	277,965	93,859	102,912	331,777	171,975	191.42	8.0	9.28
Reading	78.3	33.32	773,235	23,206	35.0	43.4	14.2	7.4	469,879	14,102	104,129	16,788	71,061	21,854	22,632	79,336	41,923	32.50	6.2	7.68
Reading Metro Area	321.7	123.03	3,776,440	30,695	26.1	38.2	19.5	16.2	1,950,830	15,857	419,058	64,703	277,965	93,859	102,912	331,777	171,975	191.42	8.0	9.28
BLAIR D-5	131.6	49.38	1,202,350	24,349	35.0	43.4	14.2	7.4	712,417	14,427	156,892	25,082	106,472	33,367	34,979	120,465	63,408	74.39	.9	.39
Altoona	52.5	20.39	475,096	23,300	35.0	43.4	14.6	7.4	288,786	14,163	63,225	10,291	43,581	13,448	13,958	48,772	25,754	26.21	.9	.15
Altoona Metro Area	131.6	49.38	1,202,350	24,349	35.0	43.4	14.2	7.4	712,417	14,427	156,892	25,082	106,472	33,367	34,979	120,465	63,408	74.39	.9	.39
BRADFORD F-3	63.9	23.03	557,343	24,201	34.4	43.4	14.2	8.1	332,061	14,419	73,136	11,694	49,638	15,550	16,298	56,148	29,556	36.69	.1	.23
BUCKS H-5	525.2	181.83	7,125,310	39,187	15.9	31.8	22.8	29.5	3,174,620	17,459	666,015	99,292	431,847	156,491	178,214	542,778	277,359	331.55	13.1	6.23
BUTLER B-5	152.0	53.51	1,488,830	27,823	27.4	43.5	17.5	11.6	826,656	15,449	178,764	27,866	119,318	39,492	42,805	140,374	73,060	90.35	.8	.52
CAMBRIA C-5	173.1	62.88	1,405,070	22,345	39.3	44.3	10.5	6.0	875,031	13,916	194,633	31,534	133,258	40,528	41,661	147,613	78,184	90.49	3.2	.90
Johnstown	31.6	13.45	244,724	18,195					173,929	12,932	39,514	6,579	27,551	7,861	7,723	29,192	15,670	13.38	2.4	.32
Johnstown Metro Area	254.6	92.69	2,049,920	22,116	39.6	44.5	10.1	5.8	1,282,870	13,840	285,789	46,397	195,935	59,314	60,782	216,334	114,693	138.16	3.3	1.14
CAMERON D-3	6.6	2.67	52,888	19,808	43.1	43.5	10.1	3.3	35,300	13,221	7,968	1,316	5,726	1,607	1,602	5,934	3,172	4.02	—	.02
CARBON G-4	54.3	20.84	496,858	23,842	34.8	45.0	12.9	7.3	298,363	14,317	65,843	10,556	44,767	13,942	14,557	50,426	26,577	31.35	.1	.34
CENTRE D-4	113.3	38.32	1,023,960	26,721	33.1	39.3	14.7	12.9	569,407	14,859	124,403	19,672	83,820	26,903	28,628	96,462	50,523	60.21	1.5	.83
State College	34.4	9.69	214,891	22,177					128,866	13,299	29,033	4,783	20,101	5,881	5,886	21,672	11,572	11.30	.8	.43
State College Metro Area	113.3	38.32	1,023,960	26,721	33.1	39.3	14.7	12.9	569,407	14,859	124,403	19,672	83,820	26,903	28,628	96,462	50,523	60.21	1.5	.83
CHESTER G-6	341.5	119.61	4,893,530	40,912	16.5	31.6	20.3	31.6	2,068,850	17,297	434,997	65,071	282,670	101,755	115,489	353,547	180,902	212.19	24.9	6.19
CLARION C-4	44.3	14.43	325,042	22,525	39.0	42.4	12.4	6.2	203,547	14,106	45,100	7,269	30,773	9,469	9,809	34,369	18,159	23.54	.2	.16
CLEARFIELD D-5	83.1	30.10	699,480	23,239	37.3	44.0	12.4	6.3	423,274	14,062	93,864	15,147	64,094	19,671	20,345	71,456	37,775	47.36	.2	.22
CLINTON F-4	37.3	13.54	294,460	21,747	38.0	47.5	9.5	4.9	185,594	13,705	41,462	6,756	28,496	8,553	8,715	31,276	16,483	21.36	.1	.13
COLUMBIA F-4	61.0	22.23	543,315	24,441	33.5	45.0	13.3	8.1	319,951	14,393	70,500	11,279	47,868	14,976	15,683	57,233	26,483	36.75	.2	.20
CRAWFORD B-3	89.3	32.50	760,226	23,392	36.9	45.0	12.0	6.6	457,480	14,076	101,433	16,364	69,252	21,205	22,600	77,233	40,825	49.32	.6	.33
CUMBERLAND E-6	192.4	71.89	2,482,830	34,537	19.1	38.4	21.2	21.3	1,198,380	16,670	254,227	38,542	166,938	58,105	65,374	204,384	105,141	123.65	2.6	.93
Carlisle	20.4	8.24	257,193	31,213					127,417	15,463	27,543	4,291	18,378	6,090	6,605	21,639	11,260	11.12	1.1	.22

County and City Data Book, Editor and Publisher Market Guide, and *State and Metropolitan Area Data Book.* Informal sources include local chambers of commerce and local advertising agency representatives. In some cases, the local sales tax department can provide estimates of local taxes paid per category of retail sales.

Distribution of Advertiser Dollars

Once an approximation has been made regarding how much money is available within the market, the next logical step is to estimate *where* local money is spent by consumers and, as a direct and indirect result, *how* that money is distributed among the sources of advertising revenue.

Foremost in the mind of a radio manager is how radio fares in comparison to the other advertising outlets in the market. The position of a particular station, as mentioned previously, varies considerably according to the configuration of media in the market. In towns and cities where there is intense competition among newspaper, radio, and television, radio stations may face a difficult job in gaining a substantial share of advertising money because much money may be diverted to other media.

And, of course, the situation differs among variously sized markets. On a nationwide basis, magazines garner 8 percent of all advertising dollars, but in small localities magazine-advertising revenue probably approaches 0 percent. Television, on average, wins about 20 to 25 percent of advertiser dollars, but the same small-market caution applies. All this is a way of prefacing the idea that the oft-quoted statement that radio gets 7 percent of all advertising dollars reflects an *average* and does not apply in every case. Because radio is a very efficient local advertising outlet and offers flexibility at a modest price, it usually does quite well in smaller communities.

Two factors apply to strategies used to gain the biggest possible slice of that advertising pie. First, it is usually difficult to take advertising away from television or newspapers. However, radio can boast a lower cost-per-person reached than most other media, as detailed in Chapters 8 and 9. Other radio stations present easier targets. Second, some products on the local level are poorly suited for radio and probably cannot improve the sales effort. Grocery stores, for example, usually favor newspaper advertising because of newspaper's ability to run long lists of specials and print coupons. Chances of the local radio station diverting much of the grocery store's advertising budget from newspapers are slim, although many such retailers do supplement their newspaper advertising with radio. In contrast, clubs offering live rock groups are ideal radio candidates. A commercial using audio from the group, run on the local rock station, would be far more efficient than an ad in the daily newspaper.

ALL ADVERTISERS REPORT

(INDEX BY PRODUCT NAME)

PRODUCT / BRAND	PARENT	CATEGORY	PAGE
SEA-LAND TRANSPORT	SEA-LAND TRANSPORT	7409	151
SEABOARD SEED CO.	SEABOARD SEED CO.	5600	117
SEAFIRST CORP.	SEAFIRST CORP.	2601	47
SEAFOOD BROILER RESTAURANT	SEAFOOD BROILER RE	3608	90
SEAFOOD SHANTY	SEAFOOD SHANTY	3608	90
SEAGRAMS GOLDEN WINE COOLER	SEAGRAMS BRANDS	1207	30
SEAGRAMS GOLDEN WINE COOLER-SP	SEAGRAMS BRANDS	1207	30
SEAGRAMS MIXERS	SEAGRAMS BRANDS	7004	137
SEAGRAMS WINE COOLERS	SEAGRAMS BRANDS	1207	30
SEALTEST ICE CREAM	DART & KRAFT, INC.	3603	76
SEALY MATTRESS	SEALY, INC.	4600	107
SEARS	SEARS ROEBUCK	6805	133
SEARS AIR CONDITIONING	SEARS ROEBUCK	4600	107
SEARS APPAREL	SEARS ROEBUCK	0402	9
SEARS AUTOMOTIVE	SEARS ROEBUCK	1001	16
SEARS BABY DAYS	SEARS ROEBUCK	0402	9
SEARS BUSINESS SYSTEMS CENTER	SEARS ROEBUCK	2004	41
SEARS CARPETS	SEARS ROEBUCK	4600	107
SEARS CATALOGUE	SEARS ROEBUCK	6803	132
SEARS DEPARTMENT STORES	SEARS ROEBUCK	6805	133
SEARS DISCOVER CARD	SEARS ROEBUCK	2602	52
SEARS ELECTRONICS	SEARS ROEBUCK	6400	128
SEARS FLOOR CARE	SEARS ROEBUCK	4600	107
SEARS FURNITURE	SEARS ROEBUCK	4600	107
SEARS HEATING	SEARS ROEBUCK	4600	107
SEARS HOME APPLIANCES	SEARS ROEBUCK	4600	107
SEARS HUMIDIFIERS & WATER HEAT	SEARS ROEBUCK	4600	107
SEARS LAWN & GARDEN	SEARS ROEBUCK	0205	6
SEARS MENSWEAR	SEARS ROEBUCK	0402	9
SEARS NATIONAL HARDWARE	SEARS ROEBUCK	1400	32
SEARS PAINT SALE	SEARS ROEBUCK	1400	32
SEARS PHOTO	SEARS ROEBUCK	5200	115
SEARS RECORDS & TAPES	SEARS ROEBUCK	6400	128
SEARS RECREATION & LEISURE	SEARS ROEBUCK	7200	141
SEARS SAVINGS BANK	SEARS ROEBUCK	2601	47
SEARS SHOES	SEARS ROEBUCK	0408	, 13
SEARS WHITE SALE	SEARS ROEBUCK	4600	107
SEARS WINDOW AIR CONDITIONER	SEARS ROEBUCK	4600	107
SEARS-BLACK	SEARS ROEBUCK	6805	133
SEARS-SPANISH	SEARS ROEBUCK	6805	133
SEATTLE BLUES	GENAUER, M. & CO.	0402	9
SEAWORLD, INC.	SEAWORLD, INC.	7404	145
SEC CHEM	SEC CHEM	0203	1
SECRETS OF MONEY	SECRETS OF MONEY	6007	123
SECURITY CHEMICALS	SECURITY CHEMICALS	0203	1
SECURITY PACIFIC NATL. BANK	SECURITY PACIFIC N	2601	47
SECURITY SAVINGS & LOAN	SECURITY SAVINGS &	2601	47
SEES CANDY	SEES CANDY	2200	43

FIRST QTR	SECOND QTR	THIRD QTR	FOURTH QTR	YTD
9,360	8,733			18,093
21,066				21,066
5,625	10,293	14,701	36,543	67,162
48,304	51,611	218		100,133
9,678				9,678
		1,273		1,273
		6,265	12,327	18,592
6,568	59,010			65,578
147,570	7,441	18,470	8,424	181,905
272,055	518,602	483,475	14,210	1,288,342
			7,123	7,123
108,119	252,321	228,748	291,753	880,941
	11,950	21,051		33,001
10,823	717,623	434,515	130,837	1,293,798
678,059	708,497		62,932	1,449,488
		41,240		41,240
495,415	454,104	624	4,299	954,442
16	3,351			3,367
1,123	6,084		1,810	9,017
1,052,264	2,136,078	2,420,551	3,430,340	9,039,233
		271,733	13,311	285,044
3,370			276,114	279,484
	51,599			51,599
69,890	90,982	93,762	3,273	257,907
		10,109		10,109
109,225	110,284	896,488	416,077	1,532,074
300,155	180,946	140,275	190,376	811,752
	133,354			133,354
			100,622	100,622
71,950	7,886	36,779	46,466	163,081
	431,800	403,213		835,013
	2,839			2,839
	3,201			3,201
		111,039		111,039
3,810	10,048	1,379	79,086	94,323
		32,225	75,311	107,536
39,335	91,338	75,169	127,159	333,001
	3,976			3,976
12,199	13,588	15,694	13,588	55,069
72,437	68,398	88,006	127,761	356,602
6,240	14,845	35,446	18,619	75,150
92,715	346,722	199,061	16,661	655,159
	390			390
		3,276		3,276
260	1,430			1,690
2,644	686,274	388,163	252,266	1,329,347
			11,029	11,029
218,423	223,727	240,460	293,647	976,257

Competition among advertising media for the available advertiser dollars has never been more intense, and from all indications severe competition will become a permanent factor in radio management and operations. This situation is forcing radio executives to *create* opportunities to sell advertising. Such alternatives are fostered by the realization that advertising budgets of local retailers are limited, but the budgets of national advertisers are extensive. The most familiar reflection of this situation is **cooperative advertising,** usually called co-op in radio verbal shorthand.

Cooperative Advertising

Co-op is a joint arrangement between a retailer and the producer of a national product that is sold in the retailer's store. Shoe manufacturers, for example, typically pay a percentage of the advertising costs. The exact percentage is variable, usually being pegged to vendor sales. In other words, a co-op arrangement might involve a shoe manufacturer placing a limit on the top-dollar amount paid; that limit is often 10 percent of sales of the product by the retailer. At one time co-op was exclusive to newspapers, but the practice has been extended to broadcasting with great success.[4] Incidentally, co-op is an excellent way to persuade a reluctant advertiser to go on the air and is a fine method for a national product to gain exposure at a local advertising rate. (Chapter 9 covers co-op from the sales perspective and offers a more thorough evaluation.)

A new variation on this theme, recently expanded by enterprising radio sales executives, is known as **vendor planning.** A particular radio station may tie together a campaign for a retailer and then approach several vendors who supply products to the retailer. One recent and highly successful such effort involved a station in a major market that put together a vendor plan based on a Superbowl promotion for a convenience store. The package involved features on the upcoming game sponsored by the convenience store and included some promotional items distributed in the store. Vendors who wholesaled the products sold in the store—soft drinks, potato chips, and other such items—financed a good portion of the campaign.

Such creative plans can work well for everyone. The store in question achieved a 16-percent increase in sales over the month-long campaign, and that retailer paid much less than if he had financed the whole plan without the aid of vendors' contributions. The manufacturers of the particular brands of potato chips and softs drinks profited, too, and found a viable outlet for funds in their discretionary advertising budgets, budgets over which in-house agencies and media buyers have great latitude in the amount and type of spending. Indeed, it is those discretionary funds that the inventive radio executive must target; some estimates place the amount of discretionary advertising funds that go unspent as high as $2.5 billion.

Impact of Competition

Some interesting aspects of competition for advertising dollars are uncovered in an examination of advertising buys at the national level. Radio stations find that their inclusion in package media buys (an overall advertising program designed by an agency, with various advertising outlets specified) is increasingly critical in economic survival. But radio has an inherent disadvantage in the media buy because inexperienced buyers simply do not recognize its strengths. Unknowledgeable buyers frequently leave radio out of a media plan or underutilize it because they regard it as an inferior medium—"television without pictures."

Another reason why advertising agency media buyers sometimes give radio short shrift is that there are so many radio stations that they simply choose to avoid the complexities of choosing radio outlets.

The radio industry seeks to deal with the first problem—the supposed inferiority of the medium—with vigorous self-promotion. Spots from the Radio Advertising Bureau, for instance, have featured comic routines that prod television for its high production costs and newspapers for their "clutter" or "bottom-of-the-bird-cage" uses. Such efforts also pertain to the local level, and sales forces are commonly armed with material highlighting radio's strengths, including the relative inexpensiveness of both production and ad placement, the flexibility in scheduling, and the ability to target highly specialized audiences.

Radio stations try to overcome the glut of radio competitors by narrowly defining their audience—targeting a precise demographic population to demonstrate that the station is a particularly good buy for a certain advertiser. And, indeed, radio can reach specific groups of buyers with precision; this, too, is touted as a strength of radio versus other media.

In fact, even radio's most bitter rivals have realized the medium's unique strengths. Newspapers, for example, frequently promote themselves on radio. David Andree, marketing services manager for the San Francisco Newspaper Agency, points to the cost effectiveness of radio: "High-quality radio spots can be produced for $3000 and be competitive with the Procter & Gambles of the world. . . . This is usually within the range of any newspaper promotion budget . . . and the quality of the commercial is important because it is rapidly associated with the quality of the product."[5]

7.3

DEVELOPING A MARKET THROUGH PROMOTION AND COMMUNITY RELATIONS

Promotion is usually thought of as a method of gaining public notice for a station. Although that assumption is correct as far as it goes, public exposure is not the entire goal of a promotion effort. In today's supersegmented radio market, promotion is strongly geared toward **positioning,** the creation and refinement of an image. Positioning also implies fitting the station into a market niche, an appropriate and profitable position in light of the competition.

Positioning is a commonly used term and is, in fact, something of a modern buzzword with a relatively imprecise definition. Probably the most important and immediate definition of positioning is the effort to form an identifiable image in the mind of the listener and to use that image to distinguish a station from competitors. Positioning also implies relating the image of station content to the name of the station. For example, stations sometimes find their call letters have little meaning to listeners and adopt an informal call such as EASY-97 or 14-Q to spur listener identification.

Gaining recognition for the station and securing its proper image and position are critical for what radio executives often term "both groups of consumers—the listeners and the advertisers." *Audience promotion* is what most of us are familiar with: contests, personal appearances, and other such methods to hike visibility among listeners. Audience promotion may be an on-air or off-air effort and is usually a combination of both. The other aspect of promotion is *sales promotion,* an effort aimed primarily at local retailers.

Audience Promotion

Audience promotion not only seeks to increase the number of individuals listening at any time but also has a goal to bring new listeners into the fold. A particular application of this strategy involves recruiting new listeners at times that will take advantage of the technical quirks in the way ratings are calculated. (See the discussion of cume in Chapter 8.)

Promotions used to be concentrated in one or two time periods during the year. Today, they are typically an ongoing affair. Another modern aspect of promotions is the inventiveness of the particular strategies. Simple giveaways are passé. Today, some typical promotions involve

—— A trip to the hairdresser and a night on the town.

—— Playing three songs in a row from a particular artist and selling the sweep to a sponsor.

—— A year's worth of child day care.

—— A "wheel of fortune" promotion where products are read off and the listeners stop the "wheel" and win the next product to be named from the list.

Promotion is a sophisticated business, and many resources are available to practitioners. The Broadcast Promotion Association is one organization that provides ideas and support to promotion directors.

Some promotions have become extremely extravagant. A Cincinnati radio station once gave away $1 million in one lump sum. WKDD in Akron, Ohio, gave away Porsche automobiles and a $10,000 credit card spree. Some promotions have been extremely successful. WHMD-FM in Hammond, Louisiana, doubled the size of its audience with a "Wheel of Meat" steak giveaway. Some promotions have been extremely bizarre. WWKA-FM in Orlando has attracted listeners by offering tickets to a maggot race.

With modern pressures to generate steady ratings numbers across traditionally slow months, programmers are using promotions heavily during lulls, such as the winter months following the holiday season. In fact, many programmers feel the slow winter months are the right time to ensure a highly rated and profitable spring season, echoing the belief that ratings reflect *past* preferences rather than current preferences.

Promotion can take many forms, and the promotion director at a radio station may have a job involving not only the on-air promotion of the station but also coordinating advertising for the station placed on other media (such as newspapers, television, and billboards), coordinating public service promotions, and producing and writing promotional materials.

In general, a promotion manager is a marketer and is charged with developing a comprehensive marketing plan. Robert A. Klein, president of a Los Angeles communications conceptual firm, states that modern marketing strategies for radio and other media have five major aspects of their design:

1. Building program popularity

2. Generating loyalty that results in extended viewing and listening

3. Appealing to the entire coverage area

4. Identifying the specific television or radio station or cable system with the needs and interests of its community

5.   Developing a competitive position in relation to the growing number of media
      alternatives on the market[6]

In addition, some observers point out that promotions, especially contests, break up
the monotony of today's standardized, clock-run formats.
      Regardless of the particulars and peculiarities, promotion is paramount in mod-
ern radio. Promotion's direct impact as an immediate audience builder is probably less
important than the overall effect of solidifying an image. (Most station executives say
only a small number of listeners actually participate in contests.)
      There is no single formula for audience promotion, but several factors apply to a
wide range of situations. To implement an audience promotion campaign, the following steps should be taken.

      DETERMINE THE APPROPRIATE PROMOTION MIX   On-air promotion, as the
name implies, is done on the air. Off-air promotion is designed to reach potential listeners who aren't aware of your station. Examples of off-air promotion are billboards,
bumper stickers, and newspaper advertising.

      PLAN THE BUDGET   It is often assumed in the industry that a competent pro-
motion can raise ratings by two or more points (ratings are explained in Chapter 8).
Assuming that this can be accomplished, does the projected revenue from two rating
points cover and/or exceed the cost of the promotion?

      CLARIFY GOALS   What do you hope the promotion will accomplish? Some pos-
sible goals are

——   *Improving image.* Many stations run highly general spots that extol the virtues
     of the community and—in a very roundabout way—the worth of the station
     to the community. As stated elsewhere, community relations is very important
     to a radio station.

——   *Audience maintenance.* A station with audience-turnover problems (too many
     listeners tuning out before the next quarter hour) may engage in various pro-
     motions to keep the audience from touching that dial. Such a strategy can be
     as simple as announcing the songs that will play during the next quarter hour.
     Internal promotion is also quite useful for promoting specialized programs or
     services such as an evening sportscast or weather reports offered at regular
     intervals.

——   *Audience building.* This is an external activity designed to attract new listeners.
     Several useful structures and methods are detailed next.

DETERMINE THE STRUCTURE OF THE CAMPAIGN   Weigh the pros and cons of the most popular promotion tactics. Some examples follow. Contests, highly effective, are expensive and involve much staff time and effort. Air people must be adept at handling the contest. A contest must be practical and simple; complex contests fall absolutely flat in radio. Beware of so-called contest pigs—people who obsessively play contests and shut out many casual listeners. (Some contest pigs go so far as to install speed dialers on their telephones so that they have a greater chance of getting through when the air personality runs a call-in contest.)

Bumper stickers are effective, but you do have to go to some effort to get drivers to use them. Some stations have a cruising vehicle that spots cars bearing the station's bumper sticker and awards cash on the spot. Stickers are sometimes distributed along with a sponsor's merchandise.

Billboards (signage) are often very useful because they reach drivers, a large part of any radio station's audience. But billboards must project a very simple image because they're only seen for a second or two. Subway and bus signs are also helpful.

Promotional remotes not only are often part of a direct-sales campaign but also are used strictly for promotion. Remotes combine on-air promotion—bolstering the station's image in the minds of listeners—with off-air promotion—being visible to people attending the event where the remote is located. Promotional remotes often are staged at fairs and public service events. Be aware that remotes take much work and involve frequent technical problems.

Public appearances often are extremely effective and involve minimal expense and personnel commitment. Having the radio morning announcer speak to a Rotary Club luncheon can reach fifty to a hundred people directly and, by extension, members of the listeners' families and acquaintances of the people attending the lunch.

Advertising in other media is effective. Advertising in newspapers often is useful. Television advertising is usually very expensive but can prove profitable if used with expertise. The amount of money spent on television—and promotion in general—is usually worthwhile if there's tight competition among stations. As a general rule of thumb, the more stations in the market, the greater the need for promotion.

Radio stations sometimes plan and stage concerts, fairs, and other events. This requires sophistication and some measure of risk; considerable money can be lost on a failed concert. Also, there is a myriad of forms to be filled out, permits to be obtained, and security details to be attended to when planning an event.

DEFINE CLEARLY THE PROCEDURES AND RULES OF ANY PROMOTION   This is particularly important in contests or in any arrangement where a sponsor buys or barters airtime. Make sure the program director is consulted about promotion procedures because the promotion must not compromise the station sound.

It is essential that contests allow absolutely no opportunity for skullduggery. You

Figure 7.3

The FCC's contest rules.

§ 73.1216   Licensee-conducted contests.

A licensee that broadcasts or advertises information about a contest it conducts shall fully and accurately disclose the material terms of the contest, and shall conduct the contest substantially as announced or advertised. No contest description shall be false, misleading or deceptive with respect to any material term.

NOTE 1: For the purposes of this rule:

(a) A contest is a scheme in which a prize is offered or awarded, based upon chance, diligence, knowledge or skill, to members of the public.

(b) Material terms include those factors which define the operation of the contest and which affect participation therein. Although the material terms may vary widely depending upon the exact nature of the contest, they will generally include: how to enter or participate; eligibility restrictions; entry deadline dates; whether prizes can be won; when prizes can be won; the extent, nature and value of prizes; basis for valuation of prizes; time and means of selection of winners; and/or tie-breaking procedures.

NOTE 2: In general, the time and manner of disclosure of the material terms of a contest are within the licensee's discretion. However, the obligation to disclose the material terms arises at the time the audience is first told how to enter or participate and continues thereafter. The material terms should be disclosed periodically by announcements broadcast on the station conducting the contest, but need not be enumerated each time an announcement promoting the contest is broadcast. Disclosure of material terms in a reasonable number of announcements is sufficient. In addition to the required broadcast announcements, disclosure of the material terms may be made in a non-broadcast manner.

NOTE 3: This rule is not applicable to licensee-conducted contests not broadcast or advertised to the general public or to a substantial segment thereof, to contests in which the general public is not requested or permitted to participate, to the commercial advertisement of non-licensee-conducted contests, or to a contest conducted by a non-broadcast division of the licensee or by a non-broadcast company related to the licensee.

[41 FR 43152, Sept. 30, 1976]

must be specific about the method of entry, how winners are chosen, and the worth of prizes. The FCC clearly spells out the requirements (Figure 7.3).

Sales Promotion

Imaging and positioning play just as significant a role when station sales personnel call on potential advertisers. The stiff competition among advertising media makes a powerful presentation essential. Many of the principles and tools of sales promotion are covered in Chapter 9; here, however, it is useful to briefly discuss that sales promotion takes many forms and some of the modern strategies are intriguingly creative.

The vendor plan discussed earlier is in part a sales promotion. Other ways to work promotions with stores include various merchandising methods such as aisle displays. Such a display may feature a combination advertisement for a soft drink and a radio station. In fact, such merchandising devices are typically an incentive for the advertiser to purchase air time in the first place; merchandising services are an added bonus to the advertisers.

Owners of sponsoring businesses frequently are involved in the promotions. The vendor plan involving the convenience store and a Superbowl promotion included a trip to the game for the store's owner. Inviting store owners to sports banquets or other appealing gimmicks also helps sell advertising.

Radio promotion on other media often can involve a tradeout—a swap of advertising time on the radio station for goods or services, sometimes including advertising time or space in another media. Trades frequently are used to supply prizes for contest promotions.

Aside from traditional sales tools, printed collateral produced by radio stations takes many creative tacks. WHEB-FM, a powerhouse New Hampshire station, publishes its own summer guide featuring station advertisers.

Community Relations

With growing competition among radio stations and media in general, there has been an increased awareness in the role of community relations. The cynic would imply a cause-and-effect relationship between those two factors. A more charitable view holds that radio managers are becoming more sophisticated in understanding operations and realize that a station has a strong obligation to the community.

In any event, the proliferation of public service announcements, community goodwill projects, and consumer affairs programs makes it evident that community relations is important to the modern radio station. Civic projects or events designed to raise money for a civic organization often can be promoted and organized by a radio station, with everyone turning a profit. Perhaps the profit that these operations produce is secondary, but profitable they are. Jim Lord Chaplin, President and General Manager of WOVV-FM and WIRA-AM in Fort Pierce, Florida, summed up a four-point plan for increasing revenues from community promotions:

— You create the illusion that you care—because you do.

— You create the illusion that you are involved—because you are.

— You create the illusion that you are everywhere—because you are.

— You create the illusion that you are the dominant radio station—because if you do the first three points of the plan with diligence, sincerity, and commitment, you are.[7]

7.4

COMMUNITY ASCERTAINMENT

An additional factor in developing community relations plans was that community groups who felt disenfranchised began to challenge station licenses, maintaining that broadcast outlets were not serving the community. Although the majority of challenges—most of which were mounted in the 1970s—failed, the FCC imposed a formal process on broadcasters, instructing them to ascertain community needs.

Regulatory Relief

Essentially, the formal **ascertainment** process called for representatives of most radio stations (the 1973 codification excluded stations in communities of under 10,000 people) to meet with community leaders and evaluate local needs and problems and devise a plan to meet those needs.

The formal ascertainment process has for all intents and purposes been dropped for radio. During the early 1980s, the FCC operated in a general atmosphere of deregulation, letting the market dictate station behavior. In essence, the FCC all but eliminated an obligation for stations to become involved with the community in which they are licensed. At the time, there was considerable concern that stations might separate themselves from their communities and operate in ways designed only to extract the largest possible profit. While some stations have indeed abandoned news and public affairs programming, the vast majority of stations remain very much involved in the affairs of the community.

Some vestige of ascertainment remains in what is known as the *Quarterly Needs and Issues Report.* This is a narrative document in which radio managers inform the FCC at three-month intervals of some of the needs they perceive within the community and how those needs are being addressed. Some stations, for example, note that AIDS is a major problem within their coverage area and list public service announcements for AIDS prevention as one way their programming speaks to that need. Other factors such as talk shows dealing with the AIDS problem would also be listed. Potholes, public works, and voter education are other typical items on needs and issues reports. The document is much briefer (up to ten pages) and less complex in its derivation than previous ascertainment reports.

As mentioned in previous discussions of the station and the community, communities typically have a negative reaction to a station that distances itself from the citizenry. The rationale behind many promotions is to focus on some sort of community involvement. It is difficult to determine whether deregulation and the withdrawal of formal ascertainment procedures have damaged the public affairs function of radio, but we must recognize that the most stringent rules did not solve the problem. Some stations, during periods of high regulation, went through the motions of public service. The local talk shows that aired at 4 AM on Sundays typified this attitude.

Value of the Ascertainment Process to Managers and Programmers

The ascertainment process was a tedious, laborious, and expensive proposition. Many broadcasters complained vigorously about ascertainment, claiming the process had little relevance to serving the community in a meaningful way.

However, the information gathered in ascertainment can be of great value to a programmer or manager. There was and is important demographic value and considerable public relations value to the information uncovered. Radio stations are to a great extent affected by public goodwill and do not operate well in a civic environment hostile to them. And there *is* a considerable interest in community affairs. What was usually perceived as indifference to public affairs programming was more often than not indifference to half-hearted, poorly produced public affairs programming. Observation in any market almost always evinces a great deal of interest in well-done news and public affairs. Even broadcasts of city council meetings can garner a loyal if not necessarily large group of listeners.

In conclusion, knowledge of the community and its needs amounts to more than simple lip service to a document. Such community knowledge can translate to valuable data for managers who wish to serve the public interest while convincing the public to maintain an interest in their stations.

EXERCISES

1. Write a brief (about 400 words) summary of economic conditions in the community in which you reside. Use the standard resources described in this chapter and other resources including the business section of the local newspaper. Briefly highlight the ability of consumers to spend money and the ability of advertisers to buy time.

2. Log your personal use of radio for two days. Keep track of when you listen to radio and to what station(s) you listen. Remember, log *all* times you listen. Briefly write down your impressions of and reactions to the following:
    a. What type of advertising did you hear? What advertising sticks in your mind?
    b. What was your level of attention to the radio? Was it as background? Did you listen intently?
    c. Do you patronize any of the establishments or buy any of the products advertised on the radio station(s) you listened to? Do you think you would buy these products as a result of the advertising?
    Discuss your listening habits with classmates or co-workers. Can you draw some conclusions about patterns of radio use among your acquaintances?

3. You are the promotion director of a 5000 watt, full-time station in a city of 110,000 people. Your city is highly industrialized but with pockets of poverty and high unemployment because of recent factory layoffs. Your boss has instructed you to come up with a promotion campaign that will (a) show the community that your station cares, and (b) induce, in a tasteful way, local residents affected by layoffs (or with family members or friends affected by

layoffs) to listen to the station. (HINT: Could an on-air job-matching program—employers describing the jobs they have available—be a possibility?
How would this or any other ideas be promoted?)

Write a paper describing your proposed program and implementation of
it. Incidentally, unlike what you would encounter in some situations, you are
perfectly free to disagree with your boss. If you don't feel that the promotion
idea is a good one, make your paper a logical argument against it. (HINT: Could
promotion aimed at unemployed people backfire somehow, particularly in
terms of the audience your boss wants to sell to advertisers?)

NOTES

1. National Association of Broadcasters estimate from printed speech. James
    Dawson, "Radio—The Natural Turn-On" (Washington, D.C.: National Asso-
    ciation of Broadcasters, 1984).

2. Charles Warner, *Broadcast and Cable Selling* (Belmont, CA: Wadsworth,
    1985), 189.

3. Figures supplied by Radio Advertising Bureau.

4. One of the initial problems concerned the difficulty of ascertaining whether
    the spot actually ran. Today, a rigorous series of affidavits is in place to ease
    advertisers' worries.

5. Quoted in "Newspapers on Radio," *Editor and Publisher* (10 January 1987): 14.

6. Susan Tyler Eastman, and Robert A. Klein (eds.), *Strategies in Broadcast and
    Cable Promotion* (Belmont, CA: Wadsworth, 1982), 33.

7. "Increasing Revenues through Community Promotions," *RadioActive Magazine*
    (October 1986): 14.

PART THREE

BUSINESS ASPECTS

CHAPTER 8

AUDIENCE

ANALYSIS

Possibly no other area of radio broadcasting seems so confusing as the use and interpretation of ratings. At first glance, a ratings report may seem very difficult to understand; after a thorough explanation from someone trying to use the numbers to prove something, the ratings report might appear virtually indecipherable.

This chapter deals with the most basic of ratings principles. Although the mechanics of sampling and interpretation of results can be extremely complex, the crux of the ratings game is simple. An understanding of the primary functions of audience analysis can be gained from careful study of this chapter. There are without question many fine points left uncovered in this treatment, but an obsession with minor details is a primary reason why so many students and emerging broadcasters gain an incomplete view of the workings of audience analysis. It is imperative to completely understand the *fundamentals* first. Then, later hands-on work with ratings reports and related sales materials will acquaint you with intimate details that relate to your particular job and market.

8.1

OVERVIEW OF THE AUDIENCE AS AN ECONOMIC FACTOR

It has been stated frequently, perhaps to the point of fatigue, that a radio station must please two audiences. This factor is so fundamental to the business as a whole that it bears reinforcement and exploration. The first audience, of course, is the listening audience, those people who tune in because they like the format, the disc jockey, or simply because of habit. The second audience is the consuming audience of advertisers, the people and institutions who purchase airtime to advertise their goods and services. They, too, must be pleased not so much by what they hear (although it helps), but by their perception of the kind of audience a radio station can deliver.

Following the Dollar

The chain of spending might begin, for example, with a beer manufacturer. The brewer, of course, wants buyers to purchase its particular brand of beer. Up to now, the issue seems reasonably clear-cut. But *who* buys the beer? *Why* do they favor that brand? And *how* can the brewer reach potential consumers?

Advertising professionals are reasonably skillful in answering each question. Who buys? Questioning by one of the ubiquitous, clipboard-toting researchers in a shopping mall might provide evidence, along with various other types of surveys. The answer, in this case, might be "mostly men, blue-collar workers in their twenties." Why do they buy this brand? An advertising agency "focus group" (a panel discussion aimed at evaluating a product and its users) might reveal that the most loyal consumers feel that it's a "quality American beer." The focus group might further reveal that typical consumers view themselves as highly independent, favor pickup trucks as their primary form of transportation, and come mostly from a predominantly rural background.

Now, the major question: How do we get the message across? Advertising professionals would design a thematic campaign to reach that group and place messages on the most efficient media.

Basics of Audience Economics

The concept of the most *efficient* media for reaching a target audience is the basis of understanding audience economics. A strong case can be made, and certainly would be made, by the representative for a country music station with a high percentage of young male listeners that station WXXX is the best vehicle for the beer company. The station representative would show figures reflecting audience composition, and indeed that station might receive a substantial order for advertising time. The particulars are not important but the concept is: Today's ratings systems deliver qualitative and quantitative information. That data is used in three important ways:

— To sell time to advertisers based on the projected audience the advertisers want to reach

— To determine the most cost-effective advertising package by showing advertisers how much it costs to reach a target audience

— To make decisions about the relative success of programming; note that in most cases this concept is subservient to the idea of delivering an audience to advertisers

Thus, the audience becomes a quantifiable and qualifiable economic factor to be packaged and sold.

8.2

RATINGS AND RESEARCH

Anyone who has ever tried to understand how a particular group votes, buys, or believes knows the inherent problem of dealing with a large collection of individuals. Barring the New England town meeting, there are few cases where a meeting of all the players can be called to express a view or validate an action. It is apparent that reliable extrapolation from an opinion sample is the only useful alternative. Sampling techniques are a relatively recent innovation, and the concept of using samples as a ratings tool has been in widespread use only for about sixty years, with varying degrees of success.

Brief History of the Ratings Services

One of the first flirtations with large-scale sampling was a virtual fiasco and is used in many statistics courses as an example of what *not* to do when sampling. The event in question was the *Literary Digest* poll of 1936, which predicted a resounding victory for Republican Alf Landon's presidential campaign. Landon lost badly to Democrat Franklin Delano Roosevelt. A postmortem indicated that an influencing variable was overlooked: The magazine sampled its readers and a randomly selected group of telephone subscribers to make the prediction. However, people with telephones in 1936 were hardly representative of the population as a whole. They tended to be economically well-off and, more often than not, Republican.

Telephone research of a more successful nature, though, had already been in use, starting in 1929 when a research company attempted to estimate the popularity of network radio shows. The results, named the Crosleys after the research firm's founder, had nothing like the impact of today's ratings. However, advertisers did want and need a mechanism to determine if their money was being spent wisely; in the late 1930s a firm known as C. E. Hooper, Inc., geared up to provide research data on a major scale. Hooper used telephone polling and counted an answer only if the person who answered the telephone was listening to the radio. This is known as *coincidental sampling.* Such a methodology faced a number of problems, not the least of which was measuring use of radio by people who did not have telephones in the 1930s and 1940s (shades of *Literary Digest*) and the fact that only in-home use could be measured by the coincidental sampling method. In 1941 a new firm known as The Pulse introduced personal interviewing to the ratings system. The Pulse system involved a highly detailed interview; it furnished useful information, but after-the-fact questioning inevitably leads to concerns about the accuracy of the respondents' memories.

What emerged as a workable compromise was developed by a firm originally known as the American Research Bureau, established in 1949, and now known as Arbitron. A pocket diary, introduced on a wide scale in the mid-1960s, was used to record listening patterns over a week. In theory, the diary solved the problems of telephone coincidental surveying (monitoring out-of-house use) and after-the-fact interviewing (memory lapse). Diary keepers could record their listening choices made at various locations (car or beach, for example) to maintain a faithful record shortly after the listening occurred. Arbitron became and remains the clear-cut winner in radio ratings services. (Pulse and Hooper went out of business.) Modern-day challengers have yet to achieve the wide acceptance accorded Arbitron by advertisers, although Birch is becoming widely accepted by stations and advertisers.

Methodologies of Audience Research

The particular workings of radio research firms are documented in a following section. As a starting point, however, it is important to note that any rating service must use a sampling technique—that is, take a sample and through statistical manipulation make that sample a reasonably reliable reflection of the whole universe of things being sampled. Ratings therefore enter the realm of statistics, the science of collecting, simplifying, and describing data as well as making inferences (drawing conclusions) based on the analysis of data.[1]

Statistical analysis and, in particular, sampling technique have come a long way from the days of the *Literary Digest* poll, but not so far that errors are impossible. Statisticians remember well the 1980 Carter–Reagan election, which was called a toss-up virtually until the eve of Reagan's landslide. However, there is a fundamental difference between ratings and opinion polls: Whereas most opinion polls are projected to predict an event (something like taking a snapshot and making a movie out of it), a rating reflects a statistical inference on what happened in the recent past.

The question is raised simply in order to deal with the issue of sampling error. Is a small sample a fair representation? Is it reasonable to make major economic judgments based on a tiny fraction of the listening audience? The answer would appear to be a reasonably unqualified yes for three reasons. First, comparison among results from various ratings services historically has shown little difference in projections made from small samples. Second, statisticians have highly reliable methods of assessing statistical inference in general and broadcasting in particular. Dr. Frank Stanton, a professional statistician who eventually rose to the presidency of CBS, was instrumental in developing many of the standard reference works used in audience research design. Anyone who works with statistics for a period of time observes that rigorous methods of demonstrating inference prove themselves time and time again. Yes, there is a standard error associated with most sampling techniques, but that error can be controlled for and the seriousness of the error estimated. For example, a statistical judgment of 100 (an arbitrary number made up for the sake of simple illustration) might have a sampling error of plus or minus 2 percent with a confidence level of 0.05. This means that, based on the historical results of millions of calculations made to compute the relevant probability factors, there is only a 5 percent chance that the actual number is 98 (2 percent less than our estimated figure of 100) or 102 (2 percent more). Close examination of a table of statistical probabilities shows that wider swings have a much lower probability of occurring.

The point is that widely accepted statistical research—be it radio ratings, opinion polls, or social research—is held to exacting and well-known mathematic standards. Now, mathematics cannot explain incorrect data being used for computation—the garbage-in-garbage-out theory popular among computer apologists—but in general the entire scope of audience research is regularly examined under a figurative microscope. In addition, an industry-supported accreditation group, the Broadcast Rating Council, closely monitors the accuracy of ratings research methods.

Finally, barring other objections, major economic decisions are based on existing ratings methodologies because they are the only games in town. No advertiser or broadcaster is willing to fund the wide-scale research provided by ratings firms, nor have broadcasters historically been willing to pay for research utilizing larger samples.

Formal and Informal Audience Research

The realm of formal research, it must be noted, is beyond the wherewithal of many stations in small markets. Ratings are not taken in many small markets; even in those small markets where ratings are undertaken, the samples are less frequent. The highly detailed breakdowns offered by various firms would not be available to small stations.

It is in those smaller markets where sales must be made without numbers, a topic addressed in Chapter 9. When formal research is not available, informal research— such as unscientific "polling" of community residents—must be brought into play.

In a broader context it is essential to realize that while results of formal or informal research efforts are an integral part of the business, they are only information. Ratings cannot be considered the final yardstick of success in radio. For example, a station with enormous investments in talent and promotions might show a smaller profit than a less-well-rated competitor that lives within its means. This is a circuitous way of illustrating that a radio station can informally garner information relative to its position in the community and the overall success of its effort without reams of quantifying figures and that a station can be a success even without top ratings in the market. The job is certainly more difficult without numbers (a term variously meaning without a rating service or with poor ratings), but it is not impossible. Having stated this, we now move on to the nuts and bolts of audience measurement.

8.3
WORKINGS OF THE RATINGS SERVICES

As mentioned earlier, there is a powerful temptation to become too heavily involved with the *technicalities* of ratings and lose sight of the overall *function* of ratings. That is precisely why the earlier discussion centered on the broadest of concepts. Now, for the particulars: The vocabulary of ratings is complex, but the ideas are simple. Familiarize yourself with the following definitions, and the upcoming section on interpreting ratings loses much of its mystery.

Definition of Terms

These definitions are presented in a sequentially layered order; that is, the most basic concepts are presented first and the ideas that build on those concepts follow.

RATING   A **rating** is a portion of the total available audience. In radio, a rating is often expressed as a percentage of the universe; the universe is statistical talk for the overall population sampled (all people who could be listening to the radio). That total population can be broken down in a number of ways, so it is important to know what the universe is for a certain rating. It might be all adults eighteen and over within the metropolitan area, or it might be for women ages twenty-five to thirty-four. The ratings page clearly indicates the universe sampled in the appropriate column. Note the general structure of the Arbitron ratings report shown in Figure 8.1. Particulars of the report are defined throughout this chapter.

Let us assume that the universe is all men ages twenty-five to forty-nine in the metropolitan area (a good target audience for our beer advertiser). A rating of 1 means that a station has 1 percent of the universe. A rating of 1.5 means that 1.5 percent of men ages twenty-five to forty-nine in the market who could listen were listening. Don't be concerned about when they were listening; that comes later.

Figure 8.1

A sample page from *Arbitron Radio.*
Reproduced with permission of Arbitron Ratings, New York, NY.

Hour by Hour
MONDAY–FRIDAY

METRO AQH(00)																			
5AM 6AM	6AM 7AM	7AM 8AM	8AM 9AM	9AM 10AM	10AM 11AM	11AM NOON	NOON 1PM	1PM 2PM	2PM 3PM	3PM 4PM	4PM 5PM	5PM 6PM	6PM 7PM	7PM 8PM	8PM 9PM	9PM 10PM	10PM 11PM	11PM MID	MID 1AM

+WAAA / WRRR

	5-6A	6-7A	7-8A	8-9A	9-10A	10-11A	11-12	12-1P	1-2P	2-3P	3-4P	4-5P	5-6P	6-7P	7-8P	8-9P	9-10P	10-11P	11-12	12-1A
P12+ SHR	3.7	6.0	8.6	10.1	9.7	9.3	8.7	9.5	9.7	9.4	8.0	6.1	6.2	9.0	9.5	9.7	6.4	5.9	8.2	4.0
P12+	20	108	218	182	158	152	136	142	136	136	126	104	98	92	78	64	42	36	38	10
TEENS	2	22	18	2	4	4	2		2	2	4	8	12	10	12	4	4			
M 16-34		6	44	34	32	26	28	28	26	24	24	16	16	26	26	20	20	16	16	4
W 18-34		30	52	54	54	58	52	54	60	62	58	44	38	36	20	24	12	10	12	2
M 25-54	8	32	70	62	52	48	44	44	36	34	32	24	24	32	34	24	24	12	20	6
W 25-54	6	34	66	56	46	54	50	54	54	50	46	34	26	22	12	14	4	10	8	2
M 35-64	10	26	38	26	26	26	22	24	20	18	14	16	14	10	10	8	6	2	6	4
W 35-64	8	24	58	44	32	32	30	34	24	28	22	16	12	8	10	8		8	4	

WBBB

	5-6A	6-7A	7-8A	8-9A	9-10A	10-11A	11-12	12-1P	1-2P	2-3P	3-4P	4-5P	5-6P	6-7P	7-8P	8-9P	9-10P	10-11P	11-12	12-1A
P12+ SHR		1.0	1.0	.7	1.2	1.0	1.0	.9	1.1	1.1	.8	1.5	1.4							
P12+		18	24	12	20	16	16	14	16	16	12	26	22							
TEENS		6	8	2	2	4	4	4	4	4	4	4	4							
M 18-34																				
W 18-34			2	2	4				2			8	14							
M 25-54		6	8		6	10	8	6	6	6	6	4	2							
W 25-54					2				2	2		10	6							
M 35-64		6	8	2	8	12	10	8	8	8	6	4	2							
W 35-64		6	6	6	6		2	2	2	4	2	10	2							

TOTALS

	5-6A	6-7A	7-8A	8-9A	9-10A	10-11A	11-12	12-1P	1-2P	2-3P	3-4P	4-5P	5-6P	6-7P	7-8P	8-9P	9-10P	10-11P	11-12	12-1A
P12+	542	1794	2526	1810	1624	1636	1566	1498	1400	1450	1572	1702	1584	1026	820	662	660	608	464	252
TEENS	36	244	252	40	36	36	44	40	58	68	138	172	168	156	128	104	124	116	58	28
M 18-34	64	326	622	396	362	346	316	344	340	358	328	374	324	290	216	146	158	160	126	64
W 18-34	60	308	560	496	400	396	398	370	326	344	386	414	404	206	160	130	126	128	96	42
M 25-54	194	516	688	508	440	430	394	390	370	370	376	410	390	268	218	158	158	116	126	74
W 25-54	174	528	738	556	470	476	472	474	404	418	454	474	442	224	158	144	126	94	74	54
M 35-64	186	398	474	338	302	308	276	272	252	232	266	296	306	168	128	102	96	68	86	58
W 35-64	180	438	498	390	358	368	364	318	284	306	314	324	280	146	120	112	96	88	70	54

Footnote Symbols: + Station(s) reported with different call letters in prior surveys - see Page 5B.

ARBITRON RATINGS

SHARE A **share** means the percentage of listeners who are *actually using the radio at a given time* and who are tuned to a particular station. A share of 7 for station WXXX means that of all the people sampled (the universe) *who were actually listening to radio at the time,* 7 percent of them were tuned in to WXXX.

AVERAGE QUARTER HOUR PERSONS **Average quarter hour (AQH) persons** measures the people (ratings services like to call them "persons") who listen for at least five minutes during a quarter hour; this is an average number and not a percentage. The quarter hour (Noon to 12:15, for example, or 12:15 to 12:30) is the basic unit of measurement in ratings. For example, between 12:30 and 1:30 there are four quarter hours. Take *all* the people who listen for at least five minutes during that hour, and then divide by four to determine the AQH persons. This figure can also be expressed as a percentage of the universe (average quarter hour *rating*) or as a share of the audience actually listening (average quarter hour *share*).

Remember that the AQH reflects the total time spent listening. If you add all the AQH persons over a given time period, you know how many people listened but you do not know how many of those people were counted twice. The following figure solves that problem.

CUME　Cumulative audience, or **cume,** is the *unduplicated* audience who listens over a predetermined period of time. Advertisers like to know the cume because they want an idea of how many *different* people they reach, as opposed to having their message played to the same listeners over and over again. (There is nothing intrinsically wrong with repetition; it just depends on the circumstance, as is explained later.)

Like people counted in AQH listeners, cume persons must listen for at least five minutes during a quarter hour.

TIME SPENT LISTENING　**Time spent listening (TSL)** is spent by the average listener who is tuned in to radio or to a particular station. Its derivation is somewhat complicated, but it suffices to remember that TSL is weighted to reflect an unduplicated audience. Cume is factored in via the complex derivation mentioned above.

TURNOVER　As you might expect, **turnover (TO)** reflects how often listenership changes from time period to time period. The Radio Advertising Bureau defines audience TO as "the number of times an average quarter hour audience is replaced by new listeners in a specified period of time." This figure can be determined by dividing the cume persons figure by the AQH persons figure. If average persons for a time period is 1000 (the number of persons who on the average will be listening at a particular time) and the weekly total of cumulative listeners for the quarter-hour time period is 15,000 (an estimation of each *separate* listener added up for the entire week), you would get 15. The number is useful for comparison among stations and can be used as an estimation of how many announcements it will take to reach about half of the cumulative audience. In other words, fifteen spots would reach about half the total cumulative listeners for the time period.

PERSONS USING RADIO　**Persons using radio (PUR)** is the number you'll arrive at by adding up the column on the ratings report that lists average persons. This means the average estimated number of persons listening to all stations in the market. Adding up the numbers estimated to be listening to each station produces a useful estimate of the people in the market who tune in to radio on a regular basis. But what exactly is the "market"?

TOTAL SURVEY AREA   The **total survey area (TSA)** includes a wide range of counties served by two or more radio stations from within a metropolitan area. Obviously, this can lead to some distortions in the definition of the survey area when a city contains two very powerful AM stations. Many broadcasters and advertisers say that TSA is becoming less useful, especially now that FM stations (which inherently have shorter signal ranges) have gained ratings dominance.

METRO SURVEY AREA   Of more use is the **metro survey area,** a local rating area defined in terms of the city and its immediate environs. It is often considered the most useful rating area for judging the penetration of radio because it gives a more realistic view of the coverage area.

CALCULATING ADVERTISING EFFECTIVENESS   Some terms that relate to the use of the ratings figures in calculating the effectiveness of advertising are presented next.

The Radio Advertising Bureau defines **gross impressions** as the total number of exposures to a schedule of announcements. Bear in mind that this figure is *not* a measurement of the number of different people exposed to a commercial over a period of time.

To calculate the gross impressions of a particular commercial, simply multiply the average persons (you can add up the AQH persons if the average persons is not broken out for the particular time period you want) and multiply by the number of the commercials.

Gross Impressions = Average Persons × Total Number of Commercials

Gross rating point (GRP) is the same idea as gross impressions, but the figure is expressed as a percentage of the universe, as a rating.

Gross Rating Point = AQH Rating × Number of Commercials

Here's an example of how the formula works. Multiply the AQH ratings by number of commercials to figure the GRPs:

Run in Quarter Hour(s) with 1 Ratings × 10 Commercials = 10 GRPs

Reach means how many *different* listeners are exposed to a message and therefore is a function of cume rather than average persons ratings. (Remember: Cume is an unduplicated audience over a period of time.) Reach means essentially the same thing as cume. Caution: Cumes are individually calculated for specific time periods and cannot be added together without some sophisticated statistical weighting. The only exception to the rule against adding cumes is when you are figuring a gross number of impressions. Why? Gross impressions is the number of exposures, *not* people. Gross impressions counts duplicated audience; therefore the cumes can be added (thus duplicating audience members) in this case.

Frequency is the average number of times a theoretical listener hears a commercial. It can be determined by dividing the gross impressions by the cume (or by the reach, which means the same thing). The formula is

$$\text{Frequency} = \frac{\text{Gross Impressions}}{\text{Cume}}$$

CALCULATING ADVERTISING EFFICIENCY   The remaining definitions deal specifically with *cost* formulas based on the relative efficiency of advertising.

Essentially, the **cost per thousand (CPM)** is the cost of reaching 1000 listeners. Remember that this reflects gross impressions, not cume. The formula is

$$\text{CPM} = \frac{\text{Cost of All Spots}}{\text{Gross Impressions}/1000}$$

Assume that your entire advertising schedule cost $500. The number of gross impressions gained during your schedule is 100,000. Divide the gross impressions by 1000 (to express it in terms of thousands), and the result is 100.

Divide the cost of all spots, $500, by 100, and you have a cost per thousand of $5—meaning that it costs you $5 to make 1000 gross impressions. Of more immediate importance than the raw figure itself is the comparison an advertiser can make between and among stations when using CPM figures for each station.

An advertiser can calculate CPM on a variety of universes, of course. He or she can compare the cost of making 1000 gross impressions in men of a certain age, for example, or teenagers of both sexes.

Cost per point (CPP) tells how much it costs to reach one rating point worth of listeners in a given demographic. It is emerging as the most frequently used cost-comparison figure. Essentially, CPP is figured in the same way as CPM except that GRPs are used instead of gross impressions.

$$\text{CPP} = \frac{\text{Cost of All Spots}}{\text{Gross Rating Points}}$$

Remember that the GRPs are the product of the number of spots run times the AQH rating. So, if you run five spots, one each on days Monday through Friday in a quarter hour with a 1.5 rating, you have $5 \times 1.5 = 7.5$ GRPs.

If each spot cost $125, you have spent $625. Divide $625 (cost of all spots) by 7.5 (GRPs) and you have $83.33. This figure—$83 a point—is what you might expect to pay on a well-rated station in a large market. Armed with the fact that this station is charging $83 per point for, let's say, women eighteen years and older, you can compare among stations. Further applications of CPP will be explored in a following section, "Interpretation of Ratings."

The Major Services

Ratings firms have come and gone—many of them have gone—in recent years. One endemic problem deals with the relative expense of such services and broadcasters' unwillingness to pay excessive sums for a ratings report. However, in recent years the highly competitive nature of radio has given birth to many specialized research firms dealing with audience measurement and, in some cases, with measurement of the effectiveness of air personalities or measurement of audience responsiveness to various pieces of music.[2]

Some brief introductions to the major firms are discussed next.

ARBITRON   The leader in radio ratings uses the previously described diary for gathering listener information. Arbitron surveys large markets four times a year; smaller markets receive one survey a year during the so-called spring sweeps. Figure 8.1 shows a sample Arbitron ratings report and descriptive material.

BIRCH   This firm uses telephone interviews to survey market listings. The methodology is sophisticated—an in-depth interview focusing on twenty-four-hour recall, conducted by a researcher trained to extract and evaluate the information. Birch is noted for supplying highly specific data on such items as location of radio listening and ethnic composition of audiences. Birch supplies a highly specialized report known as the PRIZM Cluster groups that ranks audiences on life-style factors, dividing the audiences along such lines as education, income, and type of housing. Figure 8.2 shows a sample Birch report and some descriptive data.

RADAR®   Audiences to network radio are provided in *RADAR®* (*Radio's All Dimension Audience Research*). These reports are issued twice a year. The *RADAR®* measurement uses telephone interviews for data collection. The job at *RADAR®* service is complicated by the fact that not all local stations run (or "clear," as the practice is known) network programming and/or commercials; *RADAR®* must ascertain this and must cope with the newly emerging glut of radio networks. A page of *RADAR®* report is shown in Figure 8.3.

OTHER SPECIALIZED RESEARCH FUNCTIONS   For a fee, a radio station can contract for standard audience measurement or measurement and/or interpretation of

Figure 8.2

A sample page from *Birch Radio Report*.
Reproduced with permission of Birch Research Corporation, Coral Springs, FL.

PITTSBURGH/BEAVER VALLEY PA CMSA
JUNE - AUGUST 1987

Target Demographics
ADULTS 25 - 49

AVERAGE QUARTER HOUR AND CUME ESTIMATES

	MON - SAT 6:00AM-12:00 MID				MON - SAT 6:00AM-10:00AM			
	AQH PRS (00)	AQH PRS RTG	AQH PRS SHR	CUME PRS (00)	AQH PRS (00)	AQH PRS RTG	AQH PRS SHR	CUME PRS (00)
KDKA	135	1.6	8.8	1800	253	3.1	13.4	1175
KQV	10	.1	.7	346	16	.2	.8	158
WAMO	11	.1	.7	88	12	.1	.6	80
WAMO-FM	125	1.5	8.1	1174	112	1.4	5.9	643
WBVP	3		.2	43	10	.1	.5	43
WBZZ-FM	176	2.1	11.5	1944	176	2.1	9.3	1092
WDSY-FM	85	1.0	5.5	864	90	1.1	4.8	423
WDUQ-FM	6	.1	.4	153	8	.1	.4	97
WDVE-FM	157	1.9	10.2	1980	198	2.4	10.5	1096
WEEP	19	.2	1.2	386	20	.2	1.1	169
WESA-FM	20	.2	1.3	128	29	.4	1.5	101
WHJB	2		.1	6				
WHTX-FM	85	1.0	5.5	1136	114	1.4	6.1	673
WIXZ				27				
WJAS	5	.1	.3	98	2		.1	11
WJPA	4		.3	54	7	.1	.4	39
WLTJ-FM	71	.9	4.6	637	47	.6	2.5	280
WMBS	11	.1	.7	121	18	.2	1.0	83
WMYG-FM	160	2.0	10.4	1374	187	2.3	9.9	918
WPIT	4		.3	33	10	.1	.5	33
WPIT-FM	38	.5	2.5	340	61	.7	3.2	315
WQED-FM	11	.1	.7	143	15	.2	.8	83
WSHH-FM	58	.7	3.8	575	64	.8	3.4	348
WTAE	34	.4	2.2	829	27	.3	1.4	210
WTKN	48	.6	3.1	537	62	.8	3.3	249
WWSW-FM	119	1.5	7.7	1125	161	2.0	8.6	788
WXXP-FM	11	.1	.7	286	7	.1	.4	146
WYDD-FM	47	.6	3.1	608	77	.9	4.1	320
WYTK-FM	2		.1	27				
PRS = Persons								
RTG = Rating								
SHR = Share								
PUR	1536	18.7		7806	1883	23.0		6566

* ESTIMATES ADJUSTED FOR ACTUAL BROADCAST SCHEDULE

Figure 8.3

A sample page from RADAR®.

Reproduced with permission of Statistical Research, Inc., Westfield, NJ.

```
A  6       RADAR 35 - FALL 1986/SPRING 1987

           AUDIENCE ESTIMATES FOR XXX RADIO NETWORK
           AUDIENCES TO ALL COMMERCIALS
           NUMBER OF PERSONS IN THOUSANDS

           PROGRAM QUARTER-HOUR AVERAGES BY DAYPART
```

DAYPART (PER ETZ FEED TIME)	NUM OF BCST	18+	18-54	18-49	18-34	18-24	25+	25-54	25-49	25-34	35+	35-54	35-49	50+
MONDAY-SUNDAY														
6.00A - 12.00M	140	1568	1004	890	394	84	1484	920	806	310	1174	610	496	678
6.00A - 7.00P	110	1810	1156	1027	449	97	1713	1059	930	352	1361	707	578	783
12.00M - 6.00A	42	249	151	143	56	*	249	151	143	56	193	95	87	106
6.00A - 10.00A	25	2317	1410	1213	474	87	2230	1323	1126	387	1843	936	739	1104
10.00A - 3.00P	48	1862	1174	1042	475	111	1751	1063	931	364	1387	699	567	820
3.00P - 7.00P	37	1404	967	886	400	87	1317	880	799	313	1004	567	486	518
7.00P - 12.00M	30	673	438	382	192	38	635	400	344	154	481	246	190	291
MONDAY-FRIDAY														
6.00A - 12.00M	100	1764	1140	1010	463	98	1666	1042	912	365	1301	677	547	754
6.00A - 7.00P	80	2019	1305	1157	524	113	1906	1192	1044	411	1495	781	633	862
12.00M - 6.00A	30	259	157	152	58	*	257	155	150	56	201	99	94	107
6.00A - 10.00A	20	2495	1548	1340	548	104	2391	1444	1236	444	1947	1000	792	1155
10.00A - 3.00P	35	2040	1304	1155	539	126	1914	1178	1029	413	1501	765	616	885
3.00P - 7.00P	25	1612	1114	1014	485	103	1509	1011	911	382	1127	629	529	598
7.00P - 12.00M	20	740	481	424	221	41	699	440	383	180	519	260	203	316
6A-10A + 3P-7P	45	2005	1307	1159	513	103	1902	1204	1056	410	1492	794	646	846
SATURDAY														
6.00A - 12.00M	21	1286	780	684	267	57	1229	723	627	210	1019	513	417	602
6.00A - 7.00P	16	1481	886	779	296	69	1412	817	710	227	1185	590	483	702
12.00M - 6.00A	6	315	234	211	101	*	315	234	211	101	214	133	110	104
6.00A - 10.00A	3	1760	921	760	190	*	1732	893	732	162	1570	731	570	1000
10.00A - 3.00P	7	1628	985	857	362	88	1540	897	769	274	1266	623	495	771
3.00P - 7.00P	6	1172	753	696	272	68	1104	685	628	204	900	481	424	476
7.00P - 12.00M	5	661	438	379	175	*	640	417	358	154	486	263	204	282
SUNDAY														
6.00A - 12.00M	19	850	533	484	171	42	808	491	442	129	679	362	313	366
6.00A - 7.00P	14	1001	627	578	198	40	961	587	538	158	803	429	380	423
12.00M - 6.00A	6	145	44	*	*	*	145	44	*	*	137	*	*	114
6.00A - 10.00A	2	1369	752	608	159	*	1360	743	599	150	1210	593	449	761
10.00A - 3.00P	6	1104	642	602	233	50	1054	592	552	183	871	409	369	502
3.00P - 7.00P	6	779	572	546	178	42	737	530	504	136	601	394	368	233
7.00P - 12.00M	5	424	266	219	94	45	379	221	174	49	330	172	125	205
ALL BROADCASTS	182	1263	807	717	316	65	1198	742	652	251	947	491	401	546
ALL BCSTS EX 12M-6A	140	1568	1004	890	394	84	1484	920	806	310	1174	610	496	678

```
NOTES: DAYPART DATA REFLECT PARTICULAR PROGRAMS; SEE LISTING IN VOLUME 2 OR 3, PART 1.
       NA - NOT APPLICABLE BECAUSE THERE ARE NO BROADCASTS IN ONE OR MORE COMPONENTS.
```

RADAR 35 - FALL 1986/SPRING 1987

AUDIENCE ESTIMATES FOR ALL AM AND FM RADIO STATIONS
BY DAYPART
NUMBER OF PERSONS IN THOUSANDS

MONDAY THROUGH FRIDAY
LOCAL TIME

	TOTAL PERS 12+	TOTAL ADULTS 18+	MEN TOTAL	MEN 18-49	MEN 25-54	MEN 25+	MEN 35+	WOMEN TOTAL	WOMEN 18-49	WOMEN 25-54	WOMEN 25+	WOMEN 35+	TEENS 12-17
FULL 24 HOUR DAY													
AVERAGE QUARTER HOUR	25764	23525	11589	8572	6991	9400	6047	11936	8004	6837	10038	7161	2239
AVERAGE 1 DAY CUME	160404	142181	68909	49082	41496	57197	38838	73272	49332	42270	61706	43442	18223
5 DAY WEEKLY CUME	185749	164822	78798	54844	46682	65885	45337	86024	56724	48666	72687	51621	20927
6.00 AM TO 12.00 M													
AVERAGE QUARTER HOUR	31934	29177	14221	10498	8587	11569	7417	14956	10054	8616	12601	8964	2757
AVERAGE 1 DAY CUME	158009	139992	67685	48275	40735	56170	38060	72307	48656	41675	60881	42894	18017
5 DAY WEEKLY CUME	185144	164239	78423	54601	46442	65582	45046	85816	56593	48548	72502	51505	20905
6.00 AM TO 10.00 AM													
AVERAGE QUARTER HOUR	43120	40079	18732	13282	11710	16054	10767	21347	13713	12474	18715	13849	3041
AVERAGE 1 DAY CUME	119666	107348	51951	37261	32457	44099	29896	55397	37006	32588	47474	34037	12318
5 DAY WEEKLY CUME	165301	146977	70051	49616	42328	58685	39833	76926	51218	43969	64995	46311	18324
10.00 AM TO 3.00 PM													
AVERAGE QUARTER HOUR	36451	34659	16578	12272	10041	13589	8656	18081	12187	10585	15356	10802	1792
AVERAGE 1 DAY CUME	85109	78296	37480	26977	21908	30531	20237	40816	27410	23243	34261	23927	6813
5 DAY WEEKLY CUME	145434	131609	62585	44274	36276	51261	34488	69024	46402	38882	57462	40171	13825
3.00 PM TO 7.00 PM													
AVERAGE QUARTER HOUR	33314	29934	15086	11424	9306	12163	7665	14848	10489	8860	12318	8476	3380
AVERAGE 1 DAY CUME	95032	84170	42388	31866	26558	34783	22710	41782	30148	25688	34858	23452	10862
5 DAY WEEKLY CUME	154467	136214	66129	48309	40390	54396	36387	70085	48967	41708	58537	40086	18253
7.00 PM TO 12.00 M													
AVERAGE QUARTER HOUR	17370	14372	7565	5758	4063	5489	3301	6807	4646	3366	5183	3611	2998
AVERAGE 1 DAY CUME	59173	48689	24548	18589	14037	18710	11642	24141	17080	13049	18863	12751	10484
5 DAY WEEKLY CUME	120829	102585	50792	38240	30334	40056	25470	51793	37432	29740	41415	27476	18244
12.00 M TO 6.00 AM													
AVERAGE QUARTER HOUR	7249	6564	3693	2794	2199	2890	1937	2871	1850	1498	2346	1750	685
AVERAGE 1 DAY CUME	37992	34134	17691	13161	11223	14556	9891	16443	11372	9894	13901	10094	3858
5 DAY WEEKLY CUME	74578	65220	33495	25524	20379	26365	17397	31725	22670	18297	25446	17703	9358

Figure 8.4

A sample of a report from TAPSCAN.
Reproduced with permission of TAPSCAN, Inc., Birmingham, AL.

```
           TAPSCAN  MULTI-MEDIA  REACH  AND  FREQUENCY  ANALYSIS
                   ADULTS  25-54  --  CITYNAME  METRO
                              SAMPLE RUN
                                 DEMO

SCHEDULE DESCRIPTIONS

RADIO  --  WEEKLY  SCHEDULE   (WEEKS: 4 )
=================================================================================================
          | ----- MONDAY-FRIDAY ------  -------- SATURDAY --------   -------- SUNDAY ---------  M-FRI  M-FRI  M-FRI  WKEND  M-SUN
STATION   | 6-10   10-3   3-7P  7-MID   6-10   10-3   3-7P  7-MID   6-10   10-3   3-7P  7-MID   AM+PM  6A-7P  6A-MD  6A-MD  6A-MD
..................................................................................................
KMMM         5      5      5    ....    ....   ....   ....  ....    ....   ....   ....  ....    ....   ....   ....   ....   ....
=================================================================================================


TELEVISION  --  WEEKLY  SCHEDULE   (WEEKS:  4)
=================================================================================================
DESCRIPTION              DAYTIME          EARLY FRINGE       PRIME TIME         LATE FRINGE        MULTI-DAYPART
                       SPOTS  GRP'S       SPOTS  GRP'S       SPOTS  GRP'S       SPOTS  GRP'S       SPOTS  GRP'S
..................................................................................................
KAAA,KBBB               10    15.0          6    25.0          4    75.0
=================================================================================================
NOTE: ESTIMATES WERE ENTERED BY THE USER


NEWSPAPER  --  WEEKLY  SCHEDULE   (WEEKS:  4)
=================================================================================================
NEWSPAPER NAME      = DAYS =  ==FULL PAGE==  == 3/4 PAGE==  ==HALF PAGE==  == 1/4 PAGE==  == 1/8 PAGE==  ==UNDER 1/8==  ADS
                              -ADS---RATE--  -ADS---RATE--  -ADS---RATE--  -ADS---RATE--  -ADS---RATE--  -ADS---RATE--  PER WK
..................................................................................................
ANYWHERE JOURNAL    MON-FRI   ..........    ..........       2   $2000     ..........     ..........     ..........      2
MORNING DAILY       SATURDAY  ..........    ..........     ..........      ..........     ..........     ..........
                    SUNDAY     1   $4000    ..........     ..........      ..........     ..........     ..........      1
..................................................................................................
PERCENT NOTING ADJUSTMENTS ----->  41 %        38 %           33 %           27 %           24 %           15 %
=================================================================================================
NOTE: ESTIMATES WERE ENTERED BY THE USER.  PERCENT NOTING ADJUSTMENTS REFLECT THE ESTIMATED PERCENTAGE OF THE AVERAGE-ISSUE
      READERSHIP NOTING EACH AD.

SCHEDULE COMPUTATIONS
ADULTS 25-54  (POPULATION -    894,800)

MEDIUM      SPOTS/ADS   GRP'S   GROSS IMP   REACH  FREQ   EFF RCH   --CPM--   --CPP--   CPM NR   CPM EF RCH   TOTAL COST
            WKLY  TOT
..................................................................................................
RADIO        15   60    166.1   1,486,000   18.4%   9.0   14.9%     $5.38    $48.17    $48.63    $59.93       $8,000
TELEVISION   20   80    460.0   4,116,080   81.5%   5.6   59.6%    $19.44   $173.91   $109.76   $150.09      $80,000
NEWSPAPER     3   12    161.1   1,441,312   45.0%   3.6   23.6%    $22.20   $198.66    $79.44   $151.42      $32,000
..................................................................................................
TOTALS                  787.1   7,043,392   91.7%   8.6   73.7%    $17.04   $152.45   $146.28   $181.91     $120,000

NOTE: THE EFFECTIVE REACH COMPUTATIONS REFLECT THE PERCENTAGE OF THE POPULATION EXPOSED TO THE MESSAGE 3 OR MORE TIMES.
====> NET REACH COMPUTATIONS ARE BASED UPON THE BETA-BINOMIAL STATISTICAL EXTENSION FORMULA

PREPARED BY THE TAPSCAN RATING ANALYSIS SYSTEM.  REPORT DESIGN & CONTENTS COPYRIGHT 1987 TAPSCAN, INC. (205) 987-7456
DATA FROM THE SPRING 1987 ARBITRON.  SUBJECT TO LIMITATIONS AND RESTRICTIONS STATED IN ORIGINAL REPORT.
```

specifically identified factors. Novel services such as TAPSCAN (Figure 8.4) provide a computer program to local stations containing the ratings data from Arbitron. The local stations then use their computers and the TAPSCAN program to generate promotional material utilizing the data, which can be sorted and displayed in any number of ways including visualized cost comparisons with newspapers and television. Birch-Scan uses Birch results in a similar way. Firms such as Surrey Research test music appeal by playing selections to an auditorium full of listeners. There is even a computer program available that evaluates ratings to determine whether the changes are statistically significant.[3]

8.4
INTERPRETATION OF RATINGS

Ratings are used in various ways by various people. Programmers use both quantitative and qualitative data to determine their current constituencies and, of course, to evaluate their relative level of success or failure. Radio station time salespeople use some combination of figures to show that their stations are good advertising buys. Advertising executives use ratings to determine a total media buy—that is, placement of advertising on various media.

The Numbers Game

Possibly the most direct translation of numbers into money occurs at the ad agency level where media buyers scan qualitative and quantitative data in hopes of locating the most effective vehicles for their clients' products. (Often, separate firms called media-buying agencies do the actual purchasing, even for major ad agencies.) Of prime importance to radio management is the fact that much media buying is done on a CPP basis, and it is often up to the station to pitch a package that brings in the deal at or under the going CPP. In Boston, for example, premium radio advertising runs about $100 CPP for morning drive time. But some advertising agencies balk at a total buy at $100 CPP and look for lower prices; perhaps $85 CPP is more realistic in particular cases. So the task at hand for a sales manager is to put together a package that might include some morning drive at $100 CPP, some afternoon time at $80 CPP, and some overnight time at $40 CPP. The average determined from adding up the CPP figures must be at or under the specified CPP the agency is willing to pay.

The numbers are not the only key issue. Qualitative information is essential for the radio station trying to get a piece of the agency buy. For instance, what happens if an agency is going to buy the top six stations in the market and you are number seven? There is a chance that you can persuade the buyer to include you because of your qualitative data:

—— We have a higher percentage of upper-income wage earners.

—— Our station reaches farther into the rural areas that are good markets for your client.

—— We are stronger among teenagers than many of the other higher-rated stations overall, and teenagers would be a good audience for your client's product.

Decision Making Based on Ratings

How do ad agency buyers make their final decisions? They typically weigh the factors of GRPs, CPP or CPM, reach, and frequency and try to correlate those figures with an experience-based judgment of the effectiveness of various media. As concerns the media buyer (and to some extent the knowledgeable purchaser of local advertising), radio has these pros and cons:

Pro Radio

—— Enormous penetration; almost everyone can be reached by radio

—— Highly specific target audiences

—— Low production costs

—— Good value and sometimes negotiable rates

—— Flexibility of scheduling; buying spots is simple and quick

Con Radio

—— Lack of tangibility; radio has no counterpart to a coupon or anything else that can be held in the hand and brought into a store

— Lack of ability to transmit complex information; long lists of specials or other sale items cannot be easily read or remembered; complex financial arrangements (mortgages, perhaps) are sometimes difficult to communicate effectively

— Clutter; there is a great deal of information carried during a typical hour of modern radio; it may require an extensive flight of commercials to pound the message in; conversely, the radio audience tunes in and tunes out, so a number of commercials will be necessary to reach them

These are examples of some of the factors a buyer uses when comparing research figures among various media. When comparing radio station to radio station, the concept of reach versus frequency must compound more basic comparisons of ratings figures. Two guidelines a media buyer uses in evaluating reach and frequency in relation to a station's ratings are, first, lower frequency and greater reach (remember, the two usually balance each other, varying inversely). Lower frequency and higher reach are usually most useful when the product has the following characteristics:

— High brand loyalty

— Established brand

— Longer purchase cycles

— Light competitive activity

— Simple advertising message

— High attention to medium

— Low-clutter environment

— One or fewer messages

— Broad target audience

— High product interest

Second, higher frequency and concomitant lower reach is usually most useful when the product has these characteristics:

— Low brand loyalty

— New brand introduction

— Frequent purchase cycles

— Heavy competitive activity

—— Complex advertising message

—— Low attention to medium

—— High-clutter environment

—— Multiple messages

—— Narrow target audience

—— Low product interest[4]

Certainly, the use and interpretation of ratings is a complicated affair. Remember, though, that just because the radio listenership is reduced to an accurate-sounding number, *that number is only an estimate and cannot be treated as though it is an incontrovertible, all-encompassing fact.* Americans in general have a predilection for assigning spurious precision to a number; this must be resisted when evaluating audience measurements.

It's important to balance the quest for numbers with an appreciation that those numbers are only part of the story, even—and perhaps especially—in advertising and advertising sales. Numbers do not guarantee effective advertising for a client. The believability of the message,[5] the clarity and persuasiveness of the commercial, and the proper placement of the spots (such as the reach versus frequency issue) must also be considered.

Remember that numbers do not sell the radio station by themselves. A good sales force can outsell a rival station that has similar or somewhat higher numbers, whereas an inefficient sales force could badly undersell a top-rated station. Turning those numbers into profit is the goal of the sales force and the topic of Chapter 9.

EXERCISES

1.   Using the list of reach and frequency advantages and disadvantages, construct a rationale for why those factors usually prove true. Specifically, explain why lower frequency/higher reach would be a better strategy for a product with a simple advertising message and high brand loyalty. Explain why you feel high frequency/lower reach would be appropriate for a product with a complex advertising message and low brand loyalty. Can you think of typical products that might need complicated messages or would have low brand loyalty? Explain.

2.   For the demographic women ages eighteen to forty-nine, station WXXX has an

AQH persons rating for the relevant time period (the period on which the following calculations will be based) of 2.0. You are running ten spots for a particular product at a total cost of $600.

    a.   What is the number of GRPs the ten commercials will accumulate?

    b.   What is the CPP of the advertising campaign?

3.   Station WXXX has during morning drive an AQH persons total of 20,000. Five commercials cost $50 each run during this time period.

    a.   How many gross impressions will the five commercials make?

    b.   What CPM will the five commercials have?

NOTES

1.   Warren Chase, and Fred Bown, *General Statistics* (New York: Wiley, 1986), 2. Chase and Bown's book is an excellent reference for broadcasters or researchers interested in concise definitions of statistical terms and clear-cut presentations of formulas.

2.   For a clear explanation of the workings on nonratings research, see Roger D. Wimmer, and Joseph R. Dominick, *Mass Media Research,* 2d ed. (Belmont, CA: Wadsworth, 1987), 329–340.

3.   See *Squeezing Profits Out of Ratings: A Manual for Radio Managers, Sales Managers and Programmers* (Washington, D.C.: National Association of Broadcasters, 1985). Descriptions of the computer program are contained in the appendix.

4.   Joseph W. Ostrow, "What Level Frequency?" *Advertising Age* (9 November 1981): s–4.

5.   According to one advertising expert, Coca-Cola Vice President Ira Herbert, believability is a major problem; of all consumers, 73 percent believe that ads "create a mood" rather than communicate facts. "Change Needed in People's Perception of Advertising, Says Coca-Cola's Herbert," *Broadcasting* (15 June 1987): 53, 55.

_____

_____

CHAPTER 9

_____

SALES AND

_____

ADVERTISING

_____

Selling time on a commercial radio station is a multifaceted enterprise, not without its problems but certainly not without its rewards. The subject of radio station sales is a broad one, and it is obvious that the topic cannot be covered in detail within the confines of one chapter. Instead, a highlighted broad-brush view is presented.

9.1

GENERAL OBSERVATIONS ABOUT SALES

Professional Requirements

The days of the fast-talking, plaid-jacketed salesman—if those days ever really existed—are past. The modern advertising and broadcasting climate is highly competitive and requires salespeople who can understand and use statistics, construct elaborate structures of advertising programs, interact with an eclectic variety of people, and maintain high-level internal motivation. Above all, salespeople must have the intelligence to develop a solid practical understanding of the product they are selling.

Professional Compensation

Salespeople frequently enjoy high incomes, but not everyone can reach the brass ring. Industry observers note that turnover in broadcast sales positions is high. This is partially due to the number of newcomers who never make it "over the hump" and quit after a few months. Most salespeople are paid a modest advance against anticipated commissions, and it takes some time for the accumulated sales commissions to add up to an encouraging level.

Salespeople who do hang on, however, usually do as well or better financially than anyone else. The most recent average (mean) figures for all radio stations in the United States shows that the typical account executive (salesperson) earns $22,316 per year, while the general sales manager makes $40,098. Compare this to the average salary of $17,812 for the news director, $23,446 for the program director, and $21,665 for the chief engineer. Consider, too, the fact that in a large market (serving a population of over 2.5 million), a general sales manager makes, on the average, $64,992.[1]

It is also apparent that sales offers opportunity in terms of positions available. In a typical radio station, salespeople are among the most numerous as well as the most highly paid personnel. (Table 9.1 shows average radio station salaries *by department*.)

Sales jobs, while not as innately glamorous as on-air work, usually provide greater monetary rewards. This probably explains why so many people who started on-air switched over to sales.

Table 9.1

RADIO STATION EMPLOYEE COMPENSATION FOR ALL STATIONS [2]

Department	Full-time Employees	Average Annual Department Salaries ($)
Engineering	2	25,076
Programming/Production	6	119,634
News	2	44,477
Sales	5	132,523
Advertising and Promotion	2	26,454
General and Administrative	3	82,293

Professional Growth

No other job in broadcasting offers such reward for personal initiative. Growth in most other positions is more directly limited by external factors. Clerical positions, for example, have a discrete salary cap simply because the work itself is perceived as being of limited value. The most ambitious traffic clerk in the world won't become a millionaire (from a traffic clerk's salary, anyway) regardless of ability or ambition. Talent salaries in small, medium, and many major markets are limited simply because of the competition. There are so many talented applicants for a limited number of jobs that few people can demand exorbitant incomes.

To a degree, salespeople can expand their incomes far beyond the limits imposed on radio station staff who are paid strictly on salary. We say "to a degree" because the idea that commissioned salespeople have no limits to their salaries is not strictly true within the field of radio. First, salespeople whose incomes approach that of sales managers will have accounts taken away from them; second, all communities have some sort of built-in limit as to the amount of money that feasibly can be spent on broadcast advertising.

Having prefaced the following discussion, let's now examine the mechanics of time sales, the tiers of the sales effort, sales and the modern format, the principles of effective sales, and a brief summary of the goals and structure of advertising.

9.2

MECHANICS OF TIME SALES

Quite simply, a radio station sales department's mission is to sell advertising to clients who seek to reach the station's listeners. Salespeople sell time by calling on local retailers and, through various mechanisms, selling time to national and area advertisers through advertising agencies. (An advertising agency is a firm that designs and places advertising for a client.) A radio station may also generate some income through network sales, although this is usually not a significant figure except in major markets.

Radio salespeople receive a commission based on the income they generate, usually about 15 percent of the collected revenue for the sale. The way in which they generate income is by convincing clients to purchase airtime and *by generating results* for that client. Results translate to repeat business. *Servicing* existing accounts—calling on continuing advertisers, fine-tuning their advertising, and selling them on newly created packages—is just as important as *prospecting* new accounts.

The sales department is led by the sales manager, sometimes known as the general sales manager. The sales manager's most important duty is setting quotas and seeing that those quotas are met. The sales manager is responsible for assigning accounts to the sales staff.

In some cases, particularly in large markets, there are several levels of sales personnel and sales management. This relates directly to the levels of sales. These levels usually, but not always, are classified as *retail, local,* and *national.* Retail refers to direct sales made to businesses in the area, although it is a confusing term in that local businesses are certainly not all "retail stores," as we tend to think of the term. Local sales are typically taken to mean those sales made to local businesses through their advertising agencies. National sales are those made to national accounts through firms that represent many radio stations nationwide.

In larger stations, a national sales manager works exclusively with those national firms known as rep firms. (In smaller stations the national sales effort is handled by someone else in the sales department, such as the sales manager.) The national sales manager travels to the headquarters of major buyers to make the station's presentation; usually, this is done with the representative from the rep firm. A local sales manager works closely with advertising agency buyers. In some stations, a salesperson will be assigned to work exclusively with co-op (cooperative) advertising, a mechanism whereby national advertisers pay a substantial portion of the advertising for a local retailer carrying the manufacturer's product; the local retailer, of course, receives a prominent mention in the commercial.

In any event, the commercials must be bought and scheduled; this is a much more complex affair than might, at first, be imagined. Stations charge different rates for varying dayparts, and commercials are almost always bought in packages that aim for the maximum exposure to the changing radio audience.

That, in summary, is the overall perspective. Following are close-ups of the most directly relevant details of sales practices and policies. The first item of business is the rate card, the document on which sales prices are structured.

Rate Cards

No matter how complex the **rate card**—and some can be very complicated at first glance—it contains the following basic information:

—— The price of commercial announcements in various dayparts

—— The amount of discount available for large purchases of airtime

And in many cases, the rate card contains the following data:

—— The standard prepackaged plans offered by the station for a mix-and-match arrangement of commercials

—— The amount that supply and demand will affect prices, especially as that supply and demand rises during peak advertising seasons such as the weeks before Christmas

Daypart, length of spots (thirty or sixty seconds), number of spots, and overall length of contract are the four major variables that determine a range. How that information translates to the rate card itself is presented next.

PRICE IN DAYPARTS   Highly rated parts of the listening day command a higher price; usually, the morning drive and afternoon **drive time** is listed as the highest-priced period and is known as AAA time. In an era of ever-increasing self-promotion, some stations now call it AAAA time. The rate card then classifies downward on a sliding scale from AAA, usually 6 to 10 AM and 3 to 7 PM weekdays. AA time is usually midday and evening during the week and most of Saturday. A time is everything left over, including the overnight hours. When a station uses an AAAA designation on the rate card, that usually refers to the morning drive, differentiating it from the afternoon drive, which is classified as AAA. These classifications are not universal, and rate cards vary widely in their time-classification systems.

The price listings usually provide a cost for sixty-second spots and thirty-second spots. In large markets, a thirty-second commercial usually costs between 80 and 90 percent of the price of a sixty-second spot; in small markets, a thirty-second might be closer to 60 percent. The reason a thirty costs almost as much as a sixty is that most radio stations think in terms of the amount of commercials run during an hour rather than the minutes of airtime. This relates partly to some traditional self-restrictions on numbers of spots during an hour and the ever-present desire to reduce commercial clutter and therefore the *number* of commercials. Small markets, which are usually hungrier for advertising, sometimes makes thirties almost a bargain simply because stations need advertising and clients have limited budgets. Although shorter announcements—sometimes one liners—have been used in radio, such use is now rare.

VOLUME OR FREQUENCY DISCOUNTS   A purchase of thirty-six spots might save the buyer almost a third of the cost *per spot* over a purchase of only six spots. Most rate cards indicate this by listing the per-spot price under headings for various volume purchases, usually listed "6X, 12X, 24X . . ." (meaning six times a week, twelve times a week, twenty-four times a week . . ."). Sometimes very large purchases are listed on the rate card, usually under the heading of "bulk plans."

STANDARD PLANS   Some rate cards offer **total audience plan (TAP)** packages. The TAP package offers a prepackaged schedule of spots that, in theory, has a little something for everyone. TAP packages might include a certain percentage (10 percent, perhaps) of spots in morning drive, 20 percent in the midday, 15 percent in afternoon drive, 20 percent overnight, and so on.

Run of station (ROS) packages usually carry no guarantee as to when the spots will run. In most cases, an advertiser is told that the traffic department will put commercials in good and poor time placements; indeed it is in the radio station's interest to provide advertisers with a schedule that produces results. ROS is often an excellent buy, especially during slow periods when many ROS spots find their way into drive time. But in most cases, all ROS spots are preemptible—meaning that during heavy advertising periods (the months before Christmas, for example), ROS spots frequently are "bumped" to a lower position because a higher-priced spot has been sold. ROS usually carries no guarantee that the spots will be scheduled in the best possible time to begin with.

Best time available (BTA) plans compensate for this weakness in ROS scheduling. BTA plans guarantee that a spot will be placed in the highest-rated time period that is open.

Rate cards that offer such plans usually list either ROS or BTA plans, but not both.

SUPPLY AND DEMAND   Supply and demand is sometimes adjusted for by using a grid system. This essentially means that there are various levels of advertising rates; high rates apply during periods of high demand and lower rates during times of low demand. A salesperson might use level-one (grid one) prices during peak advertising seasons, but might sell at grid four during slow months. Or, perhaps, weekends are very slow; in that case, the salesperson might sell weekend spots at grid three, even though the rest of the week is selling at grid one. Some sales experts maintain that an ideal **grid card** should have five levels and that the grid to be used should be determined after a *daily* review of grid levels and inventory to assure that the highest possible prices are being charged at any given time.[3]

Grid cards allow buyers and sellers of airtime to negotiate about prices without *appearing* to negotiate. This seemingly obtuse concept relates to the fact that broadcasters are loath to dicker about the price of airtime, preferring to hold "rate integrity." Grid cards offer a way to negotiate without sacrificing that so-called integrity.

Rate cards come in all shapes and sizes. Figure 9.1 illustrates a sample rate card.

Trade-Out and Barter

Not all advertising is bought and paid for in cash. Frequently, a station works out an arrangement with a merchant whereby a certain amount of unsold commercial spots are traded for merchandise. Station vehicles and restaurant meals are favorite **trade** items.

Most stations impose some voluntary top limit as to how much trade is carried on, and all stations prefer cash sales to trade. Trade is especially helpful to stations whose signoff time varies according to local sunset because in the summer months there is a large supply of airtime that the sales department may have trouble filling. Stations with highly labile seasonal demand such as operations in northern resort communities also can benefit from **trade-out** in slow periods.

If local advertisers do not have the merchandise that the radio station wants, the station manager can elect to enter into an arrangement with a barter firm. These companies act as clearinghouses for barter and allow indirect trades of airtime and products. In this way, a radio station might give airtime to an appliance firm that is a member of the clearinghouse, but receive restaurant meals (from another clearinghouse member) instead.

Figure 9.1

A typical radio station rate card.
Reproduced with permission of WHEB-FM/AM, Portsmouth, NH.

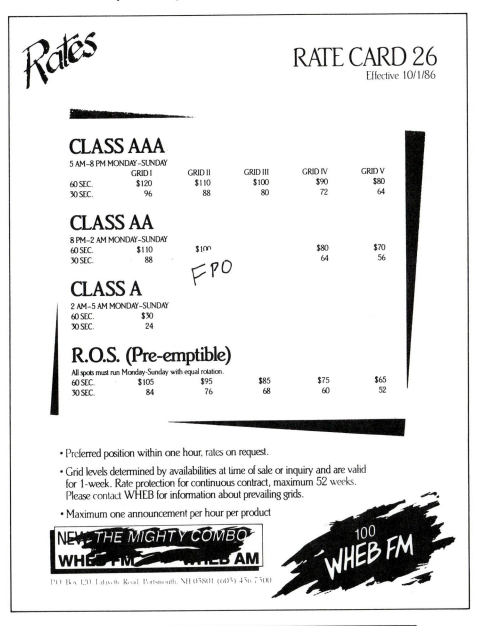

Rates

RATE CARD 26
Effective 10/1/86

CLASS AAA
5 AM–8 PM MONDAY–SUNDAY

	GRID I	GRID II	GRID III	GRID IV	GRID V
60 SEC.	$120	$110	$100	$90	$80
30 SEC.	96	88	80	72	64

CLASS AA
8 PM–2 AM MONDAY–SUNDAY

	GRID I	GRID II	GRID III	GRID IV	GRID V
60 SEC.	$110	$100		$80	$70
30 SEC.	88			64	56

FPO

CLASS A
2 AM–5 AM MONDAY–SUNDAY

	GRID I	GRID II	GRID III	GRID IV	GRID V
60 SEC.	$30				
30 SEC.	24				

R.O.S. (Pre-emptible)
All spots must run Monday-Sunday with equal rotation.

	GRID I	GRID II	GRID III	GRID IV	GRID V
60 SEC.	$105	$95	$85	$75	$65
30 SEC.	84	76	68	60	52

- Preferred position within one hour, rates on request.

- Grid levels determined by availabilities at time of sale or inquiry and are valid for 1-week. Rate protection for continuous contract, maximum 52 weeks. Please contact WHEB for information about prevailing grids.

- Maximum one announcement per hour per product

NEW! THE MIGHTY COMBO
WHEB FM   WHEB AM

100 WHEB FM

P.O. Box 120, Lafayette Road, Portsmouth, NH 03801 (603) 436-7500

Because trade-out is usually easier to produce than is cash, many employee perks come from trade and often supplement an inadequate salary. It is not unheard of for a small-market radio manager to be making a salary more befitting a restaurant busboy but be driving a traded-out car and eating traded-out food.

Advertising Agencies

In large markets, the mechanics of time sales involve heavy interaction with ad agencies at the local level. In smaller markets, the ad agency business is small or nonexistent. Recall from Chapter 8 that much of the radio station's interaction with ad agencies involves trying to work into a buy—that is, attempting to get a piece of the total media package that the ad agency is placing on behalf of its client. Often, specialized media-buying companies place the orders.

Ad agencies typically work on a 15-percent commission of billing (the amount of money spent by the client for advertising space or time purchased through the ad agency). The commission covers the cost of production and account service, although some agencies work on a fee basis in addition to, or in place of, the commission arrangement. An ad agency usually offers creative services—that is, the actual writing and production of the ad—along with media-buying services. If the agency is not capable of providing a station with air-ready ads and spot-placement orders, it may not receive as high as a 15-percent discount on rates.

Much of the work of the radio station sales department involves contact with media buyers. Media buyers are often entry-level personnel and sometimes—in poor agencies—they are not very knowledgeable about media in general and radio in particular. For example, one media buyer recently set a sales manager's teeth on edge with this response: "We decided not to buy your station because we get more spots for the same money on WXXX." WXXX was a much lower-rated station; *of course* there were more spots for the money. It is extremely unlikely that any media buyer does not know how to figure CPP or CPM, but not inconceivable in an agency unused to dealing with radio. Perhaps in this case, the agency did not want to purchase radio at all but did so to placate a client and used the massive buy on a low-rated station to show the client what a "deal" the agency had cut. The specifics do not matter as much as the advice offered by this and many other sales executives: *Do not assume that a media buyer understands the business of radio.* Make it your business to educate the buyer.

Rep Firms

The station's national sales representative, or **rep firm,** serves as a radio station's sales force to the national market. Rep firms deal with national advertisers in such advertising hotbeds as New York, Los Angeles, and Chicago, places where a local station could not afford to place a salesperson. The rep firm fills this void and charges a commission based on its sales.

Rep firms front for many stations but generally do not represent two stations in a particular geographic area; this would put the rep firm into a potential conflict of interest. The national sales manager (or whoever handles national sales) deals most closely with the rep firm and is responsible for keeping the firm up to date on the most recent rates, promotional activities, and so forth.

A rep firm is not an advertising agency. It does not prepare advertising nor plan advertising campaigns per se. The rep firm acts as intermediary between local stations and the big advertising agencies, which buy time at stations across the nation.

Some small and medium stations have traditionally charged higher rates to national advertisers, feeling that the market will bear this expense easily. However, there does appear to be a perceptible trend away from dual-price structures for national and local sales.

Our discussion to this point has dealt largely with the *things* involved in radio stations sales: airtime, rate cards, ad agencies, and rep firms. What now follows is a discussion of the *people* involved in advertising sales as we consider the tiers of the sales effort. This section then focuses on how sales efforts relate to the modern format and on principles of selling time.

9.3

TIERS OF THE SALES EFFORT

As alluded to in the opening of this chapter, some confusion exists in the nomenclature surrounding a sales department's functions and hierarchy. The term *local sales* is often taken to mean selling to local and regional advertising agencies, whereas selling to the local camera store is known as *retail sales.* National sales are typically thought of as sales made by rep firms.

The terminology sometimes varies among stations, and there are certainly some variations among staffing levels and functions. Although the individual people and their functions may differ, the overall goal is primarily the same. Reaching that goal is usually the overall responsibility of the general sales manager who might, in a large market, have several lower tiers of sales management; in a small market, the general sales manager might be the only full-time salesperson and perhaps the general manager.

Salespeople under the direction of the sales manager work in the retail, local, and national sales areas. Closeups of those people and their jobs are described next.

Retail

The salesperson who deals with local retailers is, in small markets, the linchpin of station operations. Clients must be seen and serviced, and new clients developed. In most markets, the salesperson engaged in selling to the retailer has these responsibilities:

1. *List development.* A list is among the first items handed a new salesperson; in the case of a new salesperson, that list usually contains a great many inactive accounts. Developing a list means gaining a collection of clients who buy and a collection of clients who might buy.

2. *Prospecting.* Closely related to list building is the concept of calling on potential clients, assessing their needs and their likelihood of purchasing. A part of a salesperson's prospecting is qualifying—that is, finding the right type of client for a station and a client who will benefit from radio advertising.

3. *Selling.* Selling a client is not a one-shot affair; it may take five, six, even ten calls to persuade a client to buy airtime.

4. *Servicing.* The retail salesperson's job does not end after the contract is inked; the salesperson must assure that the advertising works and that the client is happy with the results. Repeat business comprises the bulk of the salesperson's income.

Local

In many cases the same people who handle retail sales work with advertising agencies on the so-called local accounts. Typically, an advertising salesperson covets an agency account because such accounts can produce larger income with a smaller time investment than does a retail account.

Some of the functions typically handled by a salesperson dealing with an agency are evaluation, persuasion and presentation, and continuing service.

EVALUATION   This is not really as academic a subject as it might seem. Evaluation is a roll-up-the-sleeves task where agency and radio station representatives determine the target demographics, discuss the best dayparts, and frequently haggle indirectly over the price. What typically happens is this: The salesperson tries to find out the total advertising budget—both in terms of all the money to be spent and the highest CPP or CPM to be allowed—and the advertising agency representative quite reasonably declines to lay bare the workings of the purchasing plan. Then, the bits and pieces of available information are exchanged until a settlement of sorts is reached.

PERSUASION AND PRESENTATION   Selling an agency buyer is not quite the same as selling a local merchant. For one thing, most of the time an agency makes the first call, inquiring as to whether the station has a number of avails (**availabilities,** available commercial times) it can sell. As a result, the salesperson typically does not spend much time selling radio as a medium; that sale has already been made because the buyer requested airtime in the first place. This is not to say that there is no cold-calling on agencies and that agency buyers are always knowledgeable about and favorable toward radio. It simply asserts that the presentation does involve *convincing* a buyer to buy as much as *servicing* the needs of the buyer. The direct competition is against other radio stations, because the amount of money allocated to radio usually has been predetermined.

CONTINUING SERVICE   Although most sales are directly initiated by advertising buyers, those buyers need a reason to call the station in the first place. Quite often that reason is basic interpretation of ratings and demographics. However, a salesperson who services the agency—provides continuing information on such things as new promotions and format changes—usually gets *more* calls.

National

The national sales manager must be the liaison to rep firms and, by extension, to the purchasers of national advertising. This job usually involves, first, ensuring that the national sales reps have current information and monitoring to ensure that the rep firms produce adequately. Second, the job involves attending some presentations such as those made to national advertisers once a year. The national sales manager attends with the station rep. Although the rep may do a perfectly good job throughout the year, no rep knows the station as well as the national sales manager whose presence is a definite plus at a presentation for a major account.

In general terms, the national sales manager is responsible for spot and network accounts as opposed to the local sales manager who works with local and retail accounts. Some additional information on those terms and concepts is helpful.

Spot has an imprecise definition but usually is taken to mean any commercial availability not developed for any sort of special programming—that is, the standard advertising avails in a typical log. The word is further used to reflect spot sales made by media buyers approaching the radio station. In any event, sales to national advertisers come under the purview of the national sales manager.

Network sometimes defies precise definition, too, because the exact constitution of a network is changing as improved technology allows quick and relatively informal, ad-hoc formation of "networks." These arrangements are usually referred to as "unwired" networks.

Unwired network sales may or may not be national accounts because some networks such as those that carry sporting events are regional in nature. A unwired network typically secures broadcast rights to an event or program and signs up member stations. Member stations receive local availabilities—say, seven per hour—while the unwired network sells the remaining seven avails to national advertisers.

Income from traditional wired networks varies considerably according to the size of the station. In a major market, local stations are paid for running network commercials such as those contained in national network radio newscasts. There is sometimes a tendency to minimize the contribution modern wired networks make to a station, but in the case of some very large markets a network may pay a local affiliate $50 per spot cleared. Some basic arithmetic shows that networks can be a valuable source of income for the large metropolitan station.

In smaller markets, though, the networks pay less. A medium market might earn only $1 or $2 per spot cleared, and a small-market station is lucky to get away with free use of the network in exchange for clearing a certain number of spots. As an example, one actual small-market deal involved a station agreeing to clear two network spots per hour and about eighty special programming shows throughout the year. In exchange, the network paid for the $10,000 satellite dish and provided the local station with high-quality news and features.

9.4

SALES AND THE MODERN FORMAT

There is a saying in sales that no one who buys a drill really wants a drill. He wants a hole. While epigrammatic wisdom is not always totally accurate, that saying presents a memorable example of the benefit-oriented approach to sales.

A salesperson, a sales manager, and a general manager are in the business of selling benefits, which translates to *results* for the purchaser of the advertising. Selling spots is not a goal in itself because few local businesspeople have any interest in buying spots for the sake of spots, if indeed they know what a spot is. Furthermore, ineffective advertising does not spur further purchases on the part of the customer who pays money but sees few results.

This section focuses on the role and structure of radio advertising in general and, specifically, on packaging the right audience, a consideration closely related to the format. The following section deals with the actual techniques of customer contact and closing sales.

Remember that sales is a broad area that cannot be completely encapsulated within the space of a chapter. Further readings specifically devoted to sales methods are worthwhile for anyone hoping to grow beyond the basics.[4] Additional sources are listed in the bibliography at the end of the book.

Salespeople, Advertisers, and the Target Audience

Salespeople often maintain that it takes a minimum of three exposures for a commercial to make an impact. In fact, modern computer software designed to manipulate ratings figures estimates the number of times a commercial is needed to reach the desired demographic to be three.

Regardless of individual approaches, the idea of reaching a target audience with an often-repeated message is the crux of the business. Done correctly, this strategy translates into benefits for the advertiser—namely, more customers, more recognition, and more profits. Reduced to the basic elements, a successful radio advertising sales force deals in *benefits* by taking the following actions.

SELLING IDEAS, NOT SPOTS   Experienced salespeople and sales executives are unanimous in their contention that a salesperson must talk to a retailer in retailer's language, not broadcast jargon. You are selling "increased store traffic," not a "flight of spots." Telling someone he'll get "a broad rotation through the demographic" is gibberish. Instead, talk his language by telling him that he'll get "customers with disposable income, young women with a house full of children, increased floor traffic," and so forth.

SELL WORKABLE SOLUTIONS   Because radio heavily relies on repetition, a total advertising plan of four spots probably won't do a customer much if any good. A salesperson would serve the customer better by dissuading that purchase and selling a package that will work. The same principle applies to any situation where the customer does not receive value for the advertising dollar. It takes fortitude to tell a client no, but producing results accrues more income over the long term than does a quick sale of a package that may give the advertiser a lifelong aversion to radio.

SELL AND RESPECT THE FORMAT   The highly specific nature of radio programming has resulted in subtle and often rigid format guidelines and restrictions. The same guidelines and restrictions that make a station an audience grabber must apply to commercials as well. Such a consideration is hardly trivial: Program directors have become increasingly insistent on commercials that do not drive away the very audience that they have tried so diligently to capture. Salespeople must stay within the guidelines for copy and production music.

A related point is that salespeople should be very wary of offering "extras," "promotional announcements," or "bonuses" without consulting the general manager or program director. Such promised gimmicks may violate the integrity of the format and could set a poor precedent for future dealings with that particular client and other clients who want the same extras.

SELL CREATIVE SOLUTIONS   Some ideas relating to advertising packages and co-op sales have been presented elsewhere, but the subject of co-op as it specifically relates to the sales effort of the modern station is worth a final examination. Co-op, the process by which a major manufacturer agrees to underwrite a portion of a retailer's advertising budget directly advertising the manufacturer's products, is widely regarded as an undersold commodity. In particular, broadcasters have been told for years they must become as expert in their handling of co-op plans as their counterparts in newspaper. There is increasing agreement that each broadcast co-op plan should be carefully controlled and administered by knowledgeable personnel who have closely studied co-op.[5]

Experienced salespeople know that merchants often dread the paperwork and general complications involved in co-op. In many cases merchants do not know that co-op exists or even what co-op is. That, in sum, is why a sales department should have one or more co-op experts to grease the skids and educate merchants. Among other items, merchants should know that it is their (the merchants') responsibility to pay the station's bill; merchants are reimbursed by the manufacturer.

As an example of spadework the salesperson can attempt, a call to the manufacturer's home office can determine which merchants in the area are eligible and how much co-op the merchant is allowed. Also, the Radio Advertising Bureau publishes an annual list of co-op advertisers and how much of a local retailer's advertising they will cover.

If a co-op package can be created and sold, everyone benefits. In direct relation to the concept of reaching a target audience, co-op is an extremely efficient way to reach a specific demographic. The advertising package from the national firm is frequently of good caliber, and the additional funding allows a productive level of repetition.

Factors Relating to Audience Characteristics

To reiterate, a radio station sales department must sell an audience against other media and against radio. Two primary tasks are thus imposed on the sales staff:

—— Differentiating the radio medium from other media

—— Differentiating the station's audience from other radio stations in the market

Remember that it is really the *audience* that matters. Claiming that radio is intrinsically "better" than newspaper is in itself a pointless argument. (Which is *better*, basketball or football?) However, the fact that radio delivers a different type of audience than does newspaper is a perfectly lucid argument, which can in fact be supported in a number of ways.

SELLING AGAINST PRINT[6]   Knowing the strengths and weaknesses of newspapers and their audience is extremely helpful in planning the sales effort. Strengths of newspapers are the following:

1.   Habit.

2.   Tangible item (readers can bring an ad into a store).

3.   Coupons.

4.   A newspaper stays around the house.

5. One hundred percent co-op readily available.

6. Multiple items can be listed in one ad.

    Weaknesses of newspapers are the following:

1. Circulation is not keeping pace with population growth.

2. Limited target audience (mainly ages thirty-five and over).

3. High cost per thousand and rising much more quickly than other media because of increasing production and distribution costs.

4. The average advertising content of U.S. daily and Sunday newspapers is over 62 percent.

5. There is no exclusivity in the paper; your ad could run right next to a competitor's.

6. Early deadline.

7. Once the paper is printed, a mistake cannot be changed.

8. People have very little time to read.

9. Most papers are read at night; the ads are for sales that occurred that day.

10. Newspapers cannot appeal to the senses.

11. Many people cannot or do not read.

SELLING AGAINST TELEVISION AND CABLE TELEVISION[7]   VHF/UHF is usually not a prime competitor for radio advertising except in the large markets and larger medium markets. However, cable television is making larger inroads into medium and small markets. The increasing penetration of cable in many communities is expanding cable system owners' interest in selling local spots. Strengths of television/cable are the following:

1. Audience size.

2. Ego appeal (to clients who purchase television ads).

3. Incorporates sight and sound.

    Weaknesses of television/cable are the following:

1. Loose demographic appeal (difficult to isolate a demographic).

2. High production costs.

3.   Advertisements cannot be changed quickly.

4.   Cable is in competition with VHF/UHF television.

5.   Videotape recorders are now in almost 40 percent of U.S. households; people are watching more commercial-free movies or recording programs and fast forwarding through the commercial breaks.

6.   Cable television subscription is not equal to the number of people watching at any given time.

7.   Television viewing changes with the seasons; viewing is at its lowest during the summer months.

SELLING RADIO[8]   When selling against other media and especially when selling against other radio stations, it is imperative not to denigrate the competition. Etiquette aside, a salesperson who is highly critical of another radio station when presenting to a client is in effect being critical of radio in general. It is far better for a salesperson to say, "That other station does an excellent job reaching the thirty-five and over audience. But perhaps you could use our station to reach a whole different type of audience, younger people who would probably be strong buyers of your clothing line."

At all costs avoid saying, "That station is for old people! They're not going to buy clothes like the ones you sell! You're wasting your money." For one thing, the salesperson using this approach has just called his customer an idiot, and possibly an "old person" as well, and has created an atmosphere of confusion about the worth of radio in general.

It is advisable therefore to play up the strengths of your station and the strengths of all radio. Strengths of radio are the following:

1.   Affordable.

2.   Targets your customers.

3.   Commercials can be changed quickly.

4.   Free or nominal-cost production.

5.   Reaches 96 percent of people over twelve years old every week.

6.   Exclusivity in stop sets. (The advertisers's commercial is the only one for this particular business in a cluster of commercials, the stop set.)

7.   Last chance to reach customers.

8.   People do not actively participate; radio sells subliminally.

9. Ninety-nine percent of all homes have a radio.

10. Ninety-five percent of all cars have a radio.

11. Ninety-three percent of all car radios are AM/FM.

12. Consistent listenership, not affected by season.

13. Creates theater of the mind.

14. By "tagging" clients' commercials, radio can make other advertising media more effective ("see our coupon in today's paper").

15. Radio is always growing. There are more listeners every day.

Weaknesses of radio are the following:

1. It is intangible.

2. It is "blind" and cannot incorporate the visual.

9.5

PRINCIPLES OF EFFECTIVE SALES

Much of radio sales is a learned skill. Despite the adage that salespeople are "born and not made," much can be learned from the experience of other sales professionals. Many techniques have been refined, tested, and described in various literature. *They do work.*

Developing a Sales Presentation

The primary task is to construct a convincing presentation. Volumes could (and have been) written on the subject, but seven fundamental points recur.

DRESS WELL Although this advice seems something of a cliché, it is important to realize that a salesperson deals with people who place strong emphasis on appearance. Dress *does* make a difference.

USE WRITTEN PRESENTATIONS FOR IMPORTANT ACCOUNTS You cannot write up a proposal for every client, but written proposals work very well and have come into increasing favor among radio station salespeople and sales executives. In major markets, written presentations are the rule. In medium markets, they are usually reserved for the largest clients, and in small markets for major clients (if they are used at all). Word processing can make the construction of proposals simpler and can personalize the proposals with ease. Contents of a written sales proposal are discussed at greater length in the following section, "Using Research as a Sales Tool."

MAKE YOUR PRESENTATION TANGIBLE One of radio's greatest problems is that it cannot be handled, touched, or put in a scrapbook. It is fleeting, at least in the mind of the purchaser of airtime. Use of tangible items can partially overcome this problem. Three examples are the following. First, when selling radio time, have the production department make up a **speculation (spec) tape,** a sample of the kind of commercial you would like to sell to the client. Newspapers have used this tactic successfully for many years (the salesperson visits the store with a typeset ad), and radio can learn from this practice. Leave the tape with the client.

What do you include in a spec tape? Generally, you'll want to incorporate the thrust of what the client has told you about the business. You *must* use the techniques of production and advertising salesmanship in the spot; creativity in a spec tape is very important because you're attempting to show the client what radio can do for the business that other media cannot. Along these lines, it is often useful to incorporate dialogue, dramatic scenes, occasional sound effects, and other elements that radio does well.

If you have not had the opportunity to interview the client at any length, you can still prepare an effective spec tape by examining the ads placed by the client in other media. Use the information but improve on it; isolate and identify a theme.

Second, have the client handle your sales material. Instead of showing a page of figures breaking down costs for an advertising campaign, hand it to the client to hold during the presentation.

Third, secure *written* testimonials from other clients and hand them to the client you are trying to sell.

GET THE CLIENT IN THE HABIT OF SAYING YES "Powers Men's Shop used a remote to boost traffic, and they attracted over one thousand people. Wouldn't that be just the kind of result you'd like?" (What is the client going to say?) "And our station owns the men in the ages eighteen and over demographic . . . Aren't they the kind of customers you want to reach?" (What could the owner of a men's shop possibly say besides Yes?) "Can we start your ads Monday?" (You've got the client in the habit of saying Yes—maybe it will happen once more.)

LEARN TO COUNTER OBJECTIONS   A salesperson cannot argue or badger a client into purchasing airtime. Proving a client wrong—at least directly—is counterproductive. Instead, a successful sale often involves parrying objections and gracefully turning them into positive factors. For example, consider the following dialogue:

Client: Your ratings aren't very good.

You: Which ratings are those, Mr. Johnson? [You are focusing the issue.]

Client: Well, whatever the ratings are. The guy from WAAA [the other station] told me your station finished third.

You: WAAA finished ahead of us in certain categories, and we finished ahead in others. Now I certainly understand your concern with reaching as many people as possible [assuring the client that he is intelligent], and WAAA does a good job reaching large numbers of listeners in a general category. We can deliver an audience that you might be interested in, too. The ratings show that we reach more women ages eighteen to thirty-five than any other station in the market, including WAAA. Aren't women eighteen to thirty-five the most important customers for your department store? [Force a Yes; if you've done your homework, you know the answer.]

Client: Yes, that's right. [Aha! He's saying Yes. Stay tuned because this episode will be continued.]

There are many strategies for overcoming objections, and experienced sales managers have established routines that they introduce to beginning salespeople, often in a role-playing situation. Role playing is very helpful to salespeople, and anyone interested in a career in sales is advised to do as much role playing as possible.

DEVELOP TRIAL CLOSES   A trial close is a painless way to get the client to agree, or *almost* agree, to running commercials. The trial close sets the stage for the actual close, the verbal agreement and/or signing of the contract. Often, it is a question posed as if the contract were already signed, sealed, and delivered, making the actual close predestined. Here is how a trial close might work on the department store owner:

You: [after countering objections and telling the client a little more about your station's strengths] It seems as though you really know your customers, and the package we've discussed would reach those people very efficiently. Would you like to write the commercial copy, or would you rather have us do it?

Client: I should write the basics, but you should have your people check it over and punch it up. [Notice how difficult it will be at this point for the client to back up and deal with the original question of whether he wants to run ads on your station?]

Other trial closes might include:

—— Would you like prerecorded commercials or would you rather have our DJs ad lib from a fact sheet?

—— If I can co-op half your costs, can I put this schedule on the air? [You already should know, of course, if the costs can be co-oped.]

—— Would you like to start this week or next week?

These are effective strategies, but use them with caution.

GO FOR THE CLOSE "You would be amazed at how many salesmen don't get the contract *because they don't ask for it*," says Brad Murray, a successful sales manager for a highly rated station in Boston. Murray, whose experience includes general management in several small and medium markets, feels that not asking for a close is a fundamental mistake made by many novices in broadcast sales.

How do you ask for a close? Sometimes it can be a strictly straightforward matter: "I'll go ahead with the schedule, okay?" Or, it could be done with a choice close: "Should I book the schedule of all sixties or the schedule with the thirties?" (Note that this is similar to some of the trial closes, but here you are actually asking for the order.)

There are things you should *not* do when closing. Many experienced professionals such as Charles Warner, a former salesman who is now an author and teacher, warn against using the words *buy* or *order* because they frighten clients (presumably by reminding them that they are actually spending money).

Using Research as a Sales Tool

To some extent, good ratings sell themselves. Retail advertisers seek out the local ratings leader, and advertising agencies buy by the numbers. This does not mean, of course, that a top-rated station cannot be hurt by a poor sales effort. However, a poor sales effort can kill a station with middling numbers.

Conversely, competent sales can make a profit from less-than-sparkling ratings. The concept is known as *selling without numbers.* One way to sell without numbers is to recognize that somewhere, somehow, your station must have a numeric advantage. Looking at the Arbitron historical report for the previous rating periods, can you honestly say that your station shows *consistent* growth? If so, say so. Even though your numbers are low overall, do they show very low turnover? That is a strong point to make when dealing with an advertiser who has a complex message that needs repetition.

A final thought about ratings is that numbers can easily be overemphasized. Experienced professionals know that ratings can and do go down; a station that uses numbers as its *only* sales tool is heading for a fall should the next book show even a small decrease. Many radio station executives believe that goodwill, value, and *results* are the most positive attributes that can be sold to a client.

Results comprise a research and sales tool. Testimonials from satisfied clients, especially those testimonials that spell out results numerically (percentage of increase of sales or percentage of increase in customer response, for example), are fine evidence of your station's value.

Sometimes, a client elects to personally research the effectiveness of ads on your station. Known as "testing an ad," this concept can be useful but can prove disastrous. Clients frequently purchase small amounts of advertising with the promise of buying more "if it works out." Nothing is inherently wrong in this approach, but the salesperson must be sure that the test is fair. Clients who offer an essentially worthless promotion are setting up themselves and you for failure. Also, clients may have little idea of the vagaries of research into advertising response. As a rather horrifying example, consider the true case of a furniture store that pulled all its newspaper advertising for a month to "test" a flight of radio spots. Customers arriving for a special closeout were asked where they heard about the sale. Of the respondents, 67 percent said they had read about the sale in a newspaper ad, even though the store had *never* run an ad for the sale! It is fortunate that the furniture store advertising manager had the sense to suspend newspaper advertising and arrange a fair test; many merchants would not have had the wherewithal to conduct such a balanced test.[9]

Keep that example in mind when arranging a fair test. Make sure that the merchant is not predicating the test on moving merchandise that no one wanted to buy in the first place (which is exactly why many sales are held). If other media are advertising the same sale, attempt to insert a unique offer or piece of information into the radio commercials so that their effectiveness is differentiated. Possibly, you may ask the merchant to keep track of ZIP codes on checks and charge card receipts before and during the radio test so that the increased coverage area—very often an advantage of radio—can be documented.

Client Relations

In the best of situations, advertising salespeople earn the respect and friendship of their clients and enjoy those relationships for many years. Although this situation has an unexpected downside (to be explained in a moment), it can be a pleasant and lucrative aspect of the profession.

To be realistic, though, selling is not always so pleasant. The examples of overcoming objections and attempted closings were presented not only to illustrate the techniques but also to show that there is a certain amount of confrontation and competition involved in the process. There is tension, there is rejection, and there is a certain amount of fear involved in facing new people and situations.

BUILDING A CLIENT LIST   The comfortable situation felt by salespeople who deal with long-established clients is often exactly what causes lists to shrink. It is essential for a salesperson to keep making cold calls, as unpleasant as those calls may be. Successful salespeople usually are goalsetters, people who plan continuing cold calls and force themselves to make a certain quota of calls per day or per week. There are many businesses that are not being called on in any community, and each of those businesses represents a potential source of income.

SERVICING CLIENTS   Although most salespeople primarily regard servicing as continued contact with clients to straighten out problems (which are unavoidable because advertising is a complex business) and to keep relations cordial, there is another equally important aspect. Servicing is selling over the long term. In other words, the salesperson who provides conscientious service to a client is there when a client needs help in solving a promotional problem, perhaps, or overcoming a slow sales period. Also, the salesperson who stays in frequent contact has more than adequate time to inform the client of potential opportunities for seasonal or holiday promotions. Servicing is a worthwhile activity, and some successful sales leaders report that they spend up to a quarter of their time involved in servicing.

Setting Goals

An interesting aspect of radio time sales business is that while salespeople operate with a great deal of autonomy, they work under a relatively strict set of expectations. In other words, they are given a goal that they must meet, but they have quite a bit of latitude as to how they reach it.

Autonomy poses a problem for people who are not self-motivated. There is a powerful temptation to take a two-hour lunch when you make the schedule. Sales calls have a tendency to evolve into social events, and extended chats with established clients can turn into excuses not to call on new customers.

Self-motivation is a key asset of the successful salesperson. In addition to the goals a salesperson sets, certain expectations are imposed by sales management. Those who move into sales management frequently find goal setting a difficult part of the job, particularly because revenue levels are not always directly attributable to the sales department.

The practice of sales management is beyond the scope of this book, but it is worthwhile to note that many managers assert that setting clear goals and expectations is the key to keeping sales up and quotas met. For example, Ken Greenwood summarizes a sales manager's functions in a "SMART" system: **S**et performance expectations; **M**easurement methods must be defined; **A**greement on performance of goal; **R**einforcement, reprimand, praise, coach; **T**rack performance.[10]

9.6

ADVERTISING BASICS

Salespeople need a reasonably good acquaintance with the principles of advertising. After all, it is the product they sell; in some cases, salespeople actually write the script.

Now that we've explained the concept of selling time, it's worth noting that there is a continuing dilemma that faces salespeople, and it cuts directly to the heart of advertising and advertising strategy. Simply stated, radio salespeople have an obligation to provide the client with advertising that stimulates sales, fits the station's sound, and pleases the client.

Writing and producing commercials that meet all three goals is difficult because convincing the client that your intended approach is a proper one is not always easy. Many clients, particularly small-market retailers, have explicit ideas on what they want in their spots. Unfortunately, what they want may not always work. As an example, merchants frequently request extensive listings of their merchandise—a bad tactic for radio because the listener can't remember lists and the time for listing is inherently limited.

An enlightened retailer often—given the right explanation—opts for a more intelligent approach that stresses emotional appeal rather than a listing of products. Figure 9.2 demonstrates this idea.

Figure 9.2

A radio commercial script.
Courtesy of Creative Communications.

Client: Vona Shoes **Job Description:** 60-second spot **Media:** WSGO **Date:** August 19__	**Creative Communications** *Advertising and Public Relations* Box 1024 □ Oswego, New York 13126

ANNOUNCER: REMEMBER THE EXCITEMENT OF GOING BACK TO SCHOOL WHEN YOU WERE A KID? THERE WAS THE SLIGHT SADNESS THAT SUMMER WAS OVER, BUT THERE WAS ALSO THE SENSE OF ANTICIPATION. . . . NEW BEGINNINGS AND A FEELING OF GOOD TIMES AHEAD FOR THE NEW SCHOOL YEAR.

ALONG WITH THAT SENSE OF EXCITEMENT CAME THE TIME WHEN YOU WENT SHOPPING FOR NEW CLOTHES. THEY ALWAYS HAD A SPECIAL KIND OF "NEW" SMELL TO THEM. AND WHEN YOU SMELL IT TODAY, YOU PROBABLY THINK OF GOING BACK TO SCHOOL.

BEST OF ALL, THOUGH, WAS GETTING NEW SHOES. YOUR OLD RELIABLES HAD JUST ABOUT MADE IT THROUGH THE PAST YEAR. AND NOW IT WAS TIME TO GET THOSE BRAND NEW ONES THAT WOULD GET YOU OFF TO A GOOD START.

WELL VONA SHOES, 122 WEST SECOND STREET, OSWEGO, IS THE PLACE THAT CAN BUILD SIMILAR MEMORIES FOR YOUR CHILD. AND WHILE THEY'RE AT IT THEY'LL SEE TO IT THAT YOUR CHILD GETS QUALITY AND A GOOD FIT. THE TOP BRAND NAMES IN CHILDREN'S FOOTWEAR IN VONA'S EXTENSIVE INVENTORY MEANS THAT YOU'LL FIND THE SIZE YOU NEED AND YOU'LL GET VALUE.

THAT'S IMPORTANT FOR YOU. BUT FOR YOUR CHILD, THERE WILL BE EXCITEMENT AND THE FUN OF GOING TO BUY SHOES FOR BACK TO SCHOOL. A TIME FILLED WITH SIGNIFICANCE IN A YOUNG LIFE.

VONA SHOES . . . WHERE THEY UNDERSTAND YOU.

As mentioned earlier in this chapter, salespeople must avoid letting a client buy spots that won't work. In the long run, selling ineffective spots is counterproductive.

To continue another discussion introduced earlier, it is important to remember that radio advertisements are not particularly effective when placed singly—that is, a one-shot affair like a classified ad. Effective radio advertising is usually mounted in terms of a campaign, that is, a series of spots that build an image, reinforce an idea, and persuade over the long run. The idea of spot placement, reach, and frequency has been highly detailed elsewhere, but it is worth mentioning here that the goal of a radio advertising campaign is to stress a *theme*. The campaign must stress a coherent and somehow related series of ideas and appeals.

For example, a flight of ads for a local department store may stress, in various ways, that the store offers high-quality, luxury merchandise; this would be a consistent appeal to prestige. It is likely that a scattershot campaign jumping from theme to theme—a campaign with no centrally related idea—would be less effective.

Salespeople realize that appeals must be carefully structured *over the long run*. They may design a series of commercials that stress, for example,

— *Appeal to a bandwagon effect.* Note how many commercials stress the idea that "everyone else is doing/buying/joining/etc." Carried out in a coherent campaign, this appeal can be highly effective.

— *Appeal to personal fulfillment.* The U.S. Army ran an extensive campaign on radio and television imploring prospective soldiers to "be all that you can be." Such an appeal was highly effective because *the basic appeal stayed the same* even though the premises and particulars of the commercials varied.

There are many types of appeals in a radio advertising campaign, and they can be utilized effectively if the thrust is clear.

How can the salesperson plan the campaign and keep those issues clear? Basically, you must develop an easily stated theme. If you can't describe the theme of the campaign in a few words, it's probably too complex for radio. A good campaign can be summed up in a few words: "This bank has friendly loan officers who will treat you with respect." "These drugstores have fast, efficient clerks who will not waste your valuable time by making you wait in line." "This shoe store offers high fashion, but at a reasonable price."

Radio sales is not an easy job; that much should be obvious from the material presented in this chapter. What perhaps is not so clearly observed by a cursory examination of the profession is that salespeople are the ones who keep their fingers on the pulse of the station. Sales is a critical position in the modern radio station. After all, it is the sales force who provides the income to the station—figuratively translating the work of programming, engineering, management, and all other teammates into the lifeblood of any commercial enterprise.

EXERCISES

1. The following must be done as a co-operative project; if it can be managed, the experience will be worthwhile. As a class presentation, one or more class members will obtain a packet of sales materials from a local radio station and use that material in a role-playing situation. Try to "sell" a classmate or co-worker who assumes the role of the manager of an auto racetrack. Whoever takes the role of the salesperson is responsible for becoming familiar with the sales material. The role player for the auto track is assigned to investigate and uncover at least some rudimentary facts about racetracks, such as to whom they appeal, whether their business is seasonal, and if they typically offer promotional events. (HINT: A call to the local auto racing track would not be out of order.)

   If time and circumstances allow, repeat the above exercise with one role player assuming the identity of the owner of a movie theater, a lawyer specializing in personal-injury law, and the manager of a computer store.

2. Examine a copy of the telephone book "Yellow Pages" for your area. Choose five businesses of any type that you believe would be excellent prospects for a call from a radio salesperson. Choosing from among those with large display ads will help you gather information. Briefly explain why those businesses will be good prospects. (HINT: A stereo store would probably be a fine prospect; can you determine why? This counts as one of the five choices.)

   Next, choose five businesses you would be less likely to approach if you were a radio station salesperson. (Start with a small grocery store, usually not a very good bet for radio. Why?)

3. This is a group exercise that involves close cooperation among class or group members. You must develop a comprehensive ad campaign for a hypothetical— or, if circumstances allow, a real—advertising client.

   The exact methods will vary depending on the individual situation, but use this basic strategy:

   a. Elect, or have your instructor appoint, a general sales manager
   b. The sales manager will assign duties to class members, including writing,

researching, and programming. The researchers will analyze market data, target audience, availability of co-op funds, and so on. The programmers will then decide on the optimum amount and placement of the spots.

c. All class members will collaborate on a *written* presentation and summary of the campaign. The writers of the spots will produce a series of commercials that present a coherent theme.

NOTES

1. Figures are from *1985 Employees Compensation and Fringe Benefit Report* (Washington, D.C.: National Association of Broadcasters Research and Planning Dept., 1986.), 4, 5.

2. *1985 Employees Compensation and Fringe Benefit Report,* 19.

3. National Association of Broadcasters, *MegaRates: How to Get Top Dollar for Your Spots* (Washington, D.C.: The Research Group, 1986), IX.

4. Among the most worthwhile are Tom Hopkins, *How to Master the Art of Selling* (Scottsdale, AZ: Champion Press, 1980); and Charles Warner, *Broadcast and Cable Selling* (Belmont, CA: Wadsworth, 1986).

5. William McGee, *Broadcast Co-Op: The Untapped Goldmine* (San Francisco, CA: Broadcast Marketing Co., 1975), passim.

6. Analysis of strengths and weaknesses adapted from Timothy Cushman, *Sound Results: A Practical Guide to Selling Radio* (Training manual, Copyright 1987). Used with permission of the author.

7. Cushman, *Sound Results.* Used with permission of the author.

8. Cushman, *Sound Results.* Used with permission of the author.

9. Cushman, *Sound Results.* Used with permission of the author.

10. Ken Greenwood, "Excellence in Managing and Motivating Salespeople" in *Radio in Search of Excellence, Lessons from America's Best-Run Stations,* Greenwood Development Programs Inc. (Washington, D.C.: National Association of Broadcasters, 1985), 73–81.

PART FOUR

MANAGEMENT

CHAPTER 10

PERSONNEL AND

OPERATIONS MANAGEMENT

It is a cliché to state that people are the most important resource in any business setting. The fact is, however, to succeed in business today managers must be highly skilled in the process of motivating people to perform at their best. Peter F. Drucker, considered by many to be America's foremost management authority, defines the very concept of management in terms of people. "Indeed, the specific job of the manager is to make the strengths of people productive and their weaknesses irrelevant."[1] *People* make things happen for an organization. *People* produce the products or services that justify the organization's existence.

To make effective use of people, managers must understand the operations that people perform for an organization. What are the processes that go into producing a particular product or service? How do people interact with these processes? It is evident from looking at the variety of management books on the market that there are a great many ways for managers to make operations and people combine productively. The process of doing all this systematically and effectively can be extremely complex. To simplify things, it is helpful to step back and spend a moment looking at things in a broad philosophical sense.

Michael J. Jucius in his book *Personnel Management* offers a useful philosophical analysis of the problem of maximizing the productivity of people. Jucius states, "A personnel philosophy may take either of two directions. First, labor may be viewed as a factor which tends more or less passively or actively to resist managerial leadership. People must therefore be molded and controlled by management to achieve company objectives. Second, labor may be viewed as a factor with inherently constructive potentials. Management's task, then, is to provide an environment in which this force will willingly exert itself to the fullest." [2]

The first approach offered by Jucius dominated business practice for years. It assumes that workers in an organization cannot be expected to buy into the organization's goals and that management needs to exercise vigilance, lest productivity suffer. The second approach is based on a belief that employees work most effectively when they are placed in optimal circumstances. The old-style boss, who motivated through fear, has to a great extent been replaced by managers intent upon improving the working environment. Both approaches seek the same goal—increased productivity.

All the principles of effective management and all the statements of management philosophy lead ultimately to the same idea: The basic task of managers in any business enterprise is to *make things happen.* To do that managers must understand how to get people to do what is best for the business. Managers must know what tasks need to be performed and how resources are best employed in bringing about the desired results. Chapter 11 focuses on financial management; this chapter deals with the management of people and processes.

10.1

BASIC MANAGEMENT STRUCTURES

Peter Drucker, in his book *Innovation and Entrepreneurship,* uses the McDonald's hamburger chain to illustrate how effective management, applied to what had been a "mom-and-pop" type of business, resulted in making this business a major success. Drucker notes that

McDonald's first designed the end product; then it redesigned the entire process of making it; then it redesigned or in many cases invented the tools so that every piece of meat, every slice of onion, every bun, every piece of fried potato would be identical. . . . Finally, McDonald's studied what "value" meant to the customer, defined it as quality and predictability of product, speed of service, absolute cleanliness, and friendliness, then set standards for all these, trained for them, and geared compensation to them. [3]

Drucker's citation of the McDonald's success story uses a very straightforward explanation to describe operations that were by no means easy to accomplish. The value of looking at this simple statement of how McDonald's achieved success is that it gets to the essence of how managers must look at things. The whole process must start with a simple analysis of *what* it is you want to accomplish.

1. Start with the product or service you want to provide.

2. Determine how to produce that product or service; then acquire the necessary facilities and equipment to produce the product or service.

3. Look at the consumer and make adjustments designed to maximize the appeal of your product to the customer.

4. Hire and manage people to perform the operations that will turn out the product or service at the necessary level of quality to satisfy consumers and to achieve the organization's goals.

To actually accomplish what has been described is far from simple. The operations necessary to accomplish these basic goals are complex and costly. Even in small organizations, it takes skill, hard work, and careful use of resources to achieve success. But if managers are able to see beyond the complexity of day-to-day problems and focus on the essential elements that drive any business enterprise, their likelihood of success is high.

Fiscal Management Versus Operations Management

Managers must be concerned with two general areas in order to run an organization effectively: operations management—or the activities that actually get things done—and fiscal management—those aspects of the operation having to do with the financial end of the enterprise.

FISCAL MANAGEMENT   To manage the fiscal resources of the broadcast operation, it is necessary to keep a hard eye on the bottom line. Where is the revenue coming from to finance the operation? What kinds of budgeting processes ensure effective operations but avoid waste and inefficiency? How can an acceptable profit be generated? What levels of sales are necessary to meet operational expenses and return a profit? Is there a need for capital improvement that calls for long-term allocation of resources outside the normal budgetary processes? Taxes, return on investment, depreciation—these are the concerns in commercial management. They are considered in greater depth in Chapter 11.

OPERATIONS MANAGEMENT   Operations management is tied in many ways to commercial management, but the focus is different. In operations management it is necessary to consider carefully what the essential mission of the enterprise is. The task then becomes one of ensuring that people and resources are used effectively in achieving the mission. To do this, the radio manager must have a solid understanding of how each area (programming, sales, engineering, and so on) contributes to the success of the whole organization.

To fully understand the orientation of the radio manager with regard to station operations, it is necessary to clear up a common misunderstanding concerning the nature of the product of radio and to be clear about who the consumers of the product are. It has been stated often that the product of radio is its programming. The consumers therefore are the listeners. On first blush, this would seem to be the case. Listeners consume programming by turning on the radio and responding to the programming. But the situation is more complex than that.

Radio receives its revenues from advertisers. Because revenues in a profit-making organization generally come from consumers, then advertisers must consume a product. But what is the product consumed by advertisers? That can be discovered by examining the reasons why advertisers spend money on radio. They spend money in return for the use of the radio station's signal as a way to get advertising messages to the buying public. It can be said, then, that advertisers are consumers of a product called audience.

Programming becomes, in a sense, bait to attract audience. Audience is then sold to advertisers. Or, it could be said that programming is a resource used in the production process. Radio stations generate their product (audience) by efficient use of the resource (programming). Once the audience is produced, it is distributed to consumers (advertisers) by means of a distribution channel, which is also known as the broadcast channel—the frequencies assigned to the station for broadcast. Audience research is used to let advertisers know that a certain quantity of product has been delivered.

A manager must understand this clearly to separate the concern for the product from the concern for the means of distribution of the product. In radio, product quality refers to things such as income levels of target audiences and their propensity to buy certain products.

Any manager who mistakes a concern for programming quality for a concern with product quality is subject to making poor business judgments. Poor program quality may in fact result in poor product (audience) quality, but the manager who focuses on programming, when the problem is really the audience, overlooks many other factors of station operations that might be contributing to the problem. It may be, for example, that programming is basically on target and the audience problems are caused by poor station promotion. Managers who misread situations in this way squander resources and fail to find effective remedies for operational problems that can be very costly to the fiscal health of the operation.

To ensure product quality, a manager must keep a sharp watch for shifts in audience behavior. Using the tools described in Chapter 8 of this book, managers must make constant evaluations of audience levels and note any changes or shifts in the characteristics of the audiences who listen to the station. Is there a drop-off in the numbers of males during morning drive time? Have you lost teens in the evening hours? Are there any significant changes in the share of the audience for any particular time period?

The manager must keep abreast of the competition and note any changes in programming among other stations in the market. When problem areas are discovered, adjustments must be made. Perhaps a new ad campaign will help boost ratings for a new morning disc jockey. Maybe a shift of air personalities will help revive a time period that is losing the female audience to a competitor. Astute managers proceed with caution. But, by carefully monitoring the audience and adjusting operations accordingly, the product quality can be maintained so that advertisers remain satisfied that their investment in the station is productive.

Good management happens only when managers actually manage. The real arena of making things happen is in day-to-day operations of the station. It involves action—people doing things, programming going on the air, salespeople making calls, bills being sent to advertisers, collections being made, the program being transmitted. What specifically do managers do to ensure that people are being used effectively? How do they implement policy in a way that translates into productive activity? In essence, management activity is exercised through management structures.

Management Structures in Small, Medium, and Large Markets

As is the case with managers in almost every business, radio station managers work through an organizational structure (see Chapter 4). This structure is designed to make it possible for managers to respond to needs in any area of station operations while remaining somewhat removed from the dozens or hundreds of routine tasks that are performed by the people in each area. A well-thought-out organizational structure allows managers to implement station policy efficiently and to keep a clear view of the overall status of the operation as a whole.

To illustrate how a good organizational structure can help managers make good decisions, assume the following situation: An announcer expresses a need for new equipment in the on-air studio. The request is forwarded to the manager from the announcer's supervisor, the program director. At that point the manager asks the program director if this is a concern shared by other staff or if it is a trivial complaint by a hard-to-please disc jockey. If the complaint has a good basis, the chief engineer can be consulted to look into what would be needed in the way of equipment and to discern if there is money in the budget to pay for improvements.

In the discussion it may become evident that there is a problem not only in the on-air studio but also in the production studio. This may lead to a meeting of all department heads, with the manager, to see what options are available to improve things. The manager weighs the situation and decides that the situation is damaging the effectiveness of the station in fulfilling its mission. The manager decides that the entire operation must be improved if the station is to continue to grow. This leads to a reconsideration of the format and sources of programming. The program director is consulted and asked to provide information on competitive factors that might affect a change in format and to analyze the impact such a change might have on audience levels. The chief engineer is asked to look into plans for a new studio facility and new equipment. The sales manager is asked to make sales projections based on the format recommendations of the program director. And financial advisors are asked to look into the tax implications of capital expansion.

The above scenario is hypothetical and extreme, but it illustrates the value of looking at things from a broad perspective. Because of the manager's position relative to the other levels of management, he or she can analyze input from all the divisions of the station. The decisions made from this perspective take into account all factors bearing on the station's mission.

There is no one structure that provides this perspective best, and structures vary with the size of the operation. Larger stations likely have more layers of management in their organizational plans, whereas small-market stations may have very basic structures. Moreover, in small markets people may have management functions in addition to operational duties. A morning air personality, for example, may be the program director and the chief announcer. The station manager may also perform the duties of sales manager.

Interestingly, management functions vary only slightly in scope among the various-sized stations. The specific duties, however, vary greatly with the size of the operation. In a major market, for example, the local sales manager has a staff of salespeople who call on clients, write up orders, and service many accounts. The manager's duties might be largely confined to supervising the staff, keeping track of quotas, making projections, and budgeting. In a small market, the local sales manager may service half or more of the accounts. The same person may also coordinate national sales, collect delinquent bills, and produce and voice commercials among other duties. In both sizes of stations, the functions are roughly the same. The variations occur in the number of operations necessary to accomplish the mission and in the number of people assigned to specific areas.

10.2

ROLE OF THE MODERN MANAGER

Managers function in all areas of station operation. The level of involvement is broadly based. At the managerial level, the concerns with programming, for example, are broader than determining the order of records in a power rotation. The concern of the manager is with overall direction and policy. That simply means that it is the manager's job to ensure that all functions of the station contribute to the success of the whole operation. Will an additional production studio for the news operation make enough difference to the station's listeners to justify the expense of building it? In deciding on such matters, the manager reflects and implements the policies of the owners. It is the manager's job to see that the station runs in accordance with the owners' goals. One of those goals is likely to be to produce a profit for the owners. Outlays of money, then, are a matter of considerable concern. They must be viewed in terms of what they contribute to the prospect of a more profitable operation.

The manager is also obliged to keep the owners informed about operational changes that must be implemented to meet their goals. A manager must be able to push for investments in the operation that may be good in the long run even if there is a decrease in short-range revenues. A good manager can separate the nice-to-have frills from substantive improvements, which are likely to result in a better bottom line for owners.

It is the responsibility of the manager to be concerned with such things as the laws and regulations regarding fair employment and to keep up with the latest FCC regulations. The manager must keep in close touch with the community in which the station operates. This is good business and a prudent approach to good relations with the FCC. The manager must be intimately acquainted with the business aspects of the operation and must understand at least the rudiments of the technical aspects of the operation.

Manager as Personnel Administrator

In the area of personnel, the manager is ultimately responsible for hiring and firing. It is also the manager's responsibility to ensure that staffing levels are appropriate for the operational needs of the station. If there are too few people on the staff, some operations either will not be performed or they may be done in a sloppy fashion. The end result will be a diminution of quality that will result in diminished financial health. The manager must make the judgments that keep staffing adequate while not overloading the station with unneeded employees. Personnel costs are high, and efficient managers must be adept at avoiding waste in this area.

The manager must be aware of what constitutes adequate **compensation** for employees. If salaries are too low, employees feel exploited. They have little reason to feel supportive of the organization, and, when an opportunity for a better paying position comes along, they leave. If some employees are overpaid, profits suffer unnecessarily, and the manager is guilty of inefficient use of resources.

The proper level of compensation for any given staff member depends on such factors as the types of skills the individual possesses, the value of that person to the organization, and length of service. Market size has a bearing on salary levels as well.

It is helpful for managers to have information on industrywide average salaries for various positions. Organizations like the National Association of Broadcasters publish average salaries for various staff positions. Managers can also consult with managers of other stations to check on any special circumstances that might affect salaries for particular positions.

An additional salary issue is overtime pay. Overtime usually does not apply to management positions and certain other staff members. For those staff members who qualify for overtime, the rate is usually one and one-half times the standard hourly rate for hours worked in excess of the standard forty-hour week.

Arriving at salaries and negotiating annual increases may be a matter of individual negotiations with various staff members, or it may involve one or more unions.

The unions most significantly represented in radio broadcasting are the National Association of Broadcast Employees and Technicians (NABET), the American Federation of Television and Radio Artists (AFTRA), and International Brotherhood of Electrical Workers (IBEW). A radio manager may have occasion to deal with one or more of these unions at any given station. Even at the smallest of stations there may be unions representing some or all of the employees.

In the case of salespeople, the manager administers commission structures that may vary from individual to individual. Some common forms of compensation for sales personnel are straight salary, salary plus commission, draw against commission, and straight commission—the commission being a percentage of the revenue produced by the sale of advertising by a given individual.

Among these options, straight salary is the least common for salespeople. The reason for this is twofold. First, managers find that the open-ended arrangements involving commissions produce better sales results because of the direct financial incentive for better productivity by the individual. Second, good salespeople prefer commissions because they can earn as much as they are willing to work for, rather than being restricted to a set amount per week or month.

In salary plus commission, the salary is usually low with commissions making up the remainder of the salesperson's compensation. In draw against commission, a certain specified amount of money is paid regularly, and the salesperson repays that through commissions on sales. Any commission beyond the amount of the draw goes to the salesperson. Sales managers typically receive commissions on the revenue produced by salespeople working under their supervision and on any accounts they personally service.

In many cases, existing station policy stipulates which among these options are in force for which employees. The choice of one option over others is usually based on the experience levels of the salespeople, the sales objectives of the station, and the overall sales volume of the station.

Inexperienced salespeople without an established list of accounts may need to work at first on a system of draw against commission in order to make any money at all. Later, they may switch to straight commission.

Salary plus commission is often used when a station is revamping its operations and replacing many sales accounts with new advertisers. The sales volume is usually low for a while in such a situation, and salespeople may find it necessary to spend much time cultivating prospects before closing a sale. In such cases, the salary plus system allows salespeople to be compensated for time spent in cultivation. At the same time, however, there is incentive to keep pressing for orders so that the individual's salary can be augmented by commissions. Straight salary might be used by a station wishing to concentrate on attracting a particular type of client or a set of clients. Certain salespeople might be assigned to focus exclusively on just a few clients. Again, the time and attention of salespeople are likely to be more productively spent on cultivation rather than on creating high-volume sales. In such cases, the salary, if high enough, keeps salespeople from regarding it as a financial hardship, and they focus their energies on cultivation.

Compensation also includes fringe benefits. Fringe benefits are provided to employees in addition to salary. The advantage to employees is that beneficial items like health insurance and hospitalization, for example, are provided at little or no cost to the individual. And, through group rates, stations usually pay less per capita than individuals would.

Managers must be aware of industry practices as a whole in regard to fringe benefits, so that the station can remain competitive. Industry organizations such as state associations and the National Association of Broadcasters can be helpful in determining what is standard for stations of similar size. Most radio stations provide paid vacation, health insurance, sick leave, and paid holidays. Some provide retirement plans, profit-sharing plans, moving allowances, college scholarships for dependents, and various incentive plans.

Other matters pertaining to payroll considerations include withholding taxes, payment of Social Security taxes, and unemployment insurance payments. Policies must be developed to administer such things as cost-of-living increases, bonuses, and retirement and insurance plans of various sorts.

In stations that are group-owned or that are a part of corporate structures, many of the personnel duties may be administered in accordance with centralized policies and procedures. Evaluation and compensation procedures may be clearly established and written out for all employees. In such cases, the manager may function primarily as an evaluator of employee performance rather than the person directly responsible for making decisions regarding compensation of staff members. In cases where the station is locally owned, on the other hand, the manager may have full control of compensation and other personnel functions with little if any guidance from owners.

In either type of situation, it is helpful if personnel policies are clearly spelled out in an employee manual. To help stations in producing guidelines, the National Association of Broadcasters has published a set of procedures that includes information on what should be included in an employee manual.

In the NAB's publication entitled *Station Procedures: A Guide for Radio,* author Donald H. Kirkley notes that information in an employee handbook should be presented in a logical need-to-know format with information that pertains to all employees presented first. This might include

— Welcome

— General business policies and procedures

—— Employee benefits

—— Matters of salary

—— Performance appraisal and promotion

This would then be followed by information pertaining to specific departments such as news, sales, and engineering.[4]

It should also be mentioned that managers are in position to exert considerable influence on the working environment by virtue of their relationships with employees. Most experts agree that the operations with the most productive employees are those in which managers show a genuine interest in their employees and treat them with fairness and respect. Such managers expect a lot from their employees, but there is common understanding of what is expected and a general awareness of standards of performance.

Manager as Chief Programmer

In most station operations, there is a person designated as program director (PD). Increasingly, the position of PD is being replaced by a staff position called the operations director (OD). The OD's responsibilities usually extend beyond programming matters and include more broadly managerial functions such as responsibility for general-office operation and coordination with engineering, accounting, and traffic. In such operations, there is often someone designated as specifically involved with programming, but that position has less authority in programming than is the case where the PD reports directly to the general manager. In large operations, there also may be a music director, a chief of production, and a promotion director, who report to the PD or the OD. The station manager's role in programming is to ensure that programming accomplishes its intended purpose. This means that managers must know how programming is working to attract and hold an audience. This involves constant monitoring of audience levels and analysis of the competition. Every element of the station sound must be evaluated continually and measured against the programming's ability to attract the levels of audience demanded by advertisers.

The manager also must keep a close eye on the expenses of purchasing program material. The costs of format services distributed by satellite or for automation systems, for example, can be quite substantial, as can the personnel costs for top air personalities. Music services and costs of any special program material that the station purchases, such as periodically scheduled syndicated music programs, also create expenses that can put considerable strain on programming budgets. There must be constant attention to such costs to ensure that they are justified in relation to what is produced in terms of audience levels and advertising revenue.

Programming budgets must be analyzed in relation to other station expenses and against station revenues to keep costs in the proper balance. This is not to say that cost should be the only consideration in programming. The station manager who limps along with poor audience levels because of reluctance to put money into a new format will be replaced eventually with someone who knows that a wise investment in good programming can reap advertising revenues that will make the investment seem small. Moreover, programming is arguably the major factor that drives stations to higher market rankings. Higher rankings can produce exponential increases in the market value of a station.

If there are problems with programming, the manager must proceed with care. Ultimately, though, the manager is often the one who has to make the difficult decision to change air personalities, to call in a consultant, or to change the format. To do this successfully, the manager must keep abreast of what suppliers are out there and how their products have performed in other markets in terms of audience appeal. Industry trade magazines such as *Broadcasting* regularly feature articles about program suppliers and their services. And, managers can find out quickly how other markets have done with a given programming product or format by calling other managers. Even if managers who use the product in question play it close to the chest as far as particulars go, it is still possible to find out whether it is successful. One option is to call the station's competition and ask how the programming has affected them.

The manager must be knowledgeable about the characteristics of the audiences served by the station. What kinds of promotions draw a good response and increase listenership? Is there an unserved audience segment whose musical tastes are not being met? Is there a new competitive force stealing away audience from your station? Is the promotion budget adequate to support the kind of promotional activities necessary to keep the station competitive? Do you need the services of an outside firm to help with promotional activities? Should you buy into a contest service to help boost sagging audience levels? Can there be better programs of community involvement for the station? These are the kinds of questions that a manager must address constantly.

Once the questions have been asked and information has been assembled, decisions must be made and action taken. The kinds of action taken will hinge greatly on money. It costs a great deal, for example, to hire an agency to help with station promotion. Whether the outlay is a good investment depends on whether the results of better promotion will improve the station's fortunes in a way that will translate into greater profitability or will increase the overall worth of the station.

If there seem to be problems with the on-air staffing, the question of higher salaries may arise. In some markets, it may not be a good investment to pay the kind of salary that will attract top air talent. Even with improved audience levels, there may not be sufficient advertising revenues in the market to recoup the investment. Whereas in a larger market, a manager might be foolish to forego the opportunity to hire a particular personality even though the salary demands may seem exorbitant. If that air personality can raise the station's position among competing stations in the market by two places, for example, it could mean the difference between qualifying for a good part of national advertising budgets and being closed out of nearly all national advertising. Media buyers at advertising agencies often buy local radio by selecting only the top several stations in the market with the desired demographics. The object is to be above the cutoff point for national advertising. If a highly paid air personality can achieve this for a station, the high salary may be more than justified.

In the area of news, the station manager must know what types of news presentation attracts the largest audience. With the elimination of many of the FCC's public interest regulations that formerly applied to radio, many stations have abandoned news altogether. The rationale for such a move is that those interested in news have many stations in the marketplace from which to choose. Why should a music station try to compete in news when the reason its audience's tunes in is for the music it plays? News is regarded as an intrusion and a reason to twist the dial.

Managers must decide on what the goals of the station are. Is there a public service consideration for including news and public affairs in the schedule even though it is unnecessary from a regulatory standpoint? Or, is the community adequately served in this area by other journalistic outlets? There is no right answer for all situations, but the wrong decision in such matters can have damaging consequences.

For stations that do carry news, there must be an awareness of journalistic standards. The manager must be familiar with how laws of libel and slander apply to news coverage. There must be an awareness of the important issues in the community. News people often are not as attentive as they should be to the need for coverage of certain institutions and events in the community. It is the manager's job to ensure that the news is covered professionally. A great deal of damage can be done by sloppiness in news reporting, and unwary managers can find themselves in great difficulty if the news department fails to operate in a responsible manner.

At the same time, there are instances in which decisions must be made about specific issues arising from news coverage. Sometimes this boils down to being a matter of what is appropriate. Does a small station in a large market really have to provide intensive coverage of world and national news? It might be better to devote limited news time to coverage of important local stories and let the networks and other news media handle the majority of national and world news.

Another situation that sometimes arises in connection with the news operation occurs when an advertiser threatens to pull advertising if a certain story is reported. It is the manager who must face the consequences of the actions taken. Managers must be concerned with the bottom line, but sometimes the short-range gain is a long-term loss. To acquiesce to threats of an advertiser or any other party when the request involves the suppression of news stories is usually more harmful than risking the loss of revenue. To succumb to threats violates principles that are held as almost sacred by the news professions. Moreover, such advertisers often do not make good on such threats. And, if "crying wolf" succeeds once, advertisers are likely to use the strategy again. The best policy in such matters is to treat issues regarding news coverage solely in journalistic terms. Keep the business end of the operation out of such matters as much as possible.

Manager as Director of Sales and Marketing

Obviously, the sales area is one of great concern for managers. Most managers have risen to their positions through experience in sales, and many still handle sales accounts even though they are managers. Regardless of managers' background, it is axiomatic that the sales operation is going to consume a lion's share of their time and attention. The health of this segment of station operations determines the success or failure of the entire enterprise.

Managers' roles in sales can vary widely in terms of what they actually do. As mentioned, some actually sell, whereas most have a less direct involvement. At any level, the key to being an effective manager in this area is to closely monitor the sales effort. Most managers hold regular sales meetings at which the salespeople report on calls made and problems they have encountered. Good managers are familiar enough with the business climate in the community to know when opportunities are being missed. It often becomes necessary to apply gentle pressure to salespeople to get them to make difficult calls and to follow up on promising leads. The manager can assume the role of a coach, building motivation, creating a climate of enthusiasm and excitement about the idea of meeting or exceeding quotas (often called "budgets" in broadcasting), and overcoming adverse business conditions.

Managers must keep track of all advertising in the market. They must know how advertisers perceive the station and how they view competing stations and competing advertising media like television and newspaper. It's important to keep salespeople up to date on the advantages of radio over other advertising media. The Radio Advertising Bureau and the National Association of Broadcasters produce materials and sponsor seminars to educate radio people in effective selling techniques. Managers must be aware of these services and see to it that the appropriate staff people participate and are exposed to the benefits the services offer.

If the overall advertising climate is healthy and your station is not doing well, it is important to find out why and address the problem. Managers must know how this year's performance compares with last year's. They must be aware of unusual circumstances at any given time that contribute to increased or decreased sales. If a major sporting event that is a one-time-only situation is being held in the area, it may spur advertisers into increased spending on advertising to better reach this expanded imported audience. A station manager who doesn't take this into account when setting next year's sales goals may be heading for failure.

In setting sales quotas, managers work with all departments to develop a budget listing the operating expenses for the next year. Sales figures are set that will provide the revenue needed to operate and to provide a profit for the owners. Local and national sales managers will be assigned a specific amount of revenues that they are expected to produce. These figures are broken out over a twelve-month period based on the previous year's performance. Each salesperson is assigned a portion of each month's projected revenues.

It is generally estimated in some major markets that in a given year approximately 20 percent of the station's accounts will be lost. To offset that loss and still meet budgets, one leading sales manager in a major market estimates that the station must plan on about 40 to 45 percent of the advertising accounts coming from new business.

Once sales projections are established, they are monitored constantly and adjusted according to changing market conditions. A manager must be informed if sales figures do not meet projections for a given month so that expenditures do not exceed revenues.

Managers are often the only people in a station who are compelled to be realists. When sales are slumping, salespeople may complain about the format or point to a particular air personality that is "hard to sell." In fact, that may be the case. But if the problem lies with the fact that salespeople are not making enough calls or that they need more training, you won't hear that from the salespeople. The manager must be able to see what aspects of the operation are exerting an influence on sales—for good or bad—and rectify or enhance those areas. If sales are being adversely affected by the fact that clients do not receive adequate account service, for example, the manager must work through the sales manager to find why this is happening. The corrective action may be as simple as shifting accounts from one salesperson to another. It may be that additional personnel are needed to keep up with the volume.

If business is so good that you're having trouble finding commercial availabilities, perhaps it's time to raise the rates for airtime. A well-timed rate increase can improve the fiscal health of the station and clean out some of the clutter by eliminating the advertisers who find the new prices too high. Obviously, rate changes must be carefully considered before they are implemented, but often the loss of a few clients can be easily made up for by the increased revenue that the station receives. It is the manager's task to decide when a rate increase will be beneficial and when it may be harmful. The manager's ability to view the whole scope of the operation is very helpful in weighing all the factors bearing on a decision of this nature.

Manager as Financial Officer

The financial responsibilities of managers go well beyond the scope of simply monitoring revenues and determining budgets. Financial management involves consideration of such things as the invested capital of owners, profit objectives of investors and owners, tax considerations, return on investment, projecting financial growth, and determining the impact of station development on the fiscal condition of the enterprise.

Radio station managers have differing levels of fiscal responsibilities, depending on the degree of involvement that owners exercise in the operation of the station. In some operations, all major financial decisions are dealt with by corporate offices. Other stations are locally operated in every respect, and the financial decisions are made directly by the station manager. But whether the decisions are made at the top levels of corporate management or at the station level, it is incumbent upon the management of the station to be familiar with the overall financial aspects of the operation.

One of the most important things for station managers to remember is the financial goals of the owners. An owner who is interested in using station profits to produce personal income is going to view matters quite differently from an owner who is interested in getting a fast healthy return on the initial investment. The first type of owner may be hesitant to incur a heavy debt service in order to build new facilities for the station. The second type of owner may find that the debt can be a benefit in a tax sense, while increasing the value of the station for eventual sale.

A manager who is charged with turning a station around quickly in order to raise its market ranking may pour millions of dollars into building new facilities, purchasing new equipment, changing the format, and hiring highly paid air personalities in an effort to attract a top price for the station from potential buyers. Other owners might prefer a slower growth with an emphasis on a profitable bottom line.

In making operational decisions and recommendations to owners, radio managers must be conversant with the intricacies of debt management, tax laws, accounting procedures, and a host of other financial factors that impinge on how the station is developed and run. For example, a manager who is convinced that the station should switch from a standard automation system—in which the program elements are all in the station and fed into the automation equipment—to an automated format driven by a satellite feed must consider many factors. There will be considerable extra expense for **earth-station equipment** and additional signal-processing equipment needed to integrate local commercials and IDs into the programming received by satellite. There will be ongoing costs to pay for the service itself and contracts to be negotiated.

What means are available for financing the purchase of the additional equipment needed? What type of automation equipment is available, for what price? How much credit can the station get, and how will the debt affect profitability?

Debt management involves keeping current on interest rates and payback schedules. Most operations, regardless of size, avail themselves of expert advice from in-house or outside financial experts to provide guidance in this area. But managers must have a good sense of the impact of interest-rate fluctuations and options for financing. To illustrate with a simple example, if a station is carrying an old debt at a low-interest rate, it makes little sense to try to pay it off quickly. The money used to pay off the low-interest loan is often worth more if invested in an area that provides a good return based on current interest rates. Expensive debt that was incurred in a period of high rates, on the other hand, often can be refinanced at more favorable rates. Even though this involves additional handling costs, it is usually possible to save money in the long run.

Tax matters usually involve outside advice. But managers make numerous decisions that will involve tax considerations, so they must know what kinds of questions to ask and when to ask them. Many of the recent changes in federal tax legislation, for example, were not implemented immediately. It became important, therefore, for managers to consider how the timing of a given financial decision would affect tax liabilities.

In accounting, managers make decisions on how certain methods of accounting will affect station profitability. It is important to be familiar with accounting procedures affecting depreciation of capital assets, for instance. Simply put, depreciation involves assigning a value to physical property like station-owned buildings and technical equipment. A percentage of that value is subtracted over a period of years that roughly corresponds to the useful life of the building or the item of equipment. Eventually, the item depreciates to zero, and it is no longer carried on the books. In terms of accounting, the amount of depreciation is listed as a cost of doing business even though the expense does not involve an actual outlay of cash.

Managers take depreciation into account when considering expansion plans or purchase of new items of equipment. Because there are tax write-offs for depreciation, tax savings can partially offset the cost of purchasing new equipment or upgrading facilities. Given the relatively high costs of facilities and equipment in radio, managers must know how such costs can be interpreted in broad accounting terms in order to make realistic appraisals of their true impact.

It is wise for managers to have a solid knowledge about how money markets work, to be conversant with the functioning of overall economic indicators, and to be able to spot trends in interest-rate fluctuations. All these factors must be taken into account in making financial decisions. It should be noted again that radio managers are not necessarily expected to function alone in deciding on such matters and that there is no need to be a consummate expert in all financial areas. Managers would be foolish to try to function in these intricate and complex areas without professional accountants and other legal and financial advisors to examine the details of any given financial situation. But it is crucial that a manager be able to understand proposed operations in financial terms. The ability to do so greatly increases effectiveness and credibility. The obverse of that is that failure to understand the financial side of an enterprise can be disastrous.

Manager as Community Liaison

Stations are identified in the eyes of the FCC by the community to which they are licensed. Traditionally, that has meant that stations are expected to be more than trouble-free residents of the community who go about making profits without regard to the impact of the operation on the local area. Even in the current regulatory climate of deregulation, the FCC fully expects that radio stations be a major part of the life in their communities.

There are any number of ways that stations can become involved with the communities in which they are located. Many of these are considered elsewhere in this book. The rationale for involvement is simple. Setting aside the FCC mandate to serve the community, it is an obvious point that radio stations look to the community as a source of business activity.

It is in the best interests of a radio station to do what ever is necessary to keep the community healthy and vital. One of the most important functions of a radio station manager is to be involved in the kinds of community activities that contribute to making it a good place to live and do business. And, it is the manager who can best represent the station to the rest of the community. Managers can get involved in civic activities and join service organizations like Rotary and Kiwanis and can take a role in volunteer activities that benefit the community. The station can sponsor fund-raising events and make airtime available to support community activities.

In small and medium markets, the identification with the community is crucial to success. Large-markets stations are finding it increasingly beneficial to find community service tie-ins as a way of increasing listener loyalty. The manager's role is central to keeping community awareness a priority in station operations.

Manager as Implementor of Government Regulations

Chapter 12 of this book deals with government regulations that pertain to radio broadcasting. These regulations are numerous and often complex. Some managers regard the regulatory arena as the area with which they least like to deal. The tasks that must be performed by managers in meeting FCC requirements can be tedious and time-consuming. Often, they seem to be a waste of valuable time for managers. However, there is one powerful incentive for remaining on top of the regulatory situation: The failure to do so can place the station license at serious risk. No manager wants to be responsible for losing the station's license to broadcast. That rarely happens, but the mere possibility that it could is a powerful incentive for regulatory vigilance.

The manager's role in seeing to it that the station complies with regulatory requirements requires good solid knowledge of broadcast law and regulation. Most stations retain the services of outside law firms specializing in communications law. Many of these firms are located in Washington, D.C., where they can be in close touch with the FCC. They provide advice on the operational implications of federal regulations. In situations in which the station has matters coming before the FCC, the station is represented by the attorneys of the firm.

Despite the presence of such outside assistance in regulatory matters, however, the manager is responsible to see to it that operations of the station comply with federal regulations. Although recent deregulation has lessened the impact of regulatory matters on many aspects of radio operations (see Chapter 12), many operational areas remain under the purview of federal regulation.

Numerous resources are available to aid the manager in keeping abreast of current regulations, including FCC documents, textbooks on broadcasting regulation, and legal advice from attorneys. The essential tool for keeping abreast of regulatory requirements is the volume of the *Code of Federal Regulation*, which deals with regulations pertaining to telecommunications. It is designated as 47 CFR 73 and contains all FCC regulations in force as of the date of its last printing. Regulations change often, and new ones are added and old ones deleted; it is important to know what changes take place as they occur. Managers can keep up to date by reading *Broadcasting*, which reports on all FCC changes and other legal matters pertaining to radio, television, and cable television. The monthly trade publication *Broadcast Management/Engineering* contains a regular feature called "FCC Rules and Regulations," which examines particular aspects of regulation from a management perspective. Or, a station manager can subscribe to the *Federal Register*, which is issued daily by the federal government. The *Federal Register* records changes in all regulatory areas of the federal government as they occur. An index system can keep you current on any new regulations or changes in existing ones.

Perhaps the area of regulation that managers find most troublesome is the technical area. These regulations can be understood in basic terms by reading through the pertinent sections of the *Code of Federal Regulations.* But to understand them in sufficient depth to know whether your station is running afoul of limitations and specifications regarding technical operations requires the help of a trained engineer. A good manager takes the time to have his chief engineer explain what the station does to ensure compliance in the technical areas required by the FCC. With a little patience and persistence, the manager can become reasonably confident that the station is operating in accordance with FCC regulations.

In other areas of regulation, managers must be up to date on FCC requirements for handling particular types of programming such as political broadcasts and news coverage of controversial issues. There are reports that must be filed with the FCC at specified times of the year, and there is a requirement that certain documents be kept in a file for public inspection. Certain processes such as ownership changes, for example, also must be approved by the FCC before they can be legally accomplished.

In short, the regulatory area is one in which there are many responsibilities for managers. There is no greater threat to the livelihood of the station than careless disregard in this area. Although it is often viewed by managers as tedious and burdensome, the requirements that the FCC places upon broadcasters are conditions to which broadcasters willingly agree when they are issued licenses to broadcast. The license is a scarce commodity. It is an asset that many others would like to possess, and it is worth protecting with whatever degree of effort is required.

10.3

EMPLOYEE RELATIONS

Managers spend much time planning and evaluating the operations and processes that make a business run. They make sure that things get done—they execute. But the process of management, in and of itself, does not involve the actual performance of the operations that get the product or service produced. That is done by other people. The task of management, then, is to use people effectively to produce. The activities involved in doing that, often lead to conflict or they present problems of other types for managers.

The area of management activity known as employee relations deals with some of the problem areas that managers face when they go about the process of getting people to perform the tasks of production. Creating the conditions under which people will work to the best of their abilities is a task that involves a good knowledge of psychology and management theory. But it is also common sense and a consideration for human dignity. Effective managers find that they do have to work hard at employee relations, but in most cases they find that respect for workers and operational excellence go hand in hand.

Hiring and Firing

It costs much money to fire one employee and hire another. Considerations are the loss of productivity while a search is conducted for an empty position; the cost in time, money, and advertising; the time that must be invested in screening applicants and in interviewing candidates; and the cost of training a new person in the skills needed to perform the tasks required of the position. Given the expense, hiring is best done carefully, and firing is best avoided if other remedies can be found.

When a manager is faced with the task of hiring a new employee, the entire process should start with some careful planning. Before the position is advertised, the manager should pose several questions:

1. *What are the specific duties of this position?* You may be looking for an air personality who can also do some selling. If so, you'll look for different qualities than if you want a zany disc jockey for a late-evening shift aimed at teens.

2. *Where does the position fit into the overall operation? At what level is it?* You'll make salary decisions in comparison with others at the same level. Perhaps you will decide that you are expecting someone with too much experience to be hired at an entry-level salary. You'll need to reevaluate.

3. *What attributes are needed to perform the duties of this position?* List them. In a clerical position, you may find that most of the written work of the station is done using computerized word-processing equipment. In such a case, you may prefer someone who is adept at using computers and who has experience with the uses of certain software packages rather than someone who can type sixty words per minute. When you've determined all the responsibilities and duties, list the specific skills needed to perform in an acceptable manner.

4. *How will you evaluate candidates to determine their suitability for the position?* Often managers fail in this regard by looking too closely at the individual's skills

and talents without considering how they will fit in with the rest of the operation. A bright, talented engineer, for example, may be of little use to a station if the job requires working with announcers to solve production problems and the engineer cannot work with announcers. Will you ask for an audition tape for announcers? They can be unrepresentative of true talent. Perhaps a live audition would be better. How will you decide on the best candidate for a sales position? Certainly a winning personality and strong persuasive skills are important, but if the candidate requires a great deal of supervision to be productive, you may want to keep looking.

It is often helpful to develop a rating scale for each of the attributes and skills at which you are looking. Each candidate then can be rated on a numeric scale for the various categories. As a cautionary note, however, do not rely exclusively on the numeric rankings to make a final decision. Impressions and other qualities that cannot necessarily be measured should play a major part in your decision.

Once the manager has dealt with such basic questions, the position can be advertised. This can be done with a catch-all ad in the "Help Wanted" section of *Radio & Records* or *Broadcasting,* which can attract good (and poor) candidates. Or, it can be done by word of mouth. Letting key people in the business know that you're looking for a certain type of employee can attract candidates who may come with the endorsement of someone you trust. Whatever way the word is gotten out, it is important to begin the process of screening fairly quickly after you start getting responses to your advertising.

The screening process can be accomplished in four steps:

1. *Initial screening.* It is likely that the bulk of applicants for most positions can be weeded out quickly as unqualified or lacking in the types or levels of experience that you require. At this stage, eliminate only those who obviously will not fill the bill. Keep the best candidates along with those whom you think you may ultimately eliminate, but who have some possibility of making it. This allows you to compare the top prospects to less qualified ones and gives you a better sense of the overall quality of the field.

2. *Weeding-out process.* When the group is narrowed down to those who seem like possibilities, start weeding out those who look less qualified than the best. At the conclusion of this stage, you should have a few prospects who seem to be excellent possibilities. Ideally, this will be three or four individuals. This is the group with which you will want to make personal contact.

3. *Telephone contact.* Phone each of your finalists and discuss the position further.

This gives the applicant an opportunity to ask questions about the job and the station, and it gives the manager the opportunity to form impressions that will confirm or deny the positive impression conveyed by the original application. Salary should be discussed in general terms at this point so that the candidate can determine whether or not to accept the position if offered. There is no point in wasting time with an interview if there is no prospect that the applicant would come for the salary being offered.

4. *Personal interview and credentials check.* If the phone call leads to agreement that both parties want to continue the process, the next step is to bring these candidates to the station for an interview with the manager and other key personnel. An audition can be given at this time, if appropriate. When the interviews are completed, the decision will be made. Sometimes, there will be a clear-cut, top candidate; at other times it will be necessary to carefully weigh one against others. It may be that the only outcome of the interview process is that you decide that none of the candidates seem suitable and that you want to keep looking. If you decide to make an offer to one of the candidates who has been interviewed, be sure, *in all cases,* to check references. It is also a good idea to check on factual material in the résumé, such as past employment and education. It is not unknown for applicants to fudge in these areas, thinking that no one will take the trouble to check on them.

Once this process is completed, the offer can be made to the successful candidate. Settle on salary and other conditions of employment and set a date for the new employee to begin. As soon as your candidate is hired, be sure to notify your unsuccessful candidates of the fact that you have filled the position. This is nothing more than common courtesy, but it is ignored by far too many organizations. Do not notify other candidates, however, until you have secured a firm commitment from your top candidate. If that person turns down your offer, you may want to move to your second choice.

When you're firing someone, the dynamics are completely different. When firing has been done properly with plenty of advance warning and opportunities for the employee to improve have been tried and have failed, the final step out the door shouldn't come as a great surprise to the individual. Nevertheless, the process is never pleasant for either the person being fired or the person doing the firing. There are, however, some steps that can make the process less difficult for both parties.

First, a good manager should make every attempt to rectify the problems that are causing poor performance by the employee. Call the employee in at the first sign of trouble and try to determine together what is wrong. It can be very helpful to let the employee suggest solutions to the problem. The idea, though, is to come up with corrective actions to which both the manager and the employee can agree. If an employee fails to adhere to the agreed-upon actions, the manager calls him or her back in. At that point, the reasons for not meeting the agreed-upon conditions can be discussed. If there are no good reasons for the employee's failure to comply, the manager must then decide whether there is any point to giving the employee another chance. Often, it is best simply to end the relationship.

When firing someone, it is not necessary to do so in an emotional way. The best method is simply to state the problems that led to the firing and note the inability of the employee to rectify the problem. Next, state firmly that the only solution is to end the employment. It is important for the manager to resist attempts by the employee to debate the merits of the case. Be firm in your reasons for the action without being accusatory. There is little to be gained at this point by belittling the employee.

State clearly the conditions of leaving, including the effective date of the termination of employment. Keep the meeting with the employee as short as possible and give the employee the rest of the day off or schedule the meeting just prior to quitting time. Some stations require those who have been fired (and even those who resign voluntarily) to leave immediately. This policy prevents a disgruntled ex-employee from doing something to damage the station, such as sabotaging equipment or saying something embarrassing on the air.

Managers need considerable skill in judging human performance if they are to be effective in hiring and firing. In hiring, mistakes are costly because they result in poor productivity. By effective corrective actions, skillful managers can minimize the need to fire people. But when the situation calls for firing an individual, a skillful manager can ease the stress on both parties considerably.

Labor Relations

Many a manager quails at the thought of dealing with unions. But broadcasting is an industry in which managers are almost certain to have to deal with unions at some point in their careers. Announcers, technicians, and other station employees are often represented by the major national unions mentioned earlier in this chapter. Although many managers find that union requirements can seem inefficient and costly, there are managers who feel that unions contribute greatly to the professionalism of station operations.

One benefit of union activity is that many of the factors that can cause problems between management and employees have been worked out at the bargaining table. When disputes and grievances arise, the methods of dealing with them are pretty straightforward in unionized stations. The manager is relieved of the need to handle every problem as something special. There is agreed-upon policy that spells out the limits of activity available to deal with problems in the workplace. The manager's role in such situations becomes one of applying the proper procedures.

CONTRACT NEGOTIATIONS   In nonunion situations, managers are wise to develop policies of their own regarding various situations that commonly arise. For example, what are policies on overtime? What can supervisors require those under their supervision to do? Who needs to be consulted on various types of activities? These are the kinds of questions that are likely to come up in any organization. Managers must be prepared to deal with such questions fairly and effectively.

In the area of negotiating contracts with employees, managers have heavy responsibilities. It is their job to get a fair deal for the station's owners while avoiding situations in which employees feel cheated. In union situations, collective bargaining agreements are hammered out. This can be a very tedious activity, and salary is only a small part of the process. There are questions of what work should be performed by whom. The length of the work day has to be agreed upon, with provisions for overtime pay and other conditions pertaining to overtime. There are provisions that deal with fringe benefits, working conditions, and vacation.

Managers must be particularly adept at negotiating when unions are involved; remember that the union position is often represented by professionals. It is often a good idea to have professional negotiators available to management as well. Managers, however, still bear the ultimate responsibility for the results.

UNIONS: ADVANTAGES AND DISADVANTAGES   Other questions regarding union activities in broadcasting deal with the loss of flexibility that takes place when operations are structured around collective bargaining agreements. Rather than being able to work out appropriate areas of responsibility with individual technicians, for example, managers have to abide by agreements regarding the responsibilities of all technicians. This can result in situations in which it becomes difficult at times to perform tasks in the simplest way. If a microphone must be moved from one studio to another and all technicians are busy, for example, it may be against the rules for an announcer to move it. Or, it may be that announcers are prohibited from physically editing tape or running a tape machine. Announcers who have been trained to perform these activities often find it frustrating when they have to show a technician where to make a splice or when to hit the record button.

It is the opinion of many broadcast managers that unions also have advantages. Unions have been credited with bringing higher standards to the industry as a whole. There are also managers who feel that by raising the pay levels of staff people, unions have been an ally of managers who have tried to convince reluctant owners that paying higher salaries improves quality and hence profitability. Whatever the feelings of various managers may be regarding unions, however, the bottom line is that unions are a large part of the radio industry and managers must learn how to work effectively with them.

DEALING WITH UNIONS   In dealing with day-to-day operations in a station where unions represent all or most of the employees, managers should create an atmosphere of ongoing communication with union leadership. Management should try to foster the attitude that both management and the union are working to achieve similar goals and that what benefits the station as a whole can benefit all employees.

It should be equally clear to all employees that managers are aware of the essential nature of the contributions made by employees to the overall success of the operation. Such attitudes on the part of both union and management personnel can create the kind of positive atmosphere that make it easier to resolve any disputes that arise.

The types of working situations that lead to union grievances often seem surprisingly insignificant to those unfamiliar with labor relations. Seemingly major disputes can arise over issues such as inadequate parking space or proper office lighting. Managers who are sensitive to conditions that can be annoying or detrimental to employee morale and well-being can often correct deficiencies before they become union problems. Small things such as providing a room for employees to relax in while on a coffee break, for instance, can improve morale and show that management is concerned with employee comfort.

When grievances do arise, it is important to deal with them quickly and to try to get the situation resolved. This does not mean that grievances will always be resolved in favor of the union, but it does show that management regards the union's concerns as important. When demands are unreasonable or grievances are unfounded or are not dealt with in the collective bargaining agreement, managers must be firm and responsibly represent the interests of management.

Patience is extremely helpful in working through labor issues that cannot be resolved quickly. It is important to keep emotions in check and to maintain perspective on any given situation. Managers who develop skill in dealing with labor relations will thrive. But those who cannot function in such an environment will not enjoy ultimate success in the broadcasting industry.

Government Regulation in the Workplace

Besides the restrictions imposed by union contracts, the government has also imposed conditions that affect the working conditions of employees. Regulation of the workplace is quite a different matter from regulations pertaining to the station's technical operations and programming.

The philosophy behind technical and programming regulation involves a central concern with the general public. Broadcasters are obliged by such regulation to operate in ways designed to provide for the responsible use of a public resource (the so-called airways) by those to whom the privilege of broadcasting has been granted.

Regulation of the workplace is designed to protect the interests of specific categories of individuals who perform essential services that enable employers to achieve the purposes of their organizations. Legislation and regulation providing for minimum wage and fair employment practices, among many other provisions, prevent employers from taking unfair advantage of employees who are dependent on employers for their livelihoods. In essence, the laws and regulations that apply to the workplace, then, deal with ensuring fairness in employment and in protecting employees from infringements on their civil rights and from other forms of abuse.

The U.S. Department of Labor has developed policies that deal with workplace issues such as equal pay, record keeping, minimum wage, maximum hours, overtime pay, and child labor. Stations are subject to inspections by federal labor officials who spot-check from time to time, looking for violations of the labor laws. Stations are obliged to keep employee records with basic information that lists items such as working hours and compensation levels.

EQUAL EMPLOYMENT OPPORTUNITY   In hiring, the FCC specifies fair employment procedures, which stations are obliged to follow. Because broadcasting is engaged in interstate commerce, it is subject to the antidiscrimination provisions of the Civil Rights Act, which makes it illegal to discriminate on the basis of race, color, religion, national origin, or sex. Many states also have laws prohibiting discrimination and statutes that deal with other employment practices.

The FCC's regulations on fair employment practices are spelled out in Section 73.2080, entitled **Equal Employment Opportunity (EEO)** of Title 47 of the *Federal Code of Regulations*. The regulations require broadcasters with more than five full-time employees to file an annual employment report outlining programs "designed to provide equal employment opportunities for American Indians and Alaskan Natives; Asians and Pacific Islanders; Blacks, not of Hispanic Origin; Hispanics; and women. . . ." (47 CFR 73.2080).

To establish a plan of action to implement the provisions of the EEO regulations, managers must start with the premise that a good program simply will not operate well if it does not have the support of management. It is possible to develop a program that satisfies the letter of the FCC's requirements but that fails to deal effectively with the problems the regulations seek to remedy. In actual practice, a program designed only to meet the FCC's minimum requirements does not accomplish much.

The object therefore should be to develop a program that works. There are five elements that should be included in such a program. They are policy, planning, identification, implementation, and monitoring.

1.   *Policy.* The essential first step in developing an EEO or affirmative action pro-
       gram is to state clearly the obligation of all employees to observe practices
       designed to ensure compliance with EEO regulations. In enunciating this pol-
       icy, the provisions of the FCC regulations should be clearly stated; but beyond
       that, it is important to note that the policy reflects a genuine commitment of
       station management to the goals of the program. If the policy merely conveys
       a desire to achieve compliance with the regulatory requirements, it will have
       little real force in the organization. The policy statement can be relatively
       short, but it should receive wide distribution. A concise statement of this pol-
       icy should appear in all employment advertising and other public information
       regarding employment.

2.   *Planning.* Planning involves the establishment of specific procedures that will
       be followed to ensure that the policy is carried out in actual practice. The plan
       should list guidelines to be followed in hiring. It might be stated, for example,
       that in placing advertising for all positions, pertinent minority periodical pub-
       lications will be included. Or, there might be a stipulation that notification of
       any openings should be provided to trade or other organizations that represent
       the interests of women and minorities. Don't forget your own organization. By
       soliciting applications from your own employees, you let them know that there
       is room for advancement and change within the company.
           Each step in the hiring process should be described with reference to the
       actions that will be taken to ensure that equal opportunity is provided. To en-
       sure that all necessary steps are taken to conduct a fair job search, it might
       help to develop a checklist with all of the appropriate actions spelled out. The
       checklist could then be distributed to everyone who may be hiring staff mem-
       bers at any level.

3.   *Identification.* The purpose of identification is to look carefully at each position
       in the station. Spell out the qualifications needed for each position. The key
       is to look at each position in as fresh a way as possible. Many times, existing
       position descriptions contain terms that convey a predisposition toward per-
       sons of a particular sex or race. A description of a staff announcer's position,
       for example, might include the commonly used term *morning man.* Or, a secre-
       tarial position might include the term *gal Friday.* All such references can be
       easily avoided.
           This is also a good opportunity to review job descriptions to be sure that
       there are no references to tasks that are unrelated to the primary duties of the
       position. Some job descriptions may have been written long ago, and there
       may be specifications of duties that place the job holder in the position of feeling
       exploited. An example would be any description of personal services to be per-

formed for a supervisor, such as cleaning coffee cups or picking up dry cleaning. Such practices are seldom written down, but there may be phrases that convey a lack of managerial respect for the position.

In the past, demeaning duties were often attached to positions held predominantly by minorities and women. By eliminating such requirements and dropping offensive terminology, you help eliminate the stigma attached to certain job categories.

4. *Implementation.* The key to a good program is how well it operates in actual practice. When a position becomes available, every care should be taken to guarantee fairness in the hiring procedure. When the position is advertised, it should be placed carefully so that it comes to the attention of a diverse cross section of potential applicants. This can involve additional expense, but the payoff is a better chance of attracting the interest of good candidates. This doesn't necessarily mean that a national ad campaign has to be mounted for each opening regardless of level. But even within a small community, there are usually a variety of outlets for publicizing job openings.

When candidates are being reviewed, the best approach is to begin with a sole focus on qualifications. It may help to have several people review applications. It will be difficult to identify which candidates are members of minorities, and indeed no attempt should be made to do so. Remember, you're looking for a qualified employee. What you are trying to avoid is using criteria that have nothing to do with how the person will perform in the job. If the advertising has been handled well, interested and qualified minorities and women will most likely have responded to the ad, and they will be well represented as you narrow the field of candidates.

In the interview process, it is important to exercise care in choosing the kinds of questions you ask. Some of the things that it is unlawful to inquire about before hiring a person are place of birth, previous name if it has been changed by court order (maiden name is ok), or whether the candidate is a native-born American.

Beyond legal constraints, however, it is important to avoid interview questions that inquire about whether a woman will allow the fact that she has children to interfere with her ability to arrive at work on time or if being the only black member of the staff is likely to lead to feelings of resentment, for example. Such questions are based on stereotypes that do not apply to individuals. When such considerations are introduced into the hiring process, the focus shifts away from the individual and the qualifications he or she may have. Decisions made on the basis of such bogus criteria are most likely to be poor ones.

When making a final decision on which of several candidates to hire, it is helpful to have several people evaluate the candidates in relation to the stated qualifications for the position. These can be discussed among the group before the final decision is made.

5.   *Monitoring.* Unless your program is carefully monitored, there is no way of knowing whether your plan is being implemented effectively. Records must be kept to document the results of all hiring decisions. It is a simple matter to develop a form that can be filled out following each hiring decision. The form should record items such as how the position was publicized, the total number of applicants for the position, how many of the applicants were women or minorities (if known), how many of the top candidates were women or minorities, and who the successful candidate was. The form should be kept on file and used to complete an annual report on the EEO program, which is filed with the station's top management.

     The program should be reviewed periodically using the records and reports completed for each hiring situation. If the program is not producing the desired results, it may be necessary to develop new procedures or to refine the existing ones.

An EEO program based on the considerations listed above provides management with a hiring structure that can be implemented effectively. By committing itself to fairness in hiring, any station can easily comply with FCC regulations and avoid litigation that can arise when discrimination plays a part in hiring decisions. Of equal importance, however, is the fact that by ensuring full consideration of all candidates, the station benefits by hiring high-quality employees.

THE LABOR MANAGEMENT RELATIONS ACT   Another piece of federal regulation that affects broadcasting is the **Labor Management Relations Act (LMRA),** which deals with collective bargaining for businesses engaged in interstate commerce. This law protects both labor and management from unfair practices in negotiations and in working in accordance with labor contracts.

     The LMRA stipulates that management may not interfere with the employees right to organize a labor organization and that employers may not make membership in a labor organization a condition of employment. It also requires management to bargain collectively with employee representatives.

     The act protects employees from union practices such as a closed shop, which requires eligible employees to join a union. There are protections guaranteed to the employer as well, such as the right of management to call for a sixty-day cooling-off period before a strike may be called when a contract is due to expire.

     The law is administered by the National Labor Relations Board (NLRB), which consists of five presidentially appointed members. It is the task of the NLRB to decide when the law has been violated and to administer the provisions of the act.

Managers are required to submit paperwork to various agencies of the federal government to demonstrate compliance with various directives and regulations. In keeping abreast of conditions that are specified by government regulations in various areas and in ensuring to meet requirements for reporting, managers have a complex responsibility. Considerable time and energy can be devoted to dealing with these regulatory requirements of the workplace. Those who fail to take these responsibilities seriously, however, leave themselves vulnerable to lengthy and expensive litigation.

10.4

APPLYING MANAGEMENT TECHNIQUES TO RADIO

The various theories of management that have emerged from years of study and experience by many experts and would-be experts fill volumes. There are theories using elaborate formulas for making decisions, and there are procedures that detail how companies can implement concepts that involve employees in decision making. There are grids, columns, maxims, and axioms. Theories and management structures come in and out of fashion as regularly as the seasons change.

There is usually very useful information to be learned in studying those management techniques that have been shown to be effective. There are many documented success stories that attest to the efficacy of many of the best of the hundreds of management theories that have been developed over the years. Most recently, managers have been caught up in concepts that characterize successful large corporations. Books such as *In Search of Excellence* by Thomas J. Peters and Robert H. Waterman, Jr., have captured the imaginations of an American public seemingly fascinated with the idea of efficient and effective operation of complex organizations. This book and others have contributed to a redefinition of ideas about how to get people to be more effective producers.

What can radio managers learn from all this? First, it should be said that the task of assimilating all the various theories and then sorting out the ones that work from those that do not can be intimidating and frustrating. To latch on to the latest fad in management techniques can easily lead to confusion as one hot method replaces the hot method that is now passé. The answer to the dilemma is that probably no single method applies to all circumstances. But there is something to learn by considering some of the most enduring of management techniques.

There are several key concepts and themes that seem to recur in many of the best descriptions of effective management philosophy. The following five principles contain the most effective of these concepts:

—— Know what it is you do best and stick to it.

—— Try constantly to improve your product in relation to the perceived needs of your customers.

—— Do not be afraid to take calculated risks in the pursuit of doing things better. Convey that philosophy to your employees. If you fail, learn from your mistakes.

—— Hire good people and reward achievement.

—— Take seriously your responsibilities in relation to the public interest.

Read the latest books on management theory and practice. When common sense tells you that they have something to offer in your particular set of circumstances, try the concepts that work for others. Good managers are always looking for ways to make things work better. That is one attribute of the most important quality in a manager—leadership.

Theories of Effective Leadership

In their book *Leaders*, Warren Bennis and Burt Nannus take note of the fact that people have been trying to decide what constitutes leadership for some time. "Decades of academic analysis have given us more than 350 definitions of leadership. Literally thousands of empirical investigations of leaders have been conducted in the last seventy-five years alone, but no clear and unequivocal understanding exists as to what distinguishes leaders from nonleaders, and perhaps more important, what distinguishes effective leaders from ineffective leaders and effective organizations from ineffective organizations."[5]

What, then, is there to say about providing effective leadership? If the above quotation is to be believed, everything has been said and nothing has been said. There are a few things, however, that can be said about leadership, which point to how managers can be effective.

First, it is important to realize that common sense goes a long way toward increasing effectiveness in many endeavors. That simply means that managers must be able to sort out the essence of a situation from all of the things that seem to make it complicated. If problems are reduced to a basic level, it is far easier to decide what approaches to use in solving them. There always will be complexities and complications, but they can be dealt with best after you can see what has to be done in a basic sense. There is no substitute for keeping calm and working carefully to unravel things when a complicated problem needs attention.

Another attribute that contributes to effective leadership is keeping a broad perspective on situations. If you can view situations in the context of larger events, problems can be assessed as to their true significance. It is very easy to panic and see nothing but gloom when the transmitter shuts down in the middle of drive time. All missed spots must be made up, explanations must be made, people must be notified, and you can forget about that weekend fishing trip. But if you realize that the station will not lose its license, nor will bankruptcy threaten to close down the place, you can avoid trying to function with all that emotion and anxiety.

Leadership is also an ability to see possibilities and to seize opportunities. The example used in Section 10.1 (a complaint about the air studio leads to a plan to rebuild the station and change the format) illustrates the kind of style that sees the opportunity in situations. This does not mean that every cloud has a silver lining: Managers have to be realistic in assessing the state of affairs at any given time. But leadership entails the ability to see beyond the immediate situation and to look for possibilities.

There are numerous other qualities that can be listed for effective leadership, but it is not necessary to try to summarize all of them. The point that must be stressed is that leadership involves going beyond the mere concern with operational details. Many good managers can keep *things* operating in good order and avoid problems. But leaders lead *people,* not things.

Many effective managers have no leadership ability. Such managers are adept at structure. They know how work should flow through an organization, and they are good organizers. They create a constant sense of activity, and things get done. But such managers are best-suited to middle-level management where good people are needed to implement the policies of top managers. To function effectively at the top levels, managers must have a broader vision.

Managers who can view the mission of the organization as a part of the larger society are the first to see new directions for the enterprise. A few years ago, for example, savvy broadcast managers realized that advances in the field of microcomputers could drastically improve the types of information available to salespeople. When systems that linked all aspects of station operations were installed, salespeople had at their fingertips everything they needed to improve their ability to sell. The result was dramatically greater sales volume and hence better profitability.

Besides spotting the utility of this heretofore alien technology, however, those managers had to motivate people to believe in the vision. By so doing, they brought about revolutionary changes in broadcast operations. There is risk involved in such innovation. But good leaders are aware that progress seldom comes without risk. The key is to be able to assess the extent of the risk and to make decisions that result in progress.

Those managers who are able to exhibit leadership build and develop organizations. There is movement. Changes occur, and the result is that their operations thrive and grow. This is not meant to be high-blown, inspirational hype. In today's society, it is almost axiomatic that organizations that do not grow likely will die. It is particularly true in modern radio that merely minding the store is the pathway to failure.

Protecting Your Interests

Managers in radio, like all other businesses, must in essence serve two masters. Of course, it is in your interest to do your best for your employer. Few who ignore this essential fact succeed. But managers also owe something to themselves. You have an obligation to protect your interests as a professional. Good managers know what it takes to be successful, and they constantly work in ways that help to generate that success. This does not mean success at any price. Remember, you're looking out for your own interests. If you compromise your principles or sacrifice your health, for example, your success may be ultimately not worth it. But managers who develop their careers and their personal lives carefully find that their success is extremely satisfying.

It is well-known that many managers fail. In fact, to succeed in many things, it is necessary to fail in some. Enlightened modern business has come to learn that it is wise to encourage risk taking by managers. If an idea does not pan out or if a project fails, the failure becomes only a single element of the manager's performance appraisal. Of course, regular and consistent failure cannot be tolerated for very long. There must be successes to balance failure. It is increasingly realized that people often learn more from failure than they do from success.

The reason for this discussion is to point out that managers do not necessarily succeed by playing it safe. In fact, extreme caution in today's business world is far more likely to lead to failure than a certain amount of boldness. Managers who succeed do so by becoming secure in their own abilities. This is what allows them to take risks and keep the failure rate within acceptable limits.

Managers who march in lock-step with procedures that were learned long ago and who never try to experiment often seal their doom. By the same token, managers who acquiesce in all things to their superiors are likely to be limited in the areas of responsibility over which they have control. On the other side of the coin, brash managers who flit from one great idea to another and never see a direction emerging ultimately run into considerable difficulty.

Managers who are concerned with success have direction. They know where they want to go. Such managers are cautious about changing direction hastily, but they are not reluctant to get out of dead-end jobs or to challenge authority when there is good reason to do so. When change happens for such individuals, it is thoughtful change. Managers who take care to protect their own interests and who treat each job assignment as a step toward something meaningful in a larger sense are far more effective than are crisis-oriented individuals who worry about the small things that arise and seem big.

Good managers realize that they are a part of an organization and that they are most effective when they can adopt the goals of the organization as their own. In the last analysis, however, good managers are professionals whose ultimate loyalty is to themselves. Managers with this perspective serve the interests of the organizations they work for, but not at the expense of their own professional interests.

EXERCISES

1. Assume that you are the manager of a medium-market FM station. The owners have asked you to raise the ranking of the station in the market. For purposes of this exercise, it is not important to come up with a plan that will accomplish the results desired. The idea is for you to think about the kinds of managerial considerations you will have to deal with in planning how to solve the problem.

    Write a plan of action listing the activities you will undertake to deal with this problem. As an example, you might want to start with something like this. "Call a meeting of the following staff members:" List the staff members who should attend. You may want to use an actual station in your market as a guide as to what staff members to include.

You may want to write up an agenda for the staff meeting, listing the items you wish to discuss. Remember, you are looking at *procedures*. What do you need to do? What areas of managerial concern must be addressed? List them.

Try to come up with a one- or two-page plan that succinctly lays out the activities you'll be engaging in with your staff. As an extra activity, your instructor may wish to assign management roles to various members of the class. Hold the meeting and ask each member to list activities of concern. The object is to be as complete as possible in analyzing the situations from a management point of view.

2. You have just purchased the twenty-fifth-ranked radio station in a major market. It is a class II AM station with an adult contemporary format. It is your intention to do whatever is necessary to turn the station around and sell it at a sizable profit within five to eight years. You are about to meet with the manager you have just hired to run the station.

Using as a guide the organization charts found in Chapter 4, draw up an organization chart showing how you want the station staffed. List all the positions in the station. Then make a list of exactly what you want the manager to do. For example, you might list as one project, "Hire a top personality for the morning drive air shift." Or, you may list someting like, "Hire an experienced sales manager . . . preferably hire one away from the competition."

Be sure to address all areas of station operations that should be considered—engineering, sales, programming, promotion, accounting, and news. For each of these areas, spell out what must be done to develop the kind of station you wish to create. For example, you might charge the programming department with developing a format that will double the share of eighteen to thirty-four-year-old adults that listen to the station. To do that, you may want to authorize the manager to hire a consultant to analyze the market and to discover the required programming to achieve that outcome. The sales department might be required to survey the business community for clients who wish to reach that market segment.

The purpose of this exercise is for you to try to think of all the things that must be done from a management perspective to set a new direction for your station. Do not get specific with regard to format or delivery systems. Leave that to your manager to recommend.

3. You are the manager in Exercise 2. Draw up a plan of action that responds to the list developed in that exercise. If you suggest, for example, that there should be a change in the station's format, provide a brief statement about the actions necessary to bring about that change. You might want to suggest a

satellite-delivered automation service, for example. Or, you may want to raise salaries in an effort to attract better-qualified air people.

You may want to suggest things like changing the organizational structure of the station. Or, it may be necessary to increase expenditures. (If you suggest this, be sure to explain how you plan to raise the additional revenue needed to make up for the increased costs.)

To develop the specifics of your plan, refer to earlier chapters of this text for guidance. Be sure to justify each element of your plan and support your recommendations with ways that will improve the financial health of the station.

NOTES

1. Peter F. Drucker, *People and Performance: The Best of Peter Drucker on Management* (New York: Harper's College Press, 1977), viii.

2. Michael J. Jucius, *Personnel Management*, 9th ed. (Homewood, IL: Richard D. Irwin, 1979), 6.

3. Peter F. Drucker, *Innovation and Entrepreneurship: Practice and Principles* (New York: Harper & Row, 1985), 17.

4. Donald H. Kirkley, Jr., *Station Procedures: A Guide for Radio* (Washington, D.C.: National Association of Broadcasters, 1985), passim.

5. Warren Bennis, and Bert Nannus, *Leaders: The Strategies for Taking Charge* (New York: Harper & Row, 1985), 4.

CHAPTER 11

FINANCIAL

MANAGEMENT

Commercial radio is a business. This is an obvious fact, but one that is frequently overlooked or understressed in discussions of the medium. An understanding of the business aspects of radio is essential to proper operation and management of a station. The most well-conceived program schedule and the highest ideals of public service can be meaningless unless the bottom line shows a reasonable profit. Station owners simply do not tolerate operations that do not produce a profit on their investment— nor, typically, are they able to tolerate unprofitability. In the recent past, there was a more visible trend of radio owners being radio professionals, people who worked through the ranks of sales and/or on-air work into management and eventually owner- ship. But today, a radio manager may typically report to the financial officer of a large, diversified corporation. In such a case, profit—and an understanding of how profit is made—becomes paramount to the radio executive.

On balance, though, an obsession with profit without an accompanying knowledge of programming values, concern for the community, and reasonable staffing levels
provides less than adequate service. Such a situation works against the long-term financial interest of the owner. Along this line of discussion, it is worthwhile to note
that stations in small communities are typically integral elements of the communities
in which they operate. Those communities view blind pursuit of profit without community involvement as arrogant and irresponsible business practice, and communities
have ways of translating that resentment to the ledger sheet. In essence, it is crucial to
remember that shortsighted managers who ignore the requirements and obligations of
quality radio often do so at substantial peril to the bottom line. Conversely, it is important to be aware that profitability and social responsibility can go hand in hand in
radio operations.

11.1

EMERGING FINANCIAL RESPONSIBILITIES OF THE RADIO STATION MANAGER

In many cases, radio station managers of the past had little or no financial responsibility per se: That is, they supervised operations that in theory would provide an adequate return to owners. In other words, managers of the past often were not *directly*
charged with turning a profit and were not as elbow-deep in financial planning and
strategy as modern managers.

That situation has changed; in general terms, more financial sophistication is
required of modern managers. Part of the reason is that diversified corporations are
purchasing radio stations as *investments*. This contrasts with the "typical" owner of the
past who may have purchased a station as a lifetime business and income investment,
which reflected the owner's personal goals and interests.

Additional pressure to maximize profit results from the growing concern among
station owners to turn a profit *quickly*. Often, those owners have heavily financed their
purchase and need immediate returns to pay loans.

As little as ten or fifteen years ago, radio station managers were very much
troubleshooters. Largely, they would solve daily operational problems, deal with staff
personnel situations, and generally ensure that the station operated trouble-free. Today, managers must weigh the considerations outlined above and more often than not
face the problem of funds management. This involves station managers in wide ranges
of activities, including budgeting, issuing financial projections, and cutting waste.

This chapter is not intended as a substitute for a business-education program. The field is far too complex for a quick rendition. However, radio station managers do not necessarily need to be knowledgeable about all the nuances of accounting and financial manipulation. Professionals such as bankers and accountants serve these functions. What managers must be aware of is the general scope of financial operations and the basic principles involved.

Station managers in today's complex marketplace frequently are provided with opportunities for continuing education, especially in the area of finance. Also, you may currently have the opportunity to take college courses specifically dealing with finance and financial management. In either case, the general principles presented in this chapter integrate with the specific skills obtained through other educational avenues.

Survival in Today's Tight Markets

From one perspective, radio is a healthy medium. In terms of advertising revenue, radio as a whole has become a $6.6 billion-per-year industry by 1987.[1] Radio networks and individual stations can reach specialized and profitable audiences with increasing accuracy. As a result, there is a growing recognition that radio is the most effective and cost-efficient medium for certain messages. Conversely, it has also been noted that the concept of mass-marketing, broad-spectrum, mass-appeal efforts is declining.[2]

Recent trends would, on the surface, point to a healthy radio economy. For example, in 1985, Procter & Gamble tripled its network radio advertising from the previous year, spending a total of $12.8 million. Warner-Lambert doubled its spending to $16.3 million, and AT&T boosted advertising expenditures by approximately 50 percent to $24.9 million.

Even with this renewed interest, though, the *percentage* of advertising budgets allocated to radio has remained relatively flat.[3] In the long term, the industry is stable but can be characterized as sluggish in light of the greater increases posted by other media. Industry estimates for the increased radio advertising in 1986 ranged between 7 and 8 percent. In 1986 radio took an uncharacteristic lead, according to various appraisals, in the amount of advertising increase as compared to other media.

The figures change from year to year, of course, but the essential point to glean from examining revenue trends is that radio has traditionally had—and continues to have—a tough time fighting for its piece of the total advertising pie.[4] The overall picture shows a medium to which profits do not come easily.

On paper, such a discussion is an abstraction. In practice, the relative profitability of radio is a very real problem, especially in smaller stations where margins are very tight. Consider the fact that a survey conducted a few years ago showed only about six out of ten radio stations turning a profit. Consider, too, that most stations are indeed small businesses and operate with a small business' built-in financial disadvantage. More than a third of the stations in the United States employ less than fifteen people.

Add to this the problem of competition, a problem that is literally becoming worse by the day. There are at the time of this writing approximately 9000 commercial stations in the country, an exponential increase from previous years. Some industry observers feel that recent licensing decisions by the FCC may open the door to creation of 1000 or so new stations in the next decade. In realistic terms, this means that the advertising pie has to be sliced more thinly than ever among the competitors.

In terms of the financial responsibility of a manager, the foregoing serves to point up three factors:

1. Because revenue to a local station has a practical limit (discussed at various points of the book and in detail in Chapter 7) and because competition for that revenue is increasingly stiff, the financial outlay of a station must be carefully managed. In practical terms, this means that cost control is paramount in tight markets.

2. In light of radio's problems, there is a growing emphasis on sophisticated financial management. This includes the expertise available in chain-ownership situations and the ever-growing emphasis on properly constructed budgets and projections at the local level.

3. Because there is a growing realization that radio is a business, the medium has assumed many of the trappings of modern business. One such trapping, which has virtually revolutionized radio, is the view of stations as investment commodities. Buying and selling of stations has raised their sale value astronomically. It is not unheard of for a station to double its selling price in two years or so. In addition, stations in suburban areas near major markets have found their values increasing at a phenomenal rate. For example, a station in Fairfax, Virginia, recently sold for a price estimated at between $14 and $16 million. (Fairfax serves Washington, D.C.) At the same time, the prevailing view of radio as a worthwhile investment has increased opportunities for ownership. Banks and other lenders have become more receptive to radio purchase plans.

This chapter examines the role of the radio manager in cost control, financial management from the standpoint of station internal management and group-ownership responsibility, and the current trends in ownership and the ways those ownership trends have affected radio station valuation and operation.

The Growing Emphasis on Cost Control

With the realization that revenues can only be expanded so far, it becomes apparent that survival and profitability often depend on controlling expenditures. Such control is in and of itself a form of revenue. This translates to the vaunted bottom line of the business world. Unfortunately, the bottom line of the bottom line is one of the more brutal realities of the business. Personnel is almost always the largest ongoing expense of radio station operations and the most easily reduced.

From a management perspective, let's examine a confidential case study that deals with personnel reduction. Station WAAA (not the real call letters) employed a news director at a salary of $300 a week, a relatively high salary for the mid-1980s. The news director had a two-person staff and a staff of fifteen stringers—a *very* high number for a small station in the lower range of medium markets. The stringer budget alone was hundreds of dollars a month, largely spent for coverage of local meetings. The management consultant called in to evaluate the situation cut the staff by one news person and reduced the stringer budget. As a result, the news director resigned. He was replaced with a news director who was paid the same salary and instructed to either attend meetings himself or develop a relationship with local officials that would allow him to obtain the news of the meetings after the fact via telephone.

The savings were substantial, but were those savings in the best interest of the station and the community? This picture, the bottom-liner cutting staff, is not an attractive one. But was news coverage damaged? Probably, but the news situation was, in the opinion of the consultant, highly inefficient and a case of overkill for the size of the market. In the opinion of the consultant, the news director was primarily interested in showcasing himself and moving to an adjacent major market.

Another point to consider is why this audit was undertaken in the first place. Simply put, the station was in financial trouble. In this and many other cases, it is not unreasonable to assume that unbridled personnel expenditures could eventually cost the jobs of the entire staff.

This admittedly may not have been an immediate all-or-nothing situation. Perhaps cuts in the news department were too drastic. *But once a station begins running into financial problems, those problems have a habit of multiplying and coming back to haunt the owner and manager.* Take the actual case of a small station facing bankruptcy: The financial condition was well known in the community, not an ideal situation for bolstering confidence in the effectiveness of the station's advertising. To make matters worse, parties who were intent on gaining the license in the event of default on the station's loan would visit local merchants and fan the flames of the financial difficulties, hoping to accelerate the station's demise.

Such examples illustrate why the seemingly ruthless, cost-cutting measures may be a necessity. Given the slim profit margin typical to radio, any waste and inefficiency detract from survival. Although it is far less painful to identify inefficiency in the form of nonpersonnel expenditures, such as a too-expensive jingle package or an extra newswire, personnel reduction sometimes can be the only option. Even the act of refusing a yearly raise—a raise that the employee may richly deserve—may be a stressful necessity. Financial control can be a heavy burden at all levels of modern radio.

Introduction to Necessary Financial Skills

What must a manager know to assume control of a station's books? Essentially, the manager needs an understanding of

1. *Working with professionals* (accountants, attorneys, insurance people, outside payroll firms, and so on). A dilemma common to most small business and certainly not unknown in radio is a manager's inability to unload work that is not done effectively in-house. Analysis of what should or should not be done in-house is of one of the primary goals and tasks of a manager.

2. *Using facts and figures.* The manager is not always—and in many cases should not be—the person who draws up the balance sheets, projections, financial statements, and other documentation. But the manager should *understand* their use. For example, it is the manager who will be able to recognize that the high cost for talent is not being matched by a proportionate increase in sales revenue. On the other hand, a manager will know better than an accountant if the high price for a popular morning disc jockey is worthwhile in areas other than the balance sheet. Perhaps the recognition of the morning drive disc jockey carries over into profits for the entire broadcast day. The manager must make this judgment. The skill of a radio manager is not so much in adding up numbers but in being able to identify problems and evaluate potential.

3. *Analyzing operations of the station and relating them to profit and loss.* If sports remotes are killing the budget, it's the manager who must recognize the situation and take action.

4. *Identifying solutions for revenue problems.* Although anyone with a facility for numbers can locate a loss on paper, only an insightful radio professional can remedy the situation. Perhaps a format change or a personnel shift could resolve the problem; only in-depth knowledge and experience can fix what's wrong.

5. *Identifying new ways of maximizing profits.* This often involves finding what level of advertising rates the market will bear and includes developing creative promotions and sales packages.

11.2
ACCOUNTING, BUDGETING, AND CASH FLOW PRACTICES

In light of the above, we'll now take a broad overview of accounting and budgeting for modern radio. First, realize that accounting and budgeting documents in today's market are more than simple historical records. The data are used for *projection.* With the advent of modern automation, a financial or sales executive can make projections based on a wide variety of factors, including the individual account, the type of project, and the individual salesperson.

Typical Financial Structures

The basic instrument of financial management in a radio station is the operating budget. This is essentially a statement of expenses for the various departments comprising the station and a projection of income from the departments that produce revenue. The most immediate goal, of course, is to keep the budget in the black.

A radio station is an interactive financial organization. That is, the function is a complex and interactive linkage of financial operations, arcane vocabulary, tax laws, and so forth. It is probably easier to gain an initial understanding of station finances by first examining the personnel who control the dollar and then defining some of the terminology that relates to station finance.

ACCOUNTANTS   In the long run, accountants quantify the successes and failures of a business. In large radio stations, there are typically in-house accounting services or accounting services at the chain-headquarters level. Smaller stations generally rely on outside help.

Accountants are more than bookkeepers. Among other tasks, accountants must work to minimize a station's tax liability and to structure the books in such a way as to accommodate future expansion. Indeed, radio stations or ownership groups contemplating future expansion typically seek the help of established accounting firms for their guidance. Accountants dealing with radio stations are typically certified public accountants (CPAs), meaning that they have passed a rigorous series of examinations.

In some cases, the roles of accountants are expanded to that of comptrollers. In an in-house framework, comptrollers combine accounting and financial expertise with management skills to evaluate operations in terms of financial impact. Regardless of terminology and putting aside individual differences in operations, "keeping the books" has many facets. A radio station's records must include such items as tax payments, employer contributions to Social Security, retirement and health insurance, and other payroll-related activities. Insurance is a major consideration, along with the monitoring of supplies, both in terms of material and employee time. It is also essential to work with the traffic department's evaluation of airtime available to be sold and the certification, through affidavits, that commercials ran as scheduled.

All this data is honed, added, and interpreted; after many complicated machinations, the numbers are entered onto a balance sheet.

BALANCE SHEET   As the name **balance sheet** implies, this is a summary of what a station has and what it owes. A station typically lists as assets:

—— Cash

—— Inventories

—— Amounts owed to the station (called receivables)

—— Fixed assets less depreciation (meaning the worth of the physical equipment minus an allowance for a decrease in value because of age and wear and tear)

—— Intangibles

—— Prepaid expenses (fees or other expenditures paid in advance)

—— Investments

All these values are totaled to determine the station's total assets. A station typically lists as liabilities:

—— Accounts payable (the monies owed by the station)

—— Taxes and other withholdings from employees

Figure 11.1

A typical balance sheet for radio.

Balance Sheet
September 30, 1987

			LIABILITIES AND STOCKHOLDERS' EQUITY		
CURRENT ASSETS			CURRENT LIABILITIES		
Cash	1,591.95–		Accounts payable	176,952.70	
Accounts receivable	183,806.05		Payroll taxes	65,173.40	
			Unearned income	12,828.50–	
Total Current Assets		182,214.10	Total Current Liabilities		229,297.60
PROPERTY AND EQUIPMENT			LONG-TERM LIABILITIES		
Land	25,000.00		Notes payable	487,529.80	
Building	246,668.90		Covenant payable	106,250.00	
Equipment	353,100.00		Note payable	56,738.40	
Studio equipment	234,152.70		Note payable, equipment	6,613.90	
Furniture and fixtures	47,525.25		Loans from stockholders	529,282.20	
	906,446.85				
Less Accumulated Depreciation	507,841.60		Total Long-Term Liabilities		1,186,414.30
Net Property and Equipment		398,605.25			
OTHER ASSETS			STOCKHOLDERS' EQUITY		
Prepaid insurance	2,876.75		Common stock	231,250.00	
Deposits	5,500.00		Retained earnings	898,218.50–	
Covenant not to compete	125,000.00		Net loss	64,746.35–	
Accumulated amortization	120,052.75–				
Organization expense	6,205.95		Total Stockholders' Equity		731,714.85
Accumulated amortization	5,957.35–				
Goodwill	125,000.00				
Accumulated amortization	30,988.05–				
Reorganization expense	25,000.00				
Accumulated amortization	3,749.85–				
Total Other assets		128,834.70			
Total Assets		709,654.05	Total Liabilities and Stockholders' Equity		683,997.05

Balance sheets typically are highly variable in their construction and presentation. Figure 11.1 shows one example.

STATEMENT OF INCOME The **statement of income** consists of the operating expenses judged against the revenues of a station *for a specified time period.* It differs from a balance sheet in that it identifies a starting and stopping point for activity recorded and does not include a tally of fixed assets. The information from the statement of income is, of course, a major component in the balance sheet.

The typical statement of income includes the forms of revenue; depending on individual practices, they may be broken out by source such as national sales, local sales, network income, and other sources of revenue. Operating expenses are generally listed by department, often broken down into separate entries for news, programming, engineering, sales, and the "general and administrative" category. Other miscellaneous items such as royalties and repairs are also listed (Figure 11.2).

USE OF BALANCE SHEETS AND STATEMENTS OF INCOME   Although radio station managers usually are not experts in drawing up the figures, they must have an imaginative facility in evaluating those columns of numbers. The essential question is whether the station is running in the red or black. As to the whys and wherefores of operation, managers ask such questions as

1.   Is there appropriate allocation to various arms of the operation? Is any expenditure far out of proportion? If so, is such an expenditure justified?

2.   Would an increase or decrease in individual expenditures be reflected in revenues? Would cutting funds for the news department, for instance, result in cost savings or in a substantial loss of station prestige and advertising revenue?

3.   Will continuation of current revenues meet goals for the year? This is the value of month-by-month evaluation. Were these figures typical? Was there an extraordinary expenditure that will not recur?

4.   Is there adequate protection for economic downturns? Fluctuation is a fact of life in radio and a fact that must be planned for.

5.   How does this month compare with historical data *for a similar period?* Comparing a November to a February is generally pointless in that Novembers are typically high-earning months because of the Christmas season. Comparing the Novembers for previous years, though, is a highly worthwhile exercise in evaluation of revenue performance.

6.   Is the return to the ownership satisfactory? The proper return is computed on a variety of factors. In some markets, the rate of pure profit may be acceptable at 5 to 10 percent, but higher rates of return, close to 20 percent, are more commonly expected. A large, very lean operation may return as high as a 60-percent profit.

    Remember that profit is sometimes difficult to define precisely because many items are added and subtracted. In most cases, the profit is defined as the "profit margin" of money left over after all expenses are paid. To obtain a 10-percent profit margin, expenses of $162,000 could be deducted from total revenue of $180,000, leaving a profit of $18,000. The profit margin, $18,000 profit for $180,000 total revenues, would be 10 percent.

Figure 11.2

A statement of income.

Income Statement
for the Period
January 1, 1987, Through September 30, 1987

	Current Period	%	Year to Date	%
SALES	80,423.20	100.0	647,226.25	100.0
OPERATING EXPENSES	78,713.71	97.7	667,553.00	108.5
NET INCOME/LOSS	1,901.23	2.4	64,746.27–	10.0

OPERATING EXPENSES

	Current Period	%	Year to Date	%
Advertising and trades	7,416.50	9.2	12,776.10	6.6
Amortization	2,668.40	3.3	24,015.60	3.7
Commissions	4,105.50	5.1	44,668.15	6.9
Depreciation	8,684.46	10.8	78,159.60	12.1
Dues, subscriptions	0.00	0.0	1,690.00	0.3
Engineering dept.	0.00	0.0	2,493.75	0.4
Insurance	5,242.75	6.5	42,248.50	7.0
Lease expense	259.90	0.3	2,373.10	0.4
Maintenance	166.40	0.2	1,237.60	0.2
Office expense	924.70	1.2	8,920.80	1.4
Outside services	0.00	0.0	1,715.75	0.3
Program	2,518.50	3.1	24,447.15	3.8
Repairs	837.20	1.0	1,842.00	0.3
Royalties	1,437.20	1.8	12,336.70	1.9
Salaries	26,409.10	32.8	273,794.50	42.3
Promotion	5,400.00	6.7	21,703.20	3.4
Sales expense	224.25	0.3	5,999.65	0.9
Taxes, payroll	5,332.90	6.6	35,746.00	5.5
Taxes, real estate	0.00	0.0	2,984.40	0.5
Talent	627.95	0.8	10,665.00	1.7
Telephone	4,853.60	6.0	42,316.00	6.5
Utilities	1,604.40	2.0	15,419.45	2.4
Total Operating Expenses	78,713.71	97.7	667,553.00	108.5

Additional Financial Terminology

A major step in becoming familiar with financial operations is to develop an acquaintance with the lexicon. The following is a listing of some common terms as they specifically apply to radio.

AMORTIZATION   Amortization is the way in which a loan is repaid—the structure of time payments in conjunction with costs of interest on the original loan (principal). As an example, the structure of your car loan—how much you pay and when— is the way the loan is amortized.

CASH FLOW   Cash flow is all money that "passes through" the station. In many businesses, cash flow is synonymous with profits, but special considerations apply in the case of radio. A section later in the chapter offers details of cash-flow practices in a typical radio station.

DEBT   Debt is the amount of money owned. More specifically, it is money contracted to be paid back. To an accountant, there are many different types of debt, each of which carry different consequences. For example, *subordinated debt* is a type of debt that has a specified standing in the event of bankruptcy of the borrower. The holder of subordinated debt can claim repayment only after certain other specified debts are paid. *Senior debt* is the type of debt paid back first in event of bankruptcy. *Convertible debentures* are another kind of debt, carrying an option whereby the lender can take back the original debt or elect to receive stock in the company. The permutations are endless, but the single understanding that *debt is not a totally definitive category* is worthwhile for any manager.

DEBT EQUITY   Debt equity is total debt divided by total equity. This number is a ratio that simply gives a reading on how much credit has been extended to a firm and how much borrowing power is left.

DEBT SERVICE   Debt service is repayment of debt—what it costs to make loan payments. The debt service is usually expressed in an annual sum.

EQUITY   Equity is the money contributed by owners—capital contributions. Also, equity can be defined as the value of assets minus the value of liabilities.

FIXED ASSETS   Fixed assets are "hard," tangible assets such as facilities, equipment, and land.

INTANGIBLE ASSETS **Intangible assets** are valued items other than "hard" assets. Intangible assets may include a station's operating license or contracts.

RECEIVABLES **Receivables** are moneys owed to a station. Typically, receivables take the form of unpaid bills. Receivables, always a part of radio station operations, are frequently listed by their age. A station's books may carry thirty-day receivables, sixty-day receivables, ninety-day receivables, and so forth. Identifying excess receivables (the acceptable amount ranges from station to station) is one job of the station manager.

STOCKS **Stocks** are the documents that represent and comprise ownership and value of the radio station. Stock issuance, selling shares of the station, is a common method of capitalizing a radio facility.

Chain Ownership: The Manager as Financial Middleman

Radio is no longer typically a one- or two-owner, mom-and-pop operation. As addressed elsewhere in this book, there is a growing and continuing trend of individually owned stations being bought up and exchanged among group owners. Frequently, group owners are involved in an array of other business enterprises, often but not always focused in the communications industry.

One reason behind the changing face of chain involvement in broadcasting is government regulation. The FCC has, in recent years, relaxed rules that restricted ownership of AM and FM operations, a move that relates to situations created through acquisitions by Capital Cities and General Electric.[5]

What does chain ownership mean to a manager? First, there is a good chance that a manager at an individual station is working for a parent company. There are centralized policies that may govern what procedures and activities the manager will be involved with on a day-to-day basis.

Second, centralized accounting practices may make a manager's role at the local level more of a reporting function than it was in the past; supplying data to corporate management is a major responsibility of the manager. This does not change the manager's obligation to monitor the fiscal health of the operation. Management personnel interviewed in researching this section report that the fiscal practices of chain ownership do indeed remove a degree of flexibility and autonomy from the typical radio station manager's role. The positive side of the issue is that the financial procedures in place are designed by top-level experts, usually of the caliber not available to smaller stations.

Third, from the manager's standpoint, chain ownership means an enhanced opportunity for the professional manager to move to other stations in the chain, gaining experience at many different levels but not earning the label of "job-hopper" (which could be applied to a manager who makes frequent moves among unaffiliated stations). Also, there are increased opportunities for advancement into centralized management.

Fourth, from the standpoint of overall management of the station, the chain-affiliated manager generally fares better in securing products and services for the individual station because costs are usually amortized across the entire chain.

Fifth, a drawback mentioned by many who work or have worked in chain management is the rigidity of employment rules and regulations. In one extreme example, the local manager of a station was fired on the spot when it was discovered he held a minimal amount of stock in another radio station. Chain representatives literally stood over the fired manager while he cleaned out his desk.

Finally, the level of salaries and benefits is, by and large, significantly better in chain operations. Profit sharing is a common employee incentive and has proven a profitable option to many.

How Budgets Are Drawn Up and Finalized

One of the financial activities of the manager that has the greatest impact on the success of the station is the series of decisions made on the allocation of resources to the various departments of the station. These decisions directly impact the quality and financial viability of all operations.

How could operations be endangered? A manager who fails to allocate enough money to hire the appropriate number of salespeople is endangering the collection of revenues. Such a "savings" would certainly not be cost effective.

Salaries of on-air people are another consideration. The manager must factor in the reality that each position has a built-in value that is based on what the market will support. A morning announcer in a small market, for example, may be enormously popular, but there are intrinsic limits on how much revenue that announcer can generate. If every spot were sold at the maximum rate and the profit margin still were not adequate, then the owner would, in effect, take a loss on the early-morning announcer's salary.

These are the kinds of decisions you must undertake to run an efficient operation, and those decisions are the nuts and bolts of the budgeting process. What happens during that process? With some variation, the process usually begins with the manager soliciting budget requests from the heads of individual departments. More often than not, programming accounts for 30, 40, or 50 percent of the total budget.

Programming includes salaries for department personnel, jingle packages, program services such as format tapes or a music library, and licensing fees for BMI and ASCAP. Sales and engineering are generally stable in their budgets; each department typically requests about 15 percent of the total of available operating funds. However, engineering costs can spike due to unexpected repairs or purchases of new equipment such as automated gear.

News budgets vary widely according to the individual station's news effort. In terms of direct return for the money invested, news usually offers a low return in relationship to its high cost. Radio news is certainly not a money-maker in the way television news is; it simply cannot attract television's large-scale advertising revenue. In fact, with the advent of recent deregulation, many stations have dropped news coverage altogether.

In the general and administrative area (G and A in management shorthand) are budgetary requests for items such as janitorial and maintenance services and supplies, telephone bills, mailing costs, subscriptions to trade publications, and secretarial salaries. Travel and taxes are usually listed under the G and A budget.

Departmental Projections

When making projections for the budgeting process, department heads frequently peg their requested increases to the inflation rate. (Last year's budget plus 7 percent, perhaps.) Requests for extraordinary items are usually submitted independently of the overall budget.

The sales department is in charge of projecting both expenses *and* revenue. Although revenue does flow from other areas, such as rental of facilities, most revenues other than sales are negligible. Sales-revenue figures are generally projected on both a yearly and monthly basis. Revenues are projected from anticipated

— *National spot sales.* This projection is made after consultation with representatives agenting the station in the national advertising market place (the national reps).

— *Local sales.* Local projections are made by the local sales manager.

— *Network revenues.* Some stations receive a set fee for carrying network programming and advertising, and this can be reliably calculated in advance. It is worth noting, though, that some of the newer networks operate entirely on a barter arrangement, offering local availabilities in the furnished programming in lieu of payment.

Once the projections are complete, they are added together to determine a gross revenue projection for the budgeting period. The gross figure is adjusted to reflect agency commissions and other expenses directly deducted from the incoming revenues.

Budgeting Versus Income

The manager's obvious task is now to compare costs and revenue. Revenues must cover costs and provide an adequate profit margin. If the columns do not add up, then the give and take of negotiation begins. Meeting individually or collectively with department heads, the manager questions expenses and determines whether projected revenues are realistic.

First, the manager weighs the likelihood that those expected revenues will actually appear. In fact, the manager must often take the role of devil's advocate and in effect plan for the worst. To make revenue projection more difficult, external factors must be adjusted for.

BAD DEBT   The amount of money owed a station that is unlikely to be paid varies from station to station. Some stations operate with high-level bad debt because of economic difficulties in the community. Businesses in financial trouble often do not or cannot pay advertising bills. Sometimes, the bad-debt ratio is high because of lax collection practices. It is the manager's job to uncover the reason and rectify the situation if possible.

The causes of bad debt are not always obvious. In one station, intense pressure from sales management was causing salespeople to write up phony orders just to meet quotas. Because the orders were never paid, the fees were carried as bad debt until a curious manager began investigating. Another newly hired station manager dug into the bad-debt situation and found that one salesperson was stealing cash payments made by a merchant. The vast majority of salespeople are honest, but events such as these do happen and it pays to be vigilant.

OVERALL BUSINESS TRENDS   Is there any reason to anticipate a slowdown in local retail sales? The closing of a department store can seriously damage revenues in a small- or small-to-medium market station. Likewise, an alert manager must be aware of what may happen to the national economy because national trends very quickly "trickle down" to most local retail economies.

ADVERTISER ATTRITION   In a large market, advertisers can drop off a particular station's roster at the rate of 15 percent a year. Especially in cases where there is a new station or format in town, advertisers sample, and, for whatever reason, a certain number stop buying. Personnel changes in advertising agencies can have a profound impact on station revenue, in many cases through no fault of the station itself. It is therefore incumbent upon a manager who anticipates a format change or shakeups in the local advertising climate to factor in what, based on experience and judgment, the likely consequences will be.

DROPS IN PRODUCTIVITY   One advantage (or drawback, depending on your point of view) to the computer age is the ability to quickly calculate a salesperson's productivity. The individual salesperson or the department as a whole can be compared to the market average for sales productivity.

Saying No

Income is usually a finite; that is, there is no certain way to adjust the projected figure upward. Expenditure, though, can be calculated with some degree of precision. When push comes to shove in the budgeting process, it is often the manager's unpleasant task to turn down budget requests and/or trim budgets. During this process, the manager employs an overall view of the budget situation. Most departmental specialists do not have access to the overall financial big picture, nor should they. (Department heads, though, sometimes are privvy to the overall financial situation.) Expenditures for other departments and salaries of individuals working for the station must obviously remain confidential.

Indeed, the individual's view of the budget is colored by his or her particular needs. This may manifest itself, for instance, in the engineer who complains that management is shortsighted because it will not invest in a new transmitter. Or, the production manager may feel that management is taking the low road by sticking to an older, cheaper jingle package. It is not uncommon for a news director to harbor resentments against management, feeling that management is not living up to its commitment to the public because of failure to expand news operations.

Such charges may in fact be true, but often they are not. The conflict, however, is unavoidable. Station economies are ruled by the inevitable law of income versus expenditure, and each expenditure must be weighed in view of its likelihood to provide revenues. The sad fact of the matter is that in small and medium markets, and even in a few majors, overspending can result and has resulted in bankruptcies. In fact, major national networks have felt the pinch, and the trend in most media organizations is toward streamlining.

Expenditures need not always produce immediate income, of course. Tax laws make a reasonable provision for investment in long-term capital projects involving hard assets. In such a situation—long-term expansion and growth—a manager in charge of station finances must work hand in glove with an experienced accountant.

But more to the point is the concept that good financial managers can protect the interests of the organization even when their decisions are not pleasing to some or all members of the organization. Saying no can be traumatic, especially when it applies to personnel considerations. Refusing new hires or trimming existing jobs is certainly an area that should not be entered into without considerable soul searching. However, veterans of the radio business are virtually unanimous in their contention that the quickest way to bankruptcy is to carry unneeded and inefficient personnel on the payroll year after year.

Cash Flow in the Typical Radio Station

Cash flow has actually become a measure of the value of a station. A radio station, for all intents and purposes, carries very little inventory. Physical facilities such as buildings, towers, and equipment can account for only a fraction of the station's total worth. Most of the station's worth is contained in its license. The license, though, is an intangible asset; there is no standard cost attached to the license itself.

The term *cash flow* can be rather nebulous. Depending on what is added into the figures, estimations of cash flow and profit can vary from estimator to estimator. Basically, cash flow is usually considered to be the operating profit before taxes, depreciation, and interest are subtracted.[6] However, certain extraordinary costs are typically added to or subtracted from cash-flow figures. Other ways of figuring cash flow, such as discounting the value of money to be paid in the future (on the premise that money not yet paid is less valuable than money in hand), can be applied.

Setting aside the complexities of determining cash flow, remember that cash flow is useful as a valuation figure because it gives an indication of how long it will take a prospective buyer of a radio station to pay off the debt. For example, a station that takes in $5 million a year and costs $3 million a year to run (not counting taxes, depreciation, and interest)[7] has a cash flow of $2 million a year—a far more attractive option than the station with only $1 million a year. Why? That extra cash "flowing" through the station can be used to pay debt service.

The cash-flow figure is often multiplied by a certain number to provide an estimation of price. That particular multiplier is based on market trends. For example, recent figures for typical radio station valuations have been set at eight to ten times cash flow, but recent sales have pushed that proportion higher. It appears that the figures will probably keep rising.

Cash-flow estimations are often based on projected figures for two or three years, particularly in large markets.

11.3

TRENDS IN STATION OWNERSHIP AND FINANCING

One of the most exciting possibilities in radio is to become an owner of a station. One of the more visible trends in recent years is for financers to back prospective owners who are long on know-how and experience but relatively short on cash. Lenders, who today take a much more charitable view of broadcasters as businesspeople, have come to realize that sizable profits can be made from backing competent owners.

This section is not intended as a guide to buying a radio station, as that is beyond the realistic scope of this text. However, for the prospective manager interested in the finances of radio, there is no more incisive guide to the business than an examination of how stations are bought and sold, how they are financed and valued. An understanding of this provides greater insight into the overall context of financial management.

Opportunities in Ownership—Who Pays and How

More people are playing the radio ownership game today than ever before. Although this may seem odd because radio station prices have skyrocketed in recent years, it appears that lenders' greater flexibility allows more buyers into the game. Also, there are significantly greater numbers of properties to be bought and sold today than there were a few years ago. The FCC estimated in 1986 that the volume of money spent on buying radio stations was over $2.5 billion, a 700-percent increase over the previous six years.

Those who are buying stations fall into one or both of two categories: first, those with substantial financial assets who are looking for investment opportunity, and second, those who are interested in deriving long-term income from operation of a property. Historically, sales of radio stations have been less active when interest rates were high. Recent declines in interest rates have, according to industry observers, significantly fueled the fires of station sales and acquisitions. The closing months of 1986 saw brisk trading as sellers tried to take advantage of capital-gains advantages being phased out under the Tax Reform Act.

More significantly, lenders have, as mentioned, changed their approach to broadcast lending. As little as ten years ago, borrowing money for broadcast acquisition was primarily the privilege of major corporations. However, those who follow trends in broadcast lending now note that banks and other lenders are *looking* for prospective owners to whom they would like to lend capital. Those lenders are taking into account the role of experience in what many call the "management intensive" nature of broadcasting.[8]

In essence, lenders now have more knowledge of broadcasting and hence give more credibility to those who seek capital for acquisition of a property. The historical reticence of banks to deal with broadcasters has led to many a prospective owner's complaint that "the people at the bank think I'm trying to buy a shoe store—they keep asking me what my inventory is worth." And yes, there is validity in that criticism. Smaller banks, accustomed to dealing with merchants and not with broadcasters, were used to securing a loan with unsold merchandise.

Prices of Properties

At the crux of the matter is the difficulty in determining a station's worth. Whereas a shoe store is a pretty straightforward estimation (inventory, past income, physical facility, and so forth), a radio station is based on more nebulous concepts, including the cash-flow calculation. Note, too, that the calculations of cash flow may have little or no bearing on the price of a station; more than one loser station has been sold for a high price because buyers realized its unused potential. In short, a station is worth what someone thinks it's worth—as long as that person has the wherewithal to buy it.

A major point in determining a station's value is the type of station. A 1000-watt AM station in the same market as a 5000-watt FM station certainly will sell for a much lower price because the AM signal has less fidelity and is deemed less profitable and desirable than the FM. The frequency on which an AM station operates also has a bearing: An AM on 1540, for example, will be less attractive than one at 540 because—for technical reasons and licensing restrictions—the higher frequency signal has poorer coverage.

Some factors less tangible than cash flow and physical properties bear strongly on the relative worth of a station. Those factors include

—— *Potential growth of the station.* Ironically, a poorly managed station may be worth
more on the market than a well-managed one. A station operated far below
its potential has much room for growth, and buyers may be willing to assume
that risk. Other areas of potential growth include a station that is technically
limited but could perform better with a change in equipment or a change in
licensing.

—— *Location of the station.* A station on the fringes of a rapidly growing medium
market may suddenly become a hot property when investors realize that the
signal carries into a dense-population zone. Likewise, a station in an area with
a promising economy could be highly valued.

—— *Level of competition for existing advertising dollars.* A station will be of higher
value if it is not in an area saturated with radio stations, cable outlets, and
so on. Likewise, if it appears that the station is garnering an unreasonably low
share of local advertising and that low share can be attributed to a poor sales
effort, a great deal of potential may be noted.[9]

The most important factor in evaluating the competition for advertising dollars
is the performance of other radio stations. It is generally accepted that with limited
amounts of advertising revenue (and most communities do have a built-in cap on how
much advertising can be generated) it is easier to take away advertising from other
radio stations than from television or newspapers. (See Chapter 7 for additional details.) The evaluation of change therefore hinges on the likelihood that change will be
productive. This factor is typically given a long, hard look by potential purchasers. It
relates to the points above.

One point affecting price is the obvious factor of market size. Small markets generally have not been looked upon as highly prized commodities, but that is changing.
Some investors seek out stable small-market stations as a source of continued and reliable income. The small market is almost always less volatile than medium or large
markets in terms of station position. (In other words, it is not unheard of for a poorly
rated station in a medium market to shoot near the top of the pack after a format
change, while a long-time ratings leader plummets because of talent changes. In small
markets, that type of situation does not occur frequently.) Too, small markets are often
the only markets in which individual investors or smaller groups can afford to invest.

Each market size—small, medium, and large—carries pluses and minuses for the
investor. Some of the major facets of radio acquisition in those three markets are discussed next.

SMALL MARKETS   The lowest cost of a small-market station was in 1987 about
$150,000 for an AM, although $200,000 is more typical and $300,000 is not an un-

usual price for even a poorly equipped station in a small economically depressed town. Quality $500,000 FM properties are not unusual in small markets.

The advantage of a small market, as mentioned, is that these stations tend to be a relatively stable, although unspectacular, investment. They are often best-suited for an owner–operator. For those who enjoy small-town life and community involvement, ownership/operation of a radio station can be highly satisfying. Some small-market stations suffer from significant mismanagement, creating opportunities for the experienced manager/owner.

The disadvantage of a small market is that an owner–operator must be prepared to make an extensive time commitment. There is an intrinsic upper level on how much money the station can make. (A construction business in a small town can expand to the limits of how far it can drive its trucks, but a radio station can only extend its signal so far, and there is only so much revenue to be had within a certain geographic coverage area.) Many times, a small station serves as a training ground for personnel. It is difficult to maintain a loyal staff for the long term. High turnover will always be a problem.

MEDIUM MARKETS Prices in a medium market can range from $500,000 to well over $3 million.[10] An emerging trend in medium markets is the tendency of regionally based groups to hold a number of medium-market stations.

The advantage of a medium market is that there is still opportunity for those other than the wealthy to gain entry into ownership ranks. Medium markets offer the possibility of a highly profitable turnaround with moderate amounts of money invested. The ceiling for profits is not so limited as in a small market, and prices for purchases and payment of talent is not so astronomical as in a large market.

The disadvantage of a medium market is that, in light of current trends, it is safe to assume that ownership in medium markets will become less and less of a reality for most investors because of increasing prices, especially in financially healthy medium markets. A medium market is not the most stable environment. In a twenty-station market, a station's ratings and therefore its profitability can sink drastically over a short period of time. Typically, this does not happen in a small market, and in a major market there is more of an intrinsic value to the intangibles (primarily the operating license) of a station simply because it exists in a large metropolitan area.

MAJOR MARKETS The price of a major market station can range from $2 million to $40 million plus, and there is no foreseeable cap in sight.[11] Obviously, the major-market station is the most desirable product on the market because, while there is an element of risk, the potential profits are enormous. The station at the bottom of a fifty-station market could, with the right turnaround strategy, become a number three, two, or even one. This is what drives prices so high; the physical plant of a medium-market station and a major-market station could be identical, but the major market could sell for ten times the price.

It is interesting to note that the concept of a major-market station has changed somewhat in recent years, and this has altered the way in which some stations are valued. Today, many stations that have transmission facilities at the fringes of a grow- ing major market are allowed to locate studios within the major market, although those stations must make some concession to serving the original community of li- cense. A recent shake-up in technical regulations dealing with tower height and sta- tion power has allowed these so-called move-in stations to become prosperous. In effect, a station on the outskirts of a major market can become a major-market station. There is often a heavy price to pay in terms of renovations and technical adjustments, but the profits can be very large.

The advantage of a major market is that, for those select few with the available money, major-market stations are a blue-chip investment. For stations in the middle of the pack, there are many opportunities to rise to the top. Even stations at the bottom have turnaround possibilities, making them worth the gamble to some purchasers. Major markets are a fine investment simply because of their relative scarcity. As one radio professional expresses it: "It's like land—they're not making them anymore."

The disadvantage of a major market is that the cost of getting into ownership is astronomical.

Brokers

Most of the buying and selling of stations is handled by brokers. Brokers are business agents who negotiate between buyers and sellers and are paid a commission on the sale price. For the most part, the commission on the sale price is paid by sellers. The industry-standard commission paid to brokers is usually 7 or 8 percent. On some sales, especially large deals, various formulas other than flat percentages are used in calculat- ing brokers' fees.

The value of brokers to sellers is that sellers can remain anonymous to the degree that they do not have to advertise the station publicly and will deal only with inter- ested and qualified buyers. The qualification point is very important to sellers because they do not want to waste time and effort negotiating with potential buyers who really cannot afford to pay the price. Brokers will ask potential buyers for some demonstra- tion of financial worth before proceeding with contacting sellers.

The value of using brokers to buyers is that buyers need not scour the countryside looking for appropriate stations. Brokers supply lists of stations and generally send listings tailored to the demands of specific buyers. Those listings typically detail factors relating to the station, the community, and the region. For example, one flyer sent to a potential buyer reads:

> **For Sale** Station K _____ is in the city of _____, the county seat and principal community in _____ County, located sixteen miles from the geographic center of the state of _____.
>
> The economy of the area revolves around agriculture, manufacturing, and mineral production. Agriculture has been the basis of the area economy for years. The influx of new industry since World War II has lessened the county's dependence on agriculture. . . .

The listing continues with additional description of area history and economy and the impact of a regional university. Then, the flyer details some specifics of the station: facility, format, competition, frequency, power, antenna height. Existing contracts are typically listed in a broker's flyer; in this case, the tower lease is $5000 a year, the studio rents for $466 a month, and rental of the music format is $85 a month.

Also listed are items of equipment that would go with the sale, such as the transmitter, automation equipment, and consoles. Then, staffing levels are enumerated.

Now, to the nitty gritty:

> Reason for sale: Partners are splitting up. Asking price: $250,000. Terms offered: $60,000 down, assume a $50,000 bank note, with a balance of $140,000, payable over ten years at 10 percent.

How Buyers Secure Capital

It is apparent from the example above that even small-market properties require a substantial amount of up-front money. There is no way, practically speaking, that a station could be entirely purchased on credit, although substantial credit may be offered. In cases where a major proportion of money is lent, it is usually only after the borrower has demonstrated strong personal commitment, meaning a willingness to put up personal funds, often by mortgaging or selling a house, for example.

Although banks are the primary lenders, venture-capital firms have recently become key players in the radio market. Venture-capital firms are typically after equity, meaning a share of the ongoing business. Venture-capital companies are not easily convinced to invest their money and carry the additional disadvantage (from the

Table 11.1

RELATIONSHIP OF DOWN PAYMENT TO TOTAL PRICE

Down Payment ($)	Total Price ($)	Percentage
60,000	160,000	38
75,000	650,000	12
75,000	250,000	30
200,000	800,000	25

standpoint of the radio station buyer) of retaining a certain amount of control in the company.

Essentially, the functions performed by lenders and venture capitalists represent the first two levels of debt commonly encountered in broadcasting: senior debt and equity. Senior debt, as defined earlier, is the first to be paid off in the event of bankruptcy and is in some way secured with collateral. Equity debt is more hazardous for the lender but involves a higher return and a stake in the business. The next level of debt, subordinated debt, is more risky and hence a higher interest rate is attached to subordinated debt. Subordinated lenders take a bigger gamble by filling in the needed capital when the borrower's senior debt and equity do not cover the entire price. As a result, subordinated lenders want a greater return. Subordinated lenders also look for the most secure opportunities.

Seller financing is a popular option. Owners require a substantial down payment, historically in the range of 29 percent—a popular figure because of tax consequences that arise when 30 percent or more of the total purchase price is received during one year.

Some typical down payments in relation to total price are shown in Table 11.1. Many sellers offer financing of about 10 percent over several years.

It is apparent that radio is a high-stakes game, and the growing concern with return on investment has a profound impact on how a manager does the job. Some speculate that the fantastic profits to be made from sale and resale of radio stations will change the emphasis from operations to trading. Such a forecast could be possible because the profits to be made are simply phenomenal. Station WLIF in Baltimore, for example, was purchased by American Media in 1984 for $5.5 million and resold in 1986 for $30.5 million.

It is equally apparent that managers skilled in budgeting and aware of the current financial climate face unparalleled opportunities, both in career growth as an employee and as a possible future owner.

EXERCISES

1. Assume that you are the manager of a medium-market station and are facing a difficult decision concerning the budget of the news department. The revenues from sales of spots during the newscast are $14,000 short of the news department's operating budget. Ownership is pressuring you to cut the news staff by one person to make the books balance.

    What would you choose to do? Write a brief, logically ordered defense of your decision. Invent the specific facts and figures, keeping them within reason, but attempt in any case to give a realistic assessment of what you believe a situation such as this would entail. Assess the impact on the station's standing in the community, the impact on the newsperson being fired, and the impact on the station itself.

2. Using the same premise and "facts" from Exercise 1, write a brief position paper defending the opposite point of view. If possible, discuss your views with classmates or co-workers.

3. Identify a station in your local market that you believe would be good turn-around material. In a brief paper, discuss what you think are the station's weaknesses and how a new owner could remedy them. (EXAMPLES: Additional money could hire better on-air talent; new management could change format to serve the city's large black community, which is at present drastically underserved.)

NOTES

1. *Wall Street Journal*, 21 August 1986, 27:1.

2. *Wall Street Journal*, 21 August 1986, 27:1.

3. Figures such as these are obtainable from a variety of sources, two of the most useful being the *McCann–Erickson Report* and *Advertising Age*.

4. For a detailed discussion of how advertising fares against other media, see Chapter 7.

5. The so-called twelve-and-twelve rule is now in effect, and its impact on radio operations is discussed in Chapter 12.

6. *National Association of Broadcasters Guide to Investment in Broadcast Properties* (Washington, D.C.: National Association of Broadcasters, 1978), 7.

7. The reason that taxes, depreciation, and interest are not counted when using cash flow as a valuation of a station is that those items could be different for another buyer. Interest, in particular, can vary hugely depending on amount of down payment and the type of loan secured.

8. *Billboard* (24 May 1986): 75.

9. A publication known as *The Duncan Report* is useful for determining how large a share of the available advertising dollar radio obtains in individual markets.

10. For a comprehensive summary of buying and selling of stations, see *R&R* (11 April 1986): 25–66.

11. Ibid.

CHAPTER 12

REGULATION AND

DEREGULATION

Not everyone can have the opportunity to operate a radio station. There is a finite limit to the number of channels available for broadcast purposes. This physical fact implies that there must be methods to decide who will be authorized to use this limited resource and who will not. For the most part, the motivating factor that leads people to want to own and operate broadcast stations is the profit that can be produced.

Because profits for many in broadcasting have been substantial, there are, at any given period of time, more individuals wishing to operate broadcasting stations than there are channels available. It becomes the task of those who regulate broadcasting to decide who, among the many who wish to use broadcast channels, will be allowed to do so and under what conditions.

In essence, all broadcast regulation is simply a matter dealing with situations pertaining to this basic scarcity of broadcast channels. Federal legislation, FCC rules

and regulations, licensing requirements, and enforcement provisions have been established as instruments to decide how to allocate this resource and under what conditions it will be used.

12.1

REGULATION AND DEREGULATION:
ISSUES AND CONTROVERSIES

Broadcast regulation is an activity that occupies a substantial amount of time and energy for broadcast management. In one sense, management's need to be knowledgeable about regulatory matters is because those factors have a direct bearing on the
profit-making aspects of radio. In another sense, the issuance of a license to broadcast
assumes that the recipient of the license is prepared to provide a service to the public.
The public service aspect of broadcast operations is taken very seriously by the FCC. It
is therefore to the advantage of the successful broadcast manager to take the commitment seriously as well.

The degree to which the FCC specifies just how a licensee is to meet its obligations to the public has varied over the course of broadcasting's history. Currently, there
is a movement to reduce the extent to which the FCC specifies actions that it deems
necessary in meeting public service responsibilities. The licensee is still required, however, to live up to the public service obligations agreed to in principle at the time of
license issue.

Review of Major Regulatory Structures

All the regulatory structures in force today have evolved over many years (Figure
12.1). In its earliest stages of development, radio was not subject to government control of any kind. For instance, there was no need for Lee de Forest to get a license in
1907 when he placed singers before a crude microphone in New York and generated a
radio signal, which was transmitted to whomever might have been listening.

But as broadcasting moved into a stage of development in which there were
many radio transmissions being generated, things got a bit hectic. With many signals

Figure 12.1

SIGNIFICANT DATES IN RADIO REGULATION

1910

The Wireless Ship Act requires ships to have wireless operators.

1912

The Radio Act of 1912 authorizes the U.S. Secretary of Commerce to issue radio licenses.

1922–1924

Hoover's Radio Conferences held in Washington, D.C.

1926

Court decision finds that the U.S. Secretary of Commerce has no powers under Radio Act of 1912.

1927

The Radio Act of 1927 sets up regulatory framework for radio and creates the FRC.

1934

The Communications Act of 1934 reenacts the Radio Act and broadens powers of the Commission. FRC membership increased by two commissioners and becomes the FCC.

1940

FCC statement on editorializing (Mayflower Decision) forbids editorializing by licensees.

1946

FCC issues "The Blue Book," detailing public interest standards for programming.

1949

FCC's reversal on editorializing plants seeds of Fairness Doctrine.

1960

FCC issues programming statement listing fourteen program categories "usually necessary" for meeting public interest.

1969

The U.S. Supreme Court's Red Lion Decision upholds constitutionality of Fairness Doctrine.

1980

Mark Fowler becomes Chairman of the FCC and begins process of deregulation.

1987

FCC repeals the Fairness Doctrine and sparks congressional activity to codify it.

FCC enunciates a policy on indecency.

---

occupying the same group of frequencies, it eventually became difficult for anyone to be heard through the din of the jammed airways.

THE RADIO ACT OF 1912   As early as 1912, before interference among competing signals became a problem, there was recognition that the government should have a hand in deciding how radio should operate. In the Radio Act of 1912, the Secretary of Commerce was designated as the government agent responsible for radio matters.

The legislation, however, did little more than specify the requirement that radio operators be on duty at all times on American ships. This provision grew out of the sinking of the Titanic. A distress signal telegraphed by the Titanic's wireless operator went undetected by a ship that was only fifteen miles away. If the message had been received, many lives might have been saved, but the wireless operator of the nearby ship was off duty at the time of the disaster.

Under the Radio Act of 1912, however, Secretary of Commerce Herbert Hoover could not deny a license so long as the applicant was a United States citizen. Furthermore, a court ruling in 1926 found that the Secretary of Commerce could not even specify channels for use by broadcasters. This resulted in regulatory chaos, and the radio industry itself eventually requested that the federal government create new legislation to regulate broadcasting.

THE HOPE FOR INDUSTRY SELF-REGULATION   In the wake of the failure of the Radio Act of 1912, Secretary Hoover called a series of national radio conferences. Hoover's intent in convening the conferences was to encourage the radio industry to establish self-regulatory controls that would sort out the chaos that was engulfing the industry. The intentions of the industry representatives who attended the conferences, however, were to the contrary. They were focused on recommending an extension of powers for the federal government that would allow for government regulation.

Increasingly over the four years from 1922 to 1926, industry recommendations for government control of radio grew more specific in nature. The final outcome of the radio conferences was a document listing recommendations that formed the basis for the bill that ultimately became the Radio Act of 1927.

THE RADIO ACT OF 1927   The regulatory void created by the court decision of 1926 was filled when the U.S. Congress passed into law the Radio Act of 1927. With this legislation Congress asserted its power to regulate broadcasting. Congress' authority to do so derived from the commerce clause of the U.S. Constitution. Because broadcasting, by virtue of its propagation properties, was construed to be interstate commerce, Congress had the power to regulate it.

The Radio Act of 1927 was broadly conceived. Most of its provisions were far too general to provide explicit guidance in dealing with all the specific matters that might arise in enforcing the law. To make the law practical in its application, there needed to be a mechanism to translate the general intent of Congress into a form in which it could be made to apply to specific operational activities.

The key element was the establishment of a separate regulatory agency with the authority to apply the law to a variety of circumstances. To accomplish this, the Radio Act authorized the establishment of a five-person panel empowered to implement the law. Known as the Federal Radio Commission (FRC), this group of individuals was appointed by the president but subject to Senate confirmation. In providing guidance for the operation of this body, Congress borrowed a phrase from public utility legislation. That phrase called for licenses to be issued in accordance with the "public interest, convenience, and necessity."

THE COMMUNICATIONS ACT OF 1934   The Radio Act of 1927 was reenacted in 1934 to become part of the Communications Act of 1934. The new act simply added interstate and foreign wire communications to the areas covered by the original broadcast legislation. Two commissioners were added to the regulatory body, and its name was changed from the Federal Radio Commission to the Federal Communications Commission (FCC).

The Communications Act of 1934 is the law of broadcasting today. Although there have been amendments to the law, its provisions remain much as they were in 1927 when they were first conceived. This is rather remarkable, considering the fact that radio was barely out of its infancy in 1927. Remember, there was no indication that television would become a major force in the broadcasting industry. Yet it is the Communications Act that regulates television, and the first radio network was barely a year old in 1927. Almost as an afterthought, the FRC (and later the FCC) was authorized to make special regulations for stations engaged in network broadcasting, which made possible effective regulation of network operations.

The FCC's ability to control network operations provides an interesting example of how a regulatory structure can be made to apply to an area of operations that technically falls outside the limits of the legislation. The wording of the section of the Communications Act that authorizes the FCC to concern itself with network activity stipulates that the FCC has authority to regulate *stations* engaged in "chain" or network broadcasting. Stations are licensed by the FCC but networks as such are merely program suppliers. Program suppliers and hence networks do not require FCC licenses and therefore, in theory, may operate free of regulatory control.

In implementing specific regulations to deal with network operations, though, the FCC focused on placing restrictions on the kinds of agreements that stations could enter into with networks. For example, the FCC placed limits on the degree of control over the program schedule that a station could turn over to a network. The regulations also stated that affiliated stations were responsible for any network programming that was broadcast through their facilities—a situation that gave affiliates considerable clout in influencing the content of network programs.

Because networks depend on stations to broadcast their programs, the creation of regulations restricting stations in their dealings with networks had the same practical effect as would the direct regulation of networks. The intent of such regulatory activity is to ensure that licensees remain accountable for the use of the airwaves for which they have been granted licenses.

It is the great strength of the Communications Act that broad discretionary powers are given to the FCC to make rules and regulations concerning broadcast operations. This accounts for the durability of the act to deal effectively with an activity that has changed so dramatically since the law was first enacted. The largely general provisions of the Communications Act provide the authority for every action taken by the FCC. At the same time, however, the FCC is constrained by the public interest standard.

The public interest standard is expressed affirmatively. This means simply that before the FCC issues a broadcast license, for example, it must determine that to do so will serve the public interest. This does not mean that it is enough to decide that there will be *no harm* to the public interest if a license is issued. Rather, there must be *an enhancement* of the public interest.

There are certain other specifics spelled out in the Communications Act. For example, there is a stipulated prohibition against obscene or indecent broadcasts. The law also states that equal time on the air must be accorded all candidates for public office. Exceptions are made for candidates included in bona fide news coverage activities. That provision, contained in Section 315 of the act makes it incumbent upon the licensee to treat all political candidates the same. If no time is allocated to any candidate, there is no obligation. However, all candidates must be offered the same opportunity. That means that the cost to candidates must also be the same.

The Communications Act also spells out some specific areas of power allocated to the FCC, such as the power to assign frequencies, to classify stations, and to prevent interference. (Incidentally, these are all areas in which the Radio Act of 1912 failed to provide authority for the Secretary of Commerce.) Despite the existence of a few areas in which the law is specific, however, much discretion is allocated to the FCC to create specific regulations, which have the force of law.

INTERPRETING THE PUBLIC INTEREST Because the public interest standard is intentionally broad rather than specific, it has been subject to intense debate among broadcasters, legislators, regulatory officials, and others with an interest in regulatory matters. At the heart of the controversy is the question of what the public interest is and how far the government can go in establishing regulatory provisions derived from its authority.

In general, the broadcasting industry tends to view the standard strictly. This position holds that the primary intention of Congress in citing the public interest, convenience, and necessity as the rationale for regulatory action was to provide the authority for action to establish technical limitations on broadcast operations. Beyond technical matters, however, regulatory controls should be severely limited.

Critics of this position maintain that the public interest standard means that there should be regulatory attention paid to the content of broadcast services as well as to the technical area. This broad interpretation maintains that there are dangers in allowing broadcasters to be the sole decision makers on the content of the airways. Because the public owns the airways used by broadcasters, it is incumbent upon the government to ensure that these resources are used with care. That means that programming should be regulated to ensure that quality service is provided and to protect the public from inappropriate use of the airways by those few who have access to broadcast frequencies.

In practice, the FCC has interpreted its powers under the public interest standard broadly. Many regulations focus on programming and responsible use of the airways as will be seen next. In recent years, however, there has been an appetite in society and on the part of government officials to reduce the regulatory presence in the field of broadcasting. This trend toward narrowing the powers of the FCC has largely found expression through relaxation of many program-oriented regulations that have come into force over the years.

FCC RULES AND REGULATIONS The day-to-day regulation of broadcasting is accomplished by the FCC through its rules and regulations. The rules and regulations spell out in specific detail the standards that must be adhered to by licensees if they are to operate in accordance with the FCC's interpretation of the law. The enforcement power by which FCC administers these rules and regulations is exercised primarily through its licensing power.

As a means of enforcing regulations, the power of the FCC to issue and renew broadcast licenses is extremely effective. The threat of losing a license, and therefore the right and opportunity to broadcast, is a powerful incentive to station managers and owners to pay close attention to FCC requirements and to implement procedures that will guarantee compliance with regulations. On the other side of the coin, however, our legal system protects broadcasters from arbitrary and capricious behavior by the FCC by allowing for an appeal process. Licensees are entitled to hearings on licensing matters before the FCC can take official action. Ultimately, if an appeal by a licensee fails at the FCC level, the case may be taken through the federal court system. Some cases reach the U.S. Supreme Court before being finally decided.

FCC rules and regulations are wide ranging *and* specific. The bulk of FCC regulations deal with technical limitations and requirements. Others deal with standards that must be met by applicants seeking an initial broadcast license. The regulations also spell out such obligations as the requirement that broadcast stations serve the community in which they are licensed. Reporting requirements are specified, complete with dates by which various reports must be filed. There are also specifications for classification of stations and standards that must be met by various types of technical monitoring equipment.

Besides specific technical regulations, the FCC has interpreted the public interest standard to include broad regulation of programming. This has traditionally been an area of controversy and is frequently subjected to court challenges. Such challenges are usually based on the provision in the Communications Act that states that broadcasting is a form of expression protected by the First Amendment to the Constitution, which protects the press from government actions that would restrict free expression.

THE BLUE BOOK   An illustration of the sensitivity of this issue to broadcasters arose in 1946 when the FCC put together a report entitled *Public Service Responsibility of Broadcasters.* Quickly dubbed the "Blue Book" (because of the color of the cover), this report precipitated a bitter response from broadcasters who felt that their First Amendment rights had been trampled. In the Blue Book, the FCC cited numerous examples in which stations had failed to deliver on programming promises made in their original license applications. It focused particularly on the excessive number of commercials many stations were airing and criticized stations that had consistently failed to provide what the FCC called "sustaining" or noncommercial programming.

The Blue Book was FCC's first major attempt to define how it viewed the public interest standard in relation to programming. Many in the broadcasting industry believed strongly that in so doing the FCC had exceeded its authority under the Communications Act. The First Amendment was cited frequently by many broadcasters, who felt that regulation of programming was an infringement on the freedom of expression guaranteed to the press. The FCC withstood the criticism, however, and the Blue Book became the standard by which stations were judged until 1960.

THE 1960 STATEMENT   In 1960 the FCC issued its *Report and Statement of Programming Policy,* in which it delineated fourteen categories of programming that the FCC felt should be included in any broadcast program schedule that purported to meet the public interest standard. The list included educational programming, news, editorials, religious programs, programming allowing for local self-expression, and others. There were no formulas to stipulate how much of a station's broadcast schedule should be devoted to the various program types in order to satisfy the FCC's public interest standard. In fact, the FCC noted specifically that it was not trying to establish a list of what was required. The language of the statement simply stated that the categories enumerated in the document were those "usually necessary" if stations were to be regarded as meeting their public interest obligations in the programming area.

SERVING THE COMMUNITY OF LICENSE   The 1960 statement was the impetus for further FCC action that focused on ensuring that licensees took their responsibilities to the community seriously. A set of procedures that were to be followed by each station applying for a license or a renewal was developed. These procedures spelled out specific actions that local stations were obliged to take in an effort to discover what the important public issues were in the community. When the issues had been ascertained, each station had to describe how it intended to respond to these issues in its programming. The procedures were fairly specific. For instance, stations were obliged to interview leaders of the community and to survey a representative sample of the populace. All this stemmed from FCC's concern that stations not devote themselves entirely to programming that was designed solely to attract an audience for its advertisers.

EDITORIALIZING BY LICENSEES   In the matter of editorializing by stations, the FCC initially had difficulty in determining what the public interest required. It was originally thought by the FCC that it was inappropriate for the relative few who held broadcast licenses to use their broadcast facilities to espouse a particular viewpoint.

In 1940 the FCC solidified this view in its Mayflower Decision, which forbade a Boston station to broadcast editorials. In 1949, however, the FCC, apparently swayed by testimony presented in lengthy hearings, reversed itself on the matter and went so far as to make it a *duty* of broadcasters to editorialize. In so doing, the FCC stipulated that the licensee should provide the opportunity for opposing viewpoints.

THE FAIRNESS DOCTRINE   Over time the FCC's views regarding the discussion of public issues became more formalized. It eventually became what is known as the Fairness Doctrine. In effect, the Fairness Doctrine broadened considerably the FCC's position on editorialization. Under the Fairness Doctrine, stations are required to present discussion of controversial issues of public importance. In so doing, broadcasters are required to present all major viewpoints on these issues.

In enunciating the Fairness Doctrine, the FCC not only was providing guidelines as to how controversial issues should be handled but also was requiring stations to actively seek out controversial issues for broadcast treatment. The language of the doctrine notes "that broadcasters have certain obligations to afford reasonable opportunity for the discussion of conflicting views on issues of public importance" (47 CFR 73.1910).

Stations could not avoid problems with the FCC over the Fairness Doctrine by steering clear of controversy. Avoidance of controversial issues, in itself, constituted noncompliance. Stations had to get into the fray; once they did, they had to afford an opportunity for all sides to be heard. The FCC did not stipulate that all opposing views must fall within a single program or that the same amount of time be allocated to all views. In this respect, the Fairness Doctrine differed from the requirements imposed by Section 315 of the Communications Act in dealing with political candidates. Candidates were to be offered equal time. Under the rules for political candidates, stations could deny time to *all* candidates.

The Fairness Doctrine left it up to the stations to decide *how* various views would be presented. A station could, for example, present an opposing view to an opinion expressed in a documentary, in a subsequent newscast. Or, a reply to an editorial could be broadcast a week or two after the original opinion was aired. All that was required was that the station make a good-faith effort to observe fairness, but it was left to the station's discretion as to how that obligation would be met.

THE DEBATE OVER THE FAIRNESS DOCTRINE   The Fairness Doctrine has presented the most hotly contested First Amendment issue that broadcasting has faced. By requiring that broadcasters present a certain type of program in a certain way, said the critics of the doctrine, the government was in effect meddling in program content, an area in which the government is constrained from action by the First Amendment. This constitutional controversy came to a head in 1969 when the U.S. Supreme Court upheld the constitutionality of the doctrine in the Red Lion Decision.

In that case, the Court upheld the doctrine on the basis of the scarcity principle. In essence, the Court ruled that the Fairness Doctrine upheld the spirit of expression as stated in the First Amendment because to grant full freedom to those who held broadcast licenses would be to deny full freedom of expression for the overwhelming majority of citizens who do not hold licenses. By safeguarding access to broadcast outlets for the opinions of those who could not legally broadcast, the FCC was enhancing the climate for full freedom, even though limits are placed on the absolute application of the First Amendment for broadcasters.

The matter did not end in 1969, however. Those who advocate a literal reading of the First Amendment continued to maintain that the First Amendment does not allow for exceptions, no matter how good the reason. The First Amendment states simply that Congress will make *no* laws restricting freedom of the press. Moreover, aver opponents of the doctrine, the scarcity principle is rendered inapplicable in today's society by the great proliferation of broadcast outlets in this country. The bottom line, they contended, was that the Fairness Doctrine meant that broadcasting became a second-class citizen in regard to the First Amendment protection, which is applied with full force to print media.

Critics of the Fairness Doctrine also maintained that stations were inclined to steer clear of controversial programming because of the hassles presented if someone felt that his or her views had been inadequately represented, even though there was a good-faith effort to do so. The upshot of this, the argument went, was a chilling effect. To avoid litigation, stations tended to play it as safe as possible.

Defenders of the Fairness Doctrine generally endorsed the opinion put forth in the Red Lion Decision, which held that the "spirit" of the first amendment is best served by placing reasonable limits on the press freedoms of broadcast licensees in order to enhance the opportunities for free expression for those without access to the airways. Without a guarantee of access, there would be no recourse for those who were victimized by one-sided presentations of issues. Moreover, said supporters of the doctrine, when someone is issued a license to use the public airways, access is denied to others. The government has an obligation to those who are not issued broadcast licenses. To ensure that full expression is guaranteed to all viewpoints, it is necessary to place conditions on licensees that will guarantee full expression for the public at large. (After all, the public owns the airwaves, not the individual licensee.) As for the inconvenience in defending itself from those who feel that their viewpoints have been given inadequate exposure, defenders of the doctrine pointed out that this is a situation that the broadcaster should live with willingly in exchange for the privilege of having a license.

RECENT ACTION ON THE FAIRNESS DOCTRINE   The Fairness Doctrine has remained a controversial element of the regulatory apparatus of the broadcasting industry. In fighting to free themselves from the limitations imposed by this element of regulation, broadcasters were inspired to renew the fight for repeal of the doctrine by a recent climate of broadcast deregulation.

The legal status of the Fairness Doctrine has been at issue since its inception. The Red Lion Decision in 1969 settled the matter for some time, but recently the controversy resurfaced. In 1986 the U.S. Court of Appeals in Washington, D.C., ruled that the doctrine was not statutory, meaning that it is not required of broadcasters by the Communications Act. (It had previously been thought that a 1959 amendment to Section 315 of the Act had the effect of writing the doctrine into law.) In a fairness case involving WTVH-TV in Syracuse, New York, the U.S. Court of Appeals directed the FCC to clarify the question of whether the Fairness Doctrine was indeed constitutional. The FCC's perceived appetite to throw out the doctrine by repealing it sparked activity in Congress to pass it into law. Codification of the Fairness Doctrine by Congress would have made it impossible for the FCC to repeal it. In the spring of 1987, both houses of Congress passed a bill doing just that. When the bill reached President Reagan for signature, however, it was vetoed. A Congressional attempt to override the veto was considered and dropped, and the bill was referred back to committee for further consideration.

On August 4, 1987, the FCC voted unanimously to repeal the Fairness Doctrine. The FCC based its decision in part on what it called "excessive and unnecessary Government intervention into the editorial process of broadcast journalists."[1] The FCC addressed head on the constitutional question, thus complying with the directive of the U.S. Court of Appeals in Washington, D.C. "We conclude," stated the FCC, "that under the principles estabished by the Supreme Court, the doctrine fails to meet the test for constitutionality."[2]

The FCC also stated that the Fairness Doctrine did more to inhibit free speech than it did to enhance it, noting the reported tendency of the doctrine to "chill" speech.

Over sixty specific examples of chilling were presented in our recent inquiry, in contrast to only two broadcasters' claim (*sic*) that they were not chilled by the doctrine. Many of the examples go beyond individual instances of chill and set forth broadcasters' policies—under which they have shied away from covering controversial issues in news, documentaries and editorial advertisements. It can easily be seen that policies like these completely frustrate the goal of the doctrine to foster robust debate and diversity of views. They thus result in a net loss, not an enhancement, of speech.[3]

The ultimate outcome of the fairness debate is unresolved at this writing. In late 1987 there was a renewed attempt in Congress to codify the doctrine. Supporters of the Fairness Doctrine in the House of Representatives had attached the Fairness Doctrine as an amendment to an omnibus spending bill believing that President Reagan would be unlikely to veto it. The fairness provision, however, was dropped during a House-Senate conference on the bill in response to a threat of a presidential veto.

It is also quite likely that the FCC's decision will be challenged in the courts. According to *Broadcasting,* the Syracuse Peace Council, which brought the original fairness complaint in the WTVH case, plans to ask for an appeals court review of the FCC action.[4]

The issue will continue to generate strong feelings on both sides. On the side of keeping the doctrine are many public interest groups who feel that the doctrine protects holders of unpopular opinion from being denied access to broadcast media. In the effort to pass the Fairness Doctrine into law, it became clear that the Democratic majorities in both houses of Congress clearly sided with the proponents of the doctrine. In fact, defense of the Fairness Doctrine came from conservatives and liberals alike, a point noted by U.S. Representative John Dingell (D–Mich.), a co-sponsor of the bill to enact the Fairness Doctrine into law. In reacting to the presidential veto of the bill, Dingell said the veto, "flies in the face of urgings from citizens of all political persuasions and from all parts of the political spectrum."[5]

President Reagan sided with broadcasters and other journalists who felt that the doctrine should be repealed. Reagan told *Broadcasting* that his veto of the bill was motivated by his belief that it violated the First Amendment. He stated that the doctrine was not really necessary to guarantee fair treatment for controversial views. "It shouldn't take the force of law," he stated, "to compel broadcasters to be fair. The public trusts and expects those in media to provide news and information without bias. Maintenance of that trust will do far more to insure fairness than any law."[6] A *Washington Post* editorial written shortly after the presidential veto of the fairness bill summarizes the opposition to the doctrine. "However bad or unfair today's news may seem on occasion, do people really want government to step in as judge? . . . The 'fairness doctrine' undercuts free, independent, sound and responsive journalism—substituting governmental dictates. That is deceptive, dangerous and, in a democracy, repulsive."[7]

Activity will continue on the matter of the Fairness Doctrine. It will involve further action from the courts and Congress. The battle over the issue will be largely political in nature. The mood of the Democratically controlled Congress is to reign in an FCC, which is perceived by some to have exceeded its authority. The FCC, on the other hand, has the support of the overwhelming majority of broadcasters who have found renewed hope in the FCC's historical action to abolish the Fairness Doctrine. Whatever the ultimate outcome, the FCC under Dennis Patrick has recast the terms of the debate. Widespread acceptance of the idea that there are sufficient broadcast outlets to cover all points of view have dealt the scarcity principle, which undergirded the U.S. Supreme Court in the Red Lion Decision, a severe blow. The way in which this situation is resolved will have far-reaching ramifications for the future of all broadcast regulation.

Recent History of Deregulation

Throughout broadcasting's history there has been a tendency for the federal government to broaden the scope of regulation. The Radio Act of 1912 was extremely narrow in scope, but it was ineffective. The Radio Act of 1927 was considerably more comprehensive. It had to be if it was to be effective in establishing limitations that would prevent broadcasters from interfering with one another. It was widely assumed in 1927 that government regulation of broadcasting would focus largely on technical matters such as the power of transmitters, frequency assignments, and classification of stations. In fact, the earliest activities of the regulatory bodies established by the legislation were focused almost entirely on dealing with technical issues.

Later, however, after the technical aspects of broadcasting were running more smoothly, the FCC began to broaden its interpretation of the public interest to include programming. Thus, when the Blue Book and the 1960 program policy statement were promulgated, there was strong reaction from broadcasters that such infringement not only violated First Amendment protections but also that the FCC had no lawful justification to meddle in programming. But such arguments went largely unheard for many years, and the FCC steadily developed policies that made programming a very central component in ascertaining how well the public interest was being served by those to whom the commission issued licenses.

THE FCC UNDER FOWLER   The advent of the Reagan presidency in 1980, however, established a conservative political climate that resulted in the appointment of officials who were philosophically committed to reducing the role of the federal government in many activities. Because each incoming president has the prerogative to appoint the chairman of the FCC, President Reagan's choice, Mark Fowler (Figure 12.2), reflected the conservative view that it is a worthy goal of government agencies to reduce the scope of its regulatory activities wherever possible.

Figure 12.2

Mark Fowler, FCC chairman from 1976–1987, headed the commission
during a period of extensive deregulation.
Courtesy of the FCC.

This was an initiative welcomed by the overwhelming majority of broadcasters.
They had long argued that the FCC's increasingly heavy demands on broadcasters were
burdensome and that the scarcity principle on which public interest programming requirements were based no longer applied to broadcast media. This was particularly so,
they pointed out, in radio. The rise in popularity of FM had increased the scope of
radio service significantly. And the great proliferation of formats and other services
provided a far greater range of programming than there had ever been before. Cable
and other television programming initiatives also had contributed to the overall increase of broadcast services serving the public. In short, there was abundance, not
scarcity, in the broadcast industry. There was no longer any need, said broadcasters,
for the FCC to impose on licensees requirements that served no useful contemporary
purposes.

The FCC had shown receptiveness to this line of reasoning since the 1970s. It
wasn't until Fowler's chairmanship, however, that actions were taken that began to
dismantle some of the regulatory structures that pertained to what many broadcasters
viewed as the more onerous aspects of federal regulation.

The philosophy under which regulatory relief occurred was based on a belief in the efficacy of the marketplace to ensure programming that would serve the public interest. The public interest, according to this philosophy, is best defined by the American public, not by the federal government. In acting in accordance with this philosophy, the FCC under Fowler began to eliminate many of the regulatory provisions that had previously been considered necessary if the public was to be served well by its broadcast services.

The FCC has repealed requirements that radio stations engage in community ascertainment procedures as a prerequisite to license renewal, replacing it with a much shorter reporting requirement that must be filed quarterly. The FCC has dropped guidelines concerning the appropriate proportion of time that could be allotted to the broadcast of commercials. The requirement to keep a program log has been dropped, and the maximum license term has been expanded from three to seven years.

There has been a simplification in license renewal procedures for radio, including the use of a greatly simplified renewal form, which is essentially a postcard. There has been an increase in the number of broadcast properties that may be owned by a single entity from seven AM stations, seven FM stations, and seven television stations to twelve stations in each of those categories. A requirement that broadcasters must originate most of its nonnetwork programming from within their communities of license was eliminated, as was a rule requiring that a broadcaster's main studio be located in the community of license. The latter two rulings made it more convenient for stations whose signal covers a major-market area to concentrate on adjacent larger markets.

The climate of deregulation that was begun by Fowler has changed the face of broadcast regulation considerably. Broadcasters have been freed from a considerable amount of managerial energy and attention that once had applied to ensuring that complex regulatory procedures were followed carefully. In lifting the need to perform many of these time-consuming regulatory procedures, the FCC has won the support of the overwhelming majority of broadcasters in the country.

When Fowler announced his retirement as FCC chairman, there was widespread recognition of the sweeping changes he brought about. Fowler's successor, Dennis Patrick, arrived on the scene shortly after the Democratic Party gained control of both houses of Congress. In Patrick's view, the post–Fowler era at the FCC will be influenced to some extent by the differing philosophical viewpoint of the Democrats, who can make themselves felt through the mechanism of congressional oversight of the FCC.

Nevertheless, Patrick, like his predecessor, has stated a preference for the influence of the marketplace in determining the public interest. He stated in a 1987 interview with *Broadcasting,*

> I am presumptively disposed to rely on competitive marketplace mechanisms to realize that goal (of maximizing consumer welfare). In general, and there are

exceptions, markets are more effective than government in identifying the needs and interests of consumers in delivering a product.[8]

Patrick, in opening remarks presented at the first meeting of the FCC under his chairmanship, presented a list of six major objectives that he developed with the other commissioners. As reported by *Broadcasting,* they are as follows:

(1) Promote, wherever possible, a competitive marketplace for the development and use of communications facilities and services; (2) provide a regulatory framework which permits markets for communications services to function effectively, while eliminating regulations which are unnecessary or inimical to the public interest; (3) promote efficiency in the allocation, licensing and use of the electromagnetic spectrum; (4) protect and promote the interests of the American public in international communications; (5) provide service to the public in the most efficient, expeditious manner possible, and (6) eliminate government action which infringes upon freedom of speech and the press.[9]

Most observers see in this a continuation of the deregulatory trend of the recent past. There may be, however, more obstacles in the path of deregulation than were encountered in the past. Besides increased congressional opposition, there is nervousness among some broadcasters about proposals to deregulate in certain areas. The primary focus of concern by broadcasters is proposed action to make it easier for unfriendly takeovers of broadcasting operations to occur.

Some recently introduced legislation is aimed at restoring requirements for public service. Senate bill S.1277, sponsored by U.S. Senators Hollings and Inouye, is intended to ensure that broadcasters do not forsake the public interest in search of profits. Although the bill contains two provisions generally favored by broadcasters— barring competing applications for licenses up for renewal and extending cable must-carry rules—it also would require broadcasters to air "meritorious" programming to serve the public interest. A similar bill is in the House of Representatives.

The bill has been attacked as being too vague, while others believe it is an encroachment on broadcasters' rights. From all indications, though, it appears in 1987 that the administration is on the side of broadcasters.

12.2

THE FEDERAL COMMUNICATIONS COMMISSION

The origin of the FCC as an outgrowth of the federal legislation governing broadcasting meant simply that government regulation of broadcasting would be an ongoing function. It was never the intention of Congress to set down a law that would cover all contingencies and developments in the field. To protect the public from any vagueness that might result from a law that was flexible enough to allow for variations in how the industry developed, Congress established the commission to serve essentially as an interpreter of the general provisions of the law. In its interpretation, the commission was empowered to enact specific regulations that would have the force of law.

The FCC creates regulations and enforces them in accordance with the provisions of the Communications Act. It is limited in how far it may go in any of these areas by what the law says. Over the years of its existence, the FCC has put into place a considerable body of regulation that covers very specific areas of activity. These fall generally into the areas dealing with

— Transmission, such as restrictions on power or antenna height

— Operation of the station, covering things like employment practices and station ownership

— Program regulation, in which questions of indecency or coverage of controversial issues lie

The FCC has established procedures for dealing with the enforcement of the rules and regulations it has enacted. This area of activity involves handling complaints from members of the public, conducting hearings on proposed FCC actions, and providing for a process for appeal of FCC decisions. To cover the many areas of operations for which the FCC is responsible, a staff of considerable size is required (Figure 12.3).

It is important for radio station management to understand how the FCC operates and what it requires of broadcasters. To understand the rather complex procedures and requirements imposed by FCC regulation, most stations contract legal experts to guide them. Often legal experts are assisted by technical experts who help the station ensure its compliance with the very complex technical requirements of being a broadcast licensee. The obvious incentive for understanding and complying with FCC directives is the simple fact that failure to do so may result in the FCC revoking your license.

Figure 12.3

The organization of the Federal Communications Commission.

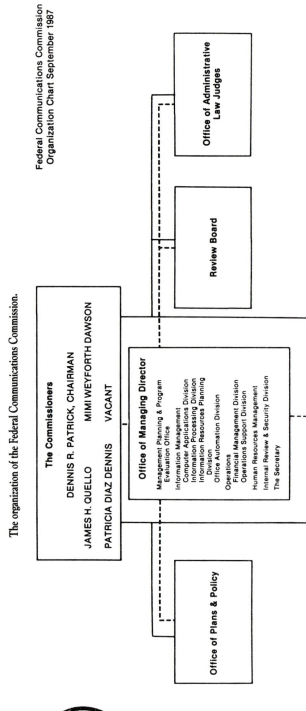

Federal Communications Commission
Organization Chart September 1987

The Commissioners

DENNIS R. PATRICK, CHAIRMAN

JAMES H. QUELLO   MIMI WEYFORTH DAWSON

PATRICIA DIAZ DENNIS   VACANT

Office of Managing Director

Management Planning & Program
Evaluation Office

Information Management
  Computer Applications Division
  Information Processing Division
  Information Resources Planning
    Division
  Office Automation Division

Operations
  Financial Management Division
  Operations Support Division
  Human Resources Management
  Internal Review & Security Division
  The Secretary

Office of Administrative Law Judges

Review Board

Office of Plans & Policy

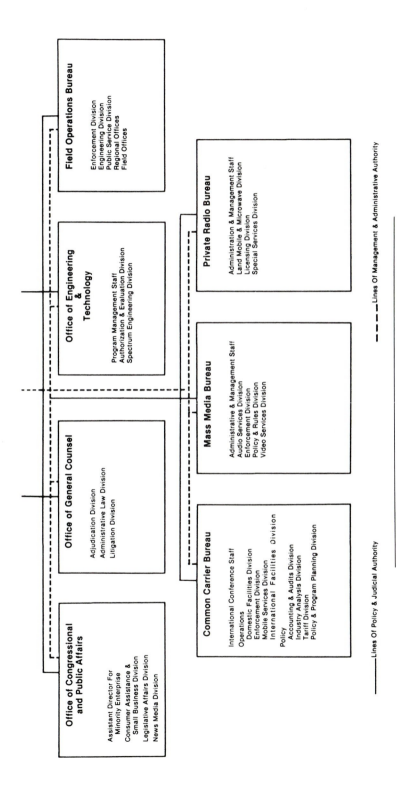

Office of Congressional and Public Affairs

Assistant Director For
Minority Enterprise
Consumer Assistance &
Small Business Division
Legislative Affairs Division
News Media Division

Office of General Counsel

Adjudication Division
Administrative Law Division
Litigation Division

Office of Engineering & Technology

Program Management Staff
Authorization & Evaluation Division
Spectrum Engineering Division

Field Operations Bureau

Enforcement Division
Engineering Division
Public Service Division
Regional Offices
Field Offices

Common Carrier Bureau

International Conference Staff
Operations
    Domestic Facilities Division
    Enforcement Division
    Mobile Services Division
    International Facilities Division
Policy
    Accounting & Audits Division
    Industry Analysis Division
    Tariff Division
    Policy & Program Planning Division

Mass Media Bureau

Administrative & Management Staff
Audio Services Division
Enforcement Division
Policy & Rules Division
Video Services Division

Private Radio Bureau

Administration & Management Staff
Land Mobile & Microwave Division
Licensing Division
Special Services Division

———— Lines Of Policy & Judicial Authority

– – – – Lines Of Management & Administrative Authority

The Operating License

In radio, operating licenses are issued for a maximum of seven years. Prior to deregulation, the license period was three years. The fact that licenses must be renewed simply gives the FCC an opportunity to review periodically the performance of the licensee to assure the FCC that the station continues to serve the public interest. The seven-year license period is the maximum term for which a license can be issued. Normally, a new license is issued for the period ending with a date at which all existing licenses for a particular region must be renewed. (All licenses for a given geographic region expire on the same date. For example, all radio station licenses in Pennsylvania and Delaware expire at seven-year intervals starting with August 4, 1984.)

Although seven years is the norm, however, the FCC reserves the right to issue licenses for shorter periods of time. The regulations state that, "If the FCC finds that the public interest, convenience, and necessity will be served thereby, it may issue either an initial license or a renewal thereof for a lesser term" (47 CFR 73.1020). Besides extending the term of the license, license renewal has been simplified since the advent of deregulation. The form has been greatly simplified (Figure 12.4), and the process of formal community ascertainment has been dropped as a requirement. Thus, once a license has been issued, it is a relatively simple matter to keep the license active for a long time as long as the licensee maintains a clean record with the FCC.

To apply for an initial license, however, is more complicated. FCC regulations specify a number of conditions that must be met by anyone applying for a new broadcast station authorization. The regulations state, for example, that "an authorization for a new AM broadcast station or increase in facilities of an existing station will be issued only after a satisfactory showing has been made in regard to the following among others:" (47 CFR 73.24). What then follows is a series of requirements including a demonstration to the FCC of things such as that the authorization will allow a "fair, efficient and equitable distribution of radio service" (47 CFR 73.24), that the "applicant is financially qualified to construct and operate" a station (47 CFR 73.24), that "the applicant is legally qualified," and that he or she is of "good character" (47 CFR 73.24). Other considerations are also listed, having to do with the quality of the technical equipment, the facilities, and the coverage of the proposed station. Special conditions applying to stations of various classifications (See Chapter 5) are stipulated. The section ends with the condition that "the public interest, convenience and necessity will be served through the operation under the proposed assignment" (47 CFR 73.24).

The above conditions assume the fact that a frequency is available in the area where the station is proposed. If so, the applicant must complete numerous forms and file an application for a construction permit that allows for installation of facilities and

Figure 12.4

The simplified radio license renewal form.

FCC 303-S
February 1983

United States of America
Federal Communications Commission
Washington, D.C. 20554

Approved by OMB
3060-0110
Expires 8/31/84

APPLICATION FOR RENEWAL OF LICENSE FOR COMMERCIAL AND NONCOMMERCIAL AM, FM OR TV BROADCAST STATION

---

1. Name of Applicant | Street Address

Call Letters | City | State | ZIP Code

---

2. Have the following reports been filed with the Commission:
(a) The Annual Employment Reports (FCC Form 395) as required by Section 73.3612 of the Commission's rules?
☐ Yes ☐ No
If No, attach as Exhibit No. _____ an explanation.

(b) The applicant's Ownership Report (FCC Form 323 or 323-E) as required by Section 73.3615 of the Commission's rules?
☐ Yes ☐ No If No, give the following information:
Date last ownership report was filed. _____
Call letters of the renewal application with which it was filed. _____

3. Is the applicant in compliance with the provisions of Section 310 of the Communications Act of 1934, as amended, relating to interests of aliens and foreign governments?
☐ Yes ☐ No
If No, attach as Exhibit No. _____ an explanation.

4. Since the filing of the applicant's last renewal application for this station or other major application, has an adverse finding been made, a consent decree been entered or final action been approved by any court or administrative body with respect to the applicant or parties to the application concerning any civil or criminal suit, action or proceeding brought under the provisions of any federal, state, territorial or local law relating to the following: any felony; lotteries; unlawful restraints or monopolies; unlawful combinations; contracts or agreements in restraint of trade; the use of unfair methods of competition; fraud; unfair labor practices; or discrimination?
☐ Yes ☐ No   If Yes, attach as Exhibit No. _____ a full description, including identification of the court or administrative body, proceeding by file number, the person and matters involved, and the disposition of litigation.

5. Has the applicant placed in its public inspection file at the appropriate times the documentation required by Section 73.3526 or 73.3527 of the Commission's rules?
☐ Yes ☐ No   If No, attach as Exhibit No. _____ a complete statement of explanation.

THE APPLICANT hereby waives any claim to the use of any particular frequency or of the ether as against the regulatory power of the United States because of the previous use of the same, whether by license or otherwise, and requests an authorization in accordance with this application. (See Section 304 of the Communications Act of 1934, as amended.)

THE APPLICANT acknowledges that all the statements made in this application and attached exhibits are considered material representations and that all the exhibits are a material part hereof and are incorporated herein as set out in full in the application.

CERTIFICATION

I certify that the statements in this application are true, complete, and correct to the best of my knowledge and belief, and are made in good faith.

Signed and dated this _____ day of _____ 19 _____

Name of Applicant _____

By Signature _____

WILLFUL FALSE STATEMENTS MADE ON THIS FORM ARE PUNISHABLE BY FINE AND IMPRISONMENT, U.S. CODE, TITLE 18, SECTION 1001

Title _____

Question-by-Question Guidelines (FCC Form 303-S)

1. The name of the applicant should be stated exactly as it appears on the station's existing license. The current street address or post office box used by the applicant for receipt of Commission correspondence should be set forth.

2. Every station with five or more full-time employees must file an employment report on or before May 31 of each year. That report is to be available locally for public inspection.

   A current and complete ownership report should be submitted with the licensee's renewal application and the question answered affirmatively. However, if the ownership report submitted with a station's last renewal application is "up-to-date" and has not been amended, a new report need not be filed with the current renewal application. The applicant should answer the question negatively and should supply the call letters of the station and the filing date of the renewal application with which the ownership report was submitted. An "up-to-date" ownership report is one that is current for *each* question on that report.

3. Aliens, foreign governments and corporations, and corporations of which any officer or director is an alien or of which less than 80% of the capital stock is owned or voted by U.S. citizens, are prohibited from holding a broadcast station license. Where a corporate licensee is directly or indirectly controlled by another corporation, of which any officer or more than 25% of the directors are aliens or of which less than 75% of that corporation's stock is owned or voted by U.S. citizens, the Commission must consider whether denial of renewal would serve the public interest. Licensees are expected to employ reasonable, good faith methods to ensure the accuracy and completeness of their citizenship representations.

4. This question is limited to adverse actions and judgments adjudicated or entered into within the preceding license term. Reportable activities consist of judgments or decrees, including settlement, consent, and like agreements, where the misconduct occurred either in the operation of the station for which renewal is requested or in the conduct of the other broadcast and non-broadcast activities of the renewal applicant and parties to that application, such as all partners and all corporate officers, directors, and stockholders with a 10% or more ownership interest in the applicant.

5. A licensee must maintain certain documents pertaining to its station in a file which should be kept at the station's main studio or other accessible place in the community of license. The file must be available for inspection by anyone during regular business hours. The documents to be maintained include applications for a construction permit and for license renewal, assignment or transfer of control; ownership and employment reports; and annual lists of local problems and responsive programming broadcast in the preceding twelve months. A complete listing of the required documents and their mandatory retention periods is set forth in Rules 73.3526 and 73.3527.

FCC NOTICE TO INDIVIDUALS REQUIRED BY THE PRIVACY ACT AND THE PAPERWORK REDUCTION ACT

The solicitation of personal information requested in this application is authorized by the Communications Act of 1934, as amended. The principal purpose for which the information will be used is to determine if the benefit requested is consistent with the public interest. The staff, consisting variously of attorneys, accountants, engineers, and application examiners, will use the information to determine whether the application should be granted, denied, dismissed, or designated for hearing. If all the information requested is not provided, the application may be returned without action having been taken upon it or its processing may be delayed while a request is made to provide the missing information. Accordingly, every effort should be made to provide all necessary information. Your response is required to obtain authority.

THE FOREGOING NOTICE IS REQUIRED BY THE PRIVACY ACT OF 1974, P.L. 93-579, DECEMBER 31, 1974, 5 U.S.C. 552a(e)(3), AND THE PAPERWORK REDUCTION ACT OF 1980, P.L. 96-511, DECEMBER 11, 1980, 44 U.S.C. 3507.

completion of the necessary performance tests to demonstrate that the proper operational conditions are met. This requires a thorough knowledge of the numerous technical regulations listed in the code. Most applicants make extensive use of consulting engineers and legal experts in completing application materials. Assuming all these hurdles are successfully overcome, the applicant will then be issued the broadcast license.

Given the considerable investment of time, energy, and money necessary to apply for a license in the first place, it is little wonder that any threat by the FCC to revoke an existing license is viewed by any broadcaster as a very serious matter. To lose a license through careless or callous disregard of FCC regulations would be a severe financial loss to most broadcasters, but it also would be a loss of something gained through prodigious effort and great expense.

Despite the considerable investment necessary to apply for a license, however, it remains the case that the issuance of a broadcast license is no more than a permit to use a public resource. The Communications Act makes it clear that FCC approval of a license application does not confer ownership. Although there is wide latitude given to broadcasters, they are still subject to limitations designed to ensure that the public benefits from the assignment of that broadcast channel to a particular applicant.

The FCC's Impact on Station Operations

Once a license has been issued and the station is on the air, it cannot be assumed that station management is free to devote full attention to making a profit for the operation while ignoring any consideration of the FCC until renewal time. Many day-to-day operations are affected greatly by the regulations the station agrees to when it receives its operating license.

As examples, the FCC requires that stations adhere to certain hiring practices designed to prevent discrimination. There are requirements that stations identify themselves once an hour as close to the hour as possible. Station management is charged with the responsibility to prevent false and misleading advertising and to identify the source of any programming for which the station has received a payment.

POLITICAL ADVERTISING   There are precise regulations pertaining to the handling of paid political advertising as well. With the exception of a station's news coverage, if time is offered to any one political candidate, a comparable amount of time must be offered to all other candidates for the same office at the same rate. The FCC also stipulates that stations can charge candidates only the lowest unit rate for a given amount of time. Many broadcasters have expressed strong opposition to the lowest unit-rate provision, feeling that it unfairly singles out broadcasters for such treatment as opposed to nonregulated advertising media such as newspapers. One effect of this provision, say opponents, is that many broadcasters will not accept paid political advertising at all, thus resulting in decreased opportunities for candidates to be heard rather than the increased opportunity that the provisions are designed to promote.

INDECENCY   Another controversial area of FCC involvement in programming is in the recent establishment of activities designed to enforce standards against indecency. In April of 1987 the FCC put forth a definition of indecency drawn from a 1978 U.S. Supreme Court decision against Pacifica Broadcasting. In a story about the FCC initiative, *Broadcasting* quoted language from the FCC decision that describes indecency as "language or material that depicts or describes, in terms patently offensive as measured by contemporary standards for the broadcast medium, sexual or excretory activities or organs" and notes that the FCC will consider such material to be in violation in broadcasts that take place during a time of day when "there is a reasonable risk that children are in the audience."[10]

In announcing its intention to regulate indecency, the FCC brought to the fore the issue of what forms of speech are protected by the First Amendment. In the Pacifica case, the U.S. Supreme Court ruled that the FCC had the power to regulate and enforce prohibitions against indecent material. In that case the FCC had acted against a Pacifica Foundation's broadcast of George Carlin's routine entitled "Seven Words You Can Never Say on Television" on WBAI-FM in New York.

In the most recent action, the FCC was reacting to complaints lodged against air personality Howard Stern on Philadelphia's WYSP-FM and against The University of California's station KCSB-FM in Santa Barbara. The Stern broadcast involved the use of such expressions as "limp dick" and the offensive use of the word *penis.* In the KCSB case, the complaint resulted from the broadcast of sexually explicit song lyrics.

There continue to be First Amendment concerns regarding the FCC initiative on indecency. These concerns focus on the difficulties encountered when selected forms of expression are deemed to be exempt from First Amendment protection. Groups such as the American Civil Liberties Union and various constitutional experts have expressed doubts about the action's constitutionality. The National Association of Broadcasters also expressed concern with the First Amendment questions raised by the FCC actions, but at the same time it registered its ongoing concern with the growing incidence of indecent broadcasts.[11]

Some in the legal community have viewed the FCC's initiative in this area as running counter to the commission's trend toward deregulation. Former FCC General Counsel Henry Geller, quoted in *Broadcasting,* noted that it seemed inconsistent that "a commission, which views the print media as a model for broadcast regulation, should take such an action."[12] Geller called the ruling a "step backward."[13]

Several industry groups have raised the issue of the "vagueness" of the standards the FCC proposes to use to determine what is indecent and what is not. In a joint petition filed with the FCC, a group, which included the major television networks, Action for Children's Television, and National Public Radio, charged that the indecency ruling was contrary to the public interest. The filing asked for a reconsideration of the indecency ruling and asked the FCC to let the licensee determine whether programming was offensive and to consider complaints concerning indecency on a case-by-case basis, using a narrower standard in deciding on the merits of each case. In a separate filing, the National Association of Broadcasters noted its own finding that indecency was contrary to the public interest and asked for a clearer standard from the FCC.[14]

In November of 1987 the FCC issued a ruling in clarification of its policy on indecency. The new ruling stated, in essence, that stations would be allowed to broadcast indecent programming between the hours of 12 Midnight and 6 AM. Obscenity continues to be banned at all times, however.[15] Also in November the Associated Press reported that the FCC was planning to step up enforcement of its indecency standards. "Actions could range from warnings to fines to license suspensions and revocations," according to the story.[16]

Although this ruling precipitated considerable public discussion, its overall impact may be minimal. According to broadcast-law specialist Marvin Bensman of Memphis State University, the new ruling doesn't represent a significant departure from the position the FCC has taken in the past. "This is really what is known as the 'raised eyebrow approach,'" said Bensman in an interview with *The Christian Science Monitor*. "It's highlighting a concern that (the FCC has) always had and is similar to a number of things they've done in the past."[17] Bensman notes that the prohibition against indecent broadcasts is a part of the Communications Act and that the FCC's ruling is in large part a reaction to pressure from public interest groups wishing to "bring back so called morality to broadcasting."[18]

Reporting Requirements

Operation under an FCC license requires broadcasters to report periodically to the FCC on certain aspects of station operation. In its Code of Federal Regulation, the FCC specifies the types of reports required and the dates when they must be filed. In general terms, the FCC leaves it to the station to maintain most required records at the station and to make certain documents available upon request. In some instances, however, the station is obliged to provide the FCC with specific documents at regular intervals.

Figure 12.5

FCC Form 395 must be filed annually on or before May 31.

SECTION V	(Section V and VI) (applicable to all respondents)												
FULL-TIME PAID EMPLOYEES JOB CATEGORIES[1]	ALL EMPLOYEES [2]			MALE					FEMALE				
				MINORITY GROUP EMPLOYEES				White, not of Hispanic origin	MINORITY GROUP EMPLOYEES				White, not of Hispanic origin
	Total Columns 2 + 3	Male	Female	Black, not of Hispanic origin	Asian or Pacific Islander	American Indian or Alaskan Native	Hispanic		Black, not of Hispanic origin	Asian or Pacific Islander	American Indian or Alaskan Native	Hispanic	
	(1)	(2)	(3)	(4)	(5)	(6)	(7)	(8)	(9)	(10)	(11)	(12)	(13)
Officials and Managers													
Professionals													
Technicians													
Sales workers													
Office and Clerical													
Craftsperson (Skilled)													
Operatives (Semi-skilled)													
Laborers (Unskilled)													
Service Workers													
TOTAL													
Total employment from previous Report (if any)													

Among the filings that the FCC requires is an annual employment report that must be filed by any station with five or more full-time employees. This report must be filed on FCC Form 395 (Figure 12.5) on or before May 31 of each year. The purpose of this report is to provide evidence that the licensee is in compliance with Section 73.2080 of the *Code of Federal Regulations* dealing with equal employment opportunities.

Besides the employment report, the FCC requires that stations file copies of certain other "contracts, instruments, and documents" as specified in Section 73.3613 of the *Code of Federal Regulations*. This requires stations to file with the FCC copies of such documents as network-affiliation contracts to ensure compliance with the FCC's "Report and Statement of Policy" and Order Docket 20721 regarding network-affiliation agreements, copies of agreements regarding ownership or control of the licensee, and personnel contracts dealing with profit-sharing or management consultancies. Radio stations are required to file the Quarterly Needs and Issues Report, which

Figure 12.6

The first page of FCC Form 323, Ownership Report.

Approved by OMB
3060-0010
Expires 04/30/89

CERTIFICATION

United States of America
Federal Communications Commission
Washington, D. C. 20554

Ownership Report

NOTE: Before filling out this form, read attached instructions

I certify that I am _____
(Official title, see Instruction 1)

of _____
(Exact legal title or name of respondent)

that I have examined this Report, that to the best of my knowledge and belief, all statements in the Report are true, correct and complete.

Section 310(d) of the Communications Act of 1934 requires that consent of the Commission must be obtained prior to the assignment or transfer of control of a station license or construction permit. This form may **not** be used to report or request an assignment of license/permit or transfer of control (except to report an assignment of license/permit or transfer of control made pursuant to prior Commission consent).

(Date of certification must be within 60 days of the date shown in Item 1 and in no event prior to Item 1 date):

_____ 19 ___
(Signature)   *(Date)*

1.   All of the information furnished in this Report is accurate as of

_____, 19 _____
(Date must comply with Section 73.3615(a), i.e., information must be current within 60 days of the filing of this report, when 1(a) below is checked.)

Telephone No. of respondent *(include area code)*:

Any person who willfully makes false statements on this report can be punished by fine or imprisonment. U.S. Code, Title 18, Section 1001.

This report is filed pursuant to Instruction *(check one)*

1 (a) ☐ Annual   1 (b) ☐ Transfer of Control, Assignment of License or Construction Permit

for the following stations:

Name and Post Office Address of respondent:

Call Letters	Location	Class of service

4.   Name of entity, if other than licensee or permittee, for which report is filed *(see Instruction 3)*:

2.   Give the name of any corporation or other entity for whom a separate Report is filed due to its interest in the subject licensee *(See Instruction 3)*:

5.   Respondent is:

☐ Sole Proprietorship

☐ For-profit corporation

☐ Not-for-profit corporation

☐ General Partnership

☐ Limited Partnership

☐ Other: _____

3.   Show the attributable interests in any other broadcast station of the respondent. Also, show any interest of the respondent, whether or not attributable, which is 5% or more of the ownership of any other broadcast station or any newspaper or CATV entity in the same market or with overlapping signals in the same broadcast service, as described in Sections 73.3555 and 76.501 of the Commission's Rules.

If a limited partnership, is certification statement included as in Instruction 4?

☐ Yes   ☐ No

FCC 323
December 1986

replaces the community ascertainment requirements. In this report, stations describe briefly some of the issues that are of current interest in the community and describe programming that responds to these needs.

The FCC requires that a complete ownership report be filed each year on the anniversary of the application for renewal. This report is filed on FCC Form 323 (Figure 12.6) and lists names of owners, partners, or certain officers of any corporation owning the broadcast facilities in question and other specified properties. Such a report is filed initially at the time of the issuance of a construction permit for a new station. Any subsequent changes in ownership that shift control of the licensee from one owner to another must receive prior approval by the FCC.

The FCC requires that certain documents be maintained at the station and provided to the FCC on request. Certain contracts specified in Section 73.3613, including agreements with "time brokers" relating to the resale of broadcast time, subchannel-leasing agreements, and sponsorship agreements for large blocks of programming for events such as sports contests. The station must keep copies of the station logs and technical records at the station and provide them to the FCC on request. The licensee is required to maintain a public inspection file containing a copy of all materials submitted in the original license application and any subsequent applications filed with the FCC. All ownership reports and all employment reports must be included in the public inspection file. Letters from the public regarding station operations and records pertaining to political broadcasts by candidates for public office must be included.

Licensees are required to post the station license and all operator licenses. The station license must be posted "in a conspicuous place and in such a manner that all terms are visible at the place the licensee considers to be the principal control point of the transmitter" (47 CFR 73.1230). Operator licenses must be posted where the operator is on duty—in other words, at the studio, not at the transmitter shack.

Defining the Public Interest for Radio

The advent of deregulation has altered the official definition of the public interest standard as it applies to radio. Prior to the Fowler era, the FCC had developed regulatory structures that reflected a broad application of the public interest concept. There was a strong belief in the centrality of the local community as the major entity to be served by licensees. Policies and regulations that were designed to assure the FCC that stations were actively providing programming that met local needs and addressed local concerns were enacted. Much of this activity was instituted in reaction to the strong influence of networks in providing programming for broadcast outlets that obviously did not directly address local communities.

Besides its concern for localness, the FCC had deemed it necessary to establish guidelines that would encourage licensees to offer public affairs programming. The Fairness Doctrine constituted an interpretation of the public interest that sought to guarantee access for a variety of views. Stations were obliged to show a considerable commitment to news programming if they were to meet the commission's criteria for having served the public interest. In its 1960 programming statement, the FCC spelled out fourteen program categories that, in its judgment, were usually necessary to fulfill public interest requirements. They were agricultural programs, children's programming, broadcast editorials, educational programs, local self-expression, local talent, entertainment, programs directed at minorities, news, political programs, public affairs programming, religious programming, sports, weather, and market reports.

Deregulation, however, brought about a dramatic reversal in this philosophy. The operative philosophy regarding the public interest standard became one of less government involvement in determining what kinds of programming would best meet the standard. Most programming decisions are now left to the licensee. There is little second guessing by the FCC at renewal time as to whether the station has proceeded properly in the programming area to effectively meet its obligations to the public interest. The assumption is that the public itself will force the licensee to meet its needs through the pressure of the marketplace. The current commission views the public as a better judge of what constitutes the public interest than the government.

The scarcity principle, which postulates that limitations on the use of broadcast channels can restrict full discussion of public issues, no longer applies with the same force it once had. The current operating assumption is that there are numerous radio and television outlets serving most localities. Therefore, the danger that a small number of licensees can exert dictatorial control over what is broadcast no longer exists, according to supporters of deregulation.

Under the current regulatory philosophy, government interference in the form of excessive regulatory control prevents the unrestricted operation of the marketplace and therefore is, in fact, contrary to the public interest. The public interest standard, then, has become focused on such things as adherence to technical standards and enhancing the climate for freer operation of the broadcast enterprise. It should be noted that radio has benefited more from deregulation than has television. Because there are by far fewer television stations than radio stations, there has been less activity to deregulate the television industry.

Major Documents of the FCC

Like many other government agencies, the FCC would have a difficult time operating without paper. It therefore becomes necessary for station management to be aware of which particular documents are the most helpful in dealing with the commission.

The entire body of FCC broadcast regulation is contained in the *Code of Federal Regulations.* The *Code of Federal Regulations* is a published collection of federal rules and regulations that have at one time been published in the *Federal Register.* The code contains fifty titles in all. Under Title 47, which is designated as "Telecommunication," there are five volumes. The volume containing parts 70 to 79 contains the rules and regulations that pertain to broadcasting (Figure 12.7). The regulations found in this document pertain to licensing requirements, technical regulation, programming regulation, and filing requirements, among others. In short, this document is the authoritative source of broadcast regulation. The code is updated each year to reflect changes that have been enacted since the last publication of the document.

To be current at any given time, it is necessary to keep abreast of new regulations as they are passed. This is done by reading the daily *Federal Register.* A "Reader Aids" section of the *Federal Register* tells how to ascertain quickly what sections of regulations may have been recently updated. By using the *Code of Federal Regulations* in conjunction with the *Federal Register,* it is possible to be up to the minute on the current state of broadcast regulation.

The FCC also publishes policy statements that elaborate on broad areas of concern. These documents are issued under various designations. Some of the general categories are "Report and Order," "Public Notice," "Memorandum Opinion and Order," "Report, Statement of Policy," and official letters. The topics of these policy statements vary. For example, the topic of network/AM, FM station affiliation agreements is addressed in "Report, Statement of Policy," and "Order," Docket 20721, FCC 77–206, adopted March 10, 1977 (63 FCC 2d 674).

The FCC issues notices of rule making in which it announces its intention to consider the implementation of new regulations. Besides informing licensees and other interested parties that the commission is about to act, the notices offer the opportunity for these parties to comment on the proposed new regulation.

For matters in which licensees are required to engage in fairly complex tasks in order to comply with FCC requirements, the commission often publishes what it designates as a "primer." These documents provide a detailed study of selected regulations. In a publication called *The Law and Political Broadcasting,* for example, the FCC provides a close examination of the rules regarding political broadcasting.

Figure 12.7

This publication contains FCC regulations pertaining to broadcasting.

code of federal regulations

Telecommunication

47

PARTS 70 TO 79
Revised as of October 1, 1986

12.3

SELF-REGULATION

The area of regulation and control of broadcasting is largely the province of the federal government. Certain state level statutes also apply in a general sense. As far back as the Radio Act of 1912, however, there was a considerable attempt in the broadcasting industry to self-regulate. When all stations occupied the same frequency, for example, it was necessary to sort out who would broadcast when, so there would be minimal interference. Because the U.S. Secretary of Commerce had no authority to specify conditions of broadcasting, the industry worked out solutions among themselves. This fragile arrangement eventually fell apart, of course. In the 1920s, preceding the enactment of the Radio Act of 1927, a series of four radio conferences was called by Secretary of Commerce Herbert Hoover to try to find a way to implement a satisfactory system of regulating broadcasting without government action. Those conferences, however, failed to produce anything other than a call from the industry for the government to enact legislation.

In more recent times, broadcasters have banded together as an industry to establish other forms of self-regulation. Partly, it is a matter of self-interest. It has been felt that if certain practices were controlled by the industry in a voluntary manner, there would be no need for the federal government to impose regulations that might be more onerous.

The Radio Code of the National Association of Broadcasters

The National Association of Broadcasters (NAB) was formed in 1923. The primary mission of the organization has been to function as a lobbying organization that attempts to influence regulatory and legislative activities pertaining to the industry. As an outgrowth of this activity, however, the NAB established a self-regulatory body known as the Code Authority. The Code Authority had as its two main areas of concern *programming practices* and *advertising*. The Authority published the Radio Code and later the Television Code. These documents provided guidelines for acceptable practices in matters pertaining to specific programming and advertising situations.

There were, for example, restrictions on types of products that could be advertised. The restriction on the advertising of hard liquor on broadcast media, for example, was a part of the codes. Programming restrictions were also stated in the codes, with listings of guidelines for handling children's programming and restrictions regarding sexual content and indecency.

The codes were voluntary, and there were no effective enforcement provisions. Not all broadcasters were code subscribers. The effort was moderately useful, though, in alerting broadcasters to social concerns and exerting industry pressure against those who ignored the standards established by the code authority.

In 1982, however, the NAB code was abolished after an antitrust suit was brought by the U.S. Department of Justice. The basis of the antitrust concern was that, because the NAB is made up entirely of broadcasters, there was danger that this form of self-regulation could become a device to reduce competition and create conditions injurious to the total advertising marketplace.

Even without the codes, however, the NAB continues to establish positions on matters that were formerly concerns of the code authorities. In the matter of indecency, the NAB board has taken a position expressing concern over the increased incidence of programming that is characterized by many as indecent. Industry jawboning can go only so far in this regard, but the effort to police itself to some degree helps in creating positive public relations, even if there is little additional effect.

Conflict: Self-Regulation Versus Profitability

Without the restraints of self-regulation, there are increased opportunities for broad-casters to be arbitrary in advertising practice and programming. The NAB codes placed restrictions on certain practices in advertising and programming. This meant that station owners were pressured to refrain from questionable practices. Now that these controls are gone, there are those who feel that there will be commercial pressures to sacrifice standards.

Some observers feel that the recent public exposure of unethical practices in the business and financial communities displays a predilection for profit-making organizations to produce profits regardless of what it takes to do so. These critics express the concern that the relaxation of FCC strictures on programming and advertising practices, combined with the loss of self-regulation, presents the danger that broadcasters are far more likely now than before to sacrifice standards to maximize profits.

There is little doubt that there is increased latitude for stations to make their own judgments regarding matters that once were prohibited or a least frowned upon by other broadcasters. Many broadcasters are finding, however, that profitability still depends to a considerable degree on observing certain standards. In advertising, for example, advertisers tend to avoid placing their advertising messages on stations where listeners are bombarded with frequent commercials. Audiences still want to be informed as well as entertained, as evidenced by the great success of many all-news stations.

In essence, it appears that profitability and accountability often go hand in hand. Unrestrained pursuit of profit without a sensitivity to what the public will tolerate seldom leads to long-range success. In the absence of strong government and self-imposed standards, it becomes the responsibility of the public to police broadcasters who exceed the bounds of what is acceptable practice. Broadcasters concerned with profitability have been given the role of setting and observing their own standards in accordance with their individual readings of what the public finds acceptable in matters of taste and decency.

Community Standards

The FCC has backed away from government insistence that radio broadcasters actively concentrate on providing programming geared specifically to the community of license. Many broadcasters have argued for years that government guidelines did not reflect reality in matters of what kinds of programming best served the public. One effect of the relaxation of some of the key regulatory strictures on programming is that it becomes the obligation of broadcasters to decide such matters as to what its community demands in terms of standards.

In today's society, it may very well be legitimate for radio broadcasters to think of community as having less to do with a geographic grouping of residents and their support systems than it does with the groupings that occur by dint of the segmentation of listening audiences. It is fundamental to success in radio that stations must serve a well-defined segment of the total potential listening audience. These various segments can be identified and characterized in respect to many different variables. Once an audience segment has been identified, it can be defined as to shared values, tastes, and interests. Teens, for example, tend to share well-defined cultural structures characterized by such things as styles of grooming and dress. There are corresponding mores that tend to make them responsive to programming that a young married adult with a family might find annoying or offensive. Indeed, the current state of audience research has enabled even the smallest of stations to know a great deal about who is listening to its programming and hence its advertising.

In the previous section of this chapter, it was stated that in the absence of centrally derived guidelines for decency and taste in relation to broadcasting, it has become necessary for individual broadcasters to determine standards that will respond to what the public demands. In light of the structure of today's radio industry as it exists in relation to its audiences, it may very well be that the criteria offered by the courts, (that is, the use of community standards to evaluate and adjudicate questions of obscenity and morality) can be applied successfully and without great difficulty by radio station operators trying to determine where to draw the line in relation to standards.

The efficacy of this approach is reflected somewhat in the FCC's obscenity ruling that has proposed that one criterion it will use to determine whether a broadcast is to be considered indecent has to do with whether children were likely to be a part of the audience. This suggests that a particular program can be judged by different standards, depending on the composition of the audience at the time of broadcast.

This concept, if embraced fully, leads to a situation in which the individual licensee becomes the best judge of what program practices are suitable, using a modern interpretation of community standards. Whether the concern is for the welfare of minors or a determination of what a particular audience segment may find offensive, this approach ultimately looks to the marketplace to exert the necessary influence to prevent abuse of the public trust that obtains to the licensee.

This view of self-regulatory practice has not been tested fully in practice because there are legal and regulatory structures in place that prevent its full implementation. If print media is a guide, it is apparent that there is a market for material that a large segment of the public finds offensive. Total self-regulation, then, fully applied to broadcasting would likely result in an increase in the incidence of what is now considered indecent program material. Despite this fact, however, the restraining influence of community standards viewed in the broad sense is a concept that must be taken into account by broadcasters and those concerned with effective regulation of the industry.

12.4

A NONTECHNICAL GUIDE TO TECHNICAL REGULATION

The majority of FCC regulations deal with technical matters. The reason for this is because, in order for many radio stations to operate without interfering with one another, fairly precise and complex standards must be established. This is known as spectrum management, referring to the fact that the natural limitations of the broadcast portion of the electromagnetic spectrum requires that conditions be placed on how broadcast channels are used. In establishing limitations and conditions on use of the AM and FM portions of the spectrum, the FCC has had to be very specific. The differing natures of these two services call for separate consideration in establishing effective technical regulations, whereas many areas of nontechnical regulation can apply to both AM and FM. The FCC's technical regulations therefore set limits and specify standards of quality for all forms of broadcast transmission. Despite their complexity, it is not necessary to be a broadcast engineer to understand the underlying intent of radio's technical regulations. It is possible to gain a sufficient understanding of this important area of regulatory activity by reading the regulations themselves. It should be noted, however, that the technical regulations of the FCC undergo constant revision as technology and engineering techniques change.

Definition of Terms

The FCC's technical regulations for radio can be extremely intimidating for the uninitiated. A glance at FCC technical documents and regulations shows them to be liberally sprinkled with terms recognizable only to engineers. There are charts and diagrams with titles like "Estimated Field Strength Exceeded at 50 Percent of the Potential Receiver Locations for at Least 50 Percent of the Time at a Receiving Antenna

Height of 9 Meters." There are formulas used to calculate "percentage modulation (amplitude)" and others used to determine "the vertical plane radiation characteristics of an AM antenna." How does a manager make sense of such a complex and specialized field?

At one time, there was a significant number of radio managers who had come to radio through the technical and engineering aspects of broadcasting. Today, however, it is far more common for managers to come from a sales background. Such managers often have an extremely limited understanding of technical matters. Although it is true that a manager need not be able to install a new transmitter or load the antenna, it is very useful to have a working knowledge of what the technical side of FCC regulation is all about. Managers with a general knowledge of FCC technical requirements, working with a competent chief engineer who has a solid technical education in broadcast engineering, can run a much more efficient and effective operation than managers who must depend on their chief operators for the answers to each and every technical question.

The *Code of Federal Regulations* spells out all technical operations and specifications with which the FCC requires compliance. It is a good idea for managers to take the time to skim through the code. Much of the material is difficult to understand for those with no technical background. But for most managers, it is possible to arrive at a general impression of what the FCC requires of radio operations.

The lists of terms in Figures 12.8 and 12.9 are reproduced directly from the FCC regulations. Figure 12.8 is taken from the section on AM broadcasting; Figure 12.9 is from the section on FM broadcasting.

Obviously, many technical matters remain beyond the nontechnical manager's scope of knowledge. The exercise of working through the definitions, however, does provide an understandable guide for gauging the scope of operations that must be taken into account in order to meet the technical requirements, which licensees agree to abide by. Managers who are conversant with the general intent of these technical areas of FCC regulation can work effectively with the station's chief engineer to ensure that the necessary operations are being performed to protect the operating license and to produce high-level quality in the transmission of the station's broadcast signal.

Management Interaction with Engineering

Of course, to be successful in staying in compliance with FCC technical regulations a manager must rely on the chief engineer and the technical staff. Among other responsibilities, the engineering section must ensure that power limitations are met, that the

Figure 12.8

AM-broadcasting terms.

§ 73.1 Scope.

This subpart contains those rules which apply exclusively to the AM broadcast service and are in addition to those rules in Subpart H which are common to all AM, FM and TV broadcast services, commercial and noncommercial.

[47 FR 8587, Mar. 1, 1982]

§ 73.14 AM broadcast definitions.

AM broadcast band. The band of frequencies extending from 535 to 1605 kHz.

AM broadcast channel. The band of frequencies occupied by the carrier and the upper and lower sidebands of an AM broadcast signal with the carrier frequency at the center. Channels are designated by their assigned carrier frequencies. The 107 carrier frequencies assigned to AM broadcast stations begin at 540 kHz and are in successive steps of 10 kHz to 1600 kHz.

NOTE: See § 73.21 for the classification of AM broadcast channels.

AM broadcast station. A broadcast station licensed for the dissemination of radio communications intended to be received by the public and operated on a channel in the band 535-1605 kilohertz (kHz). The term "AM broadcast" is synonymous with the term "standard broadcast" as may appear elsewhere in this chapter.

Amplitude modulated stage. The radio-frequency stage to which the modulator is coupled and in which the carrier wave is modulated in accordance with the system of amplitude modulation and the characteristics of the modulating wave.

Amplitude modulator stage. The last amplifier stage of the modulating wave amplitude modulates a radio-frequency stage.

Antenna current. The radio-frequency current in the antenna with no modulation.

Antenna input power. The product of the square of the antenna current and the antenna resistance at the point where the current is measured.

Antenna resistance. The total resistance of the transmitting antenna system at the operating frequency and at the point at which the antenna current is measured.

Blanketing. The interference which is caused by the presence of an AM broadcast signal of one volt per meter (V/m) or greater strengths in the area adjacent to the antenna of the transmitting station. The 1 V/m contour is referred to as the blanket contour and the area within this contour is referred to as the blanket area.

Carrier-amplitude regulation (Carrier shift). The change in amplitude of the carrier wave in an amplitude-modulated transmitter when modulation is applied under conditions of symmetrical modulation.

Combined audio harmonics. The arithmetical sum of the amplitudes of all the separate harmonic components. Root sum square harmonic readings may be accepted under conditions prescribed by the FCC.

Critical directional antenna. An AM broadcast directional antenna that is required, by the terms of a station authorization, to be operated with the relative currents and phases within the antenna elements at closer tolerances of deviation than those permitted under § 73.62 and observed with a high precision monitor capable of measuring these parameters.

Critical hours. The two hour period immediately following local sunrise and the two hour period immediately preceding local sunset.

Daytime. The period of time between local sunrise and local sunset.

Dominant station. A Class I station, as defined in § 73.21.

Effective field; Effective field strength. The root-mean-square (RMS) value of the inverse distance fields at a distance of 1 kilometer from the antenna in all directions in the horizontal plane. The term "field strength" is synonymous with the term "field intensity" as contained elsewhere in this Part.

Equipment performance measurements. The measurements performed to determine the overall performance characteristics of a broadcast transmission system from point of program origination at main studio to sampling of signal as radiated. (See § 73.1590)

Experimental period. the time between 12 midnight local time and local sunrise, used by AM stations for tests, maintenance and experimentation. However, for AM broadcast applications granted or filed before June 3, 1985, nominal power is specified in a system of classifications which include the following values: 50 kW, 25 kW, 10 kW, 5 kW, 2.5 kW, 1 kW, 0.5 kW, and 0.25 kW. The specified nominal power for any station in this group of stations will be retained until action is taken on or after June 3, 1985, which involves a change in the technical facilities of the station.

Percentage modulation (amplitude)

In a positive direction.

$$M = \frac{MAX - C \times 100}{C}$$

In a negative direction:

$$M = \frac{C - MIN \times 100}{C}$$

Where:

M = Modulation level in percent.

MAX = Instantaneous maximum level of the modulated radio frequency envelope.

MIN = Instantaneous minimum level of the modulated radio frequency envelope.

C = (Carrier) level of radio frequency envelope without modulation.

Plate modulation. The modulation produced by introduction of the modulating wave into the plate circuit of any tube in which the carrier frequency wave is present.

Primary service area. Means the service area of a broadcast station in which the groundwave is not subject to objectionable interference or objectionable fading.

Proof of performance measurements or antenna proof of performance measurements. The measurements of field strengths made to determine the radiation pattern or characteristics of an AM directional antenna system.

Secondary service area. Means the service area of a broadcast station served by the skywave and not subject to objectionable interference and in which the signal is subject to intermittent variations in strength.

Secondary AM station. Any AM station, except a Class I station, operating on a Class I frequency.

Stereophonic channel. The band of audio frequencies from 50 to 15,000 Hz containing the stereophonic information which modulates the radio frequency carrier.

Stereophonic crosstalk. An undesired signal occurring in the main channel from modulation of the stereophonic channel or that occurring in the stereophonic channel from modulation of the main channel.

Stereophonic pilot tone. An audio tone of fixed or variable frequency modulating the carrier during the transmission of stereophonic programs.

Stereophonic separation. The ratio of the electrical signal caused in the right (or left) stereophonic channel to the electrical signal caused in the left (or right) stereophonic channel by the transmission of only a right (or left) signal.

Sunrise and sunset. For each particular location and during any particular month, the time of sunrise and sunset as specified in the instrument of authorization (See § 73.1209).

"White area". The area or population which does not receive interference-free primary service from an authorized AM station or does not receive a signal strength of at least 1 mV/m from an authorized FM station.

Figure 12.9

FM-broadcasting terms.

§ 73.310   FM technical definitions.

(a) *Frequency modulation.*

Antenna height above average terrain (HAAT). HAAT is calculated by: determining the average of the antenna heights above the terrain from 3 to 16 kilometers (2 to 10 miles) from the antenna for the eight directions evenly spaced for each 45° of azimuth starting with True North (a different antenna height will be determined in each direction from the antenna); and computing the average of these separate antenna heights. In some cases less than eight directions may be used. (See § 73.313(d).) Where circular or elliptical polarization is used, the antenna height above average terrain must be based upon the height of the radiation of the antenna that transmits the horizontal component of radiation.

Antenna power gain. The square of the ratio of the root-mean-square (RMS) free space field strength produced at 1 kilometer in the horizontal plane in millivolts per meter for 1 kW antenna input power to 221.4 mV/m. This ratio is expressed in decibels (dB). If specified for a particular direction, antenna power gain is based on that field strength in the direction only.

Center frequency. The term "center frequency" means:

(1) The average frequency of the emitted wave when modulated by a sinusoidal signal.

(2) The frequency of the emitted wave without modulation.

§ 73.310

Composite baseband signal. A signal which is composed of all program and other communications signals that frequency modulates the FM carrier.

Effective radiated power. The term "effective radiated power" means the product of the antenna power (transmitter output power less transmission line loss) times: (1) The antenna field gain, or (2) the antenna field gain squared. Where circular or elliptical polarization is employed, the term effective radiated power is applied separately to the horizontal and vertical components of radiation. For allocation purposes, the effective radiated power authorized is the horizontally polarized component of radiation only.

Equivalent isotropically radiated power (EIRP). The term "equivalent isotropically radiated power (also known as "effective radiated power above isotropic) means the product of the antenna input power and the antenna gain in a given direction relative to an isotropic antenna.

FM Blanketing. Blanketing is that form of interference to the reception of other broadcast stations which is caused by the presence of an FM broadcast signal of 115 dBu (562 mV/m) or greater signal strength in the area adjacent to the antenna of the transmitting station. The 115 dBu contour is referred to as the blanketing contour and the area within this contour is referred to as the blanketing area.

FM broadcast band. The band of frequencies extending from 88 to 108 MHz, which includes those assigned to noncommercial educational broadcasting.

FM broadcast channel. A band of frequencies 200 kHz wide and designated by its center frequency. Channels for FM broadcast stations begin at 88.1 MHz and continue in successive steps of 200 kHz to and including 107.9 MHz.

FM broadcast station. A station employing frequency modulation in the FM broadcast band and licensed primarily for the transmission of radiotelephone emissions intended to be received by the general public.

Field strength. The electric field strength in the horizontal plane.

47 CFR Ch. I (10-1-86 Edition)

Free space field strength. The field strength that would exist at a point in the absence of waves reflected from the earth or other reflecting objects.

Frequency departure. The amount of variation of a carrier frequency or center frequency from its assigned value.

Frequency deviation. The peak difference between modulated wave and the carrier frequency.

Frequency modulation. A system of modulation where the instantaneous radio frequency varies in proportion to the instantaneous amplitude of the modulating signal (amplitude of modulating signal to be measured after preemphasis, if used) and the instantaneous radio frequency is independent of the frequency of the modulating signal.

Frequency swing. The peak difference between the maximum and the minimum values of the instantaneous frequency of the carrier wave during wave during modulation.

Multiplex transmission. The term "multiplex transmission" means the simultaneous transmission of two or more signals within a single channel. Multiplex transmission as applied to FM broadcast stations means the transmission of facsimile or other signals in addition to the regular broadcast signals.

Percentage modulation. The ratio of the actual frequency deviation to the frequency deviation defined as 100% modulation, expressed in percentage. For FM broadcast stations, a frequency deviation of ±75kHz is defined as 100% modulation.

(b) *Stereophonic sound broadcasting.*

Cross-talk. An undesired signal occurring in one channel caused by an electrical signal in another channel.

FM stereophonic broadcast. The transmission of a stereophonic program by a single FM broadcast station utilizing the main channel and a stereophonic subchannel.

Left (or right) signal. The electrical output of a microphone or combination of microphones placed so as to convey the intensity, time, and location of sounds originating predominately to the listener's left (or right) of the center of the performing area.

Federal Communications Commission

Left (or right) stereophonic channel. The left (or right) signal as electrically reproduced in reception of FM stereophonic broadcasts.

Main channel. The band of frequencies from 50 to 15,000 Hz which frequency-modulate the main carrier.

Pilot subcarrier. A subcarrier that serves as a control signal for use in the reception of FM stereophonic sound broadcasts.

Stereophonic separation. The ratio of the electrical signal caused in sound channel A to the signal caused in sound channel B by the transmission of only a channel B signal. Channels A and B may be any two channels of a stereophonic sound broadcast transmission system.

Stereophonic sound. The audio information carried by plurality of channels arranged to afford the listener a sense of the spatial distribution of sound sources. Stereophonic sound broadcasting includes, but is not limited to, biphonic (two channel), triphonic (three channel) and quadrophonic (four channel) program services.

Stereophonic sound subcarrier. A subcarrier within the FM broadcast baseband used for transmitting signals for stereophonic sound reception of the main broadcast program service.

Stereophonic sound subchannel. The band of frequencies from 23 kHz to 99 kHz containing sound subcarriers and their associated sidebands.

(c) *Visual transmissions.* Communications or message transmitted on a subcarrier intended for reception and visual presentation on a viewing screen, teleprinter, facsimile printer, or other form of graphic display or record.

(d) *Control and telemetry transmissions.* Signals transmitted on a multiplex subcarrier intended for any form of control and switching functions or for equipment status data and aural or visual alarms.

signal does not drift from its assigned frequency, and that all monitoring functions and technical reporting requirements are observed in a timely manner.

The manager, however, must assume the overall, final responsibility for meeting the FCC conditions of operation. If the engineering staff is not performing the functions necessary to meet FCC standards, it is incumbent upon management to be aware of the situation. To do this, the manager must communicate regularly with the chief engineer, and it is important that managers know how to ask the proper questions. Because management is generally not terribly well-versed in the nuances of technical operations, interacting with the engineering staff can sometimes be one of the most difficult management areas in radio. Many managers have been told by engineering people that a certain operation cannot be performed, only to find out later that it was really a rather simple operation. Engineers also have occasional run-ins with programming people. For example, production people, wishing to achieve a particular effect, may find that the engineer objects because it compromises sound quality. It becomes the role of the manager to settle the dispute.

Managers who have been most successful in dealing with engineering staffs are those who accord them respect, but who also refuse to be intimidated by engineers' technical knowledge. It is important to reach an understanding that lets engineers know that managers need their help to keep the station in compliance with the requirements of the FCC, but that it is ultimately the manager whose head will roll if things are not done according to what is best for the station as a whole. Final word comes from management.

Sometimes it is helpful for managers to request outside help in the form of consulting engineers who can recommend actions to improve the quality of service, to upgrade outdated equipment, or simply to help management understand new developments in technical regulation. The consulting option is especially helpful in stations where a chief engineer is not needed full-time or where existing engineering people are not highly trained. Consulting engineers understand that they are being hired by managers. They are not hesitant to report flaws in the engineering realm, and they are not interested in protecting turf for the chief engineer.

In short, management must have confidence in the engineering staff of the station. That confidence can best be obtained by constant communication. The manager who has taken the time to learn the rudiments of technical operations can ask the right questions and can pursue technical matters until satisfied that the station is operating at the proper level of technical quality.

Review of Current Technical Regulations

To gain an overview of technical regulations that apply to radio operations, it is worthwhile to view the situation from the standpoint of the FCC. The Communications Act requires that licenses be issued only if it serves the public interest, convenience, and necessity to do so. In a very basic sense, that means that the FCC's role is to make a determination in two respects: Existing public services will not be harmed in any way if a new license is issued, and there will be a positive public benefit from the issuance of the license.

From a technical standpoint, that means that the new licensee must operate without interference with existing stations and that the signal quality meets standards that contribute something positive to the nation's overall broadcasting service. All the complex formulas, charts, and diagrams illustrating performance requirements and the specifications for channel designation and station classification exist to ensure that these basic conditions exist.

A considerable portion of the FCC's technical regulations pertain to the prevention of interference. In AM broadcasting, the detailed sections dealing with station classification describe the restrictions on channel use, power limitations, and hours of operation, which deal with the problems of wave propagation that can cause interference among stations located in different parts of the country (see Chapter 5).

In another area of technical regulation, detailed specifications deal with the functions and operations for setting and monitoring power levels and patterns of radiation from antennas. Sections of the FCC Regulations—such as 73.51, "determining operating power," or 73.54, "antenna resistance and reactance measurements,"—specify conditions that must be met to operate without interference, as does 73.150, "directional Antenna Systems." The specifications listed in these and other sections make extensive use of graphs and formulas to spell out what is required. All these elements of the regulation have been carefully worked out over time to provide results that ensure proper performance.

Clearly, the bulk of technical regulation is directed to the specification of standards. Most of these conditions apply at the time a station is either installing a new operation or upgrading an existing facility. Requirements for day-to-day operations have been scaled back somewhat through deregulation. For example, the FCC once required stations to run "performance tests" regularly to show that they were meeting the standards imposed by the operating license. These are no longer required. Logging requirements have been simplified and consolidated into a single station log. This scaling back in what is required does not relieve the station from responsibility for maintaining its operations within assigned limitations, however, and periodic spot checks are made by the FCC to check on station compliance.

In terms of sheer volume, the bulk of the FCC's written regulations pertain to technical matters. Specifications are spelled out with great precision; great care is exercised in ensuring that all radio facilities operate strictly within limits that will guarantee high-quality service and prevention of interference among the many stations on the air. In the eyes of the FCC, one of station management's greatest responsibilities is to observe faithfully the technical constraints specified in the station license. If managers achieve an appreciation of this fact and keep in mind the overall rationale for regulation of technical matters, the complexity of the regulations themselves need not be an overriding concern.

Examples of Common Violations

The FCC enforces its technical regulations by spot checks and through investigation of complaints received. Penalties for violations can range from the levying of fines to the revocation of a station license. A series of violations at a single station could result in nonrenewal when the station's application is considered at renewal time. The most common violations of FCC regulations in the technical area involve some of the following situations:

—— Unauthorized operation, as in the case of daytime broadcasters who fail to sign off at the designated time of day or who sign on earlier than authorized; operating at too much power

—— Unauthorized change in operating power

—— Failure to make proper equipment-performance measurements

—— Failure to report changes in ownership

—— Operation of defective monitoring equipment and failure to keep accurate logs

Most of these violations are the result of carelessness. Others involve callous disregard of operating requirements. The tendency for stations to become careless or to disregard FCC limitations often is due to a feeling that the vigilance of the FCC has become relaxed. Stations sometimes take the attitude that as long as no one complains, the FCC will not become aware of operating violations. When the FCC decides to run a series of intensified spot checks, stations are caught unaware and penalties are exacted. Fines for violations can run anywhere from a few hundred dollars to more than $10,000. More importantly, the license is placed in jeopardy when standards are not met. Managers who risk the loss of the privilege of using the airwaves run great personal and career risks.

EXERCISES

1. Using the FCC regulations found in Title 47 of the Federal Code of Regulations, Section 73 (your instructor can help you find a copy), describe in a general sense the process by which the FCC classifies AM broadcast stations. In other words, what characteristics are used to assign a station to a particular class? To get you started, one of the characteristics is channel assignment. When you have listed the characteristics involved in classifying stations, define for each class of station the limitations imposed by that category.

   Do not be overly concerned with such things as what numeric value is assigned to the contour to which a station is protected from interference. Just formulate in your own words what it is that makes a class IV station a class IV station rather than a class II station, for example.

   Try to arrive at an explanation for each category of station that you might use to explain the concept to someone who knows nothing about radio except how to turn it on, turn it off, and tune it in to different stations.

2. This exercise is to give you additional facility in working with the FCC regulations. Use the material in Title 47 of the Federal Code of Regulation, Section 73 to look up the answers to the following questions:
   a. What information must be reported in a station log?
   b. How many days before a primary election must a station make advertising time available to political candidates at the lowest unit rates? How many days prior to a general election?
   c. Describe the conditions under which a chief operator must be an employee of a broadcast station. Under which conditions may the chief operator serve on a contract basis with a station?
   d. What are the obligations of the licensees regarding recording of a telephone conversation for broadcast?
   e. What is meant by the term territorial exclusivity?
   f. List the minimum effective radiated power for the various classifications of FM stations.
   g. List the logs and records that must be made available to the FCC on request.
   h. Describe the FCC's policy regarding broadcast of information pertaining to state lotteries.
   i. What are the minimum hours of operation required for AM and FM broadcasting stations?
   j. What are the rules regarding location of a station's public inspection file?

3. Select two radio stations in the same market. Listen to each station for one-and-one-half-hour periods at three different times of the day. You do not need

to listen to both stations on the same days. But, on any given day, listen to only one station.

The purpose of this exercise is to analyze how well each station is serving the public interest. In listening, select times when the stations are running major newscasts and community service programming.

In your evaluation consider the following:

a. How many local news items are covered in newscasts?

b. What issues are covered by newscasts and other programming?

c. How frequently does the station feature programming that can be construed as being of service to the community? What kinds of services are provided? For example, a station may run announcements of community events. Or, there may be remote broadcasts to support charitable organizations in the community.

d. Is the station engaging in any practices that could be deemed harmful to the public interest? Is there a prevalence of material that some would find morally offensive? If so, at what hours is such material broadcast?

e. How good does the station sound technically? Are there foul-ups in production of the on-air program? Are there frequent interruptions due to equipment failure?

For each station write up a one- or two-page critique of its performance as a trustee of the public interest. Then, in a paragraph or two, compare the two stations and try to make a judgment as to which is doing a better job in meeting its obligations as a licensee.

NOTES

1. "Excerpts from FCC Statement," *The New York Times*, 5 August 1987, 26.

2. *New York Times*, 26.

3. *New York Times*, 26.

4. "Fairness Held Unfair," *Broadcasting* (10 August 1987): 63–64. This issue of *Broadcasting* contains an excellent summary of the Fairness Doctrine controversy. It also includes a "Special Report" containing the complete text of the Merideth Decision, which led to the FCC's action to abolish the Fairness Doctrine.

5. "Reagan Vetoes Fairness Doctrine Bill," *Broadcasting* (29 June 1987): 27.

6. *Broadcasting* (29 June 1987): 29.

7. "Now Let That 'Fairness' Bill Die," *The Washington Post*, 24 June 1987, A14.

8. "How Far Will the Apple Fall from the Tree?" *Broadcasting* (20 April 1987): 38.

9. "Patrick Era Ushered in at FCC," *Broadcasting* (18 May 1987): 45.

10. "FCC Launches Attack on Indecency," *Broadcasting* (20 April 1987): 35.

11. *Broadcasting* (20 April 1987): 36.

12. "The Aftermath of Indecency Ruling," *Broadcasting* (27 April 1987): 35.

13. *Broadcasting* (27 April 1987): 35.

14. "FCC's Indecency Standards Too Vague, Say Commenters," *Broadcasting* (8 June 1987): 53.

15. "F.C.C. Rules on Indecent Programming," *The New York Times*, 25 November 1987, C25.

16. "FCC Sends Tough Signal on Indecency" (The Associated Press), *Syracuse Herald American*, 29 November 1987, A12.

17. "The FCC's Tougher Obscenity Standards—What Impact?" *The Christian Science Monitor*, 22 April 1987, 24.

18. *The Christian Science Monitor*, 24.

Glossary

AC Abbreviation for adult contemporary format.

Actuality The sound of an event, recorded or broadcast at the time the event took place. Sometimes used synonymously with sound bite.

AM (Amplitude modulation) A method of impressing audio on a radio signal by varying height (amplitude) of the signal.

Amortization The structure under which a loan is repaid; the structure of the time payments and interest.

Amplification Electronically increasing the power of a signal.

Amplitude The height of a wave.

AOR Abbreviation for album-oriented rock format.

ASCAP (American Society of Composers and Publishers) A music-licensing organization.

Ascertainment The formal process of determining a community's needs and how a broadcast outlet meets those needs. The ascertainment requirement, for all practical purposes, has been dropped for radio.

Attribution Statement of the source of information in a news item.

Audio A term used to denote the electrical signal that transmits sound.

Audition channel A channel separate from the program channel, used for off-the-air listening when operating an audio console.

Availability Vacant air slot for commercial announcement.

Average quarter hour (AQH) persons Measurement of the people who listen for at least five minutes during a quarter hour.

Balance sheet A summary of a station's assets and liabilities.

Best time available (BTA) A sales and programming term indicating that the spots purchased by a client will be placed into the most advantageous slots available when the schedule is constructed. This means, though, that the best times available are the ones left over after customers who have paid for specific time slots have those slots filled.

Bidirectional pickup pattern Microphone pickup pattern that is sensitive to sound from the front and back, but not from the sides.

BMI (Broadcast Music Incorporated) A music-licensing organization.

Cardioid pickup pattern Microphone pickup pattern in which sound is picked up from the front and rejected from the rear; a visual representation of this pickup pattern appears heart-shaped.

Carousel A rotary device used in automation systems to place a cartridge in position for automatic play.

Cartridge unit (cart) A continuous loop of recording tape housed in a plastic case.

Cash flow Complex term usually taken to mean operating profit before taxes, depreciation, and interest are subtracted.

Cassette Two reels of tape in a plastic housing. Cassettes differ from cartridges because they must be rewound.

Chain broadcasting Linking stations together; the original term for network broadcasting.

CHR Abbreviation for contemporary hit radio format.

Combo "Working combo" refers to an announcer hosting a show while operating the control room equipment.

Compact disc A disc that looks like a small phonograph record; it is read by laser beam and offers high-quality sound without degradation of the signal due to wear.

Compensation Fiscal term usually used to mean combination of salary and fringe benefits paid to an employee.

Condenser microphone A microphone that contains a capacitative electrical element. Changes in the vibrating diaphragm inside the mic alter the strength of the charge held by the electrical element. *Condenser* is an old-fashioned term for *capacitor*.

Console A device for amplifying, mixing, and routing audio signals.

Cooperative advertising An advertising plan in which a manufacturer of a particular product contributes to a local retailer's advertising budget.

Copywriter One who writes commercial or promotional copy.

Cost per point (CPP) Estimation of how much it costs an advertiser to reach one-rating point worth of listeners.

Cost per thousand (CPM) Estimated cost to advertisers to reach 1000 listeners.

Cue channel A channel within the audio console that allows the operator to hear, through a small speaker, the sounds of the various equipment. The most common use of a cue channel is to locate the beginning of the sound on a record or tape in order to cue the record or tape for airplay.

Cume (cumulative audience) Unduplicated audience who listens over a predetermined period of time; how many *different* people listen during a time period.

DAT Digital audio tape.

Daypart A portion of the broadcast day, such as "drive time," mid-days, or evenings.

Debt Money owed; more usually, money contracted to be paid back to a lender.

Debt equity A ratio of total debt divided by total equity.

Debt service What it costs to make loan payments. The term is usually used to indicate a monthly or yearly commitment to repaying borrowed money.

Delegation A method of controlling what sound sources are controlled by a particular potentiometer.

Demographic Statistical representation of a population.

Donut Term used in radio production to describe a recorded audio segment with an introduction, an ending, and a music bed in the middle. A local announcer reads copy over the music bed, filling in the donut "hole."

Drive time Radio's version of prime time; basically, those dayparts in which many listeners are in their autos—early morning and late afternoon.

Dubbing Copying from one source to another, as in dubbing a disc to cartridge.

Earth-station equipment Configuration of equipment for receiving a signal from a satellite.

EEO (Equal Employment Opportunity) An employment program stipulated by the FCC to ensure that applicants are not discriminated against during the hiring process.

Electronic transcription (ET) An old-style term for a type of audio disc.

Equity Money invested in a property or business; usually taken to mean the amount of a loan that has been paid off to date.

Fair comment One of the defenses against libel; basically, fair comment means that anyone has a right to express a reasonable opinion.

FCC (Federal Communications Commission) An arm of the United States government responsible for oversight of broadcast communications and certain other types of communications.

Fixed assets Hard, tangible assets such as equipment, land, and facilities.

FM (Frequency modulation) A method of impressing audio on a radio signal by varying the frequency—cycles per second—of the radio wave.

Format The overall selection and arrangement of program elements during a broadcast schedule; in other words, the type of programs a station airs.

Frequency In audience measurement, the average number of times a theoretical listener hears a commercial.

Frequency response A technical term meaning the number of times a sound wave varies in one second. Expressed as cycles per second (CPS) or Hertz (Hz).

Grid card Statement of station commercial rates (rate card) adjusted for several tiers of price; higher tier, or "grid," can be used in period of peak demand.

Gross impressions Total number of exposures to a schedule of announcements. When expressed as a percentage of the total audience, gross impressions are expressed as gross rating points.

Gross rating point A figure expressing the total number of exposures to a schedule of announcements, expressed as a percentage of all possible listeners.

Ground wave A radio wave that travels along the contour of the earth; component of the typical AM signal.

Intangible assets Assets such as contracts or the station's operating license. Differs from fixed assets, which are "hard," or "tangible."

Key (keying) Usually used as a verb, meaning to turn a sound source on or off at the console.

Labor Management Relations Act (LMRA) Federal legislation dealing with collective bargaining. Provides a "cooling-off period" for firms facing labor action.

Libel A false published or broadcast statement that damages someone's reputation.

Localness A term used to indicate FCC requirement that a radio station actively serve its community of license.

Log A record of when all program elements ran during the broadcast day. The station log is a legal document subject to FCC inspection.

Metro survey area A local rating area defined in terms of a city and its immediate environs. Smaller than the total survey area.

Mixing Combining sound sources at the audio console.

Modulation To impress a signal on a carrier wave or audio signal.

MOR Abbreviation for middle-of-the-road format.

Moving coil microphone A type of microphone that uses a coil that moves through a magnetic field in response to the movement of a diaphragm, which vibrates in response to sound waves. The movement of the coil produces an electrical signal.

Multiplexing Impressing two or more signals on one carrier. For example, the FM signal can be multiplexed with the left and right stereo signals. Sometimes a separate program will be placed on the carrier.

NAB (National Association of Broadcasters) A professional organization for broadcasters.

Narrowcasting The concept of broadcasting to a tightly defined audience.

Omnidirectional pickup pattern A microphone pickup pattern that picks up sound sources from all directions equally well.

Operations director Executive in radio station, usually second-in-command to the general manager; term is highly variable, though.

Patching A method of changing the routing of a signal through an audio system. Also, a connection that is temporarily placed between audio inputs and outputs.

Payola An undercover, illegal payment to a disc jockey or radio station programmer for playing or plugging a record.

Persons using radio (PUR) A measurement average that estimates the number of persons listening to all stations in a particular market.

Playlist The listing of the songs to be played on a radio station's schedule; today, usually computer-generated.

Positioning The programmer's attempt to place his or her station into a profitable and vacant niche in the area's radio offerings.

Potentiometer Variable resistor. A device to turn a signal up or down, just like the rheostat often used to turn lights up or down in a dining room. The term is usually shortened to "pot."

Presunrise authorization An FCC waiver allowing a certain class of radio station to begin broadcasting before local sunrise. Allows the station to maintain a regular morning schedule.

Privilege A defense against libel; basically, a privileged statement is one made in open court or on the floor of a legislative body while that body is in session. It may be made and repeated without danger of a libel suit.

Production The use of studio equipment to combine sounds into a finished product.

Program *noun:* a discrete segment of a broadcast, such as a disc jockey's show. *verb:* to construct the elements of each day's broadcasting.

Program channel The output of the console that goes over the air or to a tape recorder.

Program clock A visual representation of the station's programming strategy; usually shows what type of song will be played when. Sometimes called a "hot clock."

Program director Station executive usually in charge of all staff directly involved in putting material over the air. In some cases, a program director is limited to chief announcer duties.

Promotion Bringing the station to the attention of the public. "Audience promotion" refers to publicizing the station to the listening audience; "sales promotion" refers to publicizing the station to prospective buyers of commercials.

Psychographics Representations of life-style and mental outlook; something akin to a demographic, which is a statistical representation of a population.

Quarterly Needs and Issues Report Narrative document in which radio managers inform the FCC, at three-month intervals, of community needs and how those needs are being met. Basically, a replacement for the old ascertainment process.

Rate card A station's statement of costs for commercial airtime.

Rating A measured portion of the total available audience. Sometimes used broadly (and incorrectly) as a definition of the whole audience-measurement process.

Reach An indication of how many different members of an audience will be exposed to a message.

Receivables Money owed to a station, such as outstanding bills from commercial clients.

Reel to reel A tape machine where audiotape runs from a left hand reel to a right hand reel.

Rep firm A national sales representative firm that deals with advertisers in large cities where it would be impractical for a local station to place a salesperson.

Ribbon microphone A microphone with a thin ribbonlike element that vibrates in response to the velocity of sound waves. The element is suspended in a magnetic field that converts the sound to an electrical signal.

Routing The concept of sending a signal on a certain path via an audio console.

Run of station (ROS) Bulk commercial buying plan where station's traffic department will fit the commercials into available time locations; sometimes called run of schedule.

SESAC Society of European Stage Authors and Composers. A European agency that licenses music in the United States.

Share A measured percentage of listeners who are actually listening to radio at a particular time.

Simulcast To broadcast (or cablecast) a program on two or more media or stations.

Sky wave A type of radio wave that bounces off a layer of the atmosphere, back to earth, and back to the atmosphere, and so on. Sky waves travel a great distance and are an important component of the AM signal.

Software The program that drives a computer. A computer and related equipment are known as hardware.

Sound bite Audio portions of interviews; basically synonymous with actuality.

Sound hour A term referring to the programming strategy within an hour of radio broadcasting.

Spectrum Range of frequencies available to broadcasters.

Speculation tape Usually, a commercial tape made to impress a potential client. Used by a salesperson to show the client how a commercial might sound.

Splicing The process of joining together two pieces of recording tape; done as part of the editing process.

Spot Imprecise term usually taken to mean commercial announcement. Can also be used to mean the placement of commericals in selected markets, stations, or time periods, i.e., "spot sales."

Statement of income A document showing operating expenses and revenues of a radio station during a specific time period.

Stock Shares of a business sold to investors.

Stop set Cluster of commercial and announcements aired between sets of music.

Syndication Programs sent to a network of users. Programs can be sent by satellite or sometimes by mail.

Time spent listening (TSL) The average amount of time spent by the average listener tuned into radio or to a particular station.

Toll broadcasting The original term used by WEAF to denote selling of commercial time.

Total audience plan (TAP) A carefully designed "package" of radio spots designed to reach a broad audience. Differs from run-of-station spots in that TAP plans guarantee when the spots will run.

Total survey area (TSA) An area where ratings are taken, including a wide range of counties served by two or more radio stations from within a metropolitan area.

Trade or trade-out Bartering commercial airtime for goods or services.

Transducer A device that performs the function of converting energy from one form to another, such as the process by which a microphone changes sound energy into electrical energy.

Transduction Changing energy from one form to another. A microphone transduces the physical (motional) energy of sound waves into the electronic energy of an audio signal.

Truth A defense against libel. A reporter cannot be held liable in a libel case if the remark was provably true.

Turnover (TO) A figure reflecting how often listenership changes from time period to time period.

Turntable Device used to play discs; basically, a high-quality record player.

Vendor planning A method where a radio station may develop a campaign for a particular retailer and finance the campaign by approaching several firms whose products are marketed by the retailer.

Voice actuality A report in which an actuality, a snippet of sound from an interview, is edited into the reporter's script.

Voicer A straight reading of a news report, usually from the scene of the event being covered.

Wire service A newsgathering organization that supplies news copy and audience reports to subscribers. A vestigial term from the era when such news was supplied by wire; today, satellite delivery is more common.

———

———

———

SUGGESTED

———

READINGS

———

Listed below is a selected library for the radio professional; many of the works cross over into other disciplines but present a well-rounded view of radio and how the medium interacts with other media and society.*

Survey (Radio and General)/History

Barnouw, Eric. *A History of Broadcasting in the United States.* New York: Oxford University Press, 1966, 1968, 1970. Three-volume history; comprehensive and readable.

* Some of these books are out of print; however, they should be available at many libraries.

Busby, Linda, and Donald Parker. *The Art and Science of Radio*. Boston: Allyn and Bacon, 1984. Broad in scope but many interesting details; a good and easily accessible reference.

Douglas, George H. *The Early Days of Radio Broadcasting*. Jefferson, NC: McFarland Publishing, 1987. A narrative of radio's troubled birth and childhood.

Head, Sydney W., and Christopher H. Sterling. *Broadcasting in America: A Survey of Electronic Media*, 5th ed. Boston: Houghton Mifflin, 1987. The famous all-in-one guide to understanding the complexities of the broadcasting world.

Johnson, Joseph S., and Kenneth K. Jones. *Modern Radio Station Practices*, 2d ed. Belmont, CA: Wadsworth, 1978. An insightful but now dated survey of radio operations.

Keith, Michael C., and Joseph M. Krause. *The Radio Station*. Stoneham, MA: Focal Press, 1986. A heavily illustrated guide to radio.

Sterling, Christopher H., and John M. Kittross. *Stay Tuned: A Concise History of American Broadcasting*. Belmont, CA: Wadsworth, 1978. More than just a history— an easy-to-use, quick-reference guide to many aspects of broadcasting.

Whetmore, Edward Jay. *The Magic Medium: An Introduction to Radio in America*. Belmont, CA: Wadsworth, 1981. Comprehensive and affectionate overview of radio.

Programming, Talk Radio, and News

Dill, Barbara. *The Journalist's Handbook on Libel and Privacy*. New York: Free Press, 1986. Includes analyses of recent cases; a practical guide for journalists.

Eastman, Susan Tyler, Sydney W. Head, and Lewis Klein. *Broadcast/Cable Programming: Strategies and Practices*, 3d ed. Belmont, CA: Wadsworth, 1989. A broad but concisely analytical study of programming with specific references to radio.

Fang, Irving. *TV News, Radio News*, 4th ed. St. Paul, MN: Rada Press, 1985. An authoritative working guide.

Howard, Herbert H., and Michael S. Kievman. *Radio and TV Programming*. New York: Macmillan (originally published by Grid), 1983. A coverage of programming primarily from a historical point of view.

Keith, Michael C. *Radio Programming: Consultancy and Formatics*. Stoneham, MA: Focal Press, 1987. An analysis of strategies for different commercial radio formats.

Levin, Murray B. *Talk Radio and the American Dream*. Lexington, MA: Lexington Books, 1987. An exhaustive study of radio talk shows. Includes transcripts of broadcasts.

Routt, Edd, James B. McGrath, and Frederic A. Weiss. *The Radio Format Conundrum.* New York: Hastings House, 1978. A dated but still thoughtful view of how and why formats work.

White, Ted, Adrian J. Meppen, and Steven Young. *Broadcast News Writing, Reporting and Production.* New York: Macmillan, 1984. An incisive guide that goes beyond writing and shows the entire range of radio (and, of course, television) news operations.

Operations: Engineering

Carr, Joseph J., *The TAB Handbook of Radio Communications.* Blue Ridge Summit, PA: TAB Books, 1984. Not exactly a guide to engineering operations of a radio station, but a good self-teaching guide on radio electronics.

Crutchfield, E. B., ed. *The NAB Engineering Handbook,* 7th ed. Washington, D.C.: National Association of Broadcasters, 1985. An often updated and comprehensive book.

Operations: Production, Announcing, Promotion

Albert, James. *The Broadcaster's Legal Guide for Conducting Station Contests and Promotions.* Chicago: Bonus Books, 1986. Case studies and clear guidance of how to stay in business and out of trouble.

Alten, Stanley R. *Audio in Media,* 2d ed. Belmont, CA: Wadsworth, 1986. The most comprehensive guide available on audio; much of the content is applicable to radio production.

Bergendorff, Fred L., Charles Harrison Smith, and Lance Webster. *Broadcast Advertising and Promotion: A Handbook for Students and Professionals.* New York: Hastings House, 1983. Different perspectives on promotion strategies.

Eastman, Susan Tyler, and Robert A. Klein. *Strategies in Broadcast and Cable Promotion.* Belmont, CA: Wadsworth, 1982. Much material directly relevant or applicable to promotion in radio.

Hyde, Stuart W. *Television and Radio Announcing,* 5th ed. Boston: Houghton Mifflin, 1987. A durable book, now updated.

Nisbett, Alec. *The Technique of the Sound Studio,* 4th ed. Stoneham, MA: Focal Press, 1979. A comprehensive look at recording with an extensive glossary.

Nisbett, Alec. *The Use of Microphones,* 2d ed. Stoneham, MA: Focal Press, 1983. A very thorough study of mics and mic placement. Useful for radio, although probably more useful to recording studio engineers.

O'Donnell, Lewis B., Philip Benoit, and Carl Hausman. *Modern Radio Production.* Belmont, CA: Wadsworth, 1986. Hands-on approach to radio production; many step-by-step illustrations.

O'Donnell, Lewis B., Carl Hausman, and Philip Benoit. *Announcing: Broadcast Communicating Today.* Belmont, CA: Wadsworth, 1987. Many of the techniques discussed are applicable to radio; some chapters deal specifically with radio announcing.

Oringel, Robert S. *Audio Control Handbook: For Radio and Television Broadcasting,* 5th ed. New York: Hastings House, 1983. Good reference for audio operators; less useful for producers.

Thom, Randy, and others. *Audio Craft: An Introduction to the Tools and Techniques of Audio Production.* Washington, D.C.: National Foundation of Community Broadcasters, 1982. A practical guide.

Business: Research and Reference

Beville, Jr., Hugh M. *Audience Measurement in Transition.* New York: Television/Radio Age, 1983. An exploration of the methods and the impact of modern measurement.

Beville, Jr., Hugh M. *Audience Ratings: Radio, Television and Cable.* Hillsdale, NJ: Lawrence Erlbaum Associates, 1985. An award-winning definitive history of ratings practice.

Dominick, Joseph R., and James F. Fletcher, eds. *Broadcasting Research Methods.* Boston: Allyn and Bacon, 1985. A collection of twenty articles providing wide-ranging view of research process.

Duncan, James H. *American Radio.* Kalamazoo, MI: Duncan Media Enterprises. A twice-yearly updated report on 175 radio markets, including rating and economic information on stations. *Duncan Radio Market Guide,* issued once every two years, summarizes this information in a larger reference work.

Wimmer, Roger D., and Joseph R. Dominick. *Mass Media Research: An Introduction*, 2d ed. Belmont, CA: Wadsworth, 1987. Comprehensive and includes a valuable summary of statistics.

Business: Advertising and Sales

Heighton, Elizabeth J., and Don R. Cunningham. *Advertising in the Broadcast and Cable Media*, 2d ed. Belmont, CA: Wadsworth, 1984. Integrates advertising and research in an understandable way.

Murphy, Jonne. *Handbook of Radio Advertising*. Radnor, PA: Chilton Book, 1980. A hands-on approach.

Warner, Charles. *Broadcast and Cable Selling*. Belmont, CA: Wadsworth, 1986. A very useful and complete guide to selling time; much attention is paid to demonstrations of sales techniques.

Zeigler, Sherilyn K., and Herbert H. Howard. *Broadcast Advertising*, 2d ed. Ames: Iowa State University Press (originally published by Grid), 1984. A step-by step guide.

Business: Management and Regulation

Bittner, John R. *Broadcast Law and Regulation*. Englewood Cliffs, NJ: Prentice-Hall, 1982. A survey of regulation, now dated.

Drucker, Peter F. *People and Performance: The Best of Peter Drucker on Management*. New York: Harper's College Press, 1977. Many insights into managing and motivating people.

Kahn, Frank J., ed. *Documents of American Broadcasting*, 4th ed. Englewood Cliffs, NJ: Prentice-Hall, 1984. A useful compendium of otherwise hard-to-find documents.

Kirkley, Jr., Donald H. *Station Procedures: A Guide for Radio*. Washington, D.C.: National Association of Broadcasters, 1985. Much valuable advice on how to run a station with particular attention paid to personnel matters.

Krasnow, Erwin G., Lawrence D. Longley, and Herbert A. Terry. *The Politics of Broadcast Regulation*, 3d ed. New York: St. Martin's Press, 1982. A concise introduction to a complex field.

LeDuc, Don R. *Beyond Broadcasting: Patterns in Policy and Law.* New York: Longman, 1987. A broad view of broadcast law, focusing on entertainment.

Marcus, Norman. *Broadcast and Cable Management.* Englewood Cliffs, NJ: Prentice-Hall, 1986. Many good examples, abundance of factual information.

National Association of Broadcasters. *Radio in Search of Excellence.* Washington, D.C.: 1985. The case studies zero in on success factors in broadcast management.

McCavitt, William E., and Peter K. Pringle. *Electronic Media Management.* Stoneham, MA: Focal Press, 1986. A complete source on management with a section on new technologies.

Powe, Jr., Lucas A. *American Broadcasting and the First Amendment.* Berkeley: University of California Press, 1987. A detailed historical analysis of the derivation of First Amendment rulings and persuasive argument for full First Amendment rights.

Quaal, Ward L., and James A. Brown. *Broadcasting Management,* 2d ed. New York: Hastings House, 1978. A dated book but still quite useful; case histories are excellent.

Sherman, Barry L. *Telecommunications Management: The Broadcast and Cable Industries.* New York: McGraw-Hill, 1987. Current; stresses media business and media marketplace.

Tunstall, Jeremy. *Communication Deregulation: The Unleashing of America's Communication Industry.* New York: Basil Blackwell, 1986. Work by a prominent sociologist, analyzing the relationship between communications and politics.

Periodicals

In addition to the above books, the following periodicals are recommended as ongoing references.

Billboard. 1515 Broadway, New York, NY 10036. A source for in-depth information on the music industry, both broadcast and music stores.

Broadcasting. 1735 DeSales St. N.W., Washington, D.C. 20036–4480. A trade journal of the industry; heavy emphasis on business aspects.

Broadcast Management/Engineering. 820 Second Ave., New York, NY 10017. A resource designed for engineers but comprehensible to managers. Excellent source for keeping up with latest technologies.

Cash Box. 330 W. 58th St., Suite 5–D, New York, NY 10019. Comprehensive coverage of coin machine, music, and radio industry.

The Pulse of Broadcasting. 150 E. 58th St., New York, NY 10022. Covers radio from all angles: news, music, programming, buying and selling of stations, and interviews with radio's movers and shakers.

RadioActive. Published by National Association of Broadcasters, 1771 N St. NW, Washington, D.C., 20036. Insightful articles on a broad range of radio topics; good coverage of promotion and AM radio.

Radio and Records Weekly. 1930 Century Park West, Los Angeles, CA 90067. Especially good for coverage of music in the radio industry.

Radio Only. Published by Inside Radio Inc., 1930 East Marlton Pike, Suite S–93, Cherry Hill, NJ 08003. Provides detailed insight into programming, promotion, and sales.

Radio World Newspaper. P.O. Box 1214, Falls Church, VA 22041. Offers updated news and interesting feature material to radio professionals.

Variety. 154 E. 46th St., New York, NY 10036. Coverage of theater, TV, radio, music, records, and film.

INDEX